CALIFORNIA BANKING IN A GROWING ECONOMY: 1946–1975

CALIFORNIA BANKING IN A GROWING ECONOMY: 1946–1975

EDITED BY

HYMAN P. MINSKY

PUBLICATIONS OF THE
INSTITUTE OF BUSINESS AND ECONOMIC RESEARCH
UNIVERSITY OF CALIFORNIA

INSTITUTE OF BUSINESS AND ECONOMIC RESEARCH
BERKELEY, CALIFORNIA, 1965

INSTITUTE OF BUSINESS AND ECONOMIC RESEARCH
UNIVERSITY OF CALIFORNIA
BERKELEY, CALIFORNIA

© 1965 BY THE REGENTS OF THE UNIVERSITY OF CALIFORNIA
LIBRARY OF CONGRESS CATALOG CARD NUMBER: 65-64515

PRINTED BY THE UNIVERSITY OF CALIFORNIA PRINTING DEPARTMENT, BERKELEY

INSTITUTE OF BUSINESS AND ECONOMIC RESEARCH
University of California, Berkeley
1964–1965

The opinions expressed in this study are those of the authors. The functions of the Institute of Business and Economic Research are confined to facilitating the prosecution of independent scholarly research by members of the faculty.

Foreword

EDMUND G. BROWN, Governor of the State of California, in March 1963 appointed the Governor's Banking Study Committee to explore the place of the banking system in the growing economy of California. The membership of the committee included Paul B. Kelly, Retired Vice Chairman of the Board, Crocker-Citizens National Bank; Stanley M. Stalford, Chairman of the Board, Fidelity Bank; Jesse W. Tapp, Chairman of the Board, Bank of America, National Trust and Savings Association; Clifford Tweter, President, United California Bank; and for the State of California, Hale Champion, Director of Finance; Thomas C. Lynch, Attorney General; and John A. O'Kane, Superintendent of Banks. Allan Sproul, former President of the Federal Reserve Bank of New York, served as Chairman of the Committee.

To provide background material for the report of the Committee, arrangements were made to have a series of study papers on a number of aspects of the banking system of the state prepared by academic specialists in banking and finance. These studies were coordinated by the Institute of Business and Economic Research of the Berkeley campus of the University of California.

In view of the interest expressed in the background papers, the decision was made to publish them in book form after the Committee had presented its report to the Governor in January 1965. For this purpose, they were revised and updated, where feasible, under the editorship of Professor Hyman P. Minsky, one of the original participants in the study. The State Banking Department and the Institute of Business and Economic Research are glad to sponsor their publication in this form.

The contributors to the studies and their present institutional affiliations are as follows:

David A. Alhadeff, *Professor of Business Administration*
    University of California, Berkeley

Robert Lindsay, *Professor of Finance* and *Research Adviser to the Dean*
    New York University

Hyman P. Minsky, *Professor of Economics*
    Washington University, St. Louis, Missouri

Frederic P. Morrissey, *Professor of Business Administration and Associate Dean of the Graduate School of Business Administration*
University of California, Berkeley

Roland I. Robinson, *Professor of Financial Administration and Economics*
Michigan State University

Albert H. Schaaf, *Associate Professor of Business Administration*
University of California, Berkeley

Richard E. Towey, *Assistant Professor of Economics*
Oregon State University

Paul F. Wendt, *Professor of Finance* and *Vice Chairman of the Department of Business Administration*
University of California, Berkeley

Robert M. Williams, *Chairman, Business Economics,* and *Professor of Business Economics and Statistics*
University of California, Los Angeles

In view of the importance of the banking system in California's economy, we hope that the information and analysis presented herein will be of value to all persons interested in the banking industry in California.

JOSEPH W. GARBARINO, *Director*
Institute of Business and Economic Research

Berkeley, July 1965

Acknowledgments

THE EDITOR AND THE AUTHORS are grateful for the interest and cooperation provided by John A. O'Kane, Superintendent of Banks, in arrang-
ing for the support of these studies of various aspects of the California
banking system.

In the formulation of the project and the preparation of the studies,
the encouragement and the incisive knowledge of banking of Allan
Sproul, Chairman of the Committee, were invaluable. As Director of
the Institute of Business and Economic Research, Joseph W. Garbarino
stimulated and supported the production of the present volume. Bert-
wing C. Mah, Director of Research, represented the State Banking Department in the preparation of this volume.

The staff of the Institute of Business and Economic Research bore
with the vagaries of the independent authors and the dependent editor
during this volume's extended gestation period.

Mrs. Patricia Bragg, most valuable and meticulous research assistant,
with the help of William Rutzick brought a large portion of the data
up to date.

Two people deserve special thanks—Mrs. Jan Seibert and Professor
Robert Lindsay. Jan Seibert, Editor for the Institute of Business and
Economic Research, styled and produced this volume and relieved the
editor of myriad details. Robert Lindsay read and commented on most
of the papers. His unfailing good taste and style have left their imprint
on much that is included herein. It is a "far, far better thing" than it
would have been without his discerning assistance.

HYMAN P. MINSKY

Berkeley, July 1965

Contents

xi

Chapter III COMMERCIAL BANKING AS
AN INDUSTRY

Overview

HYMAN P. MINSKY

1. BACKGROUND

The studies in this volume were prepared for the Governor's Banking Study Committee on the Future of Banking in California. Each author, in his particular study area, was asked to explore the prospects for the commercial banks of the state in the period until 1975. Although a standard set of forecasts was prepared, the author of each study was free to use them as he saw fit. No uniformity was forced upon him. As a consequence, each author is responsible for the content of his study; editorial supervision and control have been kept to a minimum. Each paper received editorial comments, but included here is whatever the authors returned as their revised copy.

An important reason for this policy was that very little is known about banking and finance within the local economies of a state. Thus, only by allowing scholars the widest possible freedom to study the problem can steps be taken toward deeper understanding.

2. PERSPECTIVES IN BANKING

In principle, commercial banking can be studied from three perspectives. One is the interaction of commercial banking with economic growth and economic cycles. This is the essential subject matter of monetary and banking theory. The logic of this approach to banking lies in the relationship between the behavior of the economy and the supply of money—which in a modern economy is primarily a liability of commercial banks.

Another way to study commercial banking is to view it as an industry, comprised of a number of firms. These firms buy various inputs and sell various outputs. The main question industry studies attempt to answer is whether the structure and organization of the industry, given its special technical production conditions, is conducive to economic efficiency. In measuring efficiency in this context, we are usually asking if the industry behaves as if it were competitive. If monopolistic, oligopolistic, or monopsonistic features enter its behavior, there is a presump-

1

2 HYMAN P. MINSKY

tion of inefficiency, although over time the industry's tendency to innovate is also important. Moreover, given the impact of banking on the stability of an economy, it is also important to ask whether the organization of the industry helps or hinders in sustaining the stability and growth of the economy.

The third mode of looking at commercial banks is to view them as business firms designed to serve the interests of their owners. Some of the issues here are the efficiency of banks as producing units, their profitability, and the adequacy of their capital. Part of the task of viewing banks as business firms centers around the mechanics of these operations—the specification of the inputs they use to produce their outputs.

These three ways to look at banking are interdependent. It is not possible in an introduction such as this to do much more than assert the above; a complete analysis of the interactions among the three perspectives would be a large volume. However, the response of banking firms to new techniques—new production functions—can alter the industrial structure and the impact of monetary policy actions. For example, if between now and 1975 there should evolve a universal bank credit card, the link between bank accommodation of customers and central bank actions will be affected. In addition, such a credit card arrangement might draw banks together into national clubs so that even if we did not develop nationwide branch banking, we might move toward nationwide closed and exclusive correspondent systems.

Another example of interaction can be drawn from recent California experience. The rapid growth of the state has made banking profitable and has opened the way for new entrepreneurs in the industry. The foundation of new banks has made the industry more competitive. At the same time, the development of new bank instruments, such as negotiable certificates of deposit, has enabled some of the newly char-tered banks to grow rapidly. Because the full impact of this combina-tion—new banks and new instruments—was not fully analyzed, an ele-ment of instability crept into the banking system. Fortunately, this element of instability did not escalate to general instability, but obvi-ously one of the lessons of the American past is that when financial instability does become general it can do enormous harm to the Amer-ican economy and to its parts.

With the addition of a fourth class of introductory and background studies, the papers in this volume, with some forcing, fall into these three perspective classes. Although the studies will almost always over-flow their "banks," the classification seems apt.

Accordingly, the volume is organized into four chapters. The first is introductory and contains two papers, the general paper on banking and finance by Professor Roland I. Robinson, titled "Economic Role and Objectives for California's Banking and Financial Institutions" and the forecast of the California economy by Professor Robert M. Williams, "Guidelines to Economic Projections for the California Economy to 1975."

The second chapter deals with the relations between commercial banking and the California econmy. It contains two papers. One by Professor Hyman P. Minsky, "Commercial Banking and Rapid Economic Growth in California," explores how banking enters into and is affected by rapid growth. The second is a paper on the liquidity of banks and the economy by Professors Richard E. Towey and Robert Lindsay, "Liquidity of California Banks."

The third chapter deals with commercial banking as an industry. The first paper, which evaluates the structure of the industry, is by Professor David A. Alhadeff, "California Banking and Competition." Professor Frederic P. Morrissey's paper, "The Allocation of Funds by the Commercial Banks in the California Economy, 1946–1975," deals with the portfolio composition of banks. Professor Albert H. Schaaf's paper, "The Savings Function and Mortgage Investment by California Banks and Financial Institutions," centers around the market for a particular asset (mortgages) and thus examines the interaction between banks and other financial institutions.

The fourth and last chapter deals with commercial banks as businesses. Professor Paul F. Wendt investigates the adequacy of returns and the prospects for sufficient investment in the industry in his paper, "Earnings and Capital Problems of California Banks, 1946–1975." Professor Richard E. Towey, in his imaginative paper, "An Evaluation of the Payments Mechanism in California, 1946–1975," looks at banks as firms that produce an output—the payments mechanism—that is certainly one of the most vital products in the economy.

3. SYNOPSES OF THE PAPERS

The first paper in this volume, Professor Roland I. Robinson's "Economic Role and Objectives for California's Banking and Financial Systems," differs from the other papers. It is truly an introductory essay in that it is theoretical, general, and programmatic. The other papers are empirical and institutional and are concerned with specific issues related to the commercial banking system of California.

The appropriate spot in a research study for a paper such as Robinson's is in the early planning stages of the project. Usually in publishing the results of a cooperative or decentralized study such as this one, the before-the-act programmatic papers are suppressed. However, Robinson's paper became available only after the various papers included in the study either were completed or were well on their way to being completed. Thus its content does not especially illuminate that of the other papers, and most of the questions raised remain unanswered.

However, Robinson's piece is of special value if the work in this volume is viewed not as a definitive study of banking and finance in California but as the beginning of a continuing serious research effort. The aim of such an effort should be to acquire better knowledge of how financial relations affect the economy of the state and whether or not the state can guide or control the evolution of its financial system so that stable growth is facilitated.

Robinson's aim, as stated, is to summarize the "economic functions and systemic roles reasonably expected of banks and other financial institutions" [p. 27]. He divides his argument into three parts: functions banks and other financial institutions are expected to perform, criteria for judging banking and financial performance, and the objectives that can be achieved by way of state regulatory powers. In each part Robinson not only delineates the issues but also indicates questions that should be the basis for research.

Even though Robinson almost always raises general questions, he divides his discussion of the above three topics into two parts. In the first part he discusses these questions generally; in the second he relates the issues to the special problems of California—or rather to a rapidly growing geographical sector of a national economy.

It is important to note that Robinson takes as his subject matter commercial banks together with the rest of the financial system. He views the financial system as an interdependent set of institutions which can best be studied as a unit. Most of the subsequent papers take a narrower focus, emphasize commercial banking, and tend to give at best passing notice to nonbank financial institutions.

Robinson lists seven functions of commercial banks and suggests that the evaluation of the performance of commercial banks and other financial institutions should be made in the light of five criteria. As he lists them, the functions of banks and the financial system are to: (a) allocate capital funds, (b) meet legitimate credit needs, (c) provide the economy's payment system, (d) service the flow of savings, (e) abet capital importation, (f) transmit Federal Reserve credit policies to the various financial markets, and (g) provide financial service. Although this list of functions did not guide the selection of topics to be studied, all except the provision of financial services and the efficacy of California's financial system in transmitting or offsetting Federal Reserve policy actions are touched upon in the various studies.

The five criteria for judging performance discussed by Robinson are (a) efficiency in terms of costs, earnings and profits, (b) credit allocation, (c) stability, (d) efficiency in capital importation, and (e) adequate competition. At one place or another in the papers that follow, all of these criteria are applied, although not all are used in each paper. It is worth noting that Robinson transforms the criterion of the efficiency of the capital importation process into a question of the optimum interest rate differential between capital importing and capital exporting areas. Unfortunately, as no special study of interest rate patterns was undertaken, this criterion cannot be applied. Research on financing terms for various types of enterprises and contracts should be undertaken if deeper knowledge of how California grows is to be achieved.

Robinson's discussion of the objectives that can be achieved by state regulatory powers starts from the reminder that many of the economic policy aspects dealing with money and finance are the domain of the federal government operating through the Federal Reserve System and other national regulatory agencies. As a result, the state agencies are limited to chartering and branching policies. On the other hand, whereas the federal government controls monetary policy, it does not necessarily regulate other financial institutions. At present the state's responsibility for regulating nonbank institutions may very well dominate its responsibility to regulate commercial banks.

Robinson also points out that as long as banking is a regulated industry, the needs for sufficient bank capital and earnings are part of the constraints upon regulatory agencies. These agencies must take into account how their rules affect bank earnings and the ability of the banks to acquire capital. He concludes that the state's authorities, in performing their duties, must keep in mind that "the future cannot be foreseen, but in preparing for it the architects of the financial structure cannot await clearer vision. They need to plan a structure which can take advantage of the new as rapidly as it becomes visible" [p. 62].

Professor Robert M. Williams' paper, "Guidelines to Economic Projections for the California Economy to 1975," develops "economic projections as a basis for considering the role of commercial banking in the future economic growth of California . . ." [p. 63].

Williams reviews the various projections of population, employment patterns, and income that have been made for the California economy.

He not only states their results but examines their methodology. He concludes that for the forecast period California will grow somewhat faster than the country as a whole, but that the differential will not be as great as in the postwar period to date. The decrease in the differential will take place because the growth rate of the United States is expected to be higher in the forecast period than in the post-World War II period to date.

Williams forecasts a gross product originating of $123.1 billion in 1975 which implies a 5.50 percent rate of growth over the period 1963–1975. This is the same order of magnitude as the 5.42 percent rate of growth achieved by California in the 1947–1963 period.

Professor Hyman P. Minsky does three things in his paper, "Commercial Banking and Rapid Economic Growth in California." He presents a view of how rapid economic growth in a region of a national economy is generated and the relation of such growth to financial developments within the region. He describes what has taken place in the post-World War II period. Finally, he draws inferences about the prospects of the state's economy which are largely based upon his view of how the evolving financial relations affect the prospects for continuing rapid growth. His broad conclusion is that "the inferences that are made lead to skepticism that future growth will be an extrapolation of recent growth. Although the real resources of the state can readily accommodate the forecast rate of population and economic growth, it is doubtful that the recent rapid rates of growth of some critical financial flows can be maintained. However, it must be understood that this skepticism is based upon primitive theory and upon data with many gaps" [p. 80].

Minsky's view is that the major cause of California's rapid economic growth since World War II is rapid growth in the national demand for outputs in which California specializes, either because of intrinsic or accidental advantages. He writes that "as far as California is concerned, it is apparent that the income elasticity of demand for climate, retirement, vacation, and specialty foodstuffs is high, and they are among the underlying elements in California's rapid growth. However the recent rapid growth of California is more closely associated with the high rate of increase of defense related spending within the state. Hence California's growth is based upon national social or policy decisions rather than upon the intrinsic character of private demand and production function changes in a growing national economy" [pp. 89–90].

Minsky holds that the money supply within a region must grow in a manner consistent with the growth of the regional economy. As is true for the country as a whole, income velocity of demand deposits in California increased during the postwar period. However, the ratio of this velocity in California to a similar measure for the United States showed no noticeable trend. Thus the reserve base of California's banks had to grow more rapidly than the reserve base in the country as a whole.

The argument is made that the monetary behavior of a region of a country is analogous to that of a country under a very strict international gold standard. In a national state with modern central banking in the context of a relatively slack international gold standard, the increases in the reserve base and therefore in the money supply of the country can be considered as an exogenous policy variable. For a region within a country, increases in the reserve base are earned by running a surplus on its accounts with the rest of the country. That is, the money supply of a region is endogenously determined; it is not a policy variable. Thus it is necessary for a rapidly growing region, embedded in a country, to run a surplus in its balance of payments with the rest of the country large enough to make its money supply grow with the requisite speed.

Rapid growth in income implies a rapid rise in imports. Therefore, on items other than the growth inducing exports, a rapidly growing region such as California can be expected to run a large deficit. In addition, the more rapid regional growth requires a more rapid rate of investment within the region than in the country as a whole. As we can expect saving propensities to be approximately the same in the region and the country, the rapid rate of investment will require capital importation into the region. That is, in a country such as the United States, the rapidly growing sectors will import capital from the richer among the slower growing regions.

Because of the paucity of data on the size of capital imports through many markets, Minsky concentrates on the role played by those markets for which data are available. As a result, fairly heavy emphasis is placed upon the mortgage market and the closely related savings and loan associations as sources of out-of-state capital. It is hoped that further research will develop a complete view of capital flows to California, but such research will require the generation of data not now available.

After examining known sources of capital imports and the size of the federal government's deficit in California, Minsky concludes that "it seems as if, for the early part of the forecast period, the initial flow of reserves from identified sources is significantly greater than the net gain in reserves that is necessary for the money supply to grow along with the region's economy. ... However, some of the recent growth rates of financial factors obviously are not sustainable for the long haul. The question therefore remains as to how the economy of California will adjust to slower growth rates in these financial flows. One possible reaction is for the growth rate to slow down" [p. 125].

If rapid growth is financed by capital imports, and especially if debt instruments are used, payment commitments grow with the stock of outstanding indebtedness. As a result, the prospect is increased that the financial system will amplify any depressing tendencies. Because of the burden of capital imports and the way in which the growth of California depends upon the continued growth of federal expenditures in the state, the economy of California is particularly vulnerable to a slowdown or decrease in federal spending in the state. In particular, California could become a stagnant sector of an otherwise growing national economy.

Minsky notes the sophistication built into the national financial system since the great depression of the 1930's. He then says that "although we cannot expect financial institutions to act as shock absorbers if a radical change in expectations takes place, it seems likely that they will not amplify the contractionary forces to the same extent as they have in the past" [p. 134]. Thus, unfavorable income developments should not lead to a deep depression within the state, a possible result if the financial defenses crumble.

During such a stagnant period the decrease of financial commitments will set the stage for resumption of growth. "However, for those who must make the adjustments it is less than satisfactory to know that in time the difficulties will be eased. Appropriate public policies are needed which slow the withdrawal of the stimuli for rapid growth to prevent the more serious reactions from taking place" [p. 134].

Professors Robert Lindsay and Richard E. Towey, in their paper "Liquidity of California Banks," analyze a seeming paradox. Commercial banks in California appear at one and the same time to be less and more liquid than banks in other parts of the country. They seem to be less liquid in that their portfolios contain smaller proportions of primary reserves, net balances at correspondents, and treasury debt, and higher ratios of loans to assets and real estate loans to assets. They are more liquid in that they borrow less from the Federal Reserve System, and they are net lenders in the Federal Funds Market.

As Lindsay and Towey put it, "California banking must be characterized by special features which allow a more efficient management of reserves than is possible in other regions. Otherwise the comparatively tight position of these banks suggested by all the standard liquidity measures would force them to more frequent borrowing, and make such frequent lending unlikely. By the same token the existence of these special characteristics makes it clear that California banks cannot be judged by common standards. Special weight must be attached to their *appearing* to be close to the line of illiquidity when in fact they may not be any closer than other banks are" [p. 148].

The paradox is resolved by noting three structural characteristics of California banks and an attribute of California's economy. The structural attributes that enable California's banks to get along with less liquidity are their large size, the unusual incidence of branch banking, and the high ratio of time deposits to demand deposits. The "large net inflow of reserves from the rest of the country, especially the contribution of the federal government" [p. 148], is the characteristic of the economy that makes California banks appear to be more liquid.

The peculiar liquidity position of California's banks is compounded out of the following ingredients: a booming economy that makes business and real estate loan demand very strong, a banking structure that enables California's banks to economize on liquidity, and a large flow of funds on income and capital account from the rest of the country that permits California's banks to show signs of great liquidity.

The key position of the flow of funds on federal government account in the liquidity position of California's banks indicates that the economy is vulnerable in two ways to changes in federal government expenditure patterns. One is that the federal government's demand is instrumental in generating the booming California economy. The other is that the flow of funds due to federal government payments may enable California's banks safely to be less liquid in a number of ways than would be prudent in the absence of the government payments. Lindsay and Towey conclude their analysis of the implications of a slowdown or reversal in federal spending patterns by stating, "It must be stated again that we cannot define an adequate liquidity position . . . If there is a general collapse in a region, normal and prudent risks turn out to be imprudent. When collapse comes, it is a mistake to have loaned anything to anyone. In a mild stagnation, however, we can guess that California banks have sufficient secondary reserves to sustain a considerable round of reverses" [p. 154].

As a result there "is the need for special vigilance by public bodies" for, "given the very leanness of California bank liquidity by conventional standards, the potential of illiquidity must be kept actively on the agenda" [p. 155].

Professor David A. Alhadeff does two things in his paper, "California

Banking and Competition." He sets out general principles to guide any discussion of competition or market structure in banking, and he examines evidence on changes in the market structure of California banking between 1951 and 1962.

In his discussion of the general principles, Alhadeff touches upon many topics which should be subjects for full-scale papers in any continuing research effort on banking and finance in California. One of these is the use of public policy instruments to obtain an optimum structure of financial intermediaries. Alhadeff states: "Since it is public policy not to depend entirely on the market mechanism to determine the composition of the financial structure, that function must be performed, in part, by the chartering authorities. In a dynamic growth economy like that of California, it is particularly important to make a periodic review of public policy with respect to the number, kind, and legal powers of the financial institution to be authorized" [p. 171]. Another is the use of bank supervision to replace restrictions now imposed upon both bank entry and bank competition. Alhadeff states that "with or without price controls, the public interest in bank safety requires a program of effective supervision to prevent unsound practices whether induced by too much competition, by incompetence, by cupidity, by fraud, by the pressure of excessive funds, or by any other influence. Thus, further study of ways to increase the effectiveness of bank supervision would serve the public interest both in bank safety and in competition" [p. 168].

The general tone of the paper is that banks are multiproduct firms, and that markets in which banks operate have many dimensions. As a result there is no simple way to rank a bank as a firm in a monopolistic, oligopolistic, or competitive market, and the question as to whether any given change increases competition has no simple answer. A bank operates in many markets. In these markets other banks, nonbank financial firms, households, and ordinary firms may operate on the same side of the market as the bank. Hence at one and the same time a bank may be confronting a perfectly competitive situation and be a monopolist.

The complexity of bank markets has an added dimension in California where statewide branch banking is permitted. Bank customers, in addition to being in different asset and liability markets, also are segmented by their preferences for dealing with a bank that has branches throughout the state as against a bank that is mainly local.

Alhadeff points out that large branch banks also can shift funds easily among their branches. This is particularly important for Cali-

OVERVIEW 11

fornia, where local spurts in growth occur which are very large indeed. Such a locally spurting economy needs outside funds. A branch system which can draw funds from branches in slowly growing regions to branches in the locally spurting area expedites economic growth.

Evidence on the evolution of the market structure of banking in California between 1951 and 1962 is consistent with Alhadeff's formulation of the problem. The result is mixed: it is impossible to tell whether competition has increased or decreased. The percentage of the state's total of bank assets and loans in the largest bank in California decreased, yet in 1962 the largest seven or eight banks in California did the same percentage of bank business as did the largest eleven banks in 1951. In addition, whereas 61 percent of the towns had only one bank in 1951, by 1962 only 46 percent were one-bank towns. Furthermore, whereas there was only one statewide banking system in 1951, by 1962 there were three. All in all there may have been an increase in both concentration and competition in this period.

Alhadeff makes no attempt to forecast the 1975 market structure of banking. The division of banking business in 1975 between large branch systems, small branch systems, and unit banks will be the result not only of economic factors but also of the ever-changing chartering, merger, and regulatory policies of the various federal and state agencies.

Professor Frederic P. Morrissey, in his paper, "The Allocation of Funds by the Commercial Banks in the California Economy, 1946–1975," studies the changing composition of the portfolio of commercial banks in the state during the period 1946 to 1963 and estimates expected values for various portfolio items for the target year 1975. He finds that "the banking industry has responded to changes in the loan requirements in California and has devoted relatively higher proportions of their assets to loans than is reported for commercial banks throughout the United States, New York State, and Illinois" [p. 225].

Throughout, a continuing complaint of the authors has been the paucity and fragmentary nature of the available data. Morrissey notes: "It is surprising that so little information is available on the loan policies of banks—not only for California but for the nation as a whole" [p. 231]. Thus, as is true of almost every analysis in this volume, Morrissey is required to make estimates from very imperfect data about bank behavior in California.

Exploiting the available fragmentary data about interest costs, Morrissey observes that "interest costs are higher at western banks for almost any category of loans than for the nation as a whole" [p. 233]. Even though he notes that such a persistent differential may be necessary to expedite the import of capital to California, he remarks that "this persisting differential connotes an imperfection in the monetary mechanism in the country" [p. 234], for it seems to be larger than is needed in other markets when capital funds move among regions. Nevertheless to the extent that "the higher interest rates do attract more capital to a region and so provide a greater degree of loan accommodations, the continued differential may be more of a blessing than a handicap to western borrowers" [p. 234]. The forecast of slower growth rates for California as compared to the country as a whole and the expected improvements in communication "suggest the possibility of a narrowing of the differential in the future" [p. 234].

Morrissey views bank portfolios as accommodating to the dynamic growth factors in the economy. He expects California's growth to be essentially balanced over the forecast period. Thus, state and local governments, industry, and household activity will grow at basically the same rate as the state's economy while agriculture will grow somewhat more slowly. He therefore expects business loans, loans to individuals, and state and local government securities approximately to double their 1963 values by 1975. As the financing of the growth of loans by sales of federal government securities, which was available to banks in the early postwar period, will not be available to the same extent in the period to 1975, this growth in assets will have to be paralleled by a growth in deposits. For banks to meet the expected demands upon their lending and investing abilities, this implies that they will have to be able to compete effectively with savings and loan associations for time and savings deposits.

Professor Albert H. Schaaf's paper, "The Savings Function and Mortgage Investments of California Banks and Financial Institutions," focuses on two markets: savings-type deposits and mortgages. Although the ideal would be to study all mortgages issued within California, data limitations forced Schaaf to concentrate on residential mortgages to the exclusion of those on commercial and industrial property.

The competition is examined between the commercial banking industry and the other financial industries in the mortgage and savings markets during the postwar period. Although the eastern mutual savings bank industry and the national life insurance industry are both large and growing suppliers of funds to the California residential mortgage market, California savings and loan associations compete with California commercial banks both in the market for residential mortgages and in the market for savings-type deposits.

Traditionally, California commercial banks have been more heavily committed to savings-type deposits and mortgages than banks in other parts of the country. This heavier emphasis has continued throughout the postwar period. However, the difference between California commercial banks and banks elsewhere in the country has diminished during this period. Despite the upward trend in real estate loans held by California commercial banks throughout the period, both their share of the total California mortgage debt and the weight of mortgage debt in their portfolios have decreased.

Schaaf discusses the pros and cons of more active commercial bank entry into the mortgage brokerage and servicing industry. He points out that there are meaningful relative advantages for the independent mortgage brokers and that mortgage brokers, as agents for out-of-state financial institutions, are an important factor in sustaining competition in the mortgage market.

Mortgages and the closely related savings shares at savings and loan associations are major instruments used to import funds into California. For the funds supplied by commercial banks to the mortgage market, it can be assumed that all are California funds. All of the funds supplied by mutual savings banks, some 80 percent of those by life insurance companies, and approximately 25 percent of those by savings and loan associations, come from out of state. Thus the decreasing ratio of commercial bank funds to the total funds in the mortgage market implies an ever-increasing dependence of the mortgage market upon funds imported from out of state.

Looking toward 1975, Schaaf sees the weight of commercial banks in the savings and mortgage markets as being dependent upon the legal and institutional framework within which the mortgage market will function. "As long as the savings and loan associations are locked into the mortgage market, and the major interregional lenders remain active, it seems improbable that commercial banks will find it advantageous to treat permanent mortgage lending as more than a residual activity" [p. 279].

Of course the reverse side of the coin of locking the savings and loan associations into the mortgage markets is that they will not be free to compete with commercial banks, except by way of subterfuges, for non-residential consumer credit and business loans. However, the legal restrictions that lead to compartmentalization and specialization of financial markets also diminish competition. It is a matter of continuing importance for public policy makers whether compartmentalization implies adequate competition in all of the affected markets: savings, mortgage lending, consumer credit, and business loans.

Professor Paul F. Wendt, in his paper "Earnings and Capital Problems of California Banks, 1946–1975," examines the earnings experience of various classes of California commercial banks and forecasts earnings for the period to 1975. The reason for the interest in earnings is that "an adequate supply of bank capital is in the long run interest both of the public and the stockholders" [p. 287], and "bank profitability is one key to the adequacy of present and future earnings" [p. 287].

Bank profitability is a determinant of bank capital because it is a determinant both of the ability of a bank to grow by means of retained earnings and of a willingness of outside investors to acquire bank capital liabilities. Wendt argues "that high rates of economic growth in the state have sustained rapid growth of commercial banks assets and high profit levels . . ." [p. 291]. As a result of the high and rising profit levels, "approximately three-quarters of the total capital added [by insured commercial banks in California] resulted from retained profits, with the balance representing issuance of additional bank stock" [p. 305].

One aspect of the postwar expansion has been the more rapid increase of bank loans than of bank assets—portfolio shifts were one of the reasons for the profitability of banks. As a result of portfolio changes, "loan income more than doubled as a percentage of total income from 1946 to 1961 for the large California banks, and increased substantially for all California insured commercial banks. In 1961 and 1962, loan income accounted for two-thirds of total earnings for California banks with deposits in excess of $50 million. Meanwhile, interest on securities represented less than 20 percent of total earnings for the larger banks in these years, as compared with 40–50 percent in 1946" [p. 304]. The portion of the rise in bank earnings, as well as the stimulus to the California economy, due to such portfolio changes will not be available to the same extent in the period to 1975 as in the earlier postwar period. This factor places a constraint upon the expected rate of increase in bank earnings.

Wendt derives a model that relates bank earnings growth to the growth of the economy. On the basis of independent forecasts of earnings growth and expense growth, Wendt concludes that "the forecast rates of growth of various measures of bank earnings are consistently lower than the rates of growth observed in 1946 to 1962. . . . It therefore appears that retained earnings may not be as likely a source of addition to bank capital as they were in the recent past. Therefore, if the capital accounts of California banks are to grow as required by the growth of deposits, it may be expected that banks will pursue more aggressively 'new ways' of raising capital through the sale of senior securities" [pp. 325–26]. In an appendix, Wendt concludes his paper by examining "some issues associated with the use of senior securities by commercial banks" [p. 326].

"An Evaluation of the Payments Mechanism in California, 1946–1975," by Professor Richard E. Towey, investigates a rapidly changing aspect of banking usually not considered in discussion of banking policy and structure. Banks do the mechanical job of operating the economy's payments mechanism. They do it so well that the general public, and even sophisticated commentators, usually are not aware that there is any problem involved in making payments, especially payments at a distance. The growth of the economy, the rise in the importance of demand deposits relative to currency in making payments, and the increased complexity of the financial system have combined to generate a rapidly growing flood of checks. The purely mechanical problem of processing the checks threatened to lead to difficulties until banks adjusted their techniques and adopted sophisticated, computerized operations. These changes in the mechanics of banking potentially have broad implications for the structure of the banking system and the public regulatory agencies.

Banks were confronted with a serious problem of labor costs and turnover. The tedious, boring, detailed work of hand processing checks led to mounting labor costs, not only because of wage pressure and an increase in numbers but also because of a very high turnover rate of labor. The labor saving devices of the automated check handling process will tend to lower labor costs as much, or more, by decreasing labor turnover as by decreasing worker time per unit of check processing.

The computers used in the automated payments mechanism have capabilities which, if exploited, can transform traditional banking practices with regard to credit extension. That is, the transformation of the mechanics of banking may facilitate fundamental changes in banking. As an indication of the type of change that might occur, Towey notes: "The difference between present credit card plans and bank checks is more one of degree than of substance" [p. 352]. The generalization of bank credit card plans, revolving bank credit, and the automatic debiting of recurring bills (utilities, mortgages, life insurance, etc., payments), can lead to a banking system whose practices are "analogous to the British practice of overdraft banking" [p. 352].

The evolving payments mechanism may induce changes in the structure of banking. Towey notes that "with larger computers and data transmission by wire, economies of scale may become so large—perhaps because overlapping wire networks, duplicating computer facilities, and intertie complexes prove very costly—that payments functions could be performed most efficiently by a few giant banks in each area" [p. 353]. In addition, the underlying relations between money and the economy might be affected for "with the future changes the speed of making transactions probably will be increased further. A given amount of cash balances held for transactions purposes will thus be able to mediate a progressively greater volume of exchanges" [p. 355].

As a result of the potential effects of computerization, "regulatory agencies must be alert for situations where institutional changes are desirable in the interests of the general public. Moreover, it is incumbent upon regulatory agencies to acquaint themselves fully with the innovations before their actual introduction to the banks. Changes may be so extensive and rapid that society cannot afford 'wait and see' policies" [p. 354].

4. SLIGHTED AREAS

This in almost all its facets is a pilot study—i.e. a study that opens up a research territory for later more intensive exploration. In addition, the study was organized very quickly; the papers were completed in a short span of time; and the resources available were severely limited. As a result, a number of vital problem areas relating to banking in a region were slighted. In this section some of the slighted subject areas are introducted in the hope that further research on banking and finance in California will be stimulated.

a. The relation between commercial banks and other financial institutions

In setting out the frame of reference for the studies it was necessary to decide if "banking" was a shorthand for the entire set of financial institutions of an economy, if it meant strictly-defined "commercial banking," or if it was something in between, such as all depository institutions. For most of the papers the decision was made to define banking as *commercial* banking and to take as the central area of study the behavior and impact of those financial institutions that emit deposits subject to check—i.e. which have "money" among their liabilities. However, commercial banks are not only a major but also a diversified product line financial institution. Therefore, the studies of necessity had to overflow the bounds of the definition and take up aspects of other financial institutions. The other nonbank financial institutions were not studied in depth or in their entirety; they were studied only to the extent necessitated by the particular problems under investigation.

A research study of the system of financial institutionᵣ operating within California, which detailed the nature and effects of the various organizations, would be most useful to business, households, and the public authority. In fact, a complete description and the development of consistent data for the financial system should be one of the first steps taken in any continuing research effort. This is important for, as pointed out by Minsky, nonbank financial intermediaries and commercial banks are both complementary and rival institutions. The net flow of funds between California and the rest of the country is, to a large extent, a flow among financial institutions. Unless we know the magnitude of the operations within the state of, for example, sales finance companies, and have information about the sources of their financing, the part these organizations play in financing regional growth cannot be known.

Another problem relating to financial intermediaries is the role of life insurance companies lending and investing in the state as compared with the domiciles of the companies and the distributions of policy holders. Are the huge life insurance companies importers or exporters of funds to California? In addition to the extent that life insurance companies make loans to businesses, they are competitors in the main line of commercial bank business. As the rate of growth of loans by commercial banks in the state tapers off—because loans become such a large proportion of total bank assets that they no longer can grow appreciably faster than total bank assets—can the gap be filled by life insurance lending, or does it imply that a higher rate of increase in the money supply will be needed?

One particular aspect of the various financial institutions in the state is that they are "regulated" or overseen by different state agencies. Should there not be a single "Commission of Financial Institutions" which inspects, charters, licenses, and sets rules of behavior for all financial institutions operating within the state?

b. The optimal regulatory structure for banking and finance

As a result of a spate of failures by commercial banks in the winter and spring of 1964–1965, once again the issue of the optimal structure of regulating and chartering agencies for commercial banks is under discussion. From the point of view of a state government, two questions arise. One is the way in which the state's own chartering, licensing, inspecting, and regulating agencies should be organized. The second is whether the state's authorities should have economic policy as well as legal and inspection functions. The first will be discussed here, the second in the next section.

Of course, once the question of an optimal regulatory structure is raised, it is necessary to ask why regulate at all—in what way is the welfare of the community increased by regulating any particular industry? As far as banking is concerned, there are two aspects which call for regulation. Banks' demand liabilities are money, and the volume and rate of change of the money supply influence the behavior of the economy. In addition, as the general acceptability of money is a necessary condition for normal functioning of the economy, regulation of each money issuer to make sure that his monetary liabilities meet some minimum standard is necessary: regulation is a grade labeling device.

The above are arguments for regulation of banking and finances, but not for state regulation. The federal government has three agencies that regulate banks: The Controller of the Currency, the Federal Deposit Insurance Corporation, and for its member banks, the Federal Reserve System. A state could have very simple bank laws if it so wished. By issuing no state charters, only national banks would exist, and they would all be members of the Federal Reserve System and the Federal Deposit Insurance Corporation.

There is a precedent for California abstaining from chartering banks. The constitution of the State of California at the time of the Civil War forbade the practice of banking. The prohibition as contained in the state constitution was:

> The legislature shall have no power to pass any act granting any charter for banking purposes, but association may be formed, under general laws, for the deposit of gold and silver; but no such association shall make, issue, or put in circulation any bill, check, ticket, certificate, promissory note, or other paper, or the paper of any bank, to circulate as money.
>
> The legislature of this State shall prohibit by law any person or persons, association, company, or corporation from exercising the privileges of banking or creating paper to circulate as money.[1]

For example, there is no effective federal regulation of that very large and important class of financial intermediaries—insurance companies. If any effective regulation of these national concerns is to exist, the state must take action. It is a curious phenomenon that commercial banks, which typically do not have banking offices in more than one state, are to a large extent subject to control and regulation by agencies of the

---

[1] Cited in Bernard Moses, "Legal Tender Notes in California," *Quarterly Journal of Economics*, VII, October 1892, pp. 1–2.

federal government, whereas insurance companies, whose liabilities typically are sold throughout the country and which usually have offices in many states, are regulated by the individual states.

Given that the state, to protect the interests of its citizens against fraud, must regulate some financial institutions, is there any reason to have independent commissions and commissioners for the different domains? What is gained by having separate agencies for the different types of institutions, and what would be gained by having a single regulatory agency for all of finance? Robinson points out in his paper that "regulatory judgments very easily can be turned from true long-term public protection into protectionist devices for the benefit of their institutional constituents" [p. 55], which indicates that there are real advantages to a single regulatory agency for all of finance.

The above are some questions that should be answered which are not considered in this study. Inasmuch as they cover issues of policy formation and the objectives of economic policy, there are no simple right or wrong answers. All that there can be is serious discussion of the issues, including a discussion of the objectives and efficient instruments for state regulatory agencies. It would serve no useful purpose to offer off-the-cuff views in this introduction. A useful purpose is served, however, by asserting that there are serious issues of policy which should be studied.

At the same time, it should be emphasized that "perhaps the most important positive function of regulatory policy is to allow and even facilitate the kind of changes needed for the future rather than to retard them, as might occur under a mainly negative policy" [Robinson, p. 32]. To make sure that regulatory policy is not backward looking, nor narrowly based, it should be subject to independent scrutiny and review. The academic community does this for the federal regulatory agencies. Some means should be developed to interest the local academic community in the continuing critical evaluation of state policy with respect to finance.

It also should be emphasized that too often state regulatory agencies are guided by rather narrow accounting or legal precepts and frequently tend to draw their staffs from the regulated industry. Certainly, state regulation of finance is so intimately connected with the economy of the state that the regulatory body should be guided by enlightened economic analysis and research.

Once again it should be emphasized that little hard knowledge exists about how the bodies that regulate and guide financial institutions within the state operate their objectives and how instruments have not been studied. Serious, independent, critical research on regulation within the state should be undertaken.

c. Independent state economic policy

California is a very large economy—larger than many national states. For example, California had some 17½ million inhabitants in 1963; Canada's population was 19 million. However, the average per capita income in California was at least 50 percent greater than in Canada. California is a larger economy than Canada. Canada can operate a monetary and fiscal policy in the interests of its citizens. Can California have a monetary and fiscal policy that is determined by the interests of Californians? That is, is what is good for the United States necessarily good for California?

For reasons which need not be examined at this time, California has been a rapidly growing part of the American economy from 1950 to date. Within the state, business opportunities were good and plentiful; there was an ample number of vigorous expansion-minded business men; and certainly adequate financing was available to execute their plans. Unemployment rates in California were approximately the same as in the country at large during this period, but this seemingly was a special attribute of large-scale migration to California. Apparently many families come to California without a job and find work after they arrive.

Even though there is no shortage of entrepreneurial skill throughout the United States, during the last years of the 1950's and the first few years of the 1960's, the growth rate as well as the unempolyment rate in the United States were not satisfactory.

As a result, the prescription for monetary and fiscal policy for the United States called for monetary and fiscal ease. The economic situation in California called for monetary and fiscal constraint—particularly in the light of possible speculative excesses. Would it be at all possible to operate monetary and fiscal policy so that the differential required impacts were consistent with the needs of the various regions? This is a problem that has not been examined in the literature; however, regions like Appalachia, and states like California, are much larger economies than many which do have independent monetary and fiscal policies.

A number of measures that expedite the flow of financial resources among states are legacies of the Great Depression. The insurance of deposits in savings and loan associations by an "agency of the federal government" decreases the interest rate premium needed to make funds move. The FHA and VA endorsement of mortgages makes them national assets—acceptable by all without private investigation. Thus home mortgages become an instrument that can be used to import funds into the state at a relatively small premium in interest rates. Similarly— although this is not of particular importance for California—various government farm subsidy and control programs first take the form of endorsed loans.

These federal government policies, among others, make it easier for the money supply to grow rapidly in those areas where income is growing rapidly. Unlike a country, where the rate of growth of the money supply is to a large extent determined by the operations and decisions of the Central Bank, for a region within a country the growth of the money supply is determined mainly by the functioning of the economy. That is, the line of causation within a region of a national economy is more from income to money than from money to income, whereas many economists argue that the line of causation for the country is from money to income.

Inasmuch as the state's money supply is a function of its income within a context of existing financial markets, the independent monetary and fiscal policy of a state must operate upon the determinants of income and the structure of financial markets.

One determinant of income is the state's budget. If a rapidly growing state wanted to cut its rate of growth, it could do so by running a large surplus. It should minimize its dependence upon borrowing for the construction of new facilities. If there are dangers that the economic basis for the rapid growth can wither away, then it is very much to the long-run interest of the state's economy to minimize the indebtedness of the state and its citizens to the rest of the country. A budgetary surplus and constraint upon debt financing by state and local governments are ways in which the growth rate of a rapidly growing region can be restrained.

Private investment is another determinant of income within a region. Investment depends not only upon technological and demand factors but also on the conditions under which financing is available. To the extent that (1) the financing of investment within a rapidly growing area requires the importation of funds, and (2) these funds are brought in through the "mediation" of financial intermediaries, a coordinated state policy which regulates the behavior of financial intermediaries may be an effective way of constraining economic growth to a sustainable rate.

From the perspective of a rapidly growing region, the various instruments which are used to import capital are not all alike. In particular, the instruments differ in the effects they can be expected to have if the growth rate slows down. Some of the instruments can be expected to amplify a retardation whereas other instruments will have a more nearly neutral effect. In particular, the importation of capital funds by way of short-term or deposit liabilities contains the largest potential for an amplification of a slowdown in growth. The exploration of ways in which state regulatory power can be used to induce a substitution of long-term and equity for short-term and depository instruments seems very much in order.

Such a regulatory policy can be expected to slow down the rate of growth for any level of external demand stimulation and therefore ease the adjustment to a lower level of external stimulation.

The above are rather Draconian policy guidelines for a state that has been enjoying vigorous growth. However, given the national nature of the money and capital markets, the only feasible way for a state to constrain its own growth is by adopting extremely conservative fiscal and regulatory policies.

The interrelations between monetary and fiscal policy on the national level have been studied at length. Studies are needed on how state level monetary and financial policy should be integrated in order to achieve desired ends.

Of course, it must be added perhaps that the best policy for a state may not be to constrain growth; perhaps a state must get while the getting is good.

5. CONCLUSION

One of the most amazing truths uncovered by the participants in this study is how few hard facts and how little economic analysis dealing with the economy and the financial system of California exist. Certainly bits and pieces have been investigated in depth, but no study meeting modern standards of scholarship existed that could be used as a starting point for the special studies. In addition, it became evident as the studies were under way that really very little in the way of data useful for economic analysis was available for the state. In particular, there was little in the way of useful financial data. The data that do exist are by-products of legal and regulatory functions and often are not very useful for economic analysis.

One important finding of these studies, and one of the most vital recommendations of the Governor's Committee, is that a continuing program of research on the financial and economic system of California should be undertaken. Perhaps a program to support a "Center for the Study of California's Financial System" within the Institute of Business and Economic Research at Berkeley and Los Angeles would be very much in order. Certainly the studies in this volume have uncovered more problems than they have solved. It would be a pity if the start made in these studies is not followed by a continuing, serious research effort.

A second important theme running through many of these studies is that the forecast of continued growth of California at a more rapid rate than for the country as a whole should be accepted with some skepticism. Although there are no meaningful physical or real resource barriers to such growth, the financial patterns that emerged during the past decade of rapid growth are such that they cannot simply be extrapolated. The financial developments in the next decade will need to be different from those in the past decade, even if the growth of the real sectors, including "exports" to the federal government, do turn out to conform to the optimistic forecasts.

Another theme, which does not run through these studies but which should be kept in mind by the reader, is that economics is not called the "dismal science" without cause. Economists tend to see the complexity and the difficulties in a developing situation—pessimism may be a chronic shortcoming of serious economists. However, if by warning of the difficulties and perils that face the state this study makes policy makers and citizens more aware of the problems they may face, and thus arms them better and prepares them to make wise decisions, it will have served a useful purpose.

CHAPTER I

POINTS OF DEPARTURE

Economic Role and Objectives for California Banking and Financial Institutions[1]

ROLAND I. ROBINSON

THIS PAPER summarizes the economic functions and systemic roles reasonably expected of banks and other financial institutions. Given a general statement of functions and roles, our focus narrows to the more specific performance expectations of such institutions in an economy such as California. Since these expectations are qualitative as well as quantitative, part of our task is to suggest criteria for appraisal and evaluation of the functioning of these financial institutions. To be useful operationally, these criteria must be as specific as possible. The task would be incomplete if no attempt were made to evaluate functions for which quantitative or statistical testing is not possible or appropriate. Thus, at times this inquiry depends on little more than intuition. Since the survey covers not only the role or functions of the financial system but also its objectives, the treatment must be forward-looking.

This analysis is divided into three steps to correspond to the three parts of this paper: (1) functions banks and financial institutions are expected to perform, (2) criteria for banking and financial performance, and (3) objectives for the system of banks and other financial institutions which may be achieved through state regulatory power. To give the reader a simple frame of reference for devising standards for evaluating the functioning of our financial system, these areas are first examined generally and philosophically.

---

[1] The phrase "banks and other financial institutions" appears many times in this paper. For purposes of national monetary and credit policy, this dual category seems appropriate even if one gives a great deal of weight to the Gurley-Shaw thesis. In dealing with regional problems it is probably more useful to think of each type of financial institution separately: banks, savings and loan associations, insurance companies, and so forth. Nevertheless, even at a regional level commercial banks stand a bit apart from other financial institutions. This usage, therefore, seems to convey best the nature of the aggregating process.

a. Functions expected of banks and financial institutions

The financial system is a servant of the whole economic system of production and distribution. In a dominantly private economic system, finance allows saving and investment functions to be performed separately by the economic units best equipped to do so. Concurrently, finance gives individual economic units considerable strategic flexibility by supplying liquidity options and permitting them to adjust to prevailing economic conditions, to take advantage of any existing profit opportunities, to avoid economic difficulties during adverse conditions, and most of all to grow and adapt to the opportunities of a dynamic economic system. The most specialized, possibly the most important, of the liquidity roles played by the financial system is the provision of instruments—demand deposits—that serve as money.

Demand deposits, supplied by commercial banks, are "demand" in the sense that they can be converted into legal money on demand. The system operates smoothly, however, only when the algebraic total of the "demands"—the call for and restoration or redeposit of legal tender currency—is roughly in balance or is following reasonably predictable patterns. Commercial banks offer a variety of other financial services, including saving intermediation of a substantial character. Commercial banks, the most important of all financial institutions, are the most difficult to evaluate. As they have monetary significance, the government must control them more than it does other financial intermediaries. Yet, they are private institutions, and to fulfill all of their true economic roles they must be aggressive, profit-maximizing, private economic units.

The characteristics of financial intermediaries other than commercial banks are determined mainly by the needs of the savers and borrowers they serve. It can be argued that some financial institutions are oriented more toward the needs of savers than of borrowers. Certainly, the savings and loan associations, with their strong representations of liquidity to savers, are more successful than the old building and loan associations, with their primary goal of helping families become home owners. A borrower-oriented financial institution is hard to find. Although credit unions seem to have started out as such, in the course of time they also have turned their attention to the savers' side. Pension funds are highly successful because they respond to a strongly felt, but earlier unmet, need of savers.

When funds are in strong demand, it is natural that financial institutions court savers and impose stringencies on borrowers. With a different market balance, borrowers apparently enjoy better treatment.

For example, the entry of commercial banks into consumer credit and term lending during the late 1930's was an adaptation to borrower needs.

Have financial institutions, in attempting to meet the demands both of borrowers and lenders, assumed obligations not dischargeable under stress? Many savers have been given implied or outright promises of liquidity and borrowers more-assured and longer-term access to money. Under ordinary conditions financial institutions can meet both obligations. But in emergencies, do these assurances rest on expectations of governmental aid? Public policy toward economic stabilization may have made the question academic, but it is at least worthy of academic attention.

b. Financial requirements for growth

General functions of commercial banks and other financial institutions are refined to more specific terms when the problems of a large and rapidly growing area are considered. California's expansion, based on population immigration, capital import, and internal development, therefore presents a special aspect of the general financial problems caused by growth.

Most rapidly growing areas are unable to generate enough internal savings for new capital expenditures; capital must be imported. Within a sovereign nation having a homogeneous money system, regional capital movements should encounter the smallest possible degree of resistance. That some resistance remains is amply demonstrated by true interest rate differentials. Comparisons are clouded because credit risks probably are not comparable between areas of rapid and of slower but satisfactory growth.

A different type of question can be asked: does not a rapidly growing area present less credit risk than a lagging area? If it can be shown that California interest rates tend to be higher than those in areas of slower but satisfactory growth, and are also above rates in areas that are not growing, then frictions in the capital importation process presumably exist.

The exact role of financial institutions in the capital import process is hard to assess. Accordingly, criteria for performance of their function are vague. Some capital is imported directly without resort to local financial organization. If a California-based national corporation borrows on the national money markets through a New York investment banker, local financial aid is minimal. For borrowers without access to national capital markets, successful and low-cost capital importation through local financial intermediaries is more critical.

c. Criteria for banking and financial performance

Criteria for operation of the financial system are simply more explicit expressions of those which might be established for the functioning of the entire economic system. Stability, ample job opportunities, and a satisfactory growth rate, are some of our national economic goals. A further goal is freedom—freedom for the individual to achieve such economic objectives as his abilities and energies permit. The financial system should serve these ends. A simple criterion for success is how close do we come to these goals?

How can performance be tested? Even with focus narrowed from the economic system as a whole to the banking and financial system in particular, no obvious tests emerge. An abstract statement of the functions of the system may bear no relation to reality. A common test is comparison with similar situations elsewhere.

Widely variant basic conditions and economic history render it pointless to compare United States banking procedures with those of other countries. But within the United States, comparisons of states and areas are not only proper but possibly illuminating. Although business conditions and economic history have varied within the United States, all states have had a considerable period of operating under the same general legal system and a homogeneity of opportunity that present a valid basis for comparison.

Another test is examination of operating results. If the system is judged efficient on a comparison of factor input and product outputs, then costs and profits present valid evidence about economic efficiency. The problem lies, of course, in the comparison of inputs and outputs. Arbitrary and conjectural judgments of real efficiency may be the only bases for evaluation, but are better than none at all.

Complaints from sensitive areas about the malfunctioning of the financial system provide strategic, if not systematic, evidence. For example, the continued complaints about the financial problems of small business present opportunities to test and appraise the banking and financial system.

Quality of competition is hard to appraise, but an optimum degree of competition certainly seems to be a basic condition for the operation of a banking system in the public interest.

Finally, a banking and financial system, which tries new ideas and procedures in its own sphere before they are demonstrably profitable, is better prepared to accept, finance, and deal with an innovating economy.

d. Criteria and their conflicts

Once the basic functions of the financial and banking systems are identified, it is possible if not easy to set suitable criteria for judging its functional role. Financial institutions are expected to be safe *and* to finance and stimulate growth. The two objectives inherently conflict as do their criteria for judgment. A low loss experience can be regarded either as an excellent record or as a failure to take the risks expected of the financial system. It is necessary, therefore, to seek optimizing rather than maximizing criteria and to suggest common denominators for two or more objectives and the criteria for their judgment.

e. Financial system objectives achieved through state regulatory powers

The public regulation of banks and financial institutions in the United States lies somewhere between the extremes of public economic intervention encountered in other parts of the system. Most industrial companies are comparatively free of specific public regulation. Entry into such businesses is free. Exit by failure, though regrettable, is permissible. Competition is expected, and efforts to reduce it are subject to legal penalties. Public restraints on prices are few, except in wartime. Profits are subject to taxation but are not controlled. Capital structures are influenced primarily by the standards of private investors and institutions acting for them. Financing is controlled but primarily by penalizing untruthfulness.

Some exceptions exist. Public utility companies, providing electric, gas, or telephone services usually have exclusive franchise areas or operations, and the public interest is safeguarded by fairly explicit regulation of charges and financing. Public utility companies have "failed" in the financial sense, but their operations almost always continue. At present it is hard to imagine them even being allowed to fail, though they are sometimes permitted to be rather barrenly unprofitable.

Banks and financial institutions are not freely chartered, but competition is expected to prevail. Prices (interest rates) are partly controlled but are subject to considerable fluctuations. Occasional failures are permitted, but public policy is expected to avoid a general financial collapse. Despite the more negative than positive aspects of public regulation, it is a major factor in determining the characteristics of the present financial system. If modification of the financial system is contemplated, the supervisory system might administer these changes but itself be changed in the process.

To the extent that banks and financial institutions are involved in problems of general economic stability and growth, the relevant powers of government are mostly at the federal level. However, in this study it seems appropriate to focus on the important structural and supervisory problems that can be influenced at the state level. Although banks and financial institutions are chartered at both state and federal levels, state standards can have a powerful influence not only on the institutions within their own jurisdictions but also on those federally chartered. In some cases federal standards are adapted to the standards of the states in which they operate. The principal structural matters with which state authority deals are: minimum chartering requirements, powers to operate at more than one office, and the rights to merge or change corporate characteristics. The disposition of earnings by distribution or retention and the quality of assets are also subject to state influence.

In general, negative powers of regulation are stronger than positive. Banks and financial institutions can be forbidden quite successfully to do certain things, but it is hard to push them into actions not to their liking. Positive actions by financial institutions that would support growth, for example, might be hard to require of banks unless the actions were to their taste. The history of regulation has been that of prohibiting actions possibly injurious to depositors or savers. Borrowers or users of credit, on the other side, have received little aid or protection from the law except in one (doubtful) form—the usury laws.

Growth, almost the central subject of this series of papers, may require the exercise of more positive powers. The implementing of present regulatory systems with such powers may have to be considered.

f. Early use of regulatory powers to realize optimum 1975 expectations

Quite apart from regulatory action, financial institutions evolve and adapt to economic conditions and opportunities as they occur. Perhaps the most important positive function of regulatory policy is to allow and even facilitate the kind of changes needed for the future rather than to retard them, as might occur under a mainly negative philosophy. Certainly the kind of banking and financial structure needed in 1975 cannot be created suddenly at that time; it will have to grow and develop during the intervening years. Many types of regulatory decisions with respect to the financial structure are irreversible. The right choice needs to be made now.

The areas for decision are probably not new; rather decisions on familiar matters must be made for the new conditions of the future. The balance of protection for savers and borrowers should be reappraised. The optimum number and size of financial institutions need to be judged. The optimum level of competition between and among types of financial institutions needs to be encouraged. The optimum (and not maximum) amount of capital required for the financial system should be accumulated in anticipation of need. Most of all, innovational spirit needs to be encouraged, not restricted by needless regulation.

1. FUNCTIONS EXPECTED OF BANKS AND FINANCIAL INSTITUTIONS

The functions legitimately expected of banks and other financial institutions change with the evolution of the economy. What we expect of them now is indicated by the seven headings in this section. Future expectations might create a quite different and possibly much longer list.

a. Allocation of capital by the financial system

In a free market economy such as ours the price system allocates most economic resources, including that of loan capital. Concurrently, the nature of the institutional structure of finance clearly has some influence on this process, as intended by the pertinent laws and regulations. Customs and traditions also carry influence. The purpose of this subsection is to raise some critical questions about the allocation process. For example, have credit standards of the past encouraged or discouraged growth?

Economic growth can be divided into two parts: growth in the number of productive factors or units (mainly labor), and growth in the productivity of each unit of factor input. It is probably accidental that economic growth in the United States for the past seven decades appears to have been divided about equally between these two elements. Growth in factor input has been not far from $1\frac{3}{4}$ percent per annum, and productivity growth has fluctuated around the same level.

The saving which has financed both improved capital equipment and the expansion required to keep pace with the larger work force is done by business itself as well as by individuals. By custom and tradition a great deal of this capital in the business sphere is provided by internal means—business saving. Where external financing is required, such as by most public utilities, needs are quite predictable and the financial mechanism seems to have responded. The criterion of financial performance, if one is needed, is the steady availability of funds for such purposes at reasonable rates. The last proviso is not added as an escape clause; "reasonable" rates can be interpreted only in terms of the general rate structure of the market.

This balance between retained earnings and growth with occasional resort to external financing is applicable to the United States as a whole. To what extent, however, must it be modified when dealing with California which has grown not only by natural and internal increase but also by a large population in-migration? Ordinary growth needs for capital may outrun the rate of internal generation and require external financing along with some associated degree of capital importation.

To the extent this growth affects business concerns having access to national capital markets, the results lend themselves to fairly easy appraisal. Has the greater or more frequent resort to the capital markets of large nationally known corporations concentrated in California been a market disadvantage? Have they paid higher interest rates or been hamstrung with more restrictive provisions? No evidence exists that such has been the case, but the opposite is not quite assured.

The financial effects of growth on business concerns dependent on local sources of funds is a more important consideration even if the evidence is far from clear. Higher prices of goods produced in other areas and marketed in California have been attributed to cost-of-transportation differentials. The test might be in the capital costs of goods produced locally by smaller business in all areas of the country. An example might be bricks or bread. Are California capital costs of production for such goods appreciably higher than elsewhere? Is California small business less capital intensive? Is it less productive, or more?

The role of capital in increasing productivity is somewhat more difficult and complex. Presumably capital deepening—provision of a greater amount of capital for each worker—should lead to greater productivity. Although the national saving rate has been high enough to provide for some deepening, it is remarkable that in fact the ratio of capital to total factor input has increased rather slowly. The capital/output ratio has been very nearly constant for aggregates of American industry although the composition of output has changed materially. The question to be raised here is, has the financial mechanism given optimal aid to capital deepening?

Productivity is influenced by advancing technology, a factor which may or may not require added capital. When first introduced, new technology usually requires different capital equipment so that some of the old is outmoded and must be scrapped and replaced. Since rapidly changing technologies probably require external financing more often and more urgently than those changing more slowly, it is expectable that a more-than-proportionate part of loan funds placed through capital markets should go into areas of rapid technological advance. However, such areas are likely to be growing in total output as well as in productivity. Areas of stable technology are often those of shrinking market shares. Exceptions exist: agriculture has been armed with rapidly improved technology but that has had no discernible effect on the dwindling market share of agricultural products.

Advancing technology can, of course, have the effect of being capital economizing rather than capital requiring. Where this is the case, capital requirements of the financial system are unchanged. Although technology has been capital economizing in some industries (e.g. passenger transportation) this does not appear to have been true of output as a whole.

A large part of productivity is based on intangible forms of capital such as personal skills, health, dependability, and honesty. Funds spent to develop skills may be counted as capital, and one criterion of an innovating financial system is its ingenuity in working out ways to finance productive, even though intangible, advances. The relationship of financial organization to the other intangible factors seems too remote to be amenable to financial influences.

Encouragement of capital flow in directions of productivity improvement sometimes may be hampered by interest rates. High interest rates do not deter changes or improvements which pay for themselves in a short period of time and put very little strain on the system of interest rates. Changes or improvements, such as education, not yielding benefits until the more distant future cannot be accepted on quite the same terms. Because of the enormous cumulative power of discounting at high rates of interest, remote benefits have modest present value only if low rates are used in their calculation; however, low rates are generally out of keeping with those used in evaluating capital expenditures.

One of the functions of the price system is to assure the consumer that his will is respected in the market place. In totalitarian systems, capital is usually channeled into "productive" uses by fiat and consumers are forced to save beyond what appears to be their choice. In our freer economy the allocation between consumer and "productive" uses of capital is made by the market. With all due respect to the freedom represented by this process, one cannot help but wonder whether institutional characteristics of our system sometimes bias this choice. In a rapidly growing area such as California the bias could be aggravated. Consumer uses of capital tend to return high rates of interest which are particularly marked in intermediate-term uses. Profit-maximizing banks sometimes aver that no matter how tight the money markets may become they will always find money for consumer uses because of its superior profitability.

Mortgage uses of capital do not yield such sharply higher rates of return, but the differential is significant and most institutional investors, such as life insurance companies, are disposed to prefer mortgages when they are available. Have price rigidities in the rates on consumer uses of funds led to an allocation of capital to this area in excess of what it would have been with more flexible prices? This is more a national than a regional issue. It can, however, have unusually severe impacts on a growing region since the magnitude of demand for consumer capital, particularly for housing, is likely to be unusually strong. The acceleration process tends to magnify these demands in a rapidly growing area. The adverse impact is on borrowers who, for noneconomic reasons such as pride or tradition, are not prepared to outbid the consumer uses of capital.

b. Meeting legitimate credit needs

The lending process may entail substantial differences in the terms financial intermediaries are willing to grant on funds loaned and the needs of borrowers. The basic preference of commercial banks for short-term credit is very strong. Aside from their traditional preference, the demand nature of much of their liabilities is consonant with such a preference. Life insurance companies, with little or no need for liquidity, prefer rather long-term credits, particularly those in which they can safeguard or guarantee the rate of interest to be received over a long period of time. Their actuarial liabilities, however, are calculated on the assumption of a stated or given interest rate. In practice life insurance companies like to better this rate but they are desperately anxious not to default on earning it. Since their liabilities calculated on an actuarial basis run very far into the future, it can be said that their true economic liabilities are more remote than the average maturity of their loans and securities.

Other investors or financial intermediaries have specialized preferences and tastes based on institutional considerations. The net result, however, is that no financial intermediary has a clear-cut preference for maturities in the middle range of time. These so-called intermediate-term credit maturities are needed by many, particularly industrial, corporations. Cyclically vulnerable companies are subject to vacillating feelings about debt in their capital structures. They prefer to have none, but large lumpy capital expenditures force them to use debt. Because of the rates of return used in screening such capital expenditures and the margins required in estimating cash flow, these large lumpy capital expenditures often can be paid for in relatively few years. Credit may be extended originally as long-term in form, but in effect it can be and is handled as if it were intermediate-term credit. The call provisions of corporate bonds are sometimes used to convert nominally long-term into actual intermediate-term obligations.

Commercial-bank term loans are the principal credit device aimed frankly at the intermediate-term sector of this market. Combined with the general customer relationship offered by banks, the use of such credit often proves to be advantageous both to borrower and to lender. The one shortcoming of this institutional device is irregularity in availability of term-loan credit by commercial banks. During periods of high and active business when the Federal Reserve puts a ceiling on demand deposit expansion so that "money is tight," commercial banks tend to cut back more sharply on term lending than on other forms of credit expansion. In other words, intermediate-term credit is rationed more strictly at the very time when it might serve its basic purpose most usefully. Equipment leasing and trade credit may be partial substitutes for term loans but both are inferior substitutes. A steady supply of term credit may be an important element in sustained growth.

Commercial banks may have aggravated the situation for themselves by their interest charge practices. Banks usually have charged a somewhat higher rate for term loans than for short-term credit of the same size and quality. The differential, however, usually has been less than the slope of interest rate yield curves would justify. The most recent Federal Reserve survey of bank loans in the fall of 1957 showed material interest-rate differentials on small-term loans but on larger-term loans the differentials were small.

Intermediate-term credit may be particularly important in California. Rapid growth tends to be associated with capital-expansion needs which can be financed and repaid on an intermediate-term basis. Good profits and large cash flows tend to accompany growth with a resultant demand for intermediate-term credit which is larger than for other areas. Banks faced with good general loan demand may be less inclined to make such credit available, preferring to keep a flexible position and to be prepared for unexpected opportunities.

Although some big businesses have a regional income and expenditure concentration, many which are national in scope certainly have access to national capital markets and should be principal factors in leveling the availability of capital between areas of the country. Small business is regional by nature. It depends on loan credit to the extent it can be commanded, mainly from nearby commercial banks. Short-term credit needs of small business appear to have been met reasonably well, but intermediate- and longer-term needs have received less adequate provision. In a burgeoning area such as California small business is likely to assume an unusually important role. It has the agility to meet new and developing needs; its promotion is in keeping with the more adventurous and promotional atmosphere of a new and growing area.

The vigor of small business enterprise in California suggests that its credit needs have been met. The reputed ingenuity of California banks in devising imaginative credit-protection devices for marginal loans could be used to argue that small business in California has received better and more generous treatment than in most other areas of the country. California banks' large ratio of loans to total assets gives support to this conjecture.

c. Provision of a payments system

An economical payments system in which most checks are cleared at par is a more recent innovation than many recollect. Before 1914 New York funds often were quoted at a premium by midwestern banks. The currency and collection system was slow and inefficient, and dissatisfaction with it was one of the lesser but not unimportant reasons why the Federal Reserve System was established.

The establishment of a check collection system by the Federal Reserve with almost universal par collection between banks seems to have solved a great share of these problems. Collections are faster and the costs to customers are mainly in the indirect form of minimum balances used to cover the costs of operating checking accounts. However, the payments system is not beyond improvement. Service charges on deposit accounts amount to almost half a billion dollars a year. Without doubt the indirect charges covered by balance maintenance are considerably more. The check collection system accounts for the employment of about one-sixth of a million persons and costs at least a billion dollars a year to operate. These figures suggest that it is not the most efficient system possible. Furthermore the par collection system is not universal.

The number of banking offices has increased substantially in recent years, reputedly to meet the needs of a growing population that is also migrating to new homes in the suburbs. The character of banking offices also has changed, for example the addition of drive-in windows and express service devices. More modern architecture has been used to convince the public that they are welcome in banks and other financial institutions. Banking-by-mail also has been encouraged.

Magnetic ink identification coding of checks and deposit tickets has adapted the collection system to a more mechanized basis. One cannot help but wonder if further changes may not be in store. Chain grocery stores could end up doing most of the check cashing of the nation. Deposits could be made by mail. Such regular monthly bills as public utilities and charge accounts could be settled by multiple-item bank orders. Will nonborrowing bank customers find it necessary ever to visit their banks except to open an account? Is it possible that the expansion of banking offices will prove to have been excessive when the new methods are fully developed?

Another possibility should be considered: will other financial institutions develop payment devices that may compete seriously with commercial banks? Big corporate accounts probably will have to be handled by the commercial banks, but personal accounts might be serviced quite easily by other devices—and at less cost. The postal giro accounts of many European countries seem to operate very efficiently without subsidy and at amazingly low cost.

d. Servicing (and promoting?) the flow of savings

Savings institutions are expected to furnish the qualitative services needed by savers, to supply ample credit to good borrowers, and to accomplish both goals in a manner consistent with the public needs for growth and stability. This is a tall order. Savings institutions have gone far toward meeting these often conflicting needs, but some problems remain. The solution to these problems is possibly outside the system of saving-investment mediation.

Financial intermediaries working within the legal and institutional boundaries set for them may be unable to deal with major problems and needs of savers. For example, the erosion of the value of a savings fund in fixed-dollar form is well known. The probability of a continuation of this trend in the future is for each person to judge. As long as some major fraction of the population believes that further erosion in the value of the dollar is inevitable, it can be argued that savings institutions ought to try to meet the need. Although savings institutions offer savers a wide variety of instruments adapted to varying needs, they offer no purchasing power protection device adaptable to small-saver needs. If national economic policy is unable to stop value-of-money erosion, this group is particularly vulnerable. The financial innovation aimed most directly at this threat is the variable annuity. Although the logic of this device is overwhelmingly strong, so far it has made little headway. Opposition within the financial community seems to be the major deterrent, although overestimation of public demand for this protection is possible. Mutual funds furnish another example of an intermediary institution with the same aim. So far such funds appear to reach only the upper middle class as their costs and charges seem quite heavy in view of their rather frequently mediocre investment results.

Experience is still too short to demonstrate the success of mutual funds in serving their basic purpose. Their sharpest boom came during a stock-market boom which itself did *not* closely parallel a rise in the general price level; indeed this stock-market boom came during the period of greatest stability in the price level since the end of World War II. One cannot judge from present evidence if corporate equities will furnish a successful shelter from inflation. More significant is whether mutual fund stock selections have offered much inflation protection.

Should financial intermediaries be neutral with respect to the stimulation of saving and borrowing, or, if not neutral, in what fashion should such influence be exercised? Common observation makes it clear that financial intermediaries not only have not been nor tried to be neutral but have attempted to influence both saving and borrowing. If financial intermediaries stimulate saving during booms and investment during slumps, they aid in economic stabilization. If they work in the opposite direction, they tend to be destabilizing.

Dynamic macroeconomics shows that if the proportion of aggregate income saved and invested varies, the equality of the two is established by countervailing influences which sometimes reflect causation going from saving to investment, and sometimes from investment to saving. The policy question is: in which direction would it be more socially advantageous for causation to run?

Observation suggests that the institutional structure of financial intermediaries encourages a steady stream of saving with net new borrowing being made to adjust to this flow of saving. Several of the most important of the financial intermediaries—life insurance, payroll deduction saving plans, and pension plans—certainly encourage regularity of saving; the first absolutely and the others proportionally to earned income. Earned income, presumably, is more stable than total income. In terms of the psychological behavior of persons, these qualities have been and can be viewed as advantages. They encourage stability in the financial habits of persons and probably tend to increase the total amount saved. The great financial successes of these forms of saving demonstrate their popularity.

If borrowing, and therefore investment based on borrowed funds, must be adjusted to the saving level, this would seem to present a stabilizing factor as respects total income generation. If, however, investment is not responsive to interest-rate cost variations and persistently fluctuates for reasons lying outside this segment of the economy, then the regularity of saving encouraged by the institutional structure can have multiple effects on the income level.

If the institutional structure of financial intermediation for saving tends to stabilize the saving flow, then interest rates should fluctuate through wide ranges to adjust the saving-investment balance. But is this the history of interest rates? Although open market interest rates often tend to fluctuate considerably, the rates of interest or dividends paid by savings intermediaries tend to be far more constant than external conditions seem to justify. Indeed, it can be argued that both a lag and a ratchet effect work on these rates. When borrowing demand is strong, the prime loan rate usually moves up with some lag behind the flexible system of market rates. In periods of ease and open market, interest rate declines and the lag appears even greater. The financial structure has an understandable reluctance to adjust to rate declines.

The level of rates paid to savers also moves with some lag behind open-market rates. Competition among savings intermediaries sometimes tends to speed up the process, but lag remains observable. That savings institutions have been under unequal regulatory restraint with respect to the rates paid may account for some of this lag, but it seems reasonable that the lag might have been present without any or with a more uniform pattern of regulation.

When borrowing demand drops, however, there is considerable rigidity to the downward movement of lending rates. In the first place, any one savings institution hesitates to drop the announced rate it pays on deposits or savings accounts. Such an announcement exposes this leader to losses of funds—an uncomfortable possibility even if the event proves not as bad as its anticipation. With costs high, efforts to sustain earning rates are fully understandable.

A case can be made for financial intermediaries being passive factors in the pricing of money and capital. Basic economic forces should be resolved in these markets without pressure. In practice it is hard to imagine these institutions as willing to be passive forces; this is particularly true in the environment of a growth area such as California. The American managerial goal of growth and expansion is the basis for managers' pay raises. The question in practice is: do financial institutions promote with equal vigor both on the supply and demand side of the market, thus in a sense offsetting the two sides? Is their price influence neutral?

Promotion both of saving and investment is defensible as a social good as long as the balance between the two is maintained reasonably. The problem as shown by practical marketing experience is that it is far more successful to promote that side for which there is a strong basic drive. Nevertheless each financial intermediary must be in balance, hence if borrowing demands are strong, as in recent years, promotion tends to be concentrated on securing the funds to meet these demands. When borrowing demand was weak, as in the 1930's, borrowing was promoted to employ idle funds. On this score it can be argued that financial intermediaries tend to help restore the balance in financial markets.

Presumably a good tax system also is neutral in relation to the channeling of saving. In actuality tax differentials appear to be major influences in saving channels and possibly even influences on the total amount. Some of this influence is inadvertent, but in some cases it is a legacy from past efforts to use taxes to stimulate a particular sector of the economy or a particular kind of activity. Savings intermediaries themselves are subject to greatly different basic-tax assessments. The tax differential between savings and loan associations and commercial banks is the most publicized. Other differentials also exist: pension plans, for example, clearly are stimulated by the tax advantage enjoyed by their beneficiaries. Life insurance companies are taxed under complex and frequently-revised rules of assessment. Other tax differentials exist. United States savings bonds permit tax deferment, as do pension plans in part, and the sharing of contributions between employer and employee is greatly influenced by this fact. Finally, some forms of savings permit—a few almost encourage—tax avoidance on a substantial scale.

e. Capital importation

Capital importation into California has been a major constructive force. The free flow of capital among regions benefits both borrowers and lenders and furnishes an outlet for savings which might be difficult to employ at home. Also it finances expansion where the momentum of economic events is causing growth. Since interest rate differentials are the means by which capital movements are stimulated, some differentials are to be expected as long as outside funds are needed.

Capital importation into California can be accomplished by financial institutions located elsewhere *exporting* capital to California, or by

California-based financial institutions *importing*. The purchase of California mortgage loans by mutual savings banks and out-of-state life insurance companies illustrates exporting. The solicitation of out-of-state savings funds by California savings and loan associations illustrates importing.

It can be argued that California would receive a steadier inflow of funds if more of the importation process were performed by its financial institutions than by receiving capital exports from out-of-state financial institutions. The argument basis is that capital movement among areas is likely to be influenced more than proportionately by fluctuations in economic conditions and interest rates. If capital demand is strong throughout the country, including New England and the Atlantic seaboard states, mutual savings banks cannot help but prefer to place available funds in local loans. Just how much lower an interest rate they will accept is hard to say, but in high-rate periods a *satisfactory* rate of interest—one which easily permits dividend levels to be maintained or even increased slightly—is probably enough to keep money at home. The primary incentive for seeking out-of-state employment of funds by the mutual savings banks comes when home demand shrinks. In this way California tends to receive marginal import funds, funds that come in irregularly, but come when national demands as a whole have moderated.

Life insurance companies probably are more regular than mutual savings banks. They tend not to identify themselves with the areas in which their head offices are located, although it is significant that virtually every large life insurance company has a disproportionately large amount of its assets in its home state and city. However, life insurance companies do not put a constant proportion of funds into mortgages, an area in which capital movements are particularly evident. Direct placements are the other principal use of life insurance funds. No doubt direct placements are also made in California by out-of-state life insurance companies, or are made to national corporations to finance capital expansion in California.

With allowance for institutional variations, the fact remains that California-based financial institutions have strong business reasons for trying to regularize capital imports. This raises the question as to whether or not commercial banks should not be encouraged to use existing means or be given added means by which they could attract out-of-state funds rather more effectively. The issuance of more time-certificate deposits to eastern investors is one way in which present powers could be used more fully. Reinforced powers of banks to act as agents in the handling and investment of outside funds, such as in business lending, also illustrate the potentials for added business.

The correspondent banking system, which ties many banking system units together, has been cited sometimes as a substitute for branch banking. It performs some services but has relatively little influence on interregional capital movements. Although there are no data of consequence on them, overline loans and participations do so to a limited extent, but certainly far less than would be possible if branch banking on a nationwide basis were practiced.

Capital importation is aided both by deposit and savings account insurance. Without this protection, savers would be reluctant to send their money to faraway and unfamiliar institutions. Raising the limit on deposit and share insurance would increase the potential magnitude of capital importation by savings intermediaries. The guarantee and insurance of mortgages also makes these instruments more nearly fungible and adaptable to the investment needs of faraway financial institutions. Conventional mortgages are not always an acceptable instrument to facilitate mortgage fund importation.

The west coast has a long tradition of financial leadership and several commercial banks are important money wholesalers. Would the interests of California be served by even more development and independence of a west coast money market? Is this something that can be encouraged by State of California policy? Money markets tend to be national; as communications improve they are probably more national and less regional than was once the case. However, a large local wholesale market for money would have one advantage, that of helping to attract and hold more corporate funds. Next to the Treasury Department (inevitably national in character) the largest nonbanking users of the money markets are nonfinancial corporations.

The primary need for creating or strengthening a money market is a number of big banks equipped to enter the wholesale money market. Such banks exist in California; therefore isn't it quite possible that an optimum degree of local money-market development already has been achieved?

f. Transmission and distribution of Federal Reserve credit influences

As a starting point it can be assumed that anticyclical stabilization is a continuing goal of national economic policy. It can be assumed further that monetary policy will continue to play a major role in total federal government economic policy. Since the economic system continues to exhibit some basic tendencies toward economic instability, it seems just as certain that Federal Reserve credit policy (which concept is used here interchangeably with monetary policy) will shift with the tide of economic affairs.

If Federal Reserve credit policy is easy during recessions and tight during unsustainable booms, some sectors of the economy are certain to be affected. It is not reasonable to ask commercial banks or the financial system to shield the economy from these influences, but they can be expected to transmit these influences to other sectors—particularly the borrowing ones—in an equitable way. The possibility that they will not do so depends on a deeply imbedded practice of the financial system. If varying credit influences of the Federal Reserve were worked out completely in terms of fluctuating interest rates, then it could be said that the market transmits Federal Reserve credit policy. Higher interest rates would restrain borrowers, but all credit demands could be met at these higher levels of interest rates. However, the credit market does not work in this way. At the prevailing level of interest rates some borrowers are always being restrained by banks, and others bear a proportionately heavier burden, usually because they do not qualify in terms of credit quality. Rather than risking breach of usury laws by offering credit at higher rates of interest, credit is refused.

When credit market conditions tighten, credit probably is limited more by rationing than by interest rate increases. Commercial banks and other lenders choose among applicant borrowers with even more discrimination than in normal times. They may also change the type of loan acceptable; commercial banks are particularly prone to reduce term lending with the somewhat spurious argument that "they can accommodate more customers by granting only short-term credit." Short-term credit is not a substitute for intermediate-term credit, and this policy completely excludes some types of borrowers while substituting accommodation of a quite different type of borrower. Credit rationing probably is encouraged by supervisory policy since it seems to result in an upgrading of loan portfolios. Furthermore, examiners seldom show much sympathy with the idea that high interest rates can compensate for somewhat more credit risk in any part of the earning-assets portfolio even though historical experience suggests that interest-rate risk differentials usually more than compensate for variations in the quality of credit.

Federal Reserve credit pressure has been channeled by means other than credit rationing. Bank loan ratios have tended to go up in booms at the expense of secondary reserves usually in the form of short-term Treasury securities. If the Treasury usually ran a budget surplus during booms so that the aggregate amount of their outstanding securities was being reduced, the movements would be parallel and would cause few market pressures. Unfortunately, this seldom has been the case during postwar years. The reduced holdings of commercial banks have been absorbed by private buyers. In effect, holders of cash balances were persuaded by higher interest rates to economize on these balances and hold Treasury obligations instead. This process increased deposit velocities. Since increases in deposit velocities thwart the goals of a restrictive credit policy, the Federal Reserve has been obligated to exert that much more pressure on the credit structure. In other words, monetary policy has had to carry the burden of restriction which otherwise might have been shared with fiscal policy. Thus we are forced to consider in detail how credit rationing has transmitted the pressures of credit policy to the borrowing customers of banks. The exact manner of such pressure distribution in the past is not clear. Small business claims that it has borne a disproportionately large part of the pressure. Banks dispute this contention but not altogether persuasively. Most big business continues to have access to all of its requested credit although there are exceptions in cases such as sales finance companies.

The distribution of credit pressure can be an issue of particular gravity in a rapidly growing area such as California. Loan ratios tend to be higher at all times and there is less margin for accommodation of added loan demand in periods of stress. If the commercial banks cultivate national corporations and seek an increasing share of their deposit business, they are particularly hesitant to show less than alacrity in meeting any credit requests. Even though effective bank interest rates may be somewhat higher in California, the nationally-set prime loan rate furnishes a limit in dealing with national customers. An additional factor is that capital importation is likely to show cyclical swings. When credit is easy and interest rates lower in other sectors of the country, the higher rates of California can attract funds. But when rates at home increase, then local use becomes attractive even at rates below those available in California. Investors have a strong strain of satisficing in their nature. They are more attracted by interest rate differentials when rates are low than by the same differentials when rate levels are high.

Might it not be better to influence credit pressure distribution by a price effect rather than by credit rationing? Do the usury laws furnish either a useful or an effective ceiling to interest rates? Higher rates help bank earnings if they cover added credit risk, which they usually do. Small business generally has to pay a high price for any credit outside the commercial banking system; it might be preferable for it to pay the price within the banking system. The cost of capital for all levels of business size probably should be high in these circumstances (capital expenditure programming usually assumes this to be the case), and it is better to have it explicitly high. Intermediate-term borrowers, rather than curtailing capital expenditures, simply meet market prices.

Nonbank financial intermediaries encounter the influence of tight credit policy in the degree to which credit demands are shifted to them. With better earnings they are able to compete vigorously for nonmonetary savings-type financial claims. This raises the question as to whether or not commercial banks should be given even freer opportunities to compete for savings deposits and thus to regularize their growth and to allow them to acquire added assets in high interest-rate periods as well as in times of credit ease.

g. Financial services

In addition to the foregoing functions, the users of financial institutions expect them to perform a great many services, the largest single one of which at present is trust service for individuals and corporations. Banks and other financial institutions also supply safety-deposit facilities, provide credit information, transact foreign financial business both for exporting and importing customers, execute or handle customers' orders for securities, and supply information on economic conditions. There are many related services such as economic information with respect to types of credit extended and advice on case management to corporate depositors. The electronic computers installed by many banks to mechanize their own operations are now often used in their spare time to help customers solve problems such as inventory management. The list of financial services seems to be growing.

2. CRITERIA FOR BANKING AND FINANCIAL PERFORMANCE

The ultimate criterion of an economic system is its ability to meet the goals of the citizens of the nation of which it is a part. This general standard, however, is far too vague for evaluating the role played by the financial structure. More specific identification of the factors that separate proper functioning from malfunctioning is needed. Preferably standards of functional success should be quantitative.

Banking and financial systems usually have been modified under the stress of malfunctioning. Something was done because something had to be done. On a few occasions banking and financial systems have been reviewed with a considerable degree of intellectual detachment, such as by the National Monetary Commission and the Commission on Money and Credit in the United States, and in England by the McMillan and Radcliffe Committees. These inquiries, however, developed no universal standards for evaluation of satisfactory performance. The standards discussed in most cases reflected a strong flavor of the times in which the reports were written.

The subtopics in this section indicate why this probably has been true. The areas that attract attention receive it; others are neglected. The following does not pretend to be a comprehensive system of testing; it is a collection of criteria that seem relevant at this time.

a. The efficiency test: costs, earnings, and profits

The most self-evident standard by which an economic sector can be judged is efficiency. Does this sector perform its expected functions well? with the minimum use of resources? Comparative statistical data on costs, earnings, and profits furnish nearly all the available empirical evidence.

Any statistics, however, must be modified by a considerable number of nonquantitative factors. For example, if the banking structure is marred by inefficient elements, such as nonpar collections, a duplicating or overlapping Federal Reserve and correspondent banking collection system, and related inefficiencies, the whole cost structure may be too high but comparative statistics will not reveal this, nor do they tell the whole story with respect to regional variations. If California interest rates are above the average for the country, then both costs and gross income are above national averages. No efficiency significance attaches to such a fact. The same thing is true if personnel costs average higher in California.

Comparative statistics, however, can furnish very useful insights into such matters as the economies of scale in banking. Fortunately, after a long period of neglect, new work has been done on this subject. Economy of scale is a matter of profound significance in regulatory policy. If larger banks are really more efficient, denial of this advantage to the public by merger policy is not easy to justify. On the other hand, if the economies of scale are doubtful, then a more restrictive policy is defensible.

Comparative statistics of bank costs and earnings also are relevant in appraising interest rate differentials. Assuming that rates of interest in California average higher than in the nation as a whole, as appears to be the case, this differential might be widened in the passage of funds through financial intermediaries, be held constant, or even be reduced. The "pass-through" costs are an important efficiency test of financial intermediaries.

The quality of banking and financial service certainly varies. Even though the differences cannot be proven by ordinary statistical means, common observation is enough to support the proposition. The worth of quality is hard to judge, but superior financial services usually are rewarded with higher profits. This evidence suggests that the public is willing to pay the price and that the regulatory authorities should spur quality development rather than encourage spartan economy.

Differences in risk-taking also can change the form of comparative banking statistics. Since the view is expressed elsewhere that possible risk-taking should be encouraged by supervisory policy rather than inhibited, loss and earnings differences must be appraised in the light of this possibility.

The differential price/earnings ratios of bank shares might be considered indirect evidence of the markets' evaluation of efficiency. Although this idea has some relevance, it probably is not wholly valid. Differential price/earnings ratios may reflect different degrees of market power, but in practice they probably reflect more differential expectations with respect to growth. Growth expected of banks is attributed more to external economic and demographic causes than to internal efficiency. Nothing in prevailing stock analysis suggests the latter. Second, expected levels of interest rates seem to influence bank stock valuation more than matters of internal efficiency.

More selective quantitative standards of banking efficiency might be developed but at the cost of detailed and expensive research. The efficiency of the payments system is one element of banking that could be surveyed by these methods. The efficiency in credit granting would be less amenable to analysis, but since the process of consumer credit quality seems to have been reduced successfully to a computer technique, perhaps lending techniques of all types could be appraised in a similar fashion.

b. Credit allocation: positive and negative testing

New insights into the efficiency and equity of lending and investing by banks and other financial intermediaries might be found in a review of their portfolios. Who received credit and on what terms tells the story of a positive allocation policy. The regularity of availability can be determined from this evidence, although not with complete confidence.

Almost as important is the experience of those who wanted but were denied credit. A banking and financial system cannot be expected to and should not grant credit to everyone who wants it. Many applicants have neither the experience nor the background for appraising their own reasonable right of access to credit. Some rejections are inevitable under almost any system. Price can never be the sole allocator of credit. Even if formal rationing is not practiced, some screening must be done, but is the cut-off point always right?

Aggregate credit-loss statistics suggest that general standards of credit judgment as exercised by banks and other financial institutions may be neither as precise nor as equitable as would be true of an optimal financial system. Credit losses are experienced, but they are far more often due to deterioration in general economic conditions than to faults in individual borrowers during periods of reasonable prosperity. Some business fluctuations are to be expected even though national policy aims to minimize them. Credit evaluation must allow some margin for such fluctuations. Has the allowance been excessive? Has it been divided correctly among applicants? Is it possible that the interest of the economy would be served better if higher interest rates were charged and more risky loans made when credit risk is higher? For example, do the usury laws act as an inhibiting ceiling on credit granting that might benefit both borrowers and lenders? Traditionally this question has been answered affirmatively in the case of consumer credit.

Small business is one area in which the financial system has been criticized for unresponsive policies of credit granting. Those studies made suggest that short-term credit has been reasonably available to small business, but that it has been able to secure only small amounts of intermediate- and long-term credit. Experimental public programs for the relief of small-business credit needs have been tried many times, of which the Small Business Administration program is only the latest in a long line. In each case, the credit extended through these programs was less than expected and quite trivial when compared with the total equity investment in small business.

Nevertheless, small businesses and particularly *new* small businesses are so important a symbol of the philosophical ideal of free entry to business that their credit facilities should not be assumed to be adequate without repeated testing. The test lies outside the banking and financial structure; it lies in small businesses themselves. The incentives for new business organization in burgeoning California should be unusually powerful. The record of such an area cannot be judged by national standards, as local experience is more than usually important. The record is particularly important with respect to new small *innovating* businesses. Innovation, the seed of productivity and quality growth, is to be desired above almost every other characteristic. Innovating small businesses associated with the defense industries probably have access to credit through their prime contractors; the acid test is among *independent* new small innovating businesses.

Another sensitive area for testing the allocation of credit by the banking and financial system is that of intermediate-term credit. Most high-grade long-term needs for credit are met in the open capital markets or by life insurance company direct placements. Commercial banks supply short-term credit and some also is generated by trade credit within the nonfinancial business structure. But intermediate-term credit has been made available only by commercial banks, and this in rather irregular supply.

California, with rapid growth and excellent demand for bank credit, may have experienced an unusually erratic supply of intermediate-term credit. Good demand suggests good profits and fairly fast cash flows with which to retire debt over a relatively-short intermediate term. But good loan demand also suggests that banks may be under somewhat less than normal earnings pressure to extend intermediate-term credit. For concerns which can enter national money markets and have multiple bank connections, the matter may be of small consequence. For businesses not quite this large, though large by usual small-business definition, the matter may be serious.

c. Tests of stability

In dealing with the banks and financial institutions of an area, economic stability or instability at national levels is more a matter of passive recognition than one open to active control. Banks and financial institutions are influenced by these national pressures, and also feel the effects of public stabilization measures. An area itself more unstable than average does not necessarily feel any more than proportionate corrective pressure.

An area growing apace, however, runs exceptional risks with respect to local instability. For one thing, rapid growth invites an unusual degree of speculation. Speculation may serve broad economic purposes, but also it can create unusual problems of economic instability. For example, rapid advances in land value almost always invite a speculative surge. It is rare that this surge stays within the boundaries of sustainability. Credit easily becomes ensnarled within the speculative maze, and the stability of financial operations can be jeopardized all too easily.

Capital importation is also particularly liable to instability, especially if capital is brought into the area by out-of-state financial institutions. Marginal capital imports are likely to be erratic.

Growth, by itself, can be bought at too high a price. Risk-taking to support dynamic and innovating productive business may be defended, but risk-taking for price appreciation does not have as good a defense. The test that might be applied to this problem is the response of banks and financial intermediaries to varying degrees of instability to which they are exposed. On such a test, a neutral performance is satisfactory. If they mute or dampen the instability they experience, so much the better, but if they amplify it in the transmission process this should be considered an unsatisfactory performance.

Evidence as to whether banks and other financial institutions transmit an amplified or a muted degree of instability cannot be formulated in direct terms; the form in which this force bears on banks and financial institutions differs qualitatively from the way in which they pass it on. The best indirect evidence is probably in the character of credit availability. A neutral influence can be said to prevail if final borrowers seem to experience no greater variation in the availability of credit than borrowers in the open national money markets. If moderate tension in the open national money markets is accompanied by sharply curtailed supplies of funds to local borrowers, the influence has been amplified. If local borrowers continue to be accommodated steadily whatever the experience in national money markets, then the financial system can be said to have performed commendably in dampening or muting the pass-through of instability.

If the origin of instability is in local speculative excesses not generated by bank credit, it is hard to suggest measures as to the role of banks in transmitting the influence to other parts of the local economy. When the Iowa farm-land boom collapsed in 1921, and the Florida land boom in 1926, the resulting bank failures aggravated an already bad situation. On the other hand, it can be argued that banks and other financial institutions dampened the influence on the rest of the economy of the stock market break of May 1962, as a cumulative contraction was not set in motion. The recent record of financial institutions seems to be commendable.

d. Tests of efficiency in capital importation

Efficiency in capital importation can be tested by direct and available quantitative data—interest-rate differentials. A capital importing area must expect to pay some interest-rate premium to overcome market frictions. The origin of these frictions is due mainly to investors' preferences for nearby outlets. If a small interest-rate premium is sufficient to attract a large capital inflow, it can be said that the capital importation system is working very efficiently; if a large differential still fails to bring an adequate volume, then the operation appears inefficient.

What are "large" and "small" premiums? Prices for overcoming subjective preferences are not subject to direct measurement. A differential for the purpose of overcoming inertia, however, probably can be estimated from available evidence. To stimulate a movement of short-term money from New York to London on a fully-covered basis, at least a half of one percent differential appears necessary. High-grade foreign long-term borrowers (in dollar form so no exchange rate risk is involved) expect to pay more than one percentage point more than domestic borrowers of the same credit quality, more often a differential approaching one and one-half percent. Within a nation the differentials certainly should be less, probably much less. Rate differentials based on credit risk, such as the differential between Aaa and Baa bonds, have been reduced to fairly narrow ranges. Certainly the geographical movement of funds to borrowers of equal credit risk should involve even smaller differentials. How much smaller, however, is not easy to say. A significant example of interest-rate differentials is the differing discounts on FHA mortgages in secondary markets. These instruments are so nearly identical as respects basic credit standing that discount differentials are attributable almost wholly to market frictions. It seems significant that the differentials appear to be both material and fluctuating.

An interesting point for conjecture is the size of these differentials if they are expressed as "face" rates on these mortgages rather than as discounts. Some investors do not view yield income received through discounts as equivalent to yield income received via the face rate. Some avoid discounts because they cannot be reflected fully in current income; some feel that discounts might be misconstrued as "taking advantage" of unsophisticated borrowers. To the extent this is true (and on the importance of this point we have no notion at all) rate differentials might be smaller if more directly expressed.

The regularity of capital inflow also can be measured by the rate differentials but only after allowance for fluctuations in both. If investor aversion to remote investment is itself a variable, the magnitude of the system's efficiency cannot be deduced from such swings. If, however, irregularity in the inflow is due to structural characteristics of the financial institutions, then it can be said that the efficiency of the capital importing system itself varies. For most purposes the significant test of the system is its performance under pressure rather than its performance in favorable circumstances.

e. Criteria for competition

It can be said that the maximum is not necessarily the optimum degree of competition in the financial system. Competition that jeopardizes financial soundness, that amplifies instability or that leads to unsustainable customer expectations of financial institutions is less than useful in the long run. Since, however, degree of competition cannot be quantified, what tests for an optimum degree of competition can be applied?

Competition is expected to assure the users of the financial system that they receive good service at reasonable prices. If we accept the general ethic of economic freedom that individual choice outranks all other criteria, it is for financial service users to decide what constitutes good service, and price is set as they prefer. If customers warm to accommodating and attractive tellers and distrust impersonal and mechanized payments devices, that is their free choice.

If savers prefer to receive a part of their return in the form of pots and pans rather than in monetary interest rates, that is also their choice. In this sense, the final test of competitiveness is pleasing the customers of the financial system. Competitive success is the reward.

The financial system, however, cannot be entered freely, and not all of its prices are free of some supervisory or public influence. Should the public regulatory agencies use some sort of a competitive equivalence in chartering banks and financial institutions? Should regulations that influence a set price try to approximate the prices that would prevail if an optimum degree of competition existed? In other words, should public authorities try to use some sort of competitive ideal in determining their policies? The question can be illustrated by the regulation of interest rates paid on time deposits. In the banking reconstruction during the early 1930's the payment of interest on these deposits was regulated because it was thought that excessive competition for time deposits led to payment of rates that could not be earned except by taking excessive market risks. Such competition was thought to be destructive. In effect, the public authorities felt that they could exercise better judgment than the persons or savings institutions themselves with respect to their mutual long-run interests. In a similar vein the "overbanking" of the early 1920's led to more stringent chartering policies because it was felt that free entry into the banking business led to later financial difficulties; again a belief that public regulatory authorities were better judges of the long-run needs for banking facilities than banks or bank promoters themselves.

It is significant that in both cases these limitations on freedom receive the general support of bankers. They felt that competitive pressures forced them to follow policies they knew to be risky and possibly self-destructive. In the case of chartering policy, those already in the banking business could have been suspected of wishing to increase the scarcity and therefore the value of the franchise they already owned. Time-deposit interest-rate regulation also can be viewed as a method of damping a normal form of price competition. It is significant that a majority of commercial banks (by count, not by dollar volume of deposits) apparently favor public regulation of interest rates paid on time deposits even though it impairs their individual freedom.

It is hard to argue that a degree of competition which tempts financial institutions to take self-destructive risks is optimum. The view seems to prevail that financial institutions cannot be allowed to fail and pass losses along to their customers. Insurance of deposits and other claims on financial institutions, conceived primarily to be a protection only of depositors, tend also to give stockholders a greater degree of protection than was originally expected. That managers of financial institutions, as stockholder representatives, may have leaned on this fact would be difficult to document. If, however, institution managers take refuge in these regulatory shelters on the assumption that public policy will shield them from harm, the situation is hardly optimal.

On the other hand, it is not at all clear that the public authorities are wiser about the quality and direction of long-range financial developments than the managers of private financial institutions. All judgments are suspect; but it is all too apparent that regulatory judgments very easily can be turned from true long-term public protection into protectionist devices for the benefit of their institutional constituents.

Evaluating the degree of competition may have to be done by negative means. Existing legal regulation presumes that "bad" or destructive competition can be identified. At the other extreme, can it be determined if competition exists at all? If it does exist, but is not destructive, then this may have to be called the optimum degree of competition. Then how is the presence of competition to be determined? Financial institutions all aver that it exists, but what would be convincing proof of its existence? Similarity of price for similar services and variations in the price as underlying business conditions vary might appear to be a test, but not conclusive. Interest rates paid to savers and charged to borrowers are roughly similar at given points of time, but they also vary with the general economic conditions influencing these rates.

In a healthy and truly competitive situation creative innovation is used by companies or types of business as a way of increasing their share of the market. Financial innovation reflects in such things as growth of direct placements, development of new ways of offering advantageous consumer credit terms, and recently in the development of a market for large standardized certificates of deposit by the money-market banks. Active innovation can be taken as evidence of the existence of lively competition.

Failure to innovate, however, can be due to legal restraints. Life insurance companies sold annuities for many years and seemed well prepared to offer pension plans to industry, but were successful mainly among rather small companies. Since life insurance companies had limited common-stock purchase rights and even less disposition to use such rights as they had, they could not compete with trustees offering the obvious advantages of being able and willing to direct the investment of a substantial proportion of pension funds in corporate equities.

Innovation is seldom regional but the question always can be asked: are the financial institutions of a given region leaders or laggers in financial innovation?

Except for the rate of interest paid on time deposits, most banking and financial competition is expressed more in quality of service than in price. The prime loan rate sets a national anchor in the rate structure, and individual rates tend to fall into a given areal pattern. For the small customer good service may be exemplified by an accommodating teller, but for large customers the matter is much more complex. Dependability as a source of credit and conservatism in financial policies are elements in such a relationship. Giant corporations inspect the balance sheets of their depository banks as critically as bank examiners and have a material influence on banking policy. Within an area the competitive success of institutions might be judged by their ability to attract national accounts.

Apart from price and innovation, one important aspect of competition is that it deprives any one economic unit—a financial institution in this case—from holding economic power to a degree which could be used mischievously. Fortunately, recent history has disclosed almost no examples of such usage. Early economic history demonstrates that when economic power is concentrated excessively the means to accomplish such concentration are generally financial. Finance guides the allocation of resources and coordinates the various parts of the economic process. Control of the financial process often means control of the economic results. An excessive degree of power concentration is dangerous whether or not it is used exploitatively.

Dispersion of some forms of economic power can be carried to great lengths without related problems. Consumer sovereignty does not lead necessarily to apparent rational results, but the dispersion of individual choice certainly has no harmful effects and almost certainly some helpful ones. Financial power, however, probably can be overdispersed as well as overconcentrated. More complex technology and a demand for higher quality in financial services suggest that the optimum size of financial units may be quite large. Will the countervailing power implicit in larger economic units elsewhere in the economy furnish a measure of public protection? The same forces working on financial institutions are also influencing other kinds of business enterprise.

3. OBJECTIVES ACHIEVED THROUGH STATE REGULATORY POWER

The basic drive for economic achievement must come from within a financial institution. State regulatory power seldom stimulates achievement and sometimes discourages it. Financial regulatory powers are usually created as an aftermath to financial difficulties and disasters, so this negative character is natural. Since the public seems to hold the view that financial institutions cannot be allowed to fail freely, as is permitted for competitive types of business, the counterpart of protection is regulation. The somewhat critical tone with respect to regulation that might be read into this must be tempered by a recognition of the other side of the argument. Given the gravity of the failures in our financial history, could negative regulation have been avoided?

Regulation exists both at national and state levels. Because this inquiry focuses on the problems and expectations of California, most of our attention is to problems of regulation falling within state jurisdiction. The greater part of these problems intersect areas dealt with by federal regulation, but it is not our task to delve into the state-federal division of regulatory powers. One other factor lying outside the boundaries of our discussion must be mentioned as of considerable influence on banks and financial institutions—their liability to federal income taxation.

Most of the taxes influencing competition between types of financial institutions are federal in origin, therefore not directly relevant to this study, but their importance must be mentioned. Present rules of federal income taxation have stimulated savings and loan associations to seek continued growth at almost any cost. The reserve allocation exemption has been pressing many associations so that on marginal grounds they feel sharply the need for added savings accounts. This intensified competition has spilled over to stimulate other financial institutions to more than usual promotional efforts and often to increases in the interest rates paid on savings funds.

Commercial banks, fully exposed to the federal corporate income tax, have made tax-exempt securities second in importance only to direct customer loans. For many years commercial banks have bought almost no corporate bonds except rail-equipment certificates and sometimes those have been bought only as a gesture of reciprocity for railroad deposit accounts.

This section is addressed mainly to commercial banks since supervisory standards in this area are more fully developed and exposed to public view. Most of the points discussed, however, are relevant to other types of financial institutions.

a. Chartering policy

Chartering policy is the principal means by which regulatory policy influences competition, although policies relating to branch establishment, both *de novo* and by merger, are also important.

If an excessively restrictive charter policy is followed, the safety of existing banks is doubtless increased. At the same time they are sheltered from some of the rigors of competition and given a windfall gain in terms of the value of their franchise. A liberal charter policy introduces a freer spirit of competition but raises the possibility of overbanking and of greatly reduced profitability. Banking history shows that the pressure for the establishment of new banks follows a long cyclical path. The peaks of such pressure appear to be periods of higher interest rates and generally strong credit demand. In between, banking frequently suffers reduced profitability. Waves of bank failures are associated with some of these downturns. Deposit insurance and other protections against bank failures now exist, but if the long cycle in interest rates still functions, and it certainly is a likely hypothesis, then the present wave of pressure for bank establishment could be followed by one of thin bank earnings and even voluntary bank liquidations.

An optimum chartering policy seems to be one that assures active competition for existing banks and does not allow them excessive windfall gains on their franchises. If uncertain, erring on the side of liberality might not be bad. Voluntary liquidation of banks fortunately involves few social costs and often no private losses. In other words, the risk of overbanking is not necessarily serious, and retreat from such mistakes need not be costly.

b. Branching: *de novo* and by merger

The chief problem of allowing new branches to be established is their effect on existing banks. If the view is taken that all banks should be exposed to competition, a liberal branching policy is indicated. However, the use of "fighting" branches to concentrate unusual competitive pressure on individual banks unwilling to "sell out" cannot be defended. Is this possibility wholly academic?

The chief problem of branching by mergers is reduction of competition. Even if operating without direct competition in a given area, a unit bank might be aware that giving inadequate local banking service attracts the establishment of a *de novo* branch of one of the branch operating systems in that locality. Potential competition may be almost as effective as kinetic competition.

Should branch acquisition by merger be preferred over *de novo* establishment or should the two be given equal treatment? A preference for branching by merger gives existing unit banks some scarcity value for their franchise. At the same time it avoids the problem of bank-earnings starvation and voluntary liquidation in cases where existing banks do not have the managerial skill or vigor to survive in competition with branches. Voluntary liquidation, however, as noted above does not involve very great social or individual costs.

c. Bank capital and earnings

The rising stock market during the past decade made it possible for some banks to sell capital stock in the open market. During this period such sales accounted for almost one-fifth of the aggregate increase in bank capital, and retained earnings for the remainder. In the two previous decades retained earnings accounted for almost the total increase in bank capital.

Bank capital is basically a guarantee fund. The sum required for such a guarantee depends mainly on the probable character of future economic stability. Since banks and most other financial institutions are highly leveraged businesses, moderate capital requirements increase the rate of earnings on capital. In the absence of adequate capital, however, banks may be inadequately aggressive lenders. Supervisory authorities apparently never urge capital increases on banks to force them to be more aggressive credit grantors but the idea is not without merit. However, there is another side to the question.

Supervisory authorities have been pressing for larger bank capital for so many years that it is widely and unthinkingly accepted that the greater the capital, the better. This is not necessarily true. Banks need enough capital to furnish a reasonable guarantee fund to depositors and to the public in general. It is bad public policy to have a banking system excessively vulnerable to economic adversity. But each bank need not feel that it must have enough capital to protect itself against any possible extremity. If the public authorities press bankers to increase their capital beyond that which they would provide voluntarily, the public authorities assume some responsibility to pursue policies that will tend to assure earnings for this added capital.

Although bank capital is highly leveraged in compounding the net interest income received from earning assets, the rate of earnings on bank capital tends to be quite modest. At most times during the postwar years, any material expansion in the amount of bank capital would have diluted bank earnings seriously. The rising trend of interest rates could be said to have solved the problem for the banking system; the levels of rates met the added expenses of banking and maintained return on capital. The significant point, however, lies in the word "maintained." Whether one accepts the thesis of long cycles in interest rates or not, financial history shows that interest-rate levels have been materially below present levels for relatively long periods of time. Lower levels of interest rates, which could reappear, would raise questions about the sustainability of reasonable rates of return on existing bank capital. If California's needs for capital imports declined materially by 1975, the interest rate differential which benefits California bank income could disappear. Added to a lower general level of rates this would impose a double burden on California's financial institutions.

Surely bank supervisors cannot remain unaware of the market valuations of bank shares. Yet it is hard to find much evidence of regulatory aid to banks in presenting a favorable image to the investing public thereby helping to lower the cost of bank capital. This is in sharp contrast to the policies of regulatory authorities in dealing with light and power, telephone, and other public utility companies. These authorities have permitted, even encouraged, such devices as stock dividends, convertible securities, and related means used as bait for the stock-buying public. Permission to sell both ordinary and convertible capital notes is evidence that a new and welcome regulatory attitude may be emerging.

During the course of the stock market boom of the late 1950's and early 1960's bank-stock prices rose appreciably. The major factor, however, was the change in attitude of investors toward the prospects for banking growth. For a long period commercial bank stocks were viewed as having few growth potentials. It came to be recognized, however, that aggressively managed banks in growing areas were themselves growth companies. California banks were favored in this regard.

The ethics of the case is hard to judge. If banking is fundamentally not a growth industry, the public authorities could not be expected to be party to a deception. On other points, however, it is entirely possible that a slightly different attitude toward banking on the part of the regulatory authorities might have aided in attracting investors. Fairness requires one addendum: a great many banks have shown surprisingly little interest in presenting a more attractive image to stockholders. The quality of information made available to investors has been limited and the adjustment of bank share circumstances to demonstrated preferences of investors has not always been pursued vigorously.

4. A LOOK INTO THE FUTURE

Innovation usually takes unexpected forms, and some parts of the economic system seem to invite it more than others. As the cost of services is largely the cost of human labor, with rising wage levels the rewards for service, innovations certainly will be high. Banking services are thus an excellent target for new procedures.

Future developments could bring great changes to the payments system, now a costly part of the banking structure. As already suggested, the nonborrowing bank customer of the future may visit a banking office only to establish an account and thereafter may make deposits and payments by mail and cash checks (or some even more convenient credit instrument?) at chain grocery stores. Even the consumer borrower may almost never have to visit his bank; his credit will be reviewed by a computer and his credit line supervised mechanically. How many banking offices will we need? And can unit banks afford these capital-costly but laborsaving innovations?

California readily could be the first state in the union in which unit banking virtually disappears. The trend has been in that direction for many years. Several large and aggressive branch-operating banks have absorbed many of the unit banks and faced the remainder with de novo branch competition. Well-managed unit banks seem to survive and even to take advantage of anti-branch sentiments to attract some customers. But owners often must decide if their banks are worth as much in independent operation as sold for branch conversion. Sentiment aside, there may be nothing to fear in this development. If the large branch-banking systems are sufficiently competitive, the public interest may be served quite adequately. The result may be an improvement of efficiency. It is quite possible, since branch systems presumably offer greater flexibility in within-state resource movement that the tendency will be toward an even or more nearly equal availability of funds in all parts of the state. If the big systems are more efficient in capital importation, the state as a whole may enjoy greater availability of credit of all types than otherwise would be true.

The competitive safeguard to the public interest cannot be judged merely by conditions of the moment; its future requires appraising. The trend from unit to branch operations cannot easily be reversed. To what degree are we assured that active competition conditions will *continue* to prevail? Analogy to other countries and eras can be misleading, but history suggests that competition tends to weaken when growth rates slacken. Agreements for market division are easier to negotiate when the market total is fixed rather than growing and when each economic unit is optimistic about its ability to attract a larger portion of the new business. Would vigorous competition continue in California banking if unit banking disappeared and if growth rates slackened?

Is it clear that bank-capital needs will outgrow retained earnings? Shouldn't retreat lines be open for the reduction of excess bank capital if such should appear? Callable bank capital notes are a helpful way to be prepared for this contingency. The ability of the federal government to control economic stability has not been tested fully; an improvement is not impossible. If this happens, permanent bank-capital needs could be less than present capital, even if most of the earnings were distributed. This need for a reduction of bank capital would be aggravated if a long period of low interest rates should emerge. If internal financing becomes more common in the consumer sector (not an impossibility with higher incomes), low interest rates and low borrowing demand could lead to this condition more readily than now seems possible.

One development appears almost certain. The financial services of financial institutions are likely to grow relative to the remainder of their business. Until recently only a handful of upper-income groups could make good use of the trust services of banks—but growth of the solid upper-middle class promises to increase trust department customers. Savings intermediaries might furnish this service if their assets became more diversified and embraced equity ownership. Financial claims related to equity values such as the variable value annuities might become more appropriate.

The future cannot be foreseen, but in preparing for it the architects of financial structure cannot await clearer vision. They need to plan a structure which can take advantage of the new as rapidly as it becomes visible.

Guidelines to Economic
Projections for the California
Economy to 1975

1. INTRODUCTION

THE AUTHORS of a study of the New York financial community concluded that "Anyone who has attempted systematically to project the future development of an entity as complex as the Region's financial community cannot fail to come away from the experience with a sense of inadequacy and frustration."[1] Nevertheless it is axiomatic that the growth in assets and profits of commercial banks are closely related to the economic growth in the area served and that great differences in the rate of economic growth exist among different areas of the nation.[2] In *Money Metropolis* a close relationship was found between percentage increases in assets of commercial banks and in personal income from 1947 to 1956 by states.[3] In the same study expansion in employment and incomes in commercial banking was shown to bear a close relationship to changes in four measures of banking output: consumer credit, all other loans, investments, and trust functions. These fairly obvious relations focus attention upon the importance of developing regional economic projections as a basis for considering the role of commercial banking in the future economic growth of California.

For these projections to be useful in considering the future of commercial banking in California, it is necessary that they be based upon explicit assumptions concerning the prospects for national economic growth and that they provide a basis for viewing prospects in the principal sectors served by commercial banking. With this in view forecasts of consumer incomes can provide a basis for considering the outlook

---

[1] Sidney M. Robbins and Nestor E. Terleckyj, *Money Metropolis—A Locational Study of Financial Activities in the New York Region* (Cambridge, 1960), p. 177.

[2] Roland I. Robinson, *The Management of Bank Funds*, 2d ed. (New York, 1962), pp. 37, 57.

[3] *Money Metropolis . . . , op. cit.*, p. 80.

64

for consumer loans; forecasts of construction employment and population as a basis for forecasting mortgage loan volume; forecasts of employment in manufacturing, services, and trade as a key to future commercial and industrial loan volume; and finally projections of activity in the government sector may provide an indication of future potential

TABLE 1

TREND SUMMARY, POPULATION, EMPLOYMENT, AND INCOME,
CALIFORNIA AND UNITED STATES, 1947 AND 1963
AND PROJECTIONS FOR 1975[a]

Item	1947	1963	1975
CALIFORNIA			
1. Population (000)	9,912	17,600	24,830
2. Civilian labor force (000)	4,345	6,852	10,000
3. Civilian employment (000)	4,026	6,441	9,500
4. Percent unemployed	7.3	6.0	5.0
5. Gross product originating (bil. $)	27.9	64.8	123.1
6. Personal income (bil. $)	22.3	52.3	100.3
7. Disposable personal income (bil. $)	19.8	45.1	87.8
8. Per capita gross prod. orig. ($)	2,814	3,682	4,957
9. Per capita personal income ($)	2,249	2,974	4,039
10. Per capita disposable pers. inc. ($)	1,997	2,564	3,536
UNITED STATES			
11. Population (mil.)	143.7	188.5	236.0
12. Civilian labor force (mil.)	60.2	73.0	92.0
13. Civilian employment (mil.)	57.8	68.8	88.3
14. Percent unemployed	3.9	5.7	4.0
15. Gross national product (bil. $)	334.6	583.9	1,020.7
16. Personal income (bil. $)	256.7	461.6	804.7
17. Disposable personal income (bil. $)	227.9	400.3	703.4
18. Per capita GNP ($)	2,328	3,098	4,325
19. Per capita personal income ($)	1,786	2,449	3,410
20. Per capita disposable pers. inc. ($)	1,586	2,123	2,980

[a] All income and product figures are in 1963 dollars.

volumes of public financing. Although one can accept the hypothesis that such relations exist, it goes without saying that detailed forecasts for each of these sectors probably will be subject to wide margins of error because some of the variables are indeterminate and the parameters or relationships between variables are subject to change over time.

2. SUMMARY OF THE ECONOMIC PROJECTIONS

Table 1 summarizes the projections to 1975 in California population, employment, and income and also includes similar projections for the

United States as well as historical data for 1947 and 1963. In general, the projections indicate that California population and employment will continue to increase rapidly in absolute terms but at a somewhat less rapid percentage rate than that experienced from 1940 to 1962.

Table 1A compares growth rates from 1947 to 1963 and from 1963 to 1975 for population, civilian employment, and gross product in California and the United States as a whole. In both periods California

TABLE 1A

POPULATION, EMPLOYMENT, AND GROSS PRODUCT GROWTH RATES
CALIFORNIA AND UNITED STATES, 1947–1963 AND 1963–1975

	Annual average percent change	
	1947–1963	1963–1975
California		
Population......................................	3.65	2.91
Civilian employment............................	2.98	3.30
Gross product originating.......................	5.42	5.50
United States		
Population......................................	1.71	1.89
Civilian employment............................	1.10	2.10
Gross National Product.........................	3.54	4.76

growth rates substantially exceed those for the entire country. For all three items, however, growth rates for the United States are expected to increase more rapidly in the future, while those for California are expected to decline slightly. The basic explanation for this divergence between state and national growth rates lies in the lower projected rate of migration to California. Migration accounts for approximately one-half of California's growth in population and labor force. Immigration to the United States, on the other hand, accounts for a very small proportion of increases in national population and employment.

Table 1B shows California's share of national population, employment, income, and related items. Note that California's share of the civilian labor force and employment will continue to exceed its share of United States population. This reflects the fact that a larger percentage of California's population is in the 20- to 44-year age bracket than is true for the United States at large; and this difference will persist through 1975. California accounts for a still larger percentage of national product, personal income, and disposable personal income because of greater value of output per worker. Despite the existence of factors tending to equalize regional output and income per worker, Cali-

TABLE 1B

POPULATION, EMPLOYMENT, AND INCOME, CALIFORNIA
AS PERCENT OF UNITED STATES, 1947, 1963, AND 1975

	1947	1963	1975
Population............................	6.9	9.3	10.5
Civilian labor force....................	7.2	9.4	10.9
Civilian employment....................	7.0	9.4	10.8
Gross product........................	8.3	11.1	12.1
Personal income.......................	8.7	11.3	12.5
Disposable personal income..............	8.7	11.3	12.5

fornia's per capita gross product and personal income are expected to
exceed the national average in 1975, although by a smaller margin than
in 1963. The per capita data for California and the United States are
shown in Table 1C.

TABLE 1C

PER CAPITA GROSS PRODUCT, PERSONAL INCOME, AND DISPOSABLE
PERSONAL INCOME, CALIFORNIA AS PERCENT OF UNITED STATES,
1947, 1963, AND 1975

	1947	1963	1975
Per capita gross product................	121	119	115
Per capita personal income..............	126	121	119
Per capita disposable personal income.....	126	121	119

SOURCE: Tables 1A, 1B, and 1C are derived from Table 1.

3. A MORE DETAILED ANALYSIS OF THE PROJECTIONS AND THE METHODOLOGY EMPLOYED

a. Population

Several of the population projections available for California are
shown in Table 2. The first source listed is the Population Research
Unit of the California State Department of Finance, an agency experienced in analyzing California population trends. The population projections of the Department of Finance are used in this statement of
guidelines in preference to lower projections, even though some of these
are based on more sophisticated methods of analysis.

Projections of the Department of Finance are derived from detailed
analysis of birth and death rates for the California population and from
estimates of future net migration to California. The migration estimates
are considered conservative because annual net migration to the state
is limited to 300,000, a level exceeded every year since 1955. It is antici-

TABLE 2

CALIFORNIA POPULATION PROJECTIONS, 1960–1980

(thousands)

Source	Year projection made	1960	1970	1975	1976	1980
State Dept. of Finance......	1963	......	21,734	24,830	......	28,137
State Development Plan....	1963	......	21,462	24,584	......	27,880
Stanford Research Institute	1960	......	19,000	21,850[a]	......	24,700
M. I. Gershenson	1960	......	22,090	25,600	......	......
Nat'l. Planning Association	1962	......	......	......	24,186	......
ORRRC Study	1962					
Judgment Forecast.......		......	......	......	23,744	......
High U. S. population:						
High migration.........		......	......	......	24,980	......
Low migration.........		......	......	......	23,100	......
Low U. S. population:						
High migration.........		......	......	......	22,901	......
Low migration.........		......	......	......	21,111	......
W. S. Thompson[b]..........	1955					
High....................		15,204	19,466	......	......	......
Medium................		14,837	17,680	......	......	......
Low....................		13,689	15,344	......	......	......
David Weeks[b].............	1955					
Extreme upper limit......		16,373	20,736	......	......	......
Reas. upper limit.........		15,432	18,741	......	......	......
Reas. lower limit.........		15,057	17,744	......	......	......
Extreme lower limit......		13,342	15,352	......	......	......

[a] Interpolated.
[b] As reported in George A. Steiner, "U.S. Gross National Product Projections," mimeographed, March 18, 1963.

pated that crude levels of natural increase will decline somewhat in the next few years, after which a dramatic recovery will follow upon the entrance into the reproductive age groups of those born during the post-World War II baby boom. Rates of mortality are expected to maintain their present low level except in sections of the state which now enjoy abnormally low rates attributable to their favorable age compositions. No change in the military population is assumed.

The population projections used in the State Development Plan were made by the Department of Finance with the help of electronic computers at the Survey Research Center at the University of California in Berkeley. The methods used are essentially the same as those described above, and the population projection for 1975 is within one percent of that adopted in these guidelines.

The much lower population projections for 1970 and 1980 made by the Stanford Research Institute in 1960 were based on detailed analyses of employment trends and relationships. Limited space precludes a detailed explanation and criticism of this forecasting method. Essentially, the method is based on the sound assumption that new jobs are the major determinant of net additions to the population of California through migration. In detail the SRI method requires the identification and projection of "basic" or "export" employment, or more precisely "employment in each individual industry whose output is functionally independent of changes in the size of the California market."[4]

This basic employment is used then to calculate total civilian employment on the basis of expected relationships between basic and total employment. The use of this formula results only in a first approximation to total employment because the assumption is made that all changes in domestic-market-oriented employment are induced. Therefore the SRI study also allows for autonomous changes in domestic-market-oriented employment resulting from autonomous import substitution, shifts in relative demand among individual industries, and shifts in relative productivities among industries.

Finally, given projections of total civilian employment, the SRI projections of total population are made on the basis of assumptions concerning the rate of unemployment, the civilian labor force participation rates, the percent of the civilian population of working ages, and the projected number of military personnel stationed in the state.

The method used by SRI, which bases population projections on expected increases in employment, is logically sound, and the calculations were carried out with great care. Experience with such projections, however, shows that the functional relationships involved are extremely difficult to determine. Moreover, these relationships change over time in ways difficult to anticipate. Projections based on such industry-by-industry analysis of basic employment tend to underestimate future growth in regional population and employment. Our judgment that the SRI projections for 1970 and 1980 are too conservative is supported by the fact that employment and population have continued to expand at rapid rates in the five years since the study was completed.

In 1962 the National Planning Association made population projections for 1976. The NPA method is similar to that used in the SRI study in that it is based on a detailed industry analysis and assumes that population tends to follow the most favorable job opportunities. It differs from the SRI approach in the belief "that the best place to start in

---

[4] *The California Economy, 1947–1980*, Stanford Research Institute (Menlo Park, 1960), p. 439.

making state projections is from an understanding of national economic and demographic trends and the forces lying behind the pattern of national economic growth."[5]

Given the national economic projections, the NPA allocated the projected employment among states of each industry based on the relative attraction offered by each state to the people and capital engaged in the industry. Then demographic, income, and output trends for the various states were examined and related to industry-employment developments. Finally, through a process of continuous feedback among the relationships examined, the final projections were determined. The state economic projections, subjected to continual review, required a large amount of judgment by the analyst.

Although these guidelines do not adopt the NPA population projection for 1975, the NPA projections of state employment composition gross product in 1976 are used as the basis for our projections of employment and gross product for 1975. Note that the NPA population projection for California for 1976 is about 700,000 less than the figure of 24,830,000 adopted for 1975.

Table 2 includes several California population projections for 1976 made for the Outdoor Recreation Resources Review Commission (ORRRC). These include a "judgment" forecast and four alternative forecasts which combine various assumptions about the growth of United States population and the rate of interstate migration. All these projections are based on demographic factors alone and combine the analysis of various agencies including the U. S. Bureau of the Census and the U. S. Bureau of Labor Statistics. Essentially, these forecasts assume a slowing down in the growth of national population and in the level of interstate migration.

Finally, Table 2 includes two other sets of population projections for 1960 and 1970 made in 1955 by W. S. Thompson and David Weeks. Although these projections were made only five years before the 1960 Census was taken, the Census enumeration put the 1960 California population at 15,717,204, which exceeds Thompson's "high" projection and also Week's "reasonable upper limit." This indicates that the methods used by these two analysts yield projections which are too conservative.

Table 3 shows how the population increase projected in these guidelines compares with past growth in California. Our projections for 1970 and 1975 indicate that the average annual increase in population of more than 600,000 will exceed that for any previous decade. On the other hand, the percentage rate of growth will average only 3.3 between

---

[5] *State Employment Trends to 1976*, Regional Economic Projection Series, Report No. 1, National Planning Association (Washington, D.C., 1962), p. 5.

1960 and 1970 and 2.7 between 1970 and 1975. Both these figures are lower than for any decade in this century except for the depression decade of the thirties. In conclusion, it would appear that although the rate of population growth we have projected to 1975 is large, it is not unreasonable.

TABLE 3

CALIFORNIA POPULATION INCREASE, 1900–1960
AND PROJECTIONS TO 1975

	Average annual increase	Percent average annual increase
1900–1910...................	89,200	4.8
1910–1920...................	104,900	3.7
1920–1930...................	225,000	5.2
1930–1940...................	123,000	2.0
1940–1950...................	367,900	4.4
1950–1960...................	513,000	4.0
1960–1970...................	601,700	3.3
1970–1975...................	619,200	2.7

SOURCE: 1900–1960, U. S. Censuses of Population; 1970–1975, State Department of Finance.

b. Employment structure in 1975

Projections of total employment in California in 1975 are based on specific assumptions concerning the working-age population, labor force participation rates, and unemployment rates. We start with the State Department of Finance projection of the population age 14 and over of 17,740,000. The labor force participation rate is projected at 58.2 percent in 1975, slightly higher than the 57.5 percent rate reported in the 1960 Census. This increase is based on an analysis of Maurice I. Gershenson of the California Department of Industrial Relations.[6] In 1975 it is assumed that the total labor force of 10,300,000 will be divided between 300,000 military personnel and 10 million civilians.

It is assumed that the unemployment rate in California in 1975 will be 5 percent, although only 4 percent is projected for the nation as a whole. The higher unemployment rate for California is consistent with the historical record—the period 1951 to 1957 was an exception—and is accounted for by the many migrants entering California without an employment commitment. With 5 percent unemployed, total civilian employment comes to 9,500,000.

[6] M. I. Gershenson, "Labor Force Projections for California, 1960–1975," a paper presented at the annual meetings of the American Statistical Association, August 1960.

TABLE 4
PROJECTIONS OF INDUSTRIAL STRUCTURE OF CALIFORNIA EMPLOYMENT IN 1975

	Thousands of employees	Percent of civilian employment
Agriculture	285	3.0
Mining	29	0.3
Manufacturing	2,113	22.3
Food	166	1.8
Textiles	6	0.1
Apparel	75	0.8
Lumber	84	0.9
Furniture	44	0.5
Paper	46	0.5
Printing	109	1.2
Chemicals	75	0.8
Petroleum	19	0.2
Rubber	27	0.3
Leather	10	0.1
Stone, clay, and glass	50	0.5
Primary metals	86	0.9
Fabricated metals	157	1.7
Nonelectrical machinery	148	1.6
Electrical machinery	359	3.8
Transportation	490	5.2
Instruments	62	0.7
Other manufacturing	100	1.1
Transportation, Communications, Utilities	540	5.7
Trade	2,200	23.2
Services	2,235	23.5
Finance, insurance, real estate	384	4.0
Construction	704	7.4
Government	1,010	10.6
Total civilian employment	9,500	100.0
Unemployment	500	
Civilian labor force	10,000	
Military personnel	300	
Total labor force	10,300	

SOURCE: Based on NPA projections for 1976 in Table 5 adjusted for revision in employment.

The distribution of employment by industry shown in Table 4 is based on the NPA analysis of employment trends for 1976 shown in Table 5. The NPA figures are adjusted in two ways: (1) to increase total employment from 9.2 to 9.5 million and (2) to adjust the composition of employment for the changes between 1957 and 1976 indicated by long-run trends.

Although Table 4 shows the employment composition anticipated in the projection year 1975, Table 5 is useful in showing the expected changes in amount of employment and in the percent of total employment accounted for by each industry in 1957 and 1976. Employment is expected to increase substantially in all major or "one-digit" classifications except agriculture and mining, where decreases of about 25 thousand and 2 thousand, respectively, are predicted. The largest increases are expected in the trade and service industries, in both of which employment is projected to increase by more than one million. The next largest increase of nearly 800,000 is expected in manufacturing.

Within the manufacturing sector the largest increases in employment are expected in printing, chemicals, primary and fabricated metals, nonelectrical and electrical machinery, transportation equipment, and instruments. Small decreases in employment are expected in two manufacturing industries—textiles and petroleum products.

c. California gross product and personal income in 1975

The only state income or product data developed by the National Income Division of the U. S. Department of Commerce is the annual personal income series dating from 1929, and this agency provides no income forecasts. The data in these guidelines on California gross product, personal disposable income, and the projection to 1975 of personal income are based on a recent NPA study.[7] The plotted NPA gross products for states are based on its projections of GNP in 1976 and of state employment structure.

The NPA forecast of GNP in constant dollars assumes an annual growth rate of about 4.3 percent from 1957 to 1975. This rate is a little higher than the actual rate of 3.9 percent from 1947 to 1957. There has been considerable discussion recently about future growth rates of the American economy, and a number of projections of GNP are available. Some of these are listed in Table 6, including that of 4.2 percent from 1960 to 1976. This growth rate is near the median for the group.

---

[7] *State Income and Output Trends to 1976*, Regional Economic Projection Series, Report No. 2, National Planning Association (Washington, D.C., 1962).

PROJECTION GUIDELINES 73

TABLE 5
CIVILIAN EMPLOYMENT IN CALIFORNIA BY INDUSTRY, 1957 AND 1976

	Employment (thousands)		Percent of total	
	1957	1976	1957	1976
Commodity employment...............	1,605.4	2,358.7	29.7	25.6
Agriculture........................	307.0	282.4	5.7	3.1
Mining............................	31.5	29.2	0.6	0.3
Manufacturing.....................	1,266.9	2,047.1	23.5	22.2
Food............................	147.1	160.7	2.7	1.7
Tobacco.........................	0.5	0.5	0.0	0.0
Textiles.........................	6.1	5.5	0.1	0.1
Apparel.........................	57.3	72.5	1.1	0.8
Lumber.........................	57.6	82.0	1.1	0.9
Furniture.......................	28.4	43.1	0.5	0.5
Paper...........................	24.6	44.6	0.5	0.5
Printing.........................	65.0	106.3	1.2	1.2
Chemicals.......................	41.5	72.1	0.8	0.8
Petroleum.......................	29.6	18.3	0.5	0.2
Rubber..........................	18.8	26.1	0.3	0.3
Leather.........................	7.2	9.7	0.1	0.1
Stone, clay, and glass.............	38.9	49.3	0.7	0.5
Primary metals..................	51.5	82.8	1.0	0.9
Fabricated metals................	89.7	152.5	1.7	1.7
Nonelectrical machinery...........	91.5	142.6	1.7	1.5
Electrical machinery..............	88.9	347.5	1.6	3.8
Transportation equipment.........	338.1	477.0	6.3	5.2
Instruments.....................	20.8	58.9	0.4	0.5
Miscellaneous...................	63.8	95.1	1.2	1.0
Noncommodity employment...........	3,795.5	6,851.8	70.3	74.4
Transportation, communications, and utilities........................	384.0	522.6	7.1	5.7
Trade............................	1,112.9	2,132.7	20.6	23.2
Services..........................	1,066.4	2,162.9	19.8	23.5
Finance and real estate.............	234.2	372.1	4.3	4.0
Construction......................	346.0	680.8	6.4	7.4
Government.......................	652.0	980.7	12.1	10.6
Total civilian employment.......	5,400.9	9,210.5	100.0	100.0
Unemployment.....................	....	356.7	....	....
Civilian labor force.................	....	9,567.2	....	....
Total population...................	13,871	24,344	....	....

SOURCE: ORRRC Study Report 23, p. 352 (Projections made by NPA).

TABLE 6

ILLUSTRATIVE GROSS NATIONAL PRODUCT GROWTH-RATE FORECASTS

Forecaster	Period of forecast	Annual rate
Murray Shields............................	1959–70	5.25
H. H. Landsberg, et al.....................	1960–70	4.7 (high)
J. W. Knowles, et al.......................	1959–75	4.6 (high)
ORRRC (NPA)	1959–76	4.5
United California Bank	1962–70	4.4
J. W. Kendrick............................	1960–70	4.2
U. S. Dept. of Labor	1960–70	4.2
National Planning Association	1960–76	4.2
H. H. Landsberg, et al......................	1960–70	4.0 (med.)
J. W. Knowles, et al.......................	1959–75	4.0 (med.)
Stanford Research Institute..................	1962–75	3.9
G. A. Steiner	1962–72	3.8
S. W. Edmunds............................	1960–70	3.75
H. H. Landsberg, et al......................	1960–70	3.5 (low)
J. W. Knowles, et al.......................	1959–75	3.5 (low)
Dexter Keezer	1956–70	3.5
U. S. News and World Report.................	1959–70	3.5
W. C. Freund	1960–70	3.4
E. F. Denison	1960–80	3.3
R. C. Turner..............................	1956–70	3.25
C. E. Silberman and S. S. Parker in Fortune	1958–70	3.0

The NPA also computed growth rates in real gross product for regions of the United States from 1929 to 1957 as shown in Table 7. California accounts for three-fourths of the total population of the Far West, a region which had the highest average growth rate—4.4 percent—in this period. The low rate of growth in per capita gross product for the Far West is accounted for by the decrease in the percentage of the population of working age.

Total output or gross product in California is projected to reach $123 billion in 1975 compared to $65 billion in 1963. As in the past, non-commodity output is expected to grow faster than commodity output, and both faster than the national average. Output per employee in California is forecast to remain above the national average in each of the commodity and noncommodity sectors. Output per employee in California is expected to increase less than the national average because of the effect of long-run factors tending to bring regional output rates nearer the national average. These factors include the migration of labor and capital.

TABLE 7
PERCENTAGE GROWTH RATES FROM 1929 TO 1957
UNITED STATES REGIONS

Region	Total gross product	Per capita gross product
Continental U.S.	2.9	1.7
New England	2.0	1.3
Mideast	2.1	1.2
Great Lakes	2.8	1.7
Plains	2.6	2.1
Southeast	3.9	2.7
Southwest	4.0	2.6
Rocky Mountain	3.5	1.9
Far West [a]	4.4	1.3

[a] The "Far West" includes California, Nevada, Oregon, and Washington. California accounted for more than 76 percent of the population of this region in 1960.
SOURCE: Edward F. Denison, *The Sources of Economic Growth in the United States and the Alternatives Before Us*, 1962, p. 9.

Table 8 shows the percentage distribution of California gross product by major industry in 1947, 1957, and 1976. Because the industry composition of total output changes slowly, the 1976 percentages computed by the NPA can be applied to our gross product figure for 1975 with very little error. Table 8 shows that the industrial composition of California gross product will change much less from 1957 to 1976 than it did between 1947 and 1957.

TABLE 8
PERCENT DISTRIBUTION, CALIFORNIA GROSS PRODUCT
BY MAJOR INDUSTRY, 1947, 1957, AND 1976

Industry	1947	1957	1976
Manufacturing	19	25	26
Agriculture and mining	11	7	4
Trade	23	18	17
Services	13	12	14
Finance, Insurance, Real Estate	10	12	14
Construction	5	6	6
Transportation, Communications, Public Utilities	9	9	9
Government	10	11	11
Total	100	100	100

SOURCE: *State Income and Output Trends to 1976*, Regional Economic Projection Series, Report No. 2, 1962 Edition, National Planning Association, Washington, D. C., p. 77.

California personal income is projected to reach $100 billion in 1975, compared to $52 billion in 1963. This growth rate is faster than for the nation as a whole, primarily because of accelerated employment growth and a rise in the proportion of the population in the labor force. California receives a somewhat higher share of national personal income than its share of output, reflecting a net import of property income and a mix of industries which tend to be relatively labor intensive.

Per capita income in California is projected to remain above the national average, although it is expected to grow at a slower than national rate. The high per capita income in California is a direct result of the high levels of productivity and average employee compensation in the state.

All the income and product data contained in the tables discussed thus far in these guidelines are stated in 1963 prices. Although data in constant prices are required for much economic analysis, data in current prices are more useful for some purposes. For this reason Table 9 shows personal income for California and the United States from 1945 to 1961 in current prices.

TABLE 9

PERSONAL INCOME, CALIFORNIA AND UNITED STATES, 1945–1963
(billion current dollars)

Year	United States	California
1945	171.2	15.2
1946	179.3	16.1
1947	191.6	16.6
1948	210.4	17.6
1949	208.3	17.8
1950	228.5	19.6
1951	256.7	22.7
1952	273.1	25.1
1953	288.3	26.6
1954	289.8	27.4
1955	310.2	30.2
1956	332.9	33.3
1957	351.4	35.6
1958	360.3	37.2
1959	383.9	41.0
1960	400.8	43.1
1961	416.4	45.6
1962	442.1	49.2
1963	463.0	52.3

SOURCE: U. S. Department of Commerce.

CHAPTER II

BANKING AND THE ECONOMY

Commercial Banking and Rapid Economic Growth in California[1]

HYMAN P. MINSKY

1. INTRODUCTION

FOR ALL ENTERPRISE economies, commercial banks play a part in the process by which economic growth is brought about and, in turn, the characteristics of the economic growth that takes place affect commercial banks. This is true of California as well as of all other enterprise economies. However, as California is a region that has grown and is expected to continue growing much more rapidly than the larger economy of which it is a part, the interrelations between commercial banking and growth for the state are somewhat special. The particular problem of this paper is to explore the role of commercial banking in the observed and forecast growth of California and the impact of the state's growth upon banks.

The material in this paper falls under three broad headings:
(1) the pulling together of some ideas about economic growth and the relation between economic growth and financial developments;
(2) the presentation of information which seems to describe the economic growth and financial developments which have taken place; and,
(3) the drawing of inferences about the prospects of the state's economy.

The guidelines as laid down by Williams are used even though the analysis suggests that they may be unreliable because the financial factors central to California's growth are sensitive to shifts in the federal government's spending policies.

[1] I wish to thank R. Charles Vars, Mrs. Patricia Bragg, and William Rutzick for their assistance on this study, and Charles F. Haywood, Richard S. Peterson, and R. Gene Conatser for their helpful comments. In addition, I owe a special debt to Robert Lindsay whose ability to distinguish the essential from the merely interesting was of especial importance to me. Of course, the errors of fact and analysis that remain are solely my responsibility.

80

The underlying economic theory dealing with regional financial flows and the interrelations between financial variables and economic growth is not well developed. As a result only broad qualitative conclusions can be drawn from the theory. In addition, data relevant to an analysis of the role of finance in the state economy are not available. Thus, even the limited quantitative inferences which, in principle, could be drawn in fact cannot be derived because of the limitations of the data.

The inferences that are made are skeptical about future growth being an extrapolation of recent growth. Although the real resources of the state can readily accommodate the forecast rate of population and economic growth, it is doubtful that the recent rapid rates of growth of some critical financial flows can be maintained. However it must be understood that this skepticism is based upon primitive theory and upon data with many gaps.

2. ECONOMIC GROWTH

a. Introduction

Our first need is to understand how one region can grow faster than another when both are closely integrated in a national economy. In this section two propositions important for our purposes are derived. The first is that a region growing both in population and in income, at a rate significantly greater than that of the economy of which it is a part, imports capital from the rest of the economy.[2] The second is that such rapid regional growth is based upon the existence of some leading sector or sectors within the region and that the leading sectors are the result of one or a combination of the following:

(1) the pattern of increases in demand as income grows in the national economy;

(2) the nature of the technological changes that are occurring; and,

(3) the willingness of labor to take a lower nominal (monetary) income in order to live in a particular region.

The recent rapid growth of California has been based mainly upon the state's favorable location for activities for which national demand is growing more rapidly than national income. This has been supplemented by the effects of recent technological changes, particularly those related to power, communications, and transportation. In addition, some of the migration of labor to California—and the capital owned by

---

[2] For a formal argument that a more rapidly growing region will import capital see: G. H. Borts and J. L. Stein, "Regional Growth and Maturity in the United States: A Study of Regional Structural Change." *Schwerische Zeitschrift für Volkswirtschaft und Statistik*, 98th year, No. 3; 1962.

the migrating households—seems to be aided by the belief that California is a good place to live; although if this were the sole basis for the migration, wages in California would fall relative to those in the country as a whole, and this has not occurred. Another factor making for rapid growth is that rapid growth begets rapid growth—that is, the increased size of its markets makes profitable a shift of some productions to California. Nevertheless, in spite of the fact that rapid economic growth in a region is a result of a complex of factors, future prospects for rapid California growth depend upon the continued existence of some set of leading sectors which tend to pull the economy ahead expeditiously.

This chapter concentrates on the real aspects of regional economic growth: those relating to factor inputs, capital movements, and the impact of changing demand patterns and technology. In other papers the monetary and financial relations associated with the observed growth patterns are examined.

It should be noted that by economic growth we mean the percentage rate of increases in an overall measure of output, such as Gross National Product or personal income. We are not focusing on the per capita rate of increase. Hence, as we define rapid economic growth, it does not necessarily mean that the average well-being in the rapidly growing region is improving relative to the rest of the country.

Economic growth in this paper is viewed from two perspectives: "after the event" and "before the event." In the first we assume growth to have taken place and examine the relations among the various items that have changed. In the second we look more closely at how the growth was generated, at what "forces" led to growth. The after-the-event view of growth, taken up first as it is simpler, can treat the regional and national economies as entities whereas the before-the-event view, if it is to help explain differential rates of growth in the various parts of the national economy, must look at the composition of production and demand within the various regions and in the country as a whole.

The after-the-event view leads us to the conclusion that a rapidly growing region tends to import capital. The before-the-event view of regional economic growth generates the proposition that such growth is due to the existence of some leading sector. Although independent migration and technological changes which affect locational attributes are factors entering into the California growth experience, the weight of the argument is that recent rapid economic growth in California is associated with a set of leading industries which reflect rapidly growing national demand.

b. After-the-event view of economic growth

Potential output, and hence full employment income, within a region depends upon the quantity and quality of labor and capital inputs within that region. For potential output to grow, it is necessary that the quantity and quality of labor and capital also grow.[3] We will look first at the qualitative changes in labor and capital. As we are dealing with a national economy within which communication is relatively free, we assume that the qualitative contributions to growth are approximately the same throughout the country. Therefore the differences in the growth rates of the various regions depend upon differences in rates of growth of inputs. If the qualitative factors make a large contribution to overall increase, as seems to be the case,[4] the differences in the rates of growth of the quantity of inputs among regions will be greater than in the realized rates of growth of potential income.

It is useful to separate the qualitative from the quantitative aspects of economic growth in analyzing the expansion of potential output. Output at any time is considered to depend upon the product of a "technique" factor and a function that transforms the quantity of labor and capital into output. It is recognized that the technique factor includes the qualitative characteristics of the labor force associated with education and health as well as the more conventional definition of technique as know-how and the nature of capital equipment. The change in technique per period we can call an improvement factor; and we can assume that this is given independently of what happens to income within the region or the country.

It may be that the most briskly growing economies get the greater advantage from technological advance. This possibility is probably more relevant to underdeveloped countries than to any regions within an advanced economy such as the United States. Therefore, even though the more rapid rate of growth expected to take place in California will require an investment rate higher than in the country as a whole, we will ignore any implication that this may have for per capita income.[5]

---

[3] Strictly speaking, economic growth can take place as the result of qualitative changes in inputs without any increase in their quantity. However, for the foreseeable future the national labor force will grow, and at full employment saving is a substantial portion of income. Thus, we can ignore this possibility.

[4] Edward F. Denison, *The Sources of Economic Growth in the United States and the Alternatives Before Us*, Supplementary Paper No. 13; Committee for Economic Development, January 1962. Robert M. Solow, "Technical Change and the Aggregate Production Function," *The Review of Economics and Statistics*, August 1957.

[5] The experiment in higher education now underway in California, which results in a significantly larger part of the young continuing beyond high school than in the

Now we can ask how the labor force and the capital stock grow in order to achieve a given rate of growth in output. We assume that if the labor force and the capital stock develop at a particular pace, and the net result of the improvement factor is zero, then output grows at the same rate as labor and capital.[6] If the improvement factor is positive, say 2 percent per year, then the rate of growth of output, given that labor and capital expand at the same rate, will be greater, by the improvement factor, than the rate of growth of capital and labor. That is, a 2 percent per year improvement factor combined with a 2 percent per year growth rate in capital and labor will yield approximately a 4 percent per year rate of growth in output.[7]

Let us assume that the capital stock is four times the size of annual income and that the increase in capital needed to cooperate with an addition to the labor force is also four times the resultant increase in productive capacity. That is to say, for every $100 in income there is $400 in capital stock. Hence if 8 percent of income is saved and invested per year, the capital stock increases by 2 percent per year. That is, savings of $8 out of the $100 in income, when invested, will raise the capital stock from $400 to $408.

Given a 2 percent per year increase in the labor force and this increase in the capital stock, productive capacity will rise by 2 percent per year. Combining this with an annual improvement factor of 2 percent per year, a growth of income at the rate of 4 percent per year will take place.

rest of the country is, of course, investment in human resources at a rate greater than that in the rest of the country. Whether this more intensive human investment will lead to greater California, than out-of-state, increases in productive capacity is an unknown factor in estimating economic growth rates for California as compared to the United States as a whole.

[6] If the capital stock grows at one rate and the labor force at another, then, again assuming that the improvement factor is zero or independent of the rates of growth of the capital stock and the labor force, potential output (independent of whatever increase is due to the improvement factor) will grow at a rate between those of growth of the capital stock and of the labor force.

The forecast made by Williams is that per capita income will grow at a slower rate in California than in the rest of the country. This implies that, if the improvement factor is the same both in and out of California, the rate of growth of the capital stock relative to that of labor will be smaller within than outside of California during the forecast period.

The assumption that if labor and capital inputs grow at the same rate, then output will grow at this rate, is not essential to the argument. In technical language we could have postulated increasing or decreasing returns to scale and obtained the same results. It is the difference in the regional rates of growth of the labor force and the assumed constant capital-output ratios that generates the regional differences in the required rate of growth of the capital stock.

[7] A 2 percent per year rate of growth inputs and a 2 percent per year improvement factor will yield a rate of growth of 4.04 percent per year.

By contrast, consider an area in which the labor force is increasing at 3 percent per year. If per capita income is not to deteriorate in this region relative to the rest of the country, then, given the 2 percent annual improvement factor, output in this area must grow by 5 percent a year. But for this to take place the capital stock must increase by 3 percent per year to keep pace with the growth in labor force. Given the 4 to 1 capital income ratio assumed above, investment equal to 12 percent of the region's income must take place. However, the region is part of an economy that is saving and investing 8 percent of its annual income. There is no reason to believe that the population of this rapidly growing region will save at a rate relative to income different from the rest of the country.[8]

In our example, rapid growth requires 12 percent of the region's income to be saved and invested. The region's domestic sources can be expected to supply only 8 percent of its income in the form of savings. Capital equal to 4 percent of the area's income has to be imported; that is, one-third of the investment placed in the region has to be financed outside the region.[9] For this capital inflow to occur, the financial instruments generated within the area must have wide acceptability in the country as a whole—wealth owners in the rest of the country must be willing to own assets based upon the region's economy. The acceptability of the financial instruments depends in part upon the way in which financial institutions transform local into national financial assets. In the next sections we examine the financial instruments used to import capital into California in the postwar period and that are available to finance future growth.

c. Before-the-event view of economic growth

The before-the-event view of economic growth explains why growth takes place, not just what happens as growth transpires. Our special problem is to understand why California has grown more rapidly than

---

[8] It can be argued that the savings ratio in the rapidly growing region may be lower than in the country as a whole. Persons on the scene in a rapidly growing region expect to do better in terms of capital appreciation, etc., than others in the country. The higher expected future income will tend to lower current savings ratios in the surging region.

[9] The significance of the improvement factor in determining the proportion of investment in the rapidly growing region that has to be financed by imported capital can be illustrated by a numerical example. Assume 8 percent of income is saved nationally and within the rapidly growing region. Assume that for every 2 percent of income invested a 1 percent increase in income results. Hence, for income to grow 5 percent per year in a region when nationally it is growing at 4 percent per year, investment equal to 10 percent of the income of the rapidly growing region will have to be put in place within that region; that is, 20 percent of the investment put in place will have to be financed by imported capital.

the rest of the country in the past decade and whether it can be expected to continue to grow more rapidly in the future. We are interested in determining the general nature of the market conditions that induced the migration of labor and capital to California in the past decade.

In the labor market some workers will be drawn to California by the expectation of higher incomes. Others will decide to come quite independently of expected income levels. Capital, aside from safety factors, does not have preferences as to where it would like to be, hence capital will migrate to California only if the relevant combination of expected pay-off and safety is better in California than elsewhere in the country.

(1) *The patterns of population and income change.*—Since 1952 the annual percentage change of population in California has been in the neighborhood of 4 percent per year. In the nation, by contrast, the rate has been in the neighborhood of 2 percent per year (see Figure I). In the period 1948–1951 population growth in the United States was only a trifle lower than it has averaged since 1952. However, in the same period the increase in civilian population in California ranged from 2.2 to 3.3 percent. The growth rate of population in California in the immediate postwar period was thus considerably lower than in the period since 1952. The year 1952 marks an important change in the growth characteristics of California.

In 1946, 1947, and 1948 personal income grew faster in the United States than in California (see Figure II and Table 1). The recession of 1949 was mild in California. California personal income showed an increase, whereas that in the United States as a whole showed a decrease. Since 1950, in good times and in recessions, personal income in California has grown more rapidly than elsewhere in the United States. However, per capita personal income in California has at times grown faster, and at other times more slowly, than in the other states. There has been no systematic change in relative per capita personal income.

The evidence from unemployment rates, as presented in Figure III, also indicates that postwar growth of California has not exhibited the same characteristics throughout the period. Through 1953 unemployment rates in California were substantially higher than those in other states. Beginning in 1954, unemployment rates followed the same pattern and stayed at approximately the same level in California and in the balance of the nation. However, California rates were slightly below the U. S. rates in 1954–1959 whereas in 1960 and 1961 they were slightly higher.

(2) *The inducement for labor migration.*—The marked growth in employment in California in the postwar period, and the large-scale migration of labor to California have not been associated with especially tight

FIGURE I

Estimated Percent Change in Civilian and Total Population:
California and the United States, 1947–1963

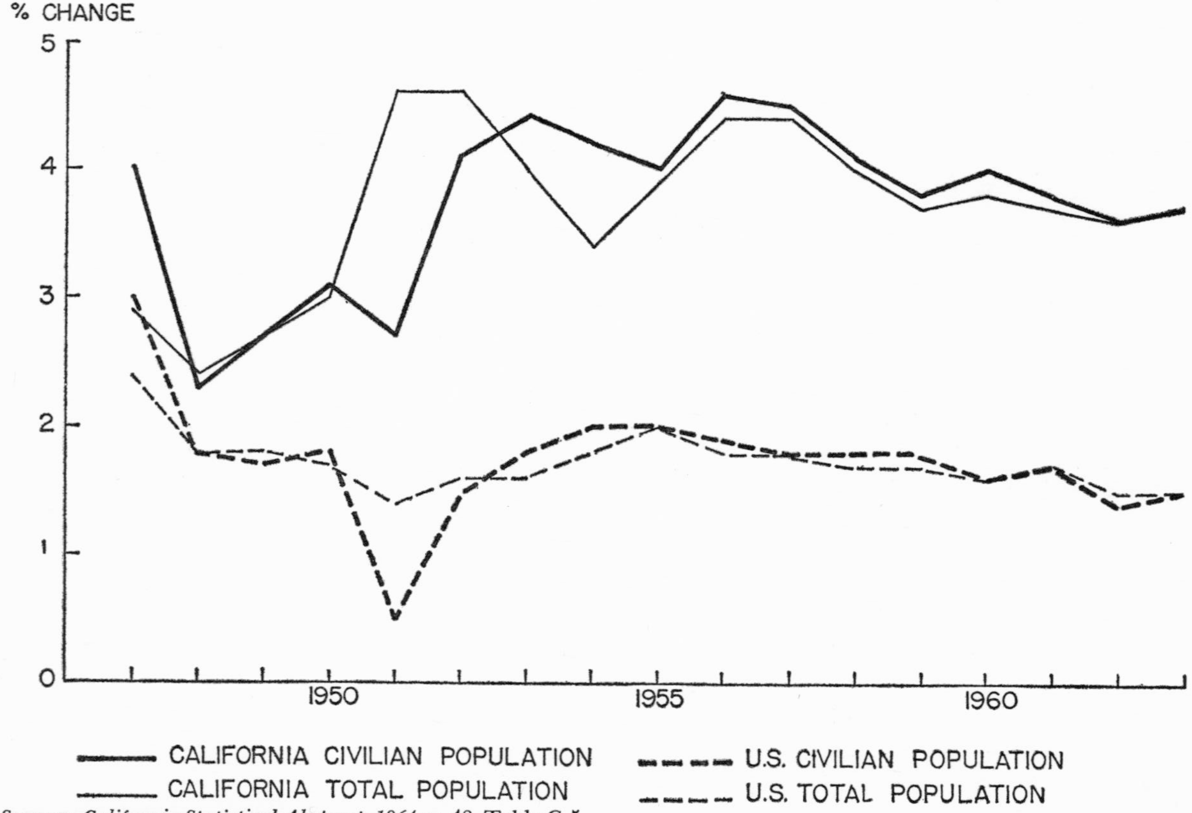

CALIFORNIA CIVILIAN POPULATION   U.S. CIVILIAN POPULATION

CALIFORNIA TOTAL POPULATION   U.S. TOTAL POPULATION

SOURCE: *California Statistical Abstract, 1964*, p. 48, Table G-5.

TABLE 1

GROWTH RATES OF PERSONAL INCOME, UNITED STATES AND CALIFORNIA
1946–1963, CURRENT DOLLARS[a, b]

Year	Personal income		Per capita personal income	
	U. S.	California	U. S.	California
1946.	6.78	5.86	1.22	4.68
1947.	7.61	3.44	5.36	1.45
1948.	9.70	5.86	7.90	4.29
1949.	−0.95	1.27	−2.68	−1.43
1950.	9.74	10.18	7.89	7.25
1951.	12.19	15.83	10.60	11.08
1952.	6.11	9.95	4.49	4.04
1953.	5.58	6.26	3.89	2.62
1954.	0.69	3.16	1.12	−1.72
1955.	7.45	10.18	5.42	6.64
1956.	7.76	10.09	5.84	5.53
1957.	5.55	6.94	3.70	3.14
1958.	2.52	4.66	0.78	1.04
1959.	6.67	9.99	4.80	5.74
1960.	4.52	5.28	2.40	1.87
1961.	3.88	5.71	2.17	2.17
1962.	6.17	7.89	4.30	3.54
1963.	4.73	6.30	3.23	3.11

[a] Alaska and Hawaii are excluded between 1946 and 1960.

[b] $\dfrac{Y_t}{Y_{t-1}} - 1$ = growth rate.

SOURCES: 1. U. S. Department of Commerce, Bureau of the Census: Current Population Reports.
2. U. S. Department of Commerce, Office of Business Economics; Survey of Current Business.

labor markets in California. In fact the migration before 1954 took place in spite of substantially greater slack in employment in California than in the rest of the country.

This early postwar migration to California in the face of high unemployment and slow growth of income suggests the importance of a belief that California is a good place to live. That this migration increased local markets indicates that migration by itself was a growth-generating factor. However, it does not appear that the pull of California was limited to its noneconomic attractions. Despite the continued inflow of workers, wages and per capita income in California did not suffer relative to the rest of the country. In 1950 average hourly earnings in manufacturing in California were 15 percent above the national average; in 1957 they had fallen to 13 percent above the national average; and by 1961 the gap had increased to 17 percent above the national

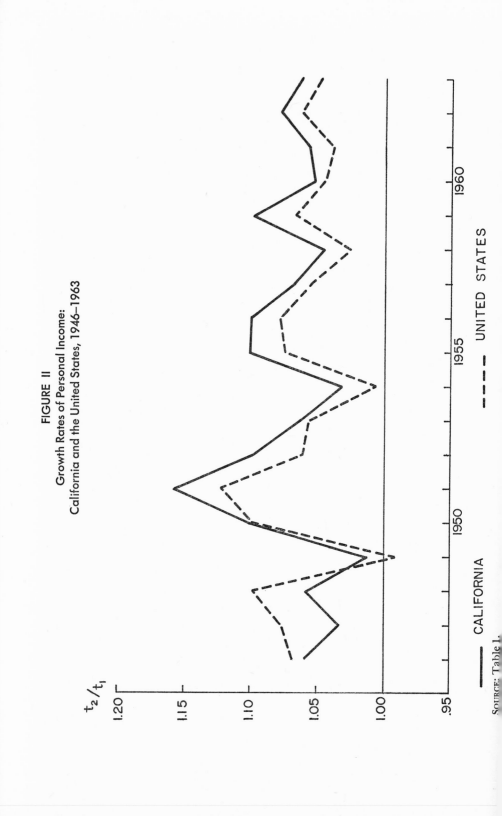

FIGURE II
Growth Rates of Personal Income:
California and the United States, 1946–1963

t_2/t_1

1.20

1.15

1.10

1.05

1.00

.95

1950

1955

1960

CALIFORNIA

UNITED STATES

Source: Table 1.

average. Demand for labor was sufficiently strong to increase the gap in average hourly wages in the last decade.

We can assume, therefore, that for most of the postwar period the migration to California has taken place because the demand for labor was expected to increase; and that since 1954 the migration and the increase in jobs have been so synchronized that the unemployment rate has been at approximately the same level in California as in the nation at large. That is, there may be a special preference for California as a place to live, but the underlying growth in the demand for labor is such that the migration has not undermined the relatively high level of manufacturing wages in California.

It is also important to note that the turn-around in the characteristics of California's growth took place in the Korean War and post-Korean War "cold war" period. The relation between federal government expenditures and California's rapid growth is investigated later.

(3) *Different kinds of growth in a region.*—For purposes of analysis we can separate the sectors in a rapidly growing region into (a) those whose rapid growth is autonomous, and (b) those which grow because they are part of a rapidly expanding economy.

(a) *Sources of autonomous growth.*—The relation between the growth of demand for an output and the growth of national income often is expressed in terms of the income elasticity of demand. The income elasticity of demand for a product states the percentage rate of growth of demand for the product relative to the percentage rate of growth of income. If national income grows at 3 percent per year, and if national demand for a particular output grows at 6 percent per year, then the annual income elasticity of demand for this output is 2. Assume, for example, that a region is a particularly good place to produce a transportable output for which the national income elasticity of demand is greater than one. Then, even if the region receives no more of the expanding market than its current share of the existing market, income in the region due to the sale of this product will grow faster than income in the country. If the income elasticity is sufficiently high in this industry, it can compensate for whatever labor- and capital-saving technological changes are taking place so that investment and employment in this industry will grow at a faster rate than in the whole economy.

As far as California is concerned, it is apparent that the income elasticity of demand for climate, retirement, vacations, and specialty foodstuffs is high, and they are among the underlying elements in California's rapid growth. However, the recent growth of California is also associated with the high rate of increase of defense-related spending

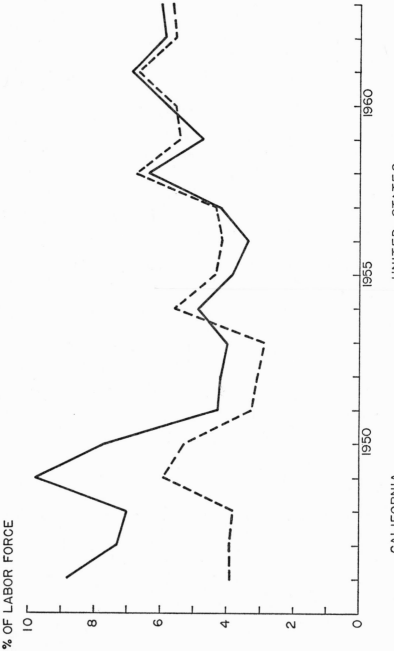

FIGURE III
Unemployment Rates:
California and the United States, 1946–1963

% OF LABOR FORCE

CALIFORNIA ————   UNITED STATES —— —— ——

SOURCES: 1962, 1963 data from *California Statistical Abstract, 1964*, p. 61, Table I-1.
1946–1961 data from *California Statistical Abstract, 1962*, p. 63, Table H-1.

within the state. Hence, California's growth is based upon national social or policy decisions rather than upon the intrinsic character of private demand and production-function changes in a growing economy.

Rapid growth may also occur even when the industry in question is not growing relative to the economy. This will come about from industrial relocation, due to the effect of technological changes. The shift of textiles production from New England to the South is a good example. So is the natural gas revolution which has made power ubiquitous throughout the United States, thus reducing the significance of previously important location-determining factors. Such relocations bring in capital and labor quite independently of the migrations resulting from income elasticities of demand.

(b) *Sources of induced growth.*—Conceptually, the induced factors can be separated into two parts: those due to the need for localized outputs to grow along with population and income, and those induced by the expectation that the prices of factors which are in inelastic supply—especially land sites—will grow most rapidly in a region that is expected to expand swiftly.

Once population and income are growing more rapidly in one region than in the country as a whole, for whatever reason, the supply of nontransportable goods and services must also increase at a faster rate. This is especially true for those nontransportable goods and services, such as housing, that seem to have high income elasticities of demand. In a region with a higher-than-average net migration of labor and incomes, the construction of housing, commercial properties, and government facilities proceeds at a faster pace than in the rest of the country. These activities lead to further demand for local labor. In addition, as construction is generally capital intensive, a further rise in local interest rates and hence an increased incentive to import capital is induced.

Moreover, as local markets grow, productions which previously were brought in from outside are shifted to the region. Once economies of scale can be realized, national organizations set up local production facilities; the growth of automobile assembly plants in California is a good example. This leads not only to an additional increase in job opportunities, but also to an immigration of capital.

The second major source of induced rapid economic growth in a region is the influx of capital drawn in by the belief that the region will expand rapidly. The expectation of rising property prices improves the quality of a mortgage—making the interest rate and the terms more favorable to the borrower than they otherwise would be. In this sense, the expectation of rapid growth facilitates a desirable importation of capital. However, above and beyond this factor, if property values are expected to rise as a result of growth, it is rational to own property in order to benefit from this expected rise in price. Moreover, the demand for property to hold because of the expected rise in its price must be added to the demand for property for current use by business firms and households in the state.

This speculative demand, however, tends to change relative prices among regions from the levels they would have attained in its absence. Hence it tends to decrease the advantages of the region. Thus, these relative price differentials may slow down the growth rate of the region and decrease the expected future, hence present, price of property. A speculative boom may feed back upon and offset in part the very production relationships which triggered the boom.

We come finally to the financial effect of a region's growth. Because of the accelerating national demands for the output of the leading sectors, on the score of these sectors the local economy enjoys, so to say, a balance-of-trade surplus. At the same time, the growth of import substitutes—industries now profitable because of the growth of the local market—also tends to improve the regional balance of trade. The faster growth of income and employment tends to generate a balance-of-trade deficit for the other demensions of demand. Thus the current account may be either in surplus or in deficit. However, as the demand for investment in a rapidly growing region is large, the expectation is that capital imports will be needed. In the next section the financial implications of rapid growth and the central role played by commercial banks in this process are examined.

3. THE GROWTH OF MONEY AND INCOME IN A REGION

a. Introduction

This section focuses on the interrelations between the growth of the money supply and income in a region growing more rapidly than the economy within which it is imbedded. The money supply of a region consists of the demand deposits at the commercial banks within its boundaries, regardless of the location of the owner of the demand deposits, and the hand-to-hand currency and coin circulating within the region.

Commercial banks, which operate the payments mechanism, play a central role in the regional growth process. Not only do "almost all" payments internal to the area pass through the books of that area's commercial banks, but in addition, so do most interregional payments.

In the process these interregional payments affect commercial bank reserves and deposits and the banks' ability to hold local and national earning assets.

Whereas demand deposits are a major liquid asset of the "public" within the region, a large part of the region's stock of national liquid assets is held by the commercial banks in the form of their primary (reserve money) and secondary reserves. In addition, nonfinancial corporations, households, and nonbank financial corporations hold deposits in non-California banks and national assets such as treasury bills. These are part of the region's stock of national liquid assets. However, these liquid assets are available only for the purposes of their owner; the national liquid assets owned by the California banks are available to make payments ordered by any owner of a demand deposit in California. Therefore, any development which puts "pressure" on the region's payments to the rest of the country (and for that matter, the world) tends to affect the commercial banks' holdings of national liquid assets.

This can be stated more precisely. A check drawn on a California bank and deposited for collection in an out-of-state bank requires the California bank to make a payment in reserve money. Symmetrically, a check deposited in a California bank drawn on an out-of-state bank brings reserve money into the California bank.[10] The ebb and flow of payments on current account and on capital account, over time, results in the net change in the reserves of banks within the state.

One business problem of a commercial bank is so to organize its portfolio that seasonal and irregular variations in the ebb and flow of payments will not force unwanted changes in its holdings of local earning assets. Given our emphasis upon the longer-run growth of commercial banking in the area, we will deëmphasize considerations dealing with cyclical, transitory, and erratic flows of bank deposits and reserves, and emphasize the net changes in bank reserves, deposits, and earning assets which accompany rapid growth.

Adequate information on demand deposits in California banks is available, but virtually none on the circulation of currency and coin in the state. We simply have to assume that the ratio of currency and coin to demand deposits is the same in our rapidly growing region, California, as in the rest of the country. This assumption may be false since the high ratio of banking offices to population in California may make the use of checks more common and so reduce the need for currency. In addition, the relatively advanced state of various currency-economizing

---

[10] As far as our level of analysis is concerned, it makes no difference whether the "outside bank" is in the rest of the country or in the rest of the world.

schemes in California may also lower the ratio of currency to demand deposits. It is not probable, however, that California is enough different from the rest of the country to influence the analysis.

To examine the factors responsible for the growth of a banking system's deposits, it is necessary to look at the sources and the determinants of the efficiency of the reserve base. Once an increase in the reserve base of a region's banks takes place, earning assets can increase. Of the earning assets acquired, one part is "secondary reserves," that is, liquid earning assets readily transformable into bank reserves, and another part is local loans.[11] An increase in local loans, especially to business, finances a rise in local spending, output, and income. Increased bank lending tends to generate a wave of expansion of local income.

It is important to note that "deposits" in savings and loan associations, and time and savings deposits in commercial banks, increase the growth of income that is attainable on the basis of a given initial increase in commercial bank reserves. In addition to making reserves more efficient in supporting income, savings and loan associations actively participate in the process by which capital (and therefore reserves) is imported into California. Thus these organizations are complementary to, as well as competitive with, the commercial banks.

It will help make clear the role of money in a growing region if we first look at the parallels between a region in a national economy and a country under a very strict gold standard. We can then examine the reserve base of commercial banks and of a region, and after that turn to the balance of trade of a region, to see how the reserve base is affected by rapid growth. The analysis can then focus on the part played by commercial banks in importing capital and in financing local business.

This is followed by a brief statement of the interrelations among money, credit, and income in a rapidly growing region. The money supply, hence the reserve base of the banks, within the region must grow more rapidly than in the rest of the country, and, for this growth to occur, the gross flow of reserves on account of the "leading" industries and the import of capital must be much larger than the net change in reserves.

b. The banking process in a region of a nation

In a national state with a modern banking system including both commercial banks and a central bank, the government authorities, within limits, can insulate the country's financial system and income

---

[11] Secondary reserves and local loans are not the only earning assets banks acquire: in particular, non-liquid national assets and loans to firms outside the region can be made. In addition it is worth noting that the rediscount windows of the Federal Reserve System transform local loans into an "emergency" source of bank reserves.

from the influences of international financial flows. Hence, in a national state with modern central banking, the overall amount of demand deposits, as well as the size and composition of the earning assets of commercial banks, are either determined or guided by the central bank.

A region within a national state does not have an independent central bank. The commercial banks within a region must conform to the national policy, both as to the minimum required deposit-reserve ratio and to the composition of portfolios. If they do not keep step, either clearing drains go against them, or they find it harder to service customers, who seek financing outside the state, by allowing them to use its good name as an endorser or correspondent.[12]

Basically the monetary system of a region is similar to that of a country under a gold standard so strict that there is no room for an independent monetary policy.[13] Deposits in the central bank, the reserve money of the country, are the analogues to gold when a region is compared with a country. That demand deposits are freely exchanged for currency (a form of reserve money), and that a dollar is a dollar throughout the country, further increase the similarity of a regional monetary system with a strict gold standard national monetary system.[14]

Three important differences exist between the financial relations among regions of a country and between most independent countries: (1) within a country, the capital market is more nearly perfect than between countries; (2) typically, it is easier for labor to move from one region to another within a country than between countries; and (3) national government taxing and spending programs can shift reserves among the areas of a country.

---

[12] Even if the banks of a state are not members of the Federal Reserve System, they have to keep their portfolios in step with the national standards.

[13] See N. N. Bowsher, J. D. Duane and R. Einzig, "The Flow of Funds Between Regions of the United States," *The Journal of Finance*, XIII, No. 1 (March 1958), p. 2. "There is a close analogy between adjustments made by the banking system in response to interregional flows of funds and the theoretical equilibrating process of a smoothly functioning international gold standard."

[14] Under a very strict gold standard, (1) gold coin circulates and provides a major share of hand-to-hand currency, and (2) each bank keeps at least a major share of its required or institutionally-necessary reserves in the form of gold coin in bullion in its vaults. That is, a bank's clearing losses are met, at least in part, by a transfer of gold.

A banking system with a central bank where the volume of central bank liabilities is tightly related to the gold supply is equivalent to a strict gold standard—especially if no possibility of sterilizing any gold gains is allowed. The central bank, if it is allowed to hold earning assets in some ratio to gold, must remain fully invested for this equivalence to hold.

Interest rate differentials can exist within a country and among countries on a strict gold standard. The interest rate differentials are determined by the direction of capital flow and the imperfections of the money and capital markets rather than by independent discount rate policies.

Due to the mobility of capital and labor, regional differences in returns set up significant factor movements. Barriers to perfect mobility exist—although the striking regional differences that occur in wage rates reflect, at least in part, markedly different investment in human capital. If a balance of payments deficit occurs for a region, whether it is due to a deficit in the balance of trade or excessive capital exports, the reserve base of the region's banks decreases. Exchange depreciation and marked change in existing wage, price, and cost differentials are not available as techniques for ending the reserve drains. The only available technique for correcting the imbalance operates by lowering income and employment within the deficit region, which decreases imports and hence tends to correct the outflow of reserves. The decrease of income within a region is brought about by some combination of three factors: (1) imports tend to lower income, (2) capital exports lower local investment, and (3) the loss of reserves decreases the willingness and ability of a region's banks to make local loans. Hence, the adjustment for a region within a country is almost entirely by way of income, and, in a growing national economy, this shows up as differentials in the rate of growth among regions.

The factors mentioned as leading to an adjustment from an initial deficit in a region's balance of payments operate in a comparable, though opposite, way for a region with a surplus. The income impact of the "export" surplus and the import of capital, as well as the secondary income wave which follows from the improved reserve position, tend to expand income. As will be shown, even though the basic income elasticities of demand are such that a surplus on trade account would result for the rapidly growing region if the various regions all grew at the same rate, any marked differentials in the rates of growth lead to a trade deficit for the rapidly growing region. Thus, capital imports are needed to support not only the more rapid rate of growth of the money supply in the rapidly growing region, but also to pay for the balance of trade deficit. However, underlying this situation is a "virtual" surplus in the balance of trade, in that, if all regions grew at the same rate the rapidly growing region would have a surplus.

c. The reserve base of the commercial banks of a region

Currency in circulation within a region, and the reserve deposits of the banks, are both reserve money. They are liabilities of the Federal Reserve System or the Treasury and are acceptable by banks throughout the country in payment for liabilities to banks. We assume that the currency in circulation depends upon the demand deposits of the region, and the rate of growth of circulating currency depends upon the rate of growth of demand deposits. Currency in circulation represents a drain of reserves out of the region's banks: hence, in a region in which income is growing rapidly, the need for concurrent increase in currency and demand deposits affects the net reserves which the region must gain.

The reserves of a region are acquired by a surplus in its balance of payments with the rest of the country and by its dealings with the central bank. Of course, the balance of payments includes financial and portfolio transactions as well as the "trade" balance. Financial transactions, which may include the sale by commercial banks and others of earning assets that are accepted nationally, are part of the process by which the local money supply grows.

We can assume that the Federal Reserve System operates so that the national reserve base rises by, say, 4 percent a year, and that the mix of available assets is such that banks remain fully "invested." In our rapidly growing region the local supply of money and national assets, such as Treasury debt, which function as secondary reserves, must rise by, say, 5 percent if the ratio of velocity in this region to that of the nation as a whole is not to change markedly.

If in the balance of payments statement the transactions of the region with the rest of the world, the Treasury and the Central Bank are consolidated, then each region will run a surplus or deficit equal to its net acquisition of reserve money and Treasury debt.[15] The surplus, on such a consolidated basis, will be larger in the more rapidly growing region than in the rest of the country.

d. The balance of trade of a region

One of the truisms of economics is that the balance of payments always balances. The national balance of payments consists of the balance of trade plus capital movements, payments on account of outstanding liabilities, and movements of a monetary nature. To get a regional balance of payments it is necessary to add the impact of Central Bank and federal government operations.

Let us assume an initial situation in which trade between a particular region and the rest of the country is in balance. Now suppose income begins to grow faster in this region than in the rest of the country. Then, assuming that the propensities to import both in the rapidly-growing region and in the rest of the country do not change, the increase

---

[15] Just as in a gold-standard world each country aside from the gold-producing country can run a surplus, so, within a country, it is possible for each region to run a surplus as measured by net acquisition of reserve money and treasury debt.

in imports will exceed the increase in exports of the rapidly expanding region.[16] The rapidly-growing region will begin to run a trade deficit.

For example, assume that California's average propensity to import from the rest of the United States is .45, and for the rest of the United States the average propensity to import from California is .05. If the income of the rest of the United States, in the original situation, is nine times California's income, then the balance of trade will be "balanced." If income in California rises by 5.5 percent a year, and income in the rest of the country by 4.3 percent a year, and the average propensity to import continues at .45, then, calling California's income Y_c, California imports will rise by $(.055)Y_c(.45) = .02475Y_c$, and California exports will rise by $(.043).9Y_c(.05) = .01935Y_c$: California will run a deficit on trade account.

The effect upon inputs of markedly different rates of growth is so large that the marginal propensity to import need not equal the average propensity to import for California to run a deficit. In our numerical example, California's marginal propensity to import can be equal to .405, and the rest of the United States' marginal propensity to import from California can be .055, and still California will run a deficit. Hence, even if the rest of the United States' demand for imports from California increases more rapidly than income, and California's imports increase less rapidly than its income, California will still run a deficit in its trade account if its relative rate of growth is sufficiently greater.[17]

Given the broad spectrum of goods traded between California and the balance of the country, it is my intuitive "guess" that the income

---

[16] The "propensity to import" is the proportion of regional income spent on goods and services from outside the region—either the rest of the country or the rest of the world. As is usual, the propensity can be either marginal—the ratio of the change in imports to the change in income, or average—the ratio of imports to income.

[17] The forecast is that California will grow at 5.5 percent per year while the country grows at 4.3 percent per year. For an initial balanced trade position to be sustained throughout the growth process, given very strict assumptions, the national income elasticity for California's output must be 1.12, whereas California's income elasticity for the demand for national output must be .88.

The assumptions are: (1) there are two types of output, that of California and of the rest of the country; (2) the income elasticities of demand for each output in the two regions are the same; and (3) the income elasticity of demand for all output is 1, so that the two income elasticities sum to 2. Under these circumstances we get

$$\frac{\Delta M_G}{M_G} \Big/ \frac{\Delta Y_G}{Y_G} = \lambda_G, \quad \frac{\Delta M_N}{M_N} \Big/ \frac{\Delta Y_N}{Y_N} = \lambda_N, \quad \lambda_G + \lambda_N = 2,$$

and as $\quad \dfrac{\Delta M_G}{M_G} = \dfrac{\Delta M_N}{M_N}$, we get $.055\,\lambda_G = .043\,\lambda_N$,

where M is imports, Y is income, λ is income elasticity of demand for imports, G is California, and N is the rest of the country.

elasticities of demand for the output of California are slightly greater than 1. Hence, at the forecast rates of growth, California would be running a deficit on current account.

California's growth, although based upon the existence of favorable income elasticities of demand, also requires that capital be imported. The markedly greater growth rate of California proportional to the rest of the country has swamped, and will continue to swamp, the export surplus that California would enjoy if the two grew at the same rate. The reserve base of the state's banks would tend to be dissipated unless it was supplemented by reserves acquired by way of capital imports. To import capital, California must either generate liabilities of the kind accepted throughout the country, or the migrants must carry with them sufficient capital to maintain the reserve base of the region's banks.[18]

e. Local and national financial instruments

To understand how commercial banks and other financial institutions make it financially feasible for a region such as California to grow appreciably faster than the national economy of which it is a part, it is necessary to distinguish between local and national financial assets.

"Local" financial assets are the liabilities of business, households, and government units whose worth can be judged only by, so to say, "on site" inspection. Intimate personal knowledge is necessary, not so much because of the innate characteristics of the unit issuing the liability, but because the total value of the liabilities emitted by this unit is so small that it is not worthwhile for public information to be made available. Hence, a small manufacturing or retail enterprise can emit only local liabilities, whereas a large national enterprise in the same line of business can emit national liabilities. Mortgages on commercial and residential real estate are "local" liabilities, in that each piece of real estate is essentially unique, and local knowledge is necessary to judge the worth of the underlying property.

National financial assets are those liabilities of financial and non-financial business, households, and government units whose worth can be judged on information which is generally available. A unit acquiring a national asset need not have intimate personal knowledge of the organization initiating the liability and the micro-environment within which it will function. Reserve money and the national debt are prime examples of national assets. They are the liabilities of debtors whose

---

[18] See: James C. Ingram, "A Proposal for Financial Integration in the Atlantic Community," *Factors Affecting the United States Balance of Payments,* Joint Economic Committee, Subcommittee on International Exchange and Payments, 87th Cong., 2d Sess. (1962), pp. 175–208.

scope is obviously nationwide. Some local liabilities can be given national scope by being taken into the portfolios of financial intermediaries which are themselves nationally recognized, and which operate throughout the country. These intermediaries finance the purchase of such local claims by issuing claims against themselves which are, by definition, national.

The existence of nationwide insurance companies and consumer credit organizations tends to blur the distinction between local and national assets within a region such as California. These organizations participate in the consumer and mortgage credit markets, which in their absence would tend to be local. When national financial organizations acquire local financial assets, their payments feed reserves into the local banking system. Whether this constitutes a net change in the reserve position of the local banks depends upon where the national organizations acquired the means of payment, i.e. on the geographic distribution of financial institutions' liabilities, such as outstanding policies, bonded indebtedness, bank loans, and open-market paper, and in the use to which the borrowed funds are put.

For example, in the case of automobile credit most of the reserves brought into California by the national lender soon leave, as the automobile dealer in turn pays for the automobiles. All that remains in the local banking system are deposits and reserves equal to that part of the automobile sale price that is local income—the dealers' profits, wages paid salesmen, and so on. In the case of mortgage credit a much larger part of the reserves initially acquired as a result of the mortgage transaction can be expected to remain in the local reserve base: a larger fraction of the materials and labor will be acquired locally.

The national government endorsement and insurance of otherwise local liabilities also operates to make these instruments more attractive to investors outside the region. Insurance by "an agency of the federal government" of deposits in savings and loan associations tends to make these deposits "default free" national assets. The existence of FHA and VA insurance on home mortgages tends to make such single-family home mortgages national assets, independent of the existence of national mortgage-lending institutions. The introduction of these insurance schemes has enabled savings and loan associations and mortgage credit emitters to import reserves into California at a lower price than would have ruled in their absence. That is, a given flow of financing can be obtained with these insurance programs at a lower rate differential than would have been necessary in their absence.

Local banks also can turn local assets into national assets. They can, for example, "accept" or endorse commercial paper, thus guaranteeing liabilities of a customer. This function also can be carried out by way of correspondent relationships with other banks and the syndication of loans. The underwriting of state- and local-government issues is another way in which commercial banks can facilitate the movement of reserves into a local economy.

With the development of national intermediaries and government guarantees, however, the essential role of commercial banks in the growth process is that they supply "loan" capital to (a) those local enterprises which must grow at least at the same rate as the local economy, and (b) those export enterprises which are too small, and perhaps too new, to be able to generate nationally-acceptable liabilities. This is especially relevant to the conjecture about the essential advantage of California as a location for the sophisticated industries that have sprung up around the core of enterprises which were originally defense-oriented. To maintain California's advantage in these industries it is important that the state offer a financial environment conducive to the creation and development of new specialized enterprises in these dynamic, sophisticated sectors. For this environment to exist it not only is necessary that an adequate supply of risk-taking equity capital exist, but that loan capital be available at nonpunitive terms. This implies that commercial bank resources must grow fast enough to make bank loans available to such new enterprises.

To summarize, the current importance of an adequate commercial-bank growth rate to a rapidly growing region centers not around banks' direct role in abetting the import of capital but rather in their significance as a source of financing for those enterprises not able to tap national credit markets yet whose growth is necessary for rapid growth of the local economy.

f. Money, income, and credit in a rapidly-growing region

In considering how commercial banks and other financial institutions participate in the process that generates rapid economic growth, it would be useful to draw on a formal model that integrates financial and nonfinancial factors into a complete theory of regional growth. There are, in fact, some models of this sort on hand.[19] Unfortunately,

---

[19] A. N. McLeod, "Credit Expansion in an Open Economy," *Economic Journal,* LXXII (Sept. 1962), pp. 611–640.

William P. Yohe, "Financial Institutions in Aggregate Models," *Saertrykk ar Statsøkonomist Tidsskrift,* IV (1963), pp. 205–233.

H. P. Minsky, "Monetary Systems and Accelerator Models," *American Economic Review,* XLVII (Dec. 1957), pp. 859–883.

these models, as they stand, are not much help. They are much too general, and the data needed to estimate the parameters of these models are not available. Thus, all that is ventured here is a partial, rather general, analysis of some of the factors relating finance and growth.

(1) *Balance of payments assumptions.*—To begin with, we assume that our rapidly growing area has the following characteristics:

(1) It has a set of leading industries whose exports to the rest of the country are growing rapidly;

(2) net, the region currently imports capital from the rest of the country;

(3) on capital account it is a debtor to the rest of the country—in the past, the region also has been a net importer of capital;

(4) in spite of the growing export industry, the rapid growth of the economy results in a current-account deficit.

The export industries leading the growth process not only generate income and employment within the region, they also generate a rising flow of reserves to the banks of the region (Assumption No. 1). Capital imports are also a source of reserves (Assumption No. 2). As a result of being a debtor (Assumption No. 3), and due to the rising imports induced by the rapid growth of income (Assumption No. 4), reserves are lost. Nevertheless the region is a net gainer of reserves, for its money supply presumably grows along with income. Thus the gross gain of reserves per period from the leading-sector exports and capital imports must be much greater than the net gain of reserves over this period.[20]

Only Assumption No. 3, that the rapidly growing region is a net debtor to the rest of the country, requires discussion. As a net debtor in each period, the state suffers a net drain of reserves.[21] The net debtor position of our region follows from the validity of Assumption No. 2 over a sufficient time period: that is, the debtor position of the region is the sum over time of the net imports of capital from the rest of the country. To be sure, net migration of households to California bring in capital, as the migrants bring their net worth with them. This capital migration tends to decrease the net-debtor position of the state's econ-

---

[20] Experiments with a model derived from McLeod's analysis (*op. cit.*) indicate that for very crude estimates of savings and import parameters the increase in the gross flow of reserves to California must be at least three times the increase in demand deposits. Given that bank cash items average about one-third of demand deposits, it appears that the increase in the gross flow of reserves over a period need be at least nine times as large as the net change in reserves during the period.

[21] The complexity of the balance-sheet interrelations among households, business firms, and financial institutions makes it very difficult to estimate the net-debtor position of a region. For example, the claims of California residents in out-of-state life insurance company reserves would be an asset of the state's economy in determining the net-debtor position of the state.

omy. However, even though no data are available on this capital flow, the assumption is made that it offsets only partly the net import of capital required by the growth and investment characteristics of the state.

(2) *Assumptions about velocity.*—With these balance-of-payments set down, we turn next to the relations between the change in income and the needed money supply.

As personal income is one of the few income concepts available on a state basis, a personal income divided by business and personal demand deposits concept of velocity is used. This concept of velocity has many weaknesses—as any "state" or "regional" concept of velocity must have. For example, demand deposits in New York are very high relative to personal income; this is so because of the large financial deposits held in New York City. These financial holdings tend to depress our measure of velocity for the nation below what a concept fully comparable to the California measure would have been.

The trends of velocity in California and the nation as a whole have been approximately the same throughout the postwar period. Velocity has always been greater in California than in the entire United States by a factor that ranged from 13 to 27 percent. This higher velocity in California is consistent with the observed interest rate differentials and the greater growth rate in the state.

During the postwar period velocity increased at a rapid rate in both the country and in California. This was a result of the initial very-liquid position of banks and the public at the end of World War II, as well as of the vigorous expansion of the economy. As a result, economic growth took place with the demand-deposit liabilities of the commercial banks growing at a rate appreciably slower than income. Income velocity is now within range of the high levels it attained during the 1920's,[22] and we can assume that the trend exhibited by velocity since 1946 cannot be maintained. Thus, it is assumed that for the forecast period of this study the growth rate of demand deposits and money income will be approximately the same: that is, velocity will not increase to any large extent even though the economy grows rapidly.

The rapid growth of velocity in the postwar period decreased the dependence of California upon net gains in reserves. For example, if California velocity in 1963 had been the same as in 1946 the California money supply necessary to support 1963 income would have been some 65 percent greater than the actual money supply. That is, the regional

[22] See H. P. Minsky, "Can 'It' Happen Again?" in D. Carson, ed., *Banking and Monetary Studies*. Homewood, Ill.: Richard D. Irwin, 1963, p. 108.

net gain from the state's balance of payments would have been some 65 percent greater than was actually achieved. Thus, what we are assuming is that for both the country and the state a growth-facilitating factor, present in the postwar period to date, will not be present to the same

TABLE 2

VELOCITY FOR UNITED STATES AND CALIFORNIA, 1946–1963

Year	Velocity (U. S.)	Velocity (Calif.)	Velocity (Calif.) / Velocity (U. S.)
1946	2.208	2.564	1.161
1947	2.219	2.666	1.201
1948	2.403	2.912	1.212
1949	2.399	3.046	1.270
1950	2.495	3.024	1.212
1951	2.641	3.149	1.192
1952	2.716	3.291	1.212
1953	2.859	3.506	1.226
1954	2.779	3.356	1.208
1955	2.845	3.415	1.200
1956	3.000	3.582	1.194
1957	3.205	3.896	1.216
1958	3.129	3.747	1.198
1959	3.303	3.854	1.167
1960	3.422	4.072	1.190
1961	3.353	3.895	1.162
1962	3.566	4.153	1.165
1963	3.735	4.213	1.128

Definition: Velocity = personal income/business and personal demand deposits.
SOURCES: 1. *Call Reports* Federal Deposit Insurance Corporation, 1946–1963.
2. Statistical Abstract of the United States.
3. California Statistical Abstract.

extent in the future. Certainly the destabilizing potentials in a high velocity economy are such that it is much safer to assume the velocity will not be allowed to increase much more than to assume that the limits of velocity will be tested by an unduly tight monetary policy.

(3) *Regional growth in the money supply by 1975.*—On December 31, 1960 there were $12,953 billion of demand deposits in California banks. As we are assuming a rate of growth of income in constant prices of 5.45 percent per year, 1975 income in California will be 2.21576 times as large as 1960 income. Assuming no increase in velocity, the 1975 money supply will have to be the same 2.21576 times as large as the 1960 money supply. However, given the behavior of the American economy in the recent past, it is not likely that the price level will remain constant if full employment is achieved and maintained. Moderate increases

in the price level of 1 and 2 percent per year, respectively, will generate a constant-velocity demand-deposit requirement of $33.5571 and $38.9015 billion respectively.[23] That is, in the fifteen-year period 1960–1975, the forecast rate of growth of income with unchanged velocity of circulation will require an increase in the money supply of from $16 to $26 billion, depending upon the assumption that is made about the behavior of the price level. We will use $20 billion as our "estimate" of the increase in demand deposits within the state which will occur if the forecast growth takes place.

On December 31, 1960, California's commercial banks held $4.5 billion in cash and due from banks: approximately 33 percent of total demand deposits. Currency was approximately 25 percent of demand deposits for the country as a whole. Thus, if demand deposits in California are to grow by $20 billion from 1960 to 1975, reserve money, assuming the ratios of 1960 still hold, will have to increase by $11.7 billion; $6.7 billion in the form of cash and due from banks of the commercial banks, and $5 billion in currency outside banks.[24]

If demand deposits grow by $20 billion over the fifteen-years 1960–1975, and of the ratio remains approximately as in Table 3, some $6.7 billion of cash and due from banks, and some $8 billion of government securities, will be acquired by the California commercial banks. This will leave some $5.3 billion for other assets—to a large extent local loans.[25]

(4) *The interaction between changes in money and income.*—Now that we know the dimensions of the required rise in money, we may inquire a bit into the qualitative relations among the various flows.

---

[23] The required money supply is computed by multiplying the initial money supply, $13.045 billion, by $(1.0545)^{15} = 2.21576$ and then multiplying the product either by $(1.01)^{15} = 1.16096$ or $(1.02)^{15} = 1.3486$.

[24] There are many heroic assumptions underlying this estimate. The cash and due from banks item includes not only reserves against demand deposits but also reserves against time deposits. We not only are assuming that Federal Reserve requirements for reserves do not change over the forecast period, but also that the ratio of time deposits to demand deposits in commercial banks will not change. In addition, the cash and due from banks item includes vault cash and correspondent balances as well as float. Once again we assume that these items in relation to demand deposits will not change appreciably.

[25] Note that in 1960, time deposits at commercial banks were some 80 percent of the demand deposits. If we assume that the same ratios will hold over the forecast period, California's commercial banks will have some $16 billion of additional time deposits outstanding in 1975. Note that *all* of the cash and due from banks and U.S. government securities was applied against demand deposits. Thus all of the time deposits would be reflected in the amount of local loans (including mortgages) acquired by the banks. Of course, cash items and U.S. government securities are held by banks because of time as well as demand deposits; however, it seems best to assume that most of these cash and secondary-reserve items are kept because of demand deposits.

This portion of our analysis would gain in precision if a satisfactory complete model of regional income could be applied to the analysis of the California data.

We can trace some of the reserve and spending flows which take place during a growth process. A dollar of "new" reserves and deposits

TABLE 3

RESERVES AND DEPOSITS, CALIFORNIA COMMERCIAL BANKS
DECEMBER 31, 1960

	Millions of dollars
California data:[a]	
Commercial banks:	
Cash and due from banks.................................	4,500
U. S. government securities..............................	5,572
Total demand deposits.....................................	12,953
Business and personal demand deposits.....................	10,590
Total "savings type" deposits	
Savings and Loan Association deposits.....................	10,794
Credit Union deposits......................................	394
Time deposits at commercial banks.........................	10,992
	22,180
National data:[b]	
Currency..	29,356
Demand deposits, business and personal....................	117,121
	144,458

SOURCES: (a) *Annual Reports*, Federal Deposit Insurance Company.
(b) Federal Reserve Bulletins.

gained by a California bank is the result either of an increase in exports or of a net capital import. To the exporter this is additional income which will be spent; to the capital-importing unit these are funds to be used. If the capital importer, directly or indirectly, spends these funds for the construction of new capital goods, income results. The resultant increased income, either from the exports or the spending of the proceeds of the capital imports, leads to a rise in imports by the region; which leads to a loss of reserves. The acquisition of national assets by the bankers also leads to a loss of reserves.

As deposits flow into the region's banks we can expect the bankers initially to use the excess reserves that result to acquire national assets— secondary reserves in the more conventional terminology. However, the rise in the region's income tends to induce a demand for bank loans from local business. The bankers, with a "large" amount of liquid assets, are in a position to accommodate local business: local loans and local demand deposits rise. The local loans finance an expansion of spending and income in addition to that due to export rise or capital import. This secondary wave of income expansion also induces imports and thus a loss of reserves.

All in all, it is obvious that the gross flow of bank reserves into and out of the state will be much larger than the net change in the reserve base of the state's commercial banks. This is true even if we ignore the flows of funds due to the international trade transactions which occur by way of San Francisco and Los Angeles.

This large ratio of gross reserve receipts to net reserve changes implies that for the forecasts of continued rapid growth of California to be realized either the state's export industries must continue to grow rapidly or that a large amount of capital will be imported into the state.

4. THE INITIAL SOURCES OF BANK RESERVES IN THE POSTWAR PERIOD

a. Introduction

If economic growth is more rapid in California than in the country as a whole, it is likely that demand deposits will also exhibit rapid growth. For this to take place, either the volume of reserve deposits or the efficiency of reserves in California banks will have to grow faster than in the country as a whole; that is, the gain of reserves must more than offset the loss of reserves. The gains will be achieved by the "income-elastic export industries," which include federal spending within the region, and by net capital imports. The losses will stem from an unfavorable trade balance on account of federal taxes and other than growth-generating industries plus the payments made necessary by the outstanding financial liabilities.

Is it probable that reserve gains from these various sources will more than offset the possible reserve losses?

b. The growth of California commercial bank reserves 1946–1963.

Major balance sheet data as of December 31 of each year for all operating banks in the United States and in California are presented. Over this period the item "cash due from banks" for all banks in the United States rose from $35.0 to $51.5 billion, an annual rate of growth of 2.85 percent. The same item in the same period, for California banks, grew from $2.7 to $5.3 billion, an annual rate of growth of 4.28 percent (see Tables 4 and 5).

TABLE 4

Assets and Liabilities, All Operating United States Banks, December 31, 1946–1963[a]

(millions of dollars)

| Year | Assets | | | | | | Liabilities and capital accounts | | | | | | | Year |
| | Cash and due from banks | U.S. gov't obligations | Other securities[b] | Loans, discounts and overdrafts | Miscellaneous assets | Total | Deposits | | | | | Miscellaneous liabilities | Total capital accounts | |
							Business and personal demand	Total business and personal[c]	Government[d]	Interbank[e]	Total demand			
1946	35,029	86,536	9,477	35,647	1,678	168,367	83,314	133,403	9,863	12,659	103,429	1,134	11,308	1946
1947	38,387	81,185	10,723	43,000	1,778	175,073	87,121	139,693	9,119	13,038	106,934	1,277	11,946	1947
1948	39,474	74,097	11,422	48,174	2,009	175,176	85,520	138,084	10,888	12,275	105,169	1,449	12,479	1948
1949	36,522	70,433	12,621	49,544	2,049	179,170	85,750	139,667	12,084	12,717	107,162	1,695	13,088	1949
1950	41,086	72,894	14,740	60,386	2,209	191,317	90,999	148,855	12,392	14,039	118,322	2,184	13,837	1950
1951	45,531	71,343	15,918	67,608	2,504	202,903	96,680	157,057	13,586	15,113	126,180	2,525	14,623	1951
1952	45,584	72,740	17,374	75,512	2,626	213,837	99,814	164,402	15,799	15,351	131,208	2,917	15,367	1952
1953	45,811	72,610	18,370	80,518	2,831	220,140	100,084	169,147	15,965	15,987	131,576	2,922	16,118	1953
1954	44,584	77,727	20,439	85,615	3,285	231,649	103,506	177,435	16,834	16,843	135,841	3,269	17,269	1954
1955	47,802	70,050	20,670	100,055	3,425	242,003	109,049	187,088	16,671	16,876	142,007	3,455	18,112	1955
1956	49,640	66,521	20,461	110,076	4,066	250,764	111,064	193,030	16,888	17,623	145,173	3,975	19,248	1956
1957	49,314	65,782	22,942	115,108	4,696	257,843	109,664	198,302	17,652	17,047	143,523	4,416	20,427	1957
1958	49,908	73,632	26,272	121,562	5,033	276,407	115,148	212,771	19,070	18,195	150,174	4,668	21,704	1958
1959	50,292	65,795	26,070	135,952	5,501	283,611	116,243	217,804	19,951	17,113	152,318	5,828	22,914	1959
1960	53,019	67,236	26,614	144,756	6,480	298,105	117,121	224,861	22,418	18,898	156,430	7,391	24,538	1960
1961	57,365	72,709	29,665	154,308	7,325	321,372	124,205	241,943	23,937	21,276	166,040	7,991	26,225	1961
1962	54,937	72,556	35,010	172,809	7,865	343,177	123,988	258,267	25,624	19,761	164,155	11,502	28,044	1962
1963	51,534	69,063	40,496	192,690	8,606	362,370	124,218	272,715	27,171	19,728	163,826	12,876	29,880	1963

a Data for 1962 are as of December 28, though data for some uninsured banks are as of December 31, 1962.
b State, subdivision, and other.
c Demand and time deposits of individuals, partnerships, and corporations, certified and officers' checks, letters of credit, etc.
d Deposits of the United States government and of states and subdivisions.
e Includes postal savings deposits, and deposits of foreign governments for 1960, 1961, 1962, and 1963.
Source: *Call Reports*, Federal Deposit Insurance Corporation, 1946–1963.

TABLE 5

Assets and Liabilities, All Operating California Banks, December 31, 1946–1963 [a]

(millions of dollars)

Year	Assets						Liabilities and capital accounts							Year
							Deposits							
	Cash and due from banks	U.S. gov't obligations	Other securities	Loans, discounts and overdrafts	Miscellaneous assets	Total	Business and personal demand	Total business and personal[b]	Government[c]	Inter-bank[d]	Total demand	Miscellaneous liabilities	Total capital accounts	
1946	2,719	6,854	773	3,333	149	13,828	6,272	11,800	856	430	7,650	106	636	1946
1947	2,793	5,835	713	4,467	162	13,970	6,240	11,905	826	427	7,535	133	679	1947
1948	2,924	5,180	741	5,019	190	14,054	6,048	11,653	1,083	453	7,459	138	728	1948
1949	2,447	5,708	902	4,942	190	14,194	5,855	11,504	1,264	469	7,341	185	771	1949
1950	2,740	5,278	1,157	5,809	211	15,193	6,491	12,162	1,322	534	8,124	281	893	1950
1951	3,120	5,274	1,231	6,523	232	16,380	7,217	13,220	1,331	623	8,841	263	944	1951
1952	3,464	5,359	1,411	7,281	251	17,766	7,624	14,149	1,598	652	9,497	369	998	1952
1953	3,528	5,419	1,482	7,554	281	18,264	7,599	14,421	1,712	690	9,529	388	1,053	1953
1954	3,380	6,645	1,593	7,653	353	19,625	8,173	15,513	1,743	765	10,100	473	1,132	1954
1955	3,689	5,994	1,668	9,140	337	20,829	8,850	16,611	1,726	792	10,944	473	1,228	1955
1956	3,929	5,238	1,530	10,451	406	21,554	9,290	17,099	1,705	847	11,251	528	1,375	1956
1957	4,036	5,400	1,771	11,021	534	22,762	9,132	17,896	2,001	880	11,274	551	1,433	1957
1958	4,102	6,596	2,085	11,515	566	24,864	9,930	19,710	2,148	930	12,058	558	1,518	1958
1959	4,543	5,462	1,938	13,521	603	26,066	10,627	20,719	2,221	883	12,950	611	1,633	1959
1960	4,500	5,572	1,969	14,079	773	26,893	10,590	20,857	2,561	920	12,953	802	1,753	1960
1961	5,196	6,590	2,335	14,882	847	29,850	11,704	23,230	2,800	993	14,232	758	2,008	1961
1962	5,313	6,089	2,928	17,010	1,010	32,349	11,844	24,848	3,098	1,072	14,426	1,206	2,124	1962
1963	5,349	5,622	3,367	19,431	1,096	34,865	12,419	26,752	3,023	1,206	14,939	1,545	2,339	1963

a Footnotes b, c, and d, and sources applicable to Table 4 are equally applicable to Table 5. For details see Table 4.

In the years since 1952 the differential in the growth rate of reserve money in California and in the United States has been even more striking. Between December 31, 1952 and December 31, 1963, the per-year growth rate of cash items was 1.9 percent for the United States and 4.4 percent for California.

TABLE 6

CHANGES IN CASH AND DUE FROM BANKS:
ALL OPERATING BANKS IN CALIFORNIA
CALENDAR YEARS 1947–1963
(millions of dollars)

Year	Change in cash and due from banks
1947	+ 74
1948	+131
1949	−477
1950	+293
1951	+380
1952	342
1953	64
1954	−148
1955	+309
1956	+240
1957	+107
1958	+ 66
1959	+431
1960	− 43
1961	+696
1962	+117
1963	+ 36

SOURCE: Federal Deposit Insurance Corporation, *Assets, Liabilities, and Capital Accounts*, 1946-1963.

Given the present level of bank cash items, net gain in the neighborhood of $300 million per year is needed if demand deposits in California are to grow as expected. This item will have to increase to more than $750 million by 1975.

Data on the annual rates of growth make it quite clear that before 1950 or 1951 cash and due from banks was growing at the same or a lesser rate in California than nationally (Table 6). Since this period, the annual rates of growth in California have been consistently, and at times substantially, greater than for the nation. The same proposition holds for demand deposits: the crossover occurred in 1949–1950, and since then California demand deposits have grown more rapidly than deposits in the country as a whole almost every year. No such marked change in relative growth rates occurred for loans, discounts, and overdrafts—the bank balance-sheet items that would include local loans (see Table 7, col. 2 and Figures IV, V, and VI).

TABLE 7

ANNUAL GROWTH RATES,

SELECTED ASSETS AND LIABILITIES OF COMMERCIAL BANKS:

UNITED STATES AND CALIFORNIA, 1947–1963

Year	Cash and due from banks		Loans, discounts and overdrafts		Total assets and liabilities		Business and personal demand deposits	
	U. S.	Calif.	U. S.	Calif.	U. S.	Calif.	U. S.	Calif.
1947	1.096	1.027	1.206	1.340	1.040	1.010	1.046	.995
1948	1.028	1.047	1.120	1.124	1.001	1.006	0.982	.969
1949	0.925	0.837	1.028	0.985	1.023	1.010	1.003	.968
1950	1.125	1.120	1.219	1.175	1.068	1.070	1.061	1.109
1951	1.108	1.139	1.120	1.123	1.061	1.078	1.062	1.112
1952	1.001	1.110	1.117	1.116	1.054	1.085	1.032	1.056
1953	1.005	1.018	1.066	1.037	1.029	1.028	1.002	.997
1954	0.973	0.958	1.063	1.013	1.052	1.075	1.034	1.076
1955	1.072	1.091	1.169	1.194	1.045	1.061	1.054	1.083
1956	1.038	1.065	1.100	1.143	1.036	1.035	1.018	1.050
1957	0.993	1.027	1.046	1.055	1.028	1.056	.987	.983
1958	1.012	1.016	1.056	1.045	1.072	1.092	1.050	1.087
1959	1.008	1.108	1.118	1.174	1.026	1.048	1.010	1.070
1960	1.054	0.991	1.065	1.041	1.051	1.032	1.008	.997
1961	1.082	1.155	1.066	1.057	1.078	1.110	1.060	1.105
1962	0.958	1.023	1.120	1.143	1.068	1.083	.998	1.012
1963	0.938	1.007	1.115	1.142	1.056	1.078	1.002	1.049

SOURCE: Federal Deposit Insurance Corporation, *Annual Reports*, 1947–1963. Calculations by the author.

Although evidence from the banking record is far from conclusive, it is consistent with the proposition that the nature of California's growth changed around 1949–1950 or so, and that only since then has California exhibited consistent rapid growth.

c. Balance of payments sources of reserve growth 1946–1963

(1) *Introduction.*—Between the end of 1946 and that of 1963, cash and due from banks of California commercial banks increased by

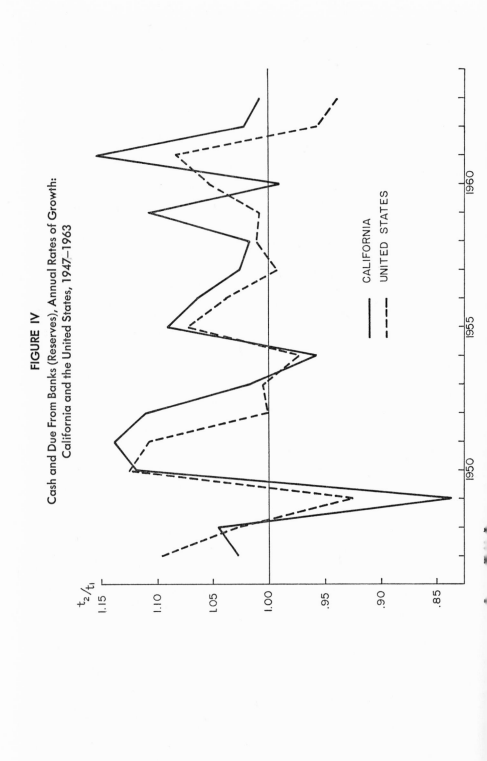

FIGURE IV

Cash and Due From Banks (Reserves), Annual Rates of Growth:
California and the United States, 1947–1963

CALIFORNIA
UNITED STATES

t_2/t_1

1.15
1.10
1.05
1.00
.95
.90
.85

1950
1955
1960

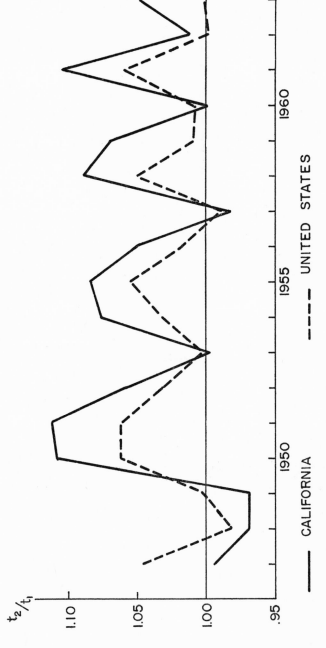

FIGURE V

Demand Deposits, Annual Rates of Growth:
California and the United States, 1947–1963

t_2/t_1

1.10

1.05

1.00

.95

1950   1955   1960

——— CALIFORNIA   - - - UNITED STATES

SOURCE: Table 7.

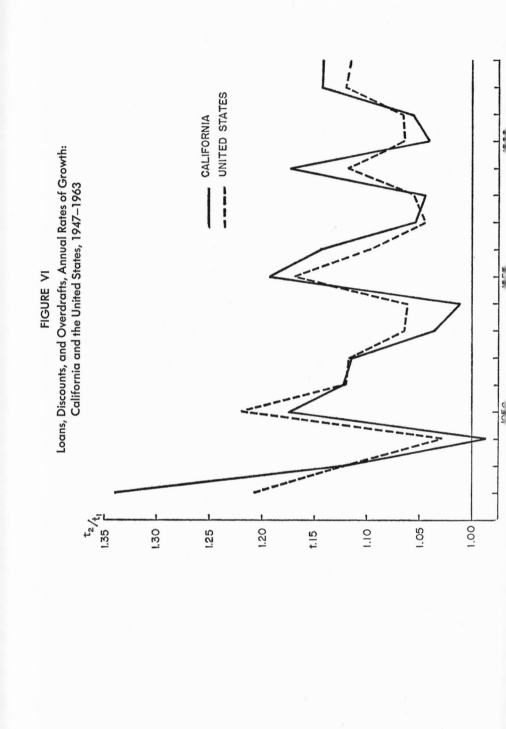

FIGURE VI

Loans, Discounts, and Overdrafts, Annual Rates of Growth:
California and the United States, 1947–1963

some $2.6 billion. As indicated in Section 3, the commercial banks' gross gain of reserves was due to rising exports and capital imports. In California's situation it is worth distinguishing the following ways in which capital can be imported:

(1) Deposits by nonresidents in California savings and loan associations and other nonbank financial institutions.

(2) The purchase, by nonresident households and firms, of:
   (a) mortgages on residential and other real estate located in California
   (b) bonds of California state and local governments, public utilities, and other business
   (c) new equity issues of California business.

(3) Direct investment in California by out-of-state firms.

(4) Migration of demand and other deposits to local financial institutions as households migrate to California.

Unfortunately, no solid data were found on the size of direct investments by out-of-state firms in California and the funds that accompanied migrants to the state. An article in the monthly review of the Federal Reserve Bank of San Francisco[26] interpreted the observed growth of deposits in member banks, population, and manufacturing, as being due to the transfer of funds by migrating households and firms.[27] However, nowhere in the article did they consider the impact of the migration of funds by way either of federal government expenditures, other exports of the state, or capital imports by way of "financial instruments" such as mortgages, "deposits" in nonbank financial institutions, and various types of bonds. As a result of the absence of evidence as to the volume of the flow of reserves to the District due to the migration of firms and households, all that can be done is to recognize that this is a factor of

---

[26] "Member Banks in Twelfth District Outpace All Others in Postwar Performance," *Monthly Review*, Federal Reserve Bank of San Francisco, July 1962, pp. 140–156.

[27] "...the much higher rate of increase in total deposits at District banks was largely due to a percentage increase in demand deposits twice that experienced by other member banks. This development reflects both the disparate rates of population growth between the District and the rest of the country and the rapid expansion in the industrial base of the District. Funds that flowed into the District from transfers of personal deposit accounts and business accounts were augmented by deposits created by the greatly expanded volume of loans extended by banks in the District during this period"; "Member Banks in Twelfth District Outpace All Others in Postwar Performance," *op. cit.*, p. 141.

116

indeterminate size which augments those flows for which we have some, albeit rough, estimates.[28]

(2) *Federal tax revenues from, and expenditures in, California.—* Our fundamental model states that for a region to grow significantly faster than the national economy of which it is a part, it must have a set of export industries growing more rapidly than the region itself.

TABLE 8

ESTIMATES OF FEDERAL TAX REVENUES ORIGINATING IN CALIFORNIA AND FEDERAL EXPENDITURES IN CALIFORNIA, FISCAL YEARS 1952, 1958, AND 1960[a]

(millions of dollars)

	Fiscal years		
	1952[b]	1958[c]	1960[d]
Federal expenditures...............	6,281	9,653	10,971
Federal tax revenues...............	6,056	7,671	8,429

[a] The estimates in this table of federal tax revenues originating in California are designed to indicate the revenue that actually can be imputed to the residents of California. This amount is not the same as that collected within the state. In addition, this table presents estimates of federal expenditures in California that are composites built upon various assumptions and procedures. Table 9 gives certain federal expenditures as well as total federal tax collections in California, 1959–1961, as reported by various government sources.

[b] Selma Mushkin, "Statistical Materials on the Distribution of Federal Expenditures among the States," U. S. Department of Health, Education, and Welfare, Public Health Service, Division of Public Health Methods (1956), Table D-2, p. 62.

[c] The Library of Congress, Legislative Reference Service, "Federal Taxation and Expenditures in the Several States" (Excerpts from a report prepared in response to specific requests from the New York State Republican Delegation in the House of Representatives) July 29, 1959, Table I, p. 7.

[d] Estimates for 1960 were made on the basis of the assumptions used in the report cited in footnote c with certain exceptions. No changes were made in the assumptions used in the above report in making the 1960 estimates of federal tax revenues in California.

These industries "pull" the economy ahead at a rapid rate. If the economic environment is favorable for continued growth, sufficient net capital imports will take place so that, in spite of the favorable growth of an export industry, the rapidly-growing region will tend to run a deficit on current trade.

The available analysis of federal government expenditures and revenues by states indicates that California runs a sizable surplus on federal government account and that between fiscal 1952 and 1960 this surplus

---

[28] An interesting study of the flows and sources of bank reserves for the Federal Reserve Districts is: Norman N. Bowsher, J. Dewey Duane, and Robert Einzig, *op. cit.*, pp. 1–20. However, they were interested in the overall district flows of reserves and did not distinguish between income and financial flows for the districts. An integration of the two approaches—the mechanical flow of funds approach used by Bowsher, Duane, and Einzig, and the income generating-banking behavior approach used here—should be feasible.

was increasing apace.[29] The estimates are that the federal government deficit in California was $225 million in fiscal 1952, $1,982 million in fiscal 1958, and by fiscal 1960 it was $2,542 million. The average annual rate of growth of federal expenditures in California was 7.4 percent during the period 1952–1958, the two years for which we have studies of the impact of federal expenditures upon the

TABLE 9

FEDERAL EXPENDITURES AND TAX COLLECTIONS IN CALIFORNIA: ESTIMATES

(millions of dollars)

Fiscal year	Military spending[a]	Income disbursed by federal government[b]	Total Internal Revenue collected[c]
1959	5,283	4,406	6,923
1960	4,839	4,832	7,998
1961	5,277	5,374	8,486

[a] From *Statistical Abstract of U. S.*, 1959, 1960, 1961. Includes military spending for supplies, services and construction.
[b] From *Survey of Current Business*, August issue. Income disbursed directly to persons by federal government. Comprised of wages and salaries (net of employee contributions for social insurance), other labor income, interest and transfer payments. Transfers include benefits from old-age and survivors insurance, state unemployment insurance, veterans' assistance, and others.
[c] From U. S., Treasury Department, *Combined Statement of Receipts, Expenditures and Balances of the U. S. Government* includes individual income taxes, individual employment taxes, old-age and disability insurance, railroad retirement, unemployment insurance, corporate income and profit taxes, estate and gift taxes, and excise taxes (alcohol, tobacco, other) collected in the State of California.

states. Personal income in California grew at a rate of 6.8 percent over this same period. As expected, the "leading" industry grew at a rate greater than that of personal income.

The dependence of the California economy on the federal government is illustrated by per capita tax and expenditure estimates. In fiscal 1958 the national per capita tax revenues were $447 and expenditures were $469—a federal government deficit of $22.00 per capita. During the same year in California the estimated per capita federal tax revenue was $553 and expenditure was $684; the federal government ran a deficit of $131 per capita in California in fiscal 1958—six times the national per capita federal deficit! This occurred even though 1957 per capita income in California was 125 percent of the national average.

[29] *Federal Taxation and Expenditures in the Several States*. The Library of Congress, Legislative Reference Service, July 29, 1959, is the basis not only of material cited in Tables 8, 9, and 10 but also of data cited in the text. It is worth noting that this document consists of "excerpts from a report prepared in response to specific requests from the New York State Republican Delegation in the House of Representatives." For New York State, in fiscal 1958, this report showed federal tax revenue of $10,101 million and expenditures of $7,565 million. The federal government collected $2,536 million more in New York than it spent in New York.

TABLE 10

Breakdown of Estimates of Federal Expenditures in California:
Fiscal Years 1958 and 1960[a]

(thousands of dollars)

	Fiscal years	
	1958	1960
Series available:		
Income disbursed directly to individuals[b]	3,762,000	4,832,000
Payments to state and local governments	464,800	536,451
Other payments reported geographically	26,000	23,866
Military procurement[c]	4,223,100	4,839,000
Net interest paid to business and others[d]	316,800	380,052
Net social insurance contributions, government personnel[e]	108,000	108,000
Offsets (deduct)[f]	(−)167,300	(−)211,927
Series unavailable:		
Estimates based on per capita distribution for the unavailable, but pertinent, statistical series	919,000	463,482
Total expenditures	9,653,000	10,970,924

[a] The assumptions, methodology, and sources of data used in making the following estimates for 1960 are identical with those used in the report cited in footnote c, Table 8: (1) income disbursed directly to individuals; (2) payments to state and local governments; (3) other payments reported geographically; and (4) estimates of unavailable, but pertinent, statistical series.

[b] U. S., Department of Commerce, Office of Business Economics, *Survey of Current Business*, August 1958 and August 1960. The figures represent income disbursed directly to persons, including nonprofit organizations but excluding incorporated enterprises and state, local and other governments. Types of income included are wages and salaries, net of employee contributions for social insurance; other labor income, interest and social security, and other transfer payments to persons. However, as shown here, the figures for 1958 and 1960 include unemployment insurance benefits payments financed from state taxes on payrolls; to exclude these benefits from the total federal expenditures in California they are included among the deductions captioned "Offsets." (See footnote f, below.)

[c] The 1960 estimate of military procurement is taken directly from the series (available publicly only since 1959) that covers awards of $10,000 or more for supplies, services, and construction.
Source: U. S., Department of Commerce, *Statistical Abstract of the U. S., 1962*, p. 260. Consequently, the estimates for military procurement for 1958 and 1960 are not strictly comparable because the 1958 estimate was based not solely on contract awards of $10,000 or more, but on a rather complex estimation procedure using contract awards and other procurement actions. The estimation procedure and techniques used in the 1958 report could not be repeated in making the 1960 estimate of military procurement in California because of the unavailability of comparable data for 1960. While the inability to follow the detailed 1958 estimation technique does raise serious objections to the 1960 estimate of military procurement in California, it must be noted that in 1958 the contract awards of $10,000 or more in California were $4,253.7 million while the 1958 reported estimate of military procurement expenditures in California was $4,223.1 million. Given our lack of information, the 1960 estimate is taken from the series covering contract awards of $10,000 or more for military procurement in the United States, cited above.

[d] Because of the unavailability of comparable data for both 1958 and 1960, the 1960 estimate is based on the assumption that the proportion of the total "net interest paid to business and others" in 1960 is the same as the proportion paid in 1958 for both California and the U. S. as a whole.

[e] Because the supporting tables used to make the 1958 estimate of "net social insurance contributions, government personnel" were not published in the 1958 report, it is assumed that the 1960 figure is equal to the estimate made for 1958.

[f] "Offsets" for 1960 include only unemployment insurance benefit payments by states, as reported in U. S. Department of Labor, Bureau of Employment Security, "The Labor Market and Employment Security," February 1961, p. 61, because the other series used in compiling total offsets in the 1958 report were based on unpublished worksheets of the National Income Division, Office of Business Economics, Department of Commerce.

(3) *The value of agricultural crops.*—Between 1950 and 1962 the cash farm receipts in California increased by $.91 billion from $2.31 to $3.22 billion.[30] The growth rate of this agricultural-output value measure was 2.8 percent per year. This was substantially smaller than the rate of growth of population and personal income over this period. Although California agriculture is a source of "reserves" for the state, the tempo of increase of California agriculture was far too small in the period under consideration for it to have served as a basis for the swift growth of the state.

(4) *The financing of nonfarm real estate in California.*—Out-of-state funds loom large in the financing of mortgages on nonfarm property in California. It is estimated that 38.5 percent of the funds invested in such mortgages by specified classes of investors at the end of 1960 came from outside the state. In the nine years 1951 to 1960, California mortgages held by these same classes of units grew at an annual rate of 14.3 percent. At this rate of growth, California nonfarm mortgage holdings of these classes of investors is increasing at some $3.3 billion a year, which means that the out-of-state funds invested in California nonfarm mortgages, assuming that roughly 40 percent of any increment comes from out of state, is increasing by approximately $1.3 billion per year at present.

That is, if past trends continue, California commercial banks presently are gaining some $1.3 billion of reserves per year due to the flow of out-of-state funds into mortgages on nonfarm California real estate (see Table 11).

Table 12 shows the growth rates of investment in nonfarm California mortgages for the six specified sources of funds for the period 1951–1960. It seems obvious that the rate of growth of investment in California mortgages by mutual savings banks is not long sustainable, for at this rate their investment in California mortgages soon would be far greater than their total assets. In addition, the rates of growth of the Cal-Vet program and savings and loan associations are far greater than the rates of growth of the economy. Hence it is questionable that their growth rates can be long sustained.

(5) *Savings and loan association deposits.*—Deposits in savings and loan associations in California grew from $503 million in 1945 to $10,794 million in 1961, an annual growth rate of 21 percent (Table 13). In 1961 these deposits grew by $1,889 million, or 21 percent. If these trends continued, then by 1964 deposits in California savings and loan associations should have increased by more than $2.5 billion per year.

---

[30] Source: *California Statistical Abstract, 1962;* Table C4, Cash Farm Receipts, p. 28.

TABLE 11

ESTIMATES OF OUT-OF-STATE FUNDS INVESTED IN CALIFORNIA NONFARM
MORTGAGE HOLDINGS OF SIX MAJOR SOURCES OF FUNDS, 1960

(millions of dollars)

Type of institution	Total nonfarm California mortgage holdings	Estimated out-of-state funds		
		Item	Amount	Percent of total
1) Savings and loan associations in California[a]	$ 9,141	Out-of-state savings accounts[b]	$1,380	18.5
		Home Loan Bank advances outstanding— 60%[c]	311	
2) Mutual savings banks	1,621	All[d]	1,621	100.0
3) Life insurance companies	5,274	Adjusted as described in footnote e	4,701	77.2
4) Commercial banks in California	5,050	None	......	....
5) FNMA	1,041	Adjusted total of California holdings[f]	989	95.0
6) Cal-Vet Program	1,061	Cal-Vet bonds held outside the state[g]	550	51.9
Total	$23,188		$8,922	38.5

[a] Insured associations which account for the bulk of all associations.

[b] In March 1960, associations responding to the Stanford Research Institute inquiry reported $430 million in "broker" savings and $950 million of direct accounts obtained from savers located more than 50 miles from the reporting offices (primarily living outside California), for a total of $1,380 million. This is a minimum estimate since not all associations responded to the inquiry. For this reason, and because mortgage investments by California associations at the end of 1960 exceeded their total savings capital, it is assumed that all funds obtained from out-of-state accounts were invested in mortgages.

[c] The total was $519 million. This was scaled down by 40 percent. Not all advances can be expected to be invested in mortgages, some of them serving liquidity needs. Also, the source of funds for advances consists in part of internal funds, such as member deposits in the Federal Home Loan Bank, or of FHLB obligations sold to California investors.

[d] The total reported was first scaled down by $800 million which is the approximate amount of mortgage holdings of California-domiciled life insurance companies. This adjustment is somewhat excessive because it assumes that companies domiciled in California do not lend outside the state. It reduces the total to $4,474 million. Second, an adjustment was made to take account of the fact that out-of-state companies obtain premiums from insurance policies originated within California. The amount of life insurance in force in California at the end of 1960 was $54.3 billion or 9.3 percent of the United States total. Consequently, the $4,474 million was scaled down by 9 percent to $4,017 million.

[e] There is no basis for estimating the out-of-state funds held by commercial banks in California and for allocating them to be banks' mortgage investments. It should be noted, however, that commercial banks outside of California hold an unknown amount of California government-underwritten loans.

[f] Assumes that 5 percent of FNMA's holdings in California are financed by FNMA stock purchases of California sellers to FNMA and California holders of FNMA obligations.

[g] According to Edward L. Rada's study of the Cal-Vet Program, 50 percent of Cal-Vet's bond obligations ($1.1 billion in mid-1960) are estimated to be held outside the state.

SOURCE: J. Gillies and T. Grebler, "Financing of Nonfarm Housing in California" in *Appendix to the Report on Housing in California*, Governor's Advisory Commission on Housing Problems (Sacramento), April 1963, pp. 379–380.

TABLE 12

NONFARM CALIFORNIA MORTGAGES
HOLDINGS OF SIX MAJOR SOURCES OF FUNDS, 1951 AND 1960
(millions of dollars)

	1951	1960	Rates of growth per year (percent)	Estimate per-cent of out-of-state funds 1960
1) Insured savings and loan associations in California........	$1,412	$ 9,141	23	18.5
2) Mutual savings banks........	32	1,621	55	100.0
3) Life insurance companies.....	2,250	5,274	9.9	77
4) Commercial banks in California........................	2,811	5,050	6.8	0
5) FNMA.....................	313	1,041	14.0	95
6) Cal-Vet program............	121	1,061	27.5	51.9
	$6,939	$23,189	14.3	38.5

SOURCE: J. Gillies and T. Grebler, op. cit., various tables in Appendix.

TABLE 13

SAVINGS AND LOAN AND FEDERAL CREDIT UNION DEPOSITS
IN CALIFORNIA, 1945–1961
(millions of dollars)

Year	Savings and loan deposits[a]	Credit Union deposits[b]
1945............................	503	13
1946............................	587	..
1947............................	691	18
1948............................	820	23
1949............................	992	32
1950............................	1,159	43
1951............................	1,386	55
1952............................	1,744	76
1953............................	2,210	101
1954............................	2,743	130
1955............................	3,405	163
1956............................	4,203	202
1957............................	4,982	235
1958............................	6,096	272
1959............................	7,353	301
1960............................	8,905	340
1961............................	10,794	394

[a] California Economic Development Agency, California Statistical Abstract, 1962, p. 199.
[b] U. S. Bureau of Federal Credit Unions, Reports of the Operations of Federal Credit Unions, 1945, 1947–61. Note: the 1946 report is missing from the University of California Library.

It has been estimated that some 18.5 percent of the deposits in California savings and loan associations are out-of-state funds. This means that roughly $.5 billion of reserves entered the state by way of savings and loan deposits by 1964.

We included the out-of-state funds on deposit with California savings and loan associations in our estimate of out-of-state funds invested in California residential real estate. However, funds invested in mortgages and funds on deposit in savings and loan associations are not the same in terms of their potential impact upon the liquidity and solvency of financial institutions in the state.

The estimate that 18.5 percent of deposits in California savings and loan associations are from out of state is an estimate of the average ratio of out-of-state to total deposits. For purposes of the analysis of the import of capital it is the marginal ratio—the ratio of out-of-state deposits in the increment of deposits—that is important. Although no data are available to support the conjecture that the marginal out-of-state ratio is greater than the average, the increased awareness of the interest-rate differential between California and eastern savings institutions, as well as some evidence that California savings and loan associations are aggressively pursuing out-of-state deposits, indicates that the marginal ratio may very well be greater than the average ratio. Hence, the estimate made above of the flow of reserves on account of savings and loan association deposits may be conservative.

(6) *State and local bonded indebtedness.*—Between 1950 and 1960, the bonded debt of the State of California grew from $263 to $2,088 million, or at an annual rate of 23 percent. During the same period the debt of counties, cities, school, and special districts grew from $1,163 to $4,417 million, or at an annual rate of 14.2 percent. That is, combining the two, in the decade of the fifties California state and local government debt increased by $4,089 million, or at an annual rate of 16.4 percent.

These debt instruments are national assets and enter into portfolios throughout the country. No information, aside from the estimate for Cal-Vet bonds, was uncovered on the proportion of California state and local bonds owned outside the state. However, given the planned programs of public works, and so on, the expectation is that California state government, and the subsidiary local government units, will continue to sell bonds at a rapid rate and that this will be a source of reserve funds for the California banks.

At the growth rates of the 1950's, California state and local debt is now increasing by more than $1 billion per year. If we use the same

TABLE 14

BONDED INDEBTEDNESS

STATE OF CALIFORNIA, CALIFORNIA LOCAL GOVERNMENTS AND
SELECTED CALIFORNIA PUBLIC UTILITIES
SELECTED POSTWAR YEARS

Year	State of California (1)	Counties, cities, school and special districts (2)	Total government in California (1) + (2)	Selected public utilities (3)
1946....	$ 170,044,000	$ 673,412,000	$ 843,456,000	$ 634,357,917
1947....	176,680,000	733,827,000	910,507,000	728,089,697
1950....	263,372,000	1,163,055,000	1,426,427,000	1,352,271,422
1960....	2,087,942,000	4,416,791,000	6,504,733,000	3,188,328,272
1962....	2,824,638,000	....	....	3,566,550,968

SOURCES:
Col. (1)—U. S. Bureau of the Census, *Summary of Government Finances*.
Col. (2)—*California Statistical Abstract, 1962*, p. 193, published by California Economic Development Agency.
Col. (3)—*Moody's*. Includes the twelve following utilities: California Electric Power Co., Pacific Gas and Electric Co., San Diego Gas and Electric Co., Southern California Edison Co., Southern California Gas Co., Southern Counties Gas of California Co., Pacific Telephone and Telegraph Co., General Telephone of California, California Interstate Telephone Co., California Water Service Co., California Water and Telephone Co., Southern California Water Co.
Some of these companies have operations in Mexico, Nevada, Oregon, Washington, and Idaho. However, corrections would change the above figures only slightly.
(a) Note: Until January 21, 1954, California Interstate Telephone Co., was part of California Electric Power Co., and prior to January 1, 1953, General Telephone of California was called Associated Telephone Co., Ltd.
(b) Note: Columns (1) and (2) contain figures as of June 30th during the selected years.
(c) Note: Column (3) contains figures as of December 31 of the year prior to the one indicated. This date was chosen for two reasons: (a) to provide as complete coverage as currently available data allow, and (b) to avoid questionable interpolation of what data are available.

TABLE 15

GROWTH RATES OF BONDED INDEBTEDNESS IN CALIFORNIA

STATE OF CALIFORNIA AND CALIFORNIA LOCAL GOVERNMENTS AND SELECTED
PUBLIC UTILITIES, SELECTED POSTWAR YEARS
(in percent)

Years	State of California	Counties, cities, school and special districts	Total government in California	Selected public utilities
1946–50........	11.56	14.65	14.04	20.81
1946–60........	19.62	14.38	15.71	12.22
1946–62........	19.20			11.20
1947–50........	14.22	16.59	16.14	22.21
1947–60........	20.93	14.81	16.33	12.03
1947–62........	20.24			11.17
1950–60........	23.00	14.21	16.39	8.96
1950–62........	21.85			8.42
1960–62........	16.30			5.77

Note: Sources and notes for Table 14 apply to Table 15.

estimate for out-of-state ownership of California state and local indebtedness as was used for Cal-Vet bonds, then about $.5 billion of reserves are gained by California commercial banks each year as a result of rising state and local indebtedness.

It is worth noting that whereas the bonded indebtedness of the state grew at an annual rate of 16.4 percent during the decade of the fifties, its personal income rose by 8.2 percent per year. The much greater rate of growth of debt than of the region's income is not long sustainable for state and local governments. At some date the growth rate of California's debt will have to be lowered to a level consistent with that of income, allowing of course for changing preferences as to relative growth of government-supplied versus privately-supplied goods and services. In the long run, state and local debt will not be as good a source of reserves for California banks, relative to other sources, as they were in the 1950's.

(7) *Private debts and equities as a source of capital.*—California firms can finance their activities by selling their liabilities to out-of-state households, nonfinancial business firms, and financial institutions. Data on these items are not readily available. However, data were collected on the bonded indebtedness of selected public utilities. The bonded debt of the twelve largest utilities in California grew from $1,352 million in 1950 to $3,188 million in 1960. During the 1950's, such debt grew at an annual rate of 8.96 percent. The growth rate for utility indebtedness was of the same order of magnitude as that of personal income. If past trends continued, this debt increased by approximately $350 million per year by 1964. If we use the 50 percent out-of-state funds estimate for these debts also, we get that at present, utility indebtedness is feeding some $175 million of reserve money into the California commercial banks each year.

(8) *Other sources of reserves.*—Many large gaps are evident in our knowledge of the financing of California's rapid economic growth. We should try to fill these gaps to be able to deal more precisely and completely with problems of financing growth. This needed knowledge should cover the way in which private business borrows out-of-state to finance expansion in California, the extent of direct investment in California by out-of-state business, and the funds brought by migrants as they move to California.

This additional information should cover the manner in which California commercial banks aid and abet the import of capital. Questions as to the extent of syndication, underwriting, endorsing, and accepting business of California banks, as well as the significance of correspondent relations, need to be answered.

d. Adequacy of the identified initial sources of reserves

In Section 4, part b, it was indicated that for growth to occur as forecast, bank cash items must increase by some $300 million per year in the early part of the forecast period, and by some $750 million per year toward the end of the period. It was argued in Section 3 that the gross increase in the flow of reserves per period has to be significantly larger than the net change in bank cash items.

The capital import items for which rough estimates were made may have been generating reserve gains at the rate of $2 billion per year in the early part of the forecast period—home financing yielding as much as $1.3 billion, state and local debt $.5 billion, and utility bonds $.2 billion. In addition, the rate of increase of federal spending in California during 1952–1958, if continued, would have been generating a $.75 billion increase in reserves gained by exports. Thus, capital imports and rising exports by the industry leading the state's growth may have been generating some $2.75 billion of reserve gains—nine times the indicated required increment in cash items. It seems as if the initial flow of reserves from identified sources is significantly greater than the net gain in reserves that is necessary for the money supply to grow along with the economy.

If our forecast is correct, by 1975 the initial reserve gains will have to be running at some $7 billion per year. However, some of the recent growth rates of financial factors are not sustainable. The question remains, how will the economy of California adjust to slower growth rates in these financial flows?

5. VULNERABILITY OF CALIFORNIA'S FINANCIAL SYSTEM

a. Introduction

How vulnerable to changes in the underlying growth-inducing relationships is the California banking and financial system? In particular, what are the effects of shocks or changes which tend to depress the California economy?

We can conceive of a financial system as: (1) absorbing, (2) amplifying, or (3) being neutral when some outside change occurs which would depress the region's economy.

A financial system acts as a shock absorber when losses and defaults in some particular sector of the economy are not passed through to the holder of claims on the financial system, i.e. the financial institutions absorb the losses, and financing terms ease, whenever income falls.

A financial system acts as an amplifier of depressing shocks when three consequences occur: (1) when losses of the financial system are passed on as widespread losses to the holders of financial system liabilities; (2) when the way in which financial organizations attempt to protect themselves against losses generates greater losses and defaults than would otherwise occur; and (3) when financing conditions tighten whenever income has fallen. A financial system is neutral when it neither absorbs nor amplifies shocks.

In the earlier analysis of income, deposits, local loans, and imports, when the region's exports and reserve-money base rose, the banking system and other financial intermediaries amplified an initial stimulus. Obviously, it is desirable for the financial system to act as a shock absorber whenever a depressing shock or change occurs. It is argued that only by restraining its "amplifying" functions can a financial system hope to "absorb" shocks; and that for shocks at all severe, the financial system, to act as an absorber, requires "central bank" support.[31]

Usually, a financial system can absorb shocks up to some limit, beyond which it becomes unstable. The financial "defenses," so to speak, are routed. The system then tends to amplify the initial disturbances. The defensive capabilities of a financial system depend upon three attributes: (1) the net worth of the institutions in the financial system; (2) the character of the system's liabilities; and (3) the extent to which the value of its assets is protected by "central bank" institutions.

Two types of possible contractions of the California economy can be identified: those due to an overall decline in the national economy and those due to a change in the special circumstances which made California a leading sector in American economic growth. The second type of shock includes charges in the income elasticities within a growing national economy, so that those industries which were erstwhile leading sectors in California's rapid growth no longer play this role. A basic aspect of a shock, insofar as California is concerned, centers around whether or not the shock changes the expectations that California's economy will continue to grow at an appreciably faster rate than the national economy. A nationwide deep depression, viewed as being unlikely to occur, might very well be more severe in California than in other states, as a deep depression would affect the expectations of rapid economic growth.

---

[31] "Central bank" institutions as used here refers to all governmental or quasi-governmental institutions which guarantee the value of specified assets. These institutions include the FHA and VA in their mortgage-guaranteeing roles, the various deposit insuring agencies, and the Federal Reserve System.

b. The behavior of California in postwar recessions

In attempting to predict the impact upon California of a national recession (or depression) it is necessary to define the dimensions of the posited recession. Suppose that we can assume the use of monetary and fiscal policies to generate sufficient aggregate demand to maintain target employment levels in the nation as a whole whenever transitory declines in income and employment do occur. Suppose further the use of central bank powers as lender-of-last-resort to prevent any overall decline in asset values. Then, as long as the underlying income elasticities are favorable to California's relatively rapid growth, nothing need happen during a recession to prevent the financial system from functioning normally.

If we assume mild recessions and favorable income elasticities, the postwar cyclical experience of the United States and California can be a guide to expected future reactions to mild cycles.

In terms of California versus the United States as a whole: during the first postwar boom personal income grew more slowly; the 1949 recession was somewhat milder; the Korean War brought appreciably faster growth; and personal income growth, since 1949, was faster through all cycle stages.

The evidence from monetary changes and from personal income is consistent. Using the chronology of the National Bureau of Economic Research, and beginning with the expansion of November 1949 to July 1953, demand deposits in California banks have grown at a faster rate than demand deposits in all United States banks during both expansions and contractions (see Table 16). Beginning with the expansion which started in September 1954, demand deposits in the United States grew faster during business cycle contractions than expansions, which was as expected if the Federal Reserve System followed a consistent contracyclical monetary policy. However, during this period demand deposits in California banks grew most rapidly during the business cycle expansion of May 1958 to May 1960, when they grew at 7.09 percent per year as opposed to countrywide growth of only 0.862 percent per year. That is, the growth-generating factors pulled sufficient reserves to California to permit demand deposits to grow rapidly even though, in the nation, they grew very slowly.

During the contraction phase of recent business cycles, time deposits grew rapidly, both in California and in the United States as a whole. This development tended to make longer-term loans available at favor-

TABLE 16
RATES OF GROWTH OF MONETARY VARIABLES
NBER BUSINESS CYCLES, 1946–1961
CALIFORNIA AND THE UNITED STATES
(in percent)

NBER dates of expansion and contraction	Call date (1)	Call date (2)	Growth rates for California				Growth rates for United States			
			Demand deposits (a)	Time deposits (b)	Total deposits (c)	Total liabilities (d)	Demand deposits (a)	Time deposits (b)	Total deposits (c)	Total liabilities (d)
Expansion, 1/46–11/48.......(P)	12/31/45	12/31/48	-3.486	5.833	-0.323	0.083	-4.322	5.762	0.321	-1.468
Contraction, 12/48–10/49....(T)	12/31/48	12/31/49	-1.26	2.46	0.35	0.97	-1.531	2.679	0.655	0.502
Expansion, 11/49–7/53........(P)	12/31/49	9/30/53	5.99	5.64	5.82	6.93	3.890	4.566	4.144	4.461
Contraction, 8/53–8/54.......(T)	9/30/53	10/7/54	4.98	8.95	6.73	5.55	1.772	7.557	4.052	2.566
Expansion, 9/54–7/57.........(P)	10/7/54	6/6/57	3.24	5.17	4.12	3.81	1.731	5.566	3.496	2.679
Contraction, 8/57–4/58.......(T)	6/6/57	6/23/58	5.65	14.78	9.85	10.43	2.664	10.611	5.960	5.933
Expansion, 5/58–5/60.........(P)	6/23/58	6/15/60	7.09	0.70	4.05	4.33	0.862	4.625	2.395	2.088
Contraction, 6/60–2/61.......(T)	6/15/60	4/12/61	6.43	12.85	9.36	8.40	3.306	10.526	5.120	3.960

SOURCES: Data for United States taken from *Federal Reserve Bulletin*. Data for California taken from (1) *Annual Report of the Comptroller of the Currency* and (2) *Annual Report of Superintendent of Banks, State of California*. (1) supplied data on California national banks, while (2) supplied data on California state banks.

able bank-interest rates and terms during contractions and thus stimulated recovery. The financial system acted as a shock absorber.

During the postwar business cycles it seems as if the commercial banks in California not only did not act to amplify contractions but, by generating rapid increases in the availability of bank loans during contractions, they acted as true shock absorbers (which not only absorb shocks but tend to return the system to the preshock condition). Certainly the postwar evidence indicates that the California financial system has nothing to fear from national business contractions of the order of magnitude so far experienced in the postwar period, given that these contractions are associated with no change in the general expectations that California will grow rapidly.

6. THE DAY THE FEDERAL MONEY STOPS

This rather dramatic heading serves to emphasize the significance of the federal government as the leading factor both in the demand and in the financial relations associated with the recent rapid growth of California. The development within the state of vigorous industries in defense and related productions, including the production of sophisticated defense-linked systems involving large research and development components, has brought reserves into the California banking system and has been a key element in allowing California banks to help finance the rapid expansion of complementary and local industries.

Under the pressure of public commitments to defense, space, and health research, the country has gone far toward socializing research and development—if not in the organizations carrying out these activities then certainly in the source of demand for these outputs. Whether the rapid growth of such federal expenditures will continue, if defense and space spending no longer grow rapidly, is an open question. Another open question is whether California will continue to be a good location for research-and-development-related industries if the output mix of these industries shifts from defense and space-related industries toward a "civilian" mix.

It is important to emphasize that from our limited observations, federal government expenditures, especially those related to defense and space, appear to have grown rapidly in California throughout the fifties and sixties. A change in the economic environment of California would take place even if the present level of government-related expenditures in the state were stabilized—either as a result of a conscious program of "contract distribution" or international agreements to restrain defense expenditures. A more serious change would take place if there was a cutback in the level of government spending in California.

If defense expenditures were cut back or stabilized, national problems relating to the maintenance of adequate levels and growth rates of aggregate demand would become more acute than at present. Even if we assume vigorous action on the part of the government to maintain ever-growing demand, there would be no special reason why the federal government should be committed to California growing rapidly by way of net-migration of labor and large federal deficits in California. In fact, we could expect the per capita federal deficit in California to tend toward, or even fall below, the national average, and we would expect migration to slow down and halt as relative job opportunities improve in the rest of the country as compared to California.[32]

California's current financial flow relations can be summarized as follows (partly conjectural):

(1) Deficit on civilian private balance of trade.

(2) Deficit on payments due to ownership of California assets by non-Californians being greater than national assets owned by Californians.

(3) Surplus on federal government account.

(4) Surplus on current investment account. As a result of the need for California banks to gain reserves, the sum of the surplus items is greater than the sum of the net deficit items.

To this point there has been no discussion of the magnitude of the net payments which California has to make to the rest of the country because of its net debtor position. Mortgages, state and local debt, corporate bonds, and deposits in California savings and loan associations all generate payments which are committed by contracts. On mortgages and bonds the payments are contractual, whereas deposits in savings and loan associations are demand liabilities: even the interest paid on such deposits is usually credited to the accounts and paid in money only when "demanded."

As an example of the mortgage payments, for a fully-amortized mortgage, 6 percent, twenty years original maturity, the payments during the first year amount to 8.8 percent of the initial face amount. This is both an interest payment and a repayment of principal. As the typical outstanding contract has an amount due which is less than the initial face value, we can assume that the annual payment as a percent of the value of debt outstanding is in excess of 8.8 percent. Let us assume that it is

---

[32] If we assume that California is a "very good place to live" so that people would willingly move to or remain in California even though their income expectations were poorer there than elsewhere, then California could become a low-wage and low-per capita income region. Under these circumstances, it might enjoy advantages in production due to lower labor costs. A new basis for population and income growth then would be created.

10 percent, which makes most of the mortgages fairly new and allows for refinancing as homes are traded. Then, given that $7.3 billion of mortgages were held by out-of-state institutions and FNMA in 1960, some $730 million of the reserves of commercial banks in California are lost each year as a result of payments on these mortgages. As another $2,241 million of out-of-state funds were on deposit in savings and loan associations in 1960, assuming an average 4½ percent interest rate on these funds, $100 million of reserve losses or additions to deposits took place due to this factor. Similar payments have to be made on state, local, and private indebtedness. In addition, direct investments result in payments being made outside the state on account of balance sheet relations as income is earned.

As an offset to the contractual payments made on account of debts, there are the contractual and contingent receipts which California persons, financial institutions, and business enterprises receive per period because of the ownership of assets based outside of California. This includes common stock of national or out-of-state corporations as well as interest and principal on debt owned. The assumption that California is a net debtor state means that these receipts are smaller than the contractual payments which must be made.

Mortgage and bond investments in the state are forms of contractual payment commitments. For these commitments, there is no way for the debt holder to change the amount due per period as a result of a change in his estimation of the worth of assets based upon the California economy, although, of course, any particular debt holder can sell out his position in California liabilities. Deposits in savings and loan associations are demand liabilities. The amount of foreign and domestic deposits withdrawn in any period for transfer to out-of-state institutions depends upon the estimate, by the deposit owner, of the worth of assets based upon the California economy.

Two determinants of the value of a California-based asset, as compared to assets based on other economies, are relative interest rates and relative certainty of the asset's capital value. As long as California is expected to continue to grow faster than the national economy, both interest rate and capital certainty aspects of deposits based upon California real estate liabilities compare favorably with deposits in other parts of the country, and there will be no reason for exercising the withdrawal privilege. If the expectation of California's more-rapid growth ceases, then the interest-rate and capital-value certainty of a California-based asset will no longer be superior to an asset based in another economy.

What can break the expectation that California will grow faster than the rest of the country? One way is by a severe depression producing a "no growth" expectation throughout the land. Another is by lowered income elasticity for outputs for which California has production advantages, so that national economic growth no longer means an amplified growth rate for California exports. In the context of our admittedly imperfect knowledge of California's exports and imports, it seems that this can occur if the national demand for defense and space commodities and services decreases or decelerates.

Let us assume that federal expenditures in the state are stabilized. This, of course, means that the demand for the products of those industries with high growth rate due to government demand no longer will increase—at least in California—and the California firms in these industries will stop expanding at the former rate. This decrease in their growth rate will lead immediately to a decline in the value of these firms' equities and in the value of sites which would have benefited most directly from the expansion of these firms. Hence, an income-expansion force will be eliminated, and an income-contraction factor will be brought into play, as a result of a decrease in these industries' growth rates.

At the previous year's level of income and capital flow a given net increment of bank reserves was achieved. However, in this year the payments due to outstanding debts were greater than during last year, for some net import of capital took place last year. In order to generate the same arithmetic increase in income as transpired last year with the stabilized federal expenditures, a larger import of capital or a smaller import of goods and services is needed. However, with the elimination of a factor making for growth, the likelihood is small that the import of capital will continue to grow for long. If for a time capital is imported at a sufficiently rapid rate so that income growth can be maintained, then the payment commitments in succeeding years will continue to increase —calling for ever-increasing capital imports to maintain the base for demand deposit accretion.

The continued expansion of demand deposits is necessary if bank financing is to be available for investments in local and new enterprises. But, if the net reserves acquired by the banks decreases, then the increase in demand deposits and local loans made by the banking system declines. This leads to a decline in the rate of increase of local investment, of local income, and of imports. In addition, if local income declines while national income is sustained or grows, California is not a good place for investment and the rate of capital importation falls. A "floor" level of income exists at which the payments on contractual commitments, plus the private net imports of goods and services, equals the stabilized federal government deficit in California.

The value of a long-lived asset, such as real estate, is a capitalized value of future returns. If "r" is the rate of interest, the value of a piece of property which will yield $1 next year and $$(1 + g)^t$$ in the following years is $\dfrac{\$1}{r - g}$. If the safety of deposits in institutions such as savings and loan associations is a function of the expectation that the value of the underlying property will increase, then as California's growth rate expectation is affected by the change in the growth rate of government spending in California, some withdrawal of deposits from California savings and loan associations can be expected as a reaction to its growth rate decline.

The further development of a "softer" market for new housing as migration decreases not only will affect income and employment within the state, it will also affect the demand for financing by California savings and loan associations. An attempt to lower interest rates on deposits will tend to increase the flow of deposits, both resident and out-of-state, to other, now more rapidly growing, areas. The nonresident deposits in California savings and loan associations can be considered as a type of hot money, money which would leave the state if the interest rate differential disappeared.

The existence of specialized agencies which enable savings and loan associations to meet large-scale cash drains without a dumping of earning assets, means that such financial flows can be weathered. The commercial banks, by selling their national assets and borrowing from the Federal Reserve Bank, can meet the drains imposed upon them by the out-of-state payments by savings and loan associations whose deposits they hold.

However, borrowing from Home Loan Banks, sale of local mortgages to FNMA, selling of positions in national assets such as government bonds, and borrowing from the Federal Reserve System, all of which may be needed if the local financial system is to meet its commitments due to the withdrawal of out-of-state deposits, leave behind a residue of obligations which tend to constrain the expansion of the economy in subsequent periods. Commercial banks and savings and loan associations heavily in debt, or with "unbalanced" portfolios as a result of the flight of hot money, use the funds they receive due to their assets to repay debts and correct portfolios rather than to acquire new local loans and mortgages. That is, financial institutions, in an effort to put their "house in order," will further depress the local economy beyond that caused by the change in federal government spending.

That secondary contractions can be set off is, of course, possible. Even without such a wave a major result of a change in the underlying growth-generating forces—from favorable to unfavorable for rapid growth—is a tendency to generate local deep depression or stagnation. The build-up of contractual and demand payment commitments during an era of rapid growth tends to magnify the repercussions of any change in the economic environment which decreased the fundamental export surplus and the ability of the area to import capital. Before the creation of the central bank institutions which protect and maintain the value of the liabilities of financial institutions, the transition from a rapid to a slow, or even a normal-growth, economy was associated with large scale defaults on contracts by financial institutions. As most financial institutions are now protected, in that either the value of their liabilities is guaranteed or they mainly purchase heavily-protected assets (FHA or VA mortgages, conventional mortgages with large equities), the expectation is that these institutions will not again amplify the losses which follow a change from a rapid- to a slow-growth expectation. Although we cannot expect financial institutions to act as shock absorbers if a radical change in expectations takes place, it seems likely that they will not amplify the contractionary forces to the same extent as they have in the past.

As financial commitments are met during a period in which there are no net capital imports, future financial commitments are decreased—especially if they consist of payments on fully-amortized contracts. Hence, the local income level, sustainable on the basis of a fixed receipt of reserves from out-of-state, increases as the debt burden is eased. As this takes place, the rate of growth of income in the state recovers and moves toward the national rate. Thus, the impact even of the most radical changes in the structure of national demand is transitory in the long run. However, for those who must make the adjustments it is less than satisfactory to know that in time the difficulties will be eased. Appropriate public policies are needed which slow the withdrawal of the stimuli for rapid growth to prevent the more serious reactions from taking place.

Liquidity of California Banks

RICHARD E. TOWEY

ROBERT LINDSAY

LIQUIDITY is a primary concern of commercial banks because they must always stand ready to meet their "debt" obligations.

Some of these "debts" (the demand deposits) must be discharged immediately upon notice from creditors. Others fall due on specific dates, or after a waiting period which the bank may or may not choose to invoke. Still a third possibility is the need to create new debts—i.e. the deposits created to meet the credit needs of borrowers.

To meet these various needs banks may rely on both a "stock liquidity and a "flow" liquidity. For the stock liquidity they can hold assets that either are cash or can be sold quickly for cash without significant loss. For flow liquidity they can arrange the maturities of these assets so that repayment inflows coincide with predictable withdrawals of deposits. In most of this discussion, stock liquidity takes center stage because the data tell us so little of flow liquidity.

1. LIQUIDITY NEEDS OF THE INDIVIDUAL BANK: THE GENERAL PROBLEM[1]

Banks issue perfectly liquid demand claims. They also encourage the general public to view bank savings deposits as being, for practical purposes, readily transferable into demand claims. They also want most borrowers to feel their needs will be met when they arise.[2]

Bank customers tend to take out only part of their deposit balances in any given business day, and in the normal course of business, deposits

---

[1] For extended treatment see, for example, Howard D. Crosse, *Management Policies for Commercial Banks* (Prentice-Hall, Englewood Cliffs, N.J., 1962), Chapters 7 and 8, and Roland I. Robinson, *The Management of Bank Funds*, 2d ed. (McGraw-Hill, 1962), Chapters 4 through 7.

[2] The public may view commercial bank savings deposits as a closer substitute for money than are the claims of savings and loan associations and mutual savings banks. Turnover of bank demand deposits was about 41 times per year in 1962; commercial bank savings deposits turn over once every two years, and savings and loan shares and mutual savings bank deposits about once every three years and ten months.

135

flow in and more or less offset these payment demands. But deposit inflows and outpayments vary according to type of customer, type of local economy, national economic developments, and so forth. Loan repayments and security retirements may add to the irregularity. Similarly, some loan demand may also be irregular and nonsystematic.

Bankers have developed general principles and rules of thumb to provide ample liquidity for these purposes. Banking textbooks supply additional information on tailoring these principles to individual needs. Here it is sufficient to note that in acquiring assets a bank must strive for an optimal balance among the conflicting requirements of liquidity and income.

a. A bank's primary liquidity

Although liquidity is important in most of the assets a bank acquires, it is customary to distinguish primary and secondary liquidity segments of a portfolio from those parts acquired chiefly for income. Primary reserves usually are defined to include cash in vault and deposits with the Federal Reserve and correspondents. These nonearning assets are held mainly to meet legal reserve requirements, although correspondent balances are held partly as secondary reserves and might be included in that category.

All banks except the very largest tend to hold surplus deposit balances with correspondents and with the Federal Reserve—in anticipation of net withdrawals of deposits or increased loan requests. But drawing down excess balances and borrowing at the Federal Reserve are not the only means of adjustment. Much of the provision banks make for deposit losses, as well as for satisfying credit demand, is through the sale of readily marketable assets that provide interim earnings.

b. Secondary reserve balances

To achieve an optimal balance between income and liquidity, a bank tries to keep down its holdings of nonearning assets. To provide some earnings while protecting itself against near-term uncertainties of deposit losses and loan demands, it holds sizable amounts of assets that mature shortly or are readily marketable. Treasury securities of short maturity generally serve these ends, but they may be supplemented by short-term municipal securities, commercial papers, bankers acceptances, brokers loans and participations therein, and correspondent balances not required to meet state legal reserve requirements. Of course the size of correspondent balances affects the degree to which one bank can rely on other banks to provide it with desired services, but in most parts of the nation existing correspondent balances could be reduced for some time without impairing their ability to have these services performed.

Since the early 1950's the larger banks have engaged in an increased volume of trading in federal funds; a bank with excess reserves may acquire an earning asset through lending this balance to another bank with a reserve deficiency. To be sure, the size of the minimum unit of federal funds traded is high ($1 million), and thus the market is concentrated among larger banks. Even so, growing expertise in this market has made it possible for relatively small banks to participate advantageously.[3] Also, a small bank may enter repurchase agreements with a government security dealer, when lending in the federal funds market would cause the bank to exceed its unsecured loan limit.

Some deposit losses and customer loan demands will follow reasonably predictable patterns, with much of the drain not expected to occur until weeks and months ahead. Liquidity for these needs is provided by short- and intermediate-range Treasury securities and the like. The pattern of loan demand is not strictly periodic, of course, and many banks find that purchases of intermediate Treasuries at low interest rates are followed, sooner than expected, by sales at high interest rates, resulting in undesired capital losses.[4]

c. Lending and investing for earnings

Once its legal and other liquidity requirements are satisfied, a bank can begin to acquire assets primarily for earnings. Even here liquidity is important. Moreover, in contrast to virtually all previously-considered assets, loans require the bank to assume some risk of default as a necessary part of the transaction. Therefore, banks tend to lend at short maturities, and to require collateral and other safeguards. With the growth of term lending, mortgages, and consumer credit, periodic repayments of principal and interest are stipulated and thus provide a flow of liquidity to a bank.[5]

The composition of earning assets arises chiefly from the business opportunities offered the bank. Loans desired by good customers tend to come first. High-quality and high-earning loans from other areas may

---

[3] See Crosse, *op. cit.*, pp. 153–155.

[4] See Crosse, *op. cit.*, pp. 236–239 and Robinson, *op. cit.*, Chapter 7, and especially pp. 123–126.

[5] In view of these provisions and the fact that "demand" loans generally are among the slowest on a bank's books, Crosse concludes that loan liquidity has not deteriorated in recent years. *Op. cit.*, pp. 121–122.

also be important—government-backed mortgages and loan participations, for example. High-grade securities, particularly municipals and Treasuries, are also attractive.[6]

If these high-earning assets also have high liquidity, so much the better. Their liquidity, however, is a distinctly subordinate point of their appeal. Except where the risk of default is high, or regulatory bodies insist on some measure of marketability, an asset can be completely illiquid, prior to maturity, and still be deliberately acquired by a well-run bank.

d. Liquidity of the nationwide banking system

The liquidity problem of the banking system in the nation as a whole is the ability to meet short-run changes in credit demands. Deposit losses at one bank generally mean deposit gains at others. Decisions by the public on holding currency affect the total amount of reserves available to the banking system, but there is little danger of any large-scale attempt to rush into currency because of fears for bank solvency. Moreover, bank reserve changes from international transactions, and shifts in the location of Treasury cash balances are largely offset by monetary policy.

Among the various types of financial institutions, commercial banks have the greatest degree of impact on the national economy over the business cycle. The demand for the most profitable forms of bank credit —business and consumer loans—has a pattern of change roughly parallel to the national business cycle. Also, business and consumer loan demands usually undergo cyclical swings of wider amplitude than most other types of credit demand. Under present Federal Reserve policies, commercial banks are assured of plentiful additions to their reserves only when overall economic activity and business loan demands are slack. When economic activity is booming and business loan demand is brisk, the authorities apply the strongest pressure to bank-reserve positions. Thus the banks must rely largely upon already-held resources when business and consumer loan demands surge upward. Yet most banks do not hold sizable amounts of excess reserves in periods of slack demand for consumer and business loans. Instead they switch partly into other types of loans, but even more into highly-marketable earning assets which bolster earnings and give needed flexibility when recovery occurs in preferred-type loan demand. Thus, measures of liquidity for the banking system as a whole undergo cyclical swings which more or less correspond inversely with loan demand.

---

[6] For some purposes local municipal security acquisitions follow the principles of ordinary lending rather than those of the investment portfolio.

e. Liquidity of the regional banking system

The banking system of a well-defined geographical region is closely tied to the fortunes of that region. The monetary authorities will supply extra reserves to the *national* network of banks when lean times come to the *national* economy. But if the region suffers economic slump while prosperity continues elsewhere, the banking system of a region by and large must shift for itself. These banks may turn to central banks for some aid, but mostly they must rely on their own resources.

Liquidity in this setting takes on an extra dimension. To acquire needed reserves the banks of the region must hold, as assets, some claims issued *outside* the region. The best candidates are claims on the United States government itself, whose marketability will never depend on the cyclical fortunes of any particular region. Other possibilities are the issues of state and local governments in other parts of the country, and those of corporations with limited dependence on the region in question.

2. THE RECORD FOR CALIFORNIA BANKS

Most of the standard measures of liquidity suggest that California banks are less liquid than those elsewhere in the country. As with so many other things in the state, however, banking also operates in a special climate which makes it possible for California banks to *look* less decently dressed while underneath they maintain the same standards prevailing in other regions.

a. Evidence of apparent illiquidity

(1) *Some ground rules.*—At the outset, a couple of general observations should be made. First, the data for California banks often do not apply to exactly the group of banks it would be most appropriate to judge. The figures most nearly fitting the need are those published by the FDIC for insured banks in California. As these data do not provide some of the most critical measures of liquidity, the analysis sometimes rests on data for member banks of the Federal Reserve System. For some information the member banks covered are in California, but for other data totals for all member banks in the Twelfth Federal Reserve District are used. Again, at other times the figures come from a sample of member banks in the District.

These overlapping and underlapping coverages are something of a nuisance but not crippling. Member banks in California account for a large portion of all insured banks in the state, and these same member banks represent the bulk of all member banks in the Twelfth District.

Table 1 shows these kinship patterns in the bank populations for which data are used.

A second ground rule deals with the line between liquidity and illiquidity. No one can draw that line. We can establish the end zones but not the midfield stripe, and the only technique open to us is a comparison of liquidity measures at California banks with those of the rest of the country, or in selected centers elsewhere. If the banking system of the United States as a whole overstretches itself, then California banks may be in trouble for no more than going along with the crowd. We use this yardstick because it is all we have. But it is only a beginning—the first few inches of the yardstick we should like to have.

TABLE 1

BANK CLASSIFICATIONS: TWELFTH FEDERAL RESERVE DISTRICT

Total commercial banks	366	
In California	129	
Member banks		62
Nonmember banks		67
Elsewhere	237	
Member		92
Nonmember		145

SOURCE: *Federal Reserve Bulletin*, April 1963.

(2) *Primary reserves.*—Excess reserves held by California banks are a relatively small part of their total reserves. The figures for member banks of the Twelfth District are shown in Table 2. Country banks in the District have larger relative holdings of excess reserves than do reserve city banks, and both have higher ratios than the banks in New York City and Chicago. Compared with the rest of the country, excluding these two money-market centers, the West Coast banks in both groups tend to have lower ratios than similarly-classified banks in the rest of the nation.

A California tendency toward lower primary reserves also is indicated by the size of their deposits with correspondents (see Table 3). These deposits might be viewed as earning assets since they yield as a return the various services rendered by the correspondent, yet they are demand obligations which may be drawn down almost immediately to meet reserve drains or liquidity needs. Moreover, there is no evidence to suggest that California banks enjoy less of these services from their correspondents despite their smaller balances. This pattern can be assumed to mean that California banks are less liquid by this measure too.

TABLE 2

MEMBER BANK EXCESS RESERVES AS A PERCENTAGE OF TOTAL RESERVES HELD:
TWELFTH DISTRICT AND OTHER PARTS OF THE UNITED STATES

Date	Twelfth District		Other parts of the United States			
	Reserve city banks	Country banks	New York City	Chicago	Other reserve city banks	Country banks
1953.....	0.9	6.5	0.6	...	1.6	9.4
1954.....	1.0	7.6	0.9	0.4	1.7	10.9
1955.....	0.5	5.9	0.4	0.1	1.0	9.2
1956.....	0.5	5.2	0.2	0.2	1.1	8.5
1957.....	0.4	4.3	0.2	0.2	0.9	7.8
1958.....	0.6	4.6	0.7	0.5	1.3	8.5
1959.....	0.4	3.3	0.3	0.2	0.7	6.8
1960.....	0.6	4.0	0.5	0.4	0.8	7.9
1961.....	0.7	3.8	0.6	0.4	0.9	7.9
1962.....	0.3	3.1	0.6	0.3	0.6	6.7
1963.....	0.3	3.2	0.6	0.3	0.5	6.0

SOURCE: Board of Governors of the Federal Reserve System, *Deposits, Reserves and Borrowings of Member Banks*.

TABLE 3

DEMAND BALANCES WITH OTHER UNITED STATES BANKS HELD BY MEMBER BANKS:
CALIFORNIA AND UNITED STATES, 1946–1962

(millions of dollars)

End of December	Member banks in California		Member banks in United States other than California	
	Amount of demand balances with U. S. banks	As percent of total demand deposits less interbank	Amount of demand balances with U. S. banks	As percent of total demand deposits less interbank
1946..............	$318.9	4.5	$5,580.7	7.6
1948..............	273.9	4.0	5,368.9	7.1
1950..............	299.0	4.0	6,540.6	7.8
1952..............	420.0	4.8	6,928.2	7.5
1954..............	364.8	4.0	7,217.9	7.5
1956..............	382.0	3.8	7,677.2	7.5
1958..............	321.3	2.9	7,615.9	7.3
1960..............	369.9	3.2	8,170.2	7.6
1962..............	318.9[a]	2.4[a]	7,383.2	6.5[a]

[a] Because the Call Report date was earlier than usual in 1962, some "windowdressing" through the use of Inter-Bank Demand Deposits was not possible; therefore the data for this year are probably lower than would otherwise have been expected.
SOURCE: Federal Deposit Insurance Corporation: *Call Reports*.

(3) *Secondary reserves and other earning assets.*—Moving further out the liquidity spectrum, the California banks are again found to be less liquid than their fellows in most other regions. This is evident in at least two ways. First, California banks consistently have had a higher ratio of loans to total assets. Second, they have tended to hold relatively longer maturities of Treasury issues.

TABLE 4

INSURED BANKS LOAN-ASSET RATIOS: LEADING INDUSTRIAL STATES

END-OF-YEAR 1946 TO 1962

States	1946	1948	1950	1952	1954	1956	1958	1960	1962
California	24.1	35.8	38.3	41.0	39.1	48.5	46.3	52.4	52.6
Florida	15.9	19.9	22.9	24.2	27.4	33.9	35.0	37.5	39.3
Illinois	19.0	22.2	24.5	28.4	29.2	36.6	35.7	42.3	43.4
Indiana	16.0	21.6	24.2	25.8	27.8	33.2	34.9	40.2	42.0
Massachusetts	24.4	29.2	33.0	36.6	39.1	46.0	44.6	47.9	49.8
Michigan	18.9	24.5	27.2	28.6	31.3	38.0	39.5	44.6	45.5
Missouri	23.6	29.8	34.2	34.5	35.4	38.0	37.0	42.3	44.9
New Jersey	17.3	22.6	27.2	31.5	34.1	39.6	40.0	45.4	47.2
New York	23.0	29.4	33.8	39.3	38.0	47.8	45.0	47.5	48.5
Ohio	20.7	24.7	28.3	31.1	32.8	39.7	40.9	45.5	47.2
Pennsylvania	18.6	26.1	28.7	34.1	35.4	43.7	43.3	48.5	48.0
Texas	23.7	28.6	32.0	33.0	35.9	38.0	39.8	42.0	44.6

SOURCE: Federal Deposit Insurance Corporation: *Call Reports.*

(a) The loan pattern.—The ratio of loans to assets, seen in Table 4, compares the California experience with that in a number of other industrial states. California banks had just under the highest percentage of loans in 1946, and in every year thereafter have led the list. The *growth* in loans as a portion of all assets has been pronounced in all states shown in the table, but in California the climb has been faster than in most of the other states. Even those states showing a sharper rise in the ratio—e.g. New Jersey and Pennsylvania—have not yet caught up to California.

The liquidity characteristics of various kinds of loans also call for comment. The booming real estate market in the region gives California banks both the opportunity and the incentive to make large volumes of mortgage loans. They are not the major suppliers of this need (as Professor Schaaf makes clear in his paper in this volume), but they sink a much larger portion of their assets into mortgages than do banks over the country as a whole (see Table 5). The table also makes clear that

California banks remain much more heavily invested in mortgages than banks elsewhere, despite steady or rising ratios in the rest of the country and falling ratios in California.

The large-scale acquisition of mortgages does not automatically make a bank less liquid than its neighbors, but large holdings of mortgages make a bank more illiquid than do comparable holdings of most other assets traditionally acquired by commercial banks. Running over long years, they cannot produce instant liquidity in large amounts, even when installments are carefully timed and firmly policed.

TABLE 5

REAL ESTATE LOANS AS A PERCENTAGE OF INSURED COMMERCIAL BANK ASSETS AND LOANS: CALIFORNIA AND ALL OTHER UNITED STATES

| | Real estate loans as a percentage of | | | |
| Selected year-ends | Total assets | | Total loans | |
	California banks	Other U. S. banks	California banks	Other U. S. banks
1945................	6.9	2.6	43.3	15.8
1948................	16.9	6.0	46.7	22.2
1956................	20.7	9.3	42.1	22.2
1962................	19.0	10.7	35.5	22.5

SOURCE: Federal Deposit Insurance Corporation.

Much the same must be said for so-called term loans. California banks have not taken these up with the same fervor as have the large money-market banks in New York and elsewhere. Nonetheless, from the meager data available, the California banks appear to have extended such loans in significant quantities. In the business loan survey taken by the Federal Reserve System in 1955, member banks in the Twelfth District had term loans accounting for about 37 percent of their total business loans as compared with 34 percent for all member banks together. In the survey conducted in 1957, member banks in the region had about 39 percent of their business loans in the form of term loans. For the system as a whole the proportion was 38 percent. Given the much higher percentages for the large New York banks, large in overall totals as well, the California involvement in term loans can be assumed to be at least something above the average.

A different sort of measure of loan liquidity is the delinquency experience of banks. Failure by the borrower to make repayments when due serves to lengthen the maturity of the loan, which in itself makes the loan less liquid. The flow of repayments is part of a bank's planning in meeting its own liquidity needs. In addition, of course, a rise in delinquency may foreshadow a greater incidence of absolute default, again reducing liquidity.

The evidence is sketchy indeed, but data collected by the American Bankers Association could be interpreted to mean that West Coast banks in recent years have suffered somewhat greater delinquency than banks in other regions.[7] The difference, however, is not pronounced. In addition, the California banks appear to experience comparatively higher delinquency rates in the first three months following due dates, but rates thereafter are lower than the national average. Without a great deal more study, one is perhaps entitled to conclude only that California banks do not in general have lower delinquency rates than those in other regions, although there may be some tendency toward slightly higher rates.

(b) The investment pattern.—The large and growing slice of total assets taken by loans in itself would tend to squeeze secondary reserves, with consequent pressure on liquidity. This pressure on liquidity could be offset only if banks moved to rearrange their security holdings into more liquid combinations. One way to accomplish this would be an upward shift in the proportion of total investments accounted for by U. S. Treasury issues. These issues are in general more readily marketable than other issues, hence provide greater certainty of the amount of cash realizable if they are sold before maturity. In addition, being federal obligations they carry virtually zero risk of default at time of maturity.

California banks do not seem to have made this shift. Through the postwar period they, as banks everywhere, have continued to reduce the role played by Treasury issues within their total investment portfolios and to expand their holdings of other securities. Indeed, at California banks the share of total investments represented by Treasury issues has been only slightly below the comparable figure for banks over the country as a whole. However, California banks hold fewer securities of any kind, per dollar of total assets. Their government holdings are thus smaller relative to total assets, or relative to deposits, than are the holdings at U. S. banks in general. These patterns may be seen in Table 6.

Shorter maturities of investment holdings also can improve liquidity. This is particularly likely to make them more liquid if the shortening occurs in their holdings of government obligations.

---

[7] See "Delinquency Rates on Bank Installment Loans," a monthly report.

Information on maturities of securities not issued by the U. S. Treasury is not available, beyond a few wisps here and there. However, the maturity of government security holdings is reported, and the record for California banks, relative to the national average, is somewhat ambiguous. As shown in Table 6, the share of short-term issues (defined as bills, certificates, and notes) in the California banks' total holdings of Treasury obligations has fluctuated considerably over the postwar years. This

TABLE 6

UNITED STATES GOVERNMENT SECURITIES IN BANK PORTFOLIOS:
CALIFORNIA AND UNITED STATES AS A WHOLE

| Year | Governments as percent of | | | | Bills, certificates, and notes as percent of total governments | |
| | Total assets | | Total investments | | | |
	Calif.	U. S.	Calif.	U. S.	Calif.	U. S.
1946..........	49.6	49.9	89.8	90.4	36.9	28.7
1951..........	32.2	34.2	81.0	82.2	42.4	42.9
1956..........	24.3	26.8	77.4	78.4	27.5	33.7
1958..........	26.5	27.7	76.0	76.5	37.4	40.7
1959..........	21.0	24.0	73.8	74.3	32.6	39.9
1960..........	20.7	23.6	73.9	74.7	43.1	49.2
1961..........	22.1	23.8	73.8	73.7	58.8	32.8
1962..........	18.8	22.3	67.5	69.5	52.3	32.6

SOURCE: Federal Deposit Insurance Corporation.

reflects in part the cyclical swings in private demand for bank credit, and in part the debt-management strategies followed by the Treasury. Through the bulk of this period, however, California banks kept a smaller portion of their government holdings in the form of bills, certificates, and notes than did commercial banks generally. In the last two years reported in the table, they reversed themselves and moved heavily into these shorter issues. During these same two years banks over the nation as a whole were lengthening their maturities.

Until 1961–1962 the investment portfolios of California banks were, by every count, less liquid than the national average. In 1961 and 1962 their government holdings became much more heavily concentrated in the shorter maturities. Whether this shift toward greater liquidity was enough to offset the continuing relative illiquidity, as represented by the low investment in governments overall, is difficult to say. It seems doubtful.

146 RICHARD E. TOWEY AND ROBERT LINDSAY

b. Some counter evidence

The patterns emerging up to this point suggest a group of banks with heavy pressure on their liquidity positions, relative to banks in the country as a whole. With liquidity pressed down to such apparently thin ribbons, this group of banks might be expected to run short of reserves with somewhat greater frequency than otherwise. By the same

TABLE 7

MEMBER BANK BORROWINGS AS PERCENTAGE OF TOTAL RESERVES HELD:
TWELFTH DISTRICT BANKS AND OTHER PARTS OF THE COUNTRY

Year	Twelfth District		New York City	Chicago	Other Reserve city	Other country
	Reserve city banks	Country banks				
1953.....	3.2	1.4	2.4	8.4	5.5	2.6
1954.....	0.9	0.1	0.4	1.0	0.9	0.9
1955.....	1.4	0.8	2.3	6.7	5.1	2.2
1956.....	1.0	1.3	3.7	11.4	6.7	2.6
1957.....	1.4	1.0	4.0	9.5	6.6	3.0
1958.....	0.4	0.2	1.1	1.2	2.4	1.8
1959.....	1.4	1.3	3.1	6.2	6.8	3.7
1960.....	0.8	1.5	0.7	6.0	3.5	2.4
1961.....	0.1	0.1	0.2	1.0	0.4	0.5
1962.....	0.2	...b	0.4	0.9	0.6	0.5
1963a....	0.5	...b	1.0	1.6	1.5	0.7

a Based on data for the first half of the year.
b Less than .1.
SOURCE: Board of Governors of the Federal Reserve System, *Deposits, Reserves and Borrowings of Member Banks.*

logic these banks might also be expected to borrow more frequently, whether from the Federal Reserve or from other commercial banks, through the federal funds market.

In fact, California banks have borrowed very little. As Table 7 makes clear, member banks in the Twelfth District have used the discount window less than banks elsewhere in the Reserve System. The segment of total reserves acquired through borrowing is appreciably lower at country banks in this District than at their out-of-state counterparts. In a number of years the proportion has been less than half as high as elsewhere, and often a still smaller fraction, Borrowing by reserve city banks also has been much leaner in this District. For these banks the rate rarely has been as much as one-fifth the level experienced in the other Districts taken together, and in several years less than a tenth as much as other banks have borrowed, relative to their total reserves. It should be noted, moreover, that these figures are free of the window-dressing activity common to year-end reports. They are not subject to that bias because they are averages of levels reported for each day throughout the year.

Commercial banks also borrow from each other through the sale and purchase of federal funds. In many cases the acquisition of such funds is followed almost immediately by their sale, since many banks active in this market act essentially in accommodation of their correspondents. Their own borrowing—i.e. purchase of federal funds—is offset against virtually simultaneous selling as they follow through in their role as middlemen. At other times these same banks buy federal funds to supply reserves to temporarily-deficient correspondents who prefer not to borrow from the Reserve Bank. Ultimately, however, there must be some bank, or banks, who are net purchasers or sellers of federal funds, and these become the real borrowers and lenders. It is they whose liquidity needs are reflected in the federal-funds market.

For one reason and another there are about two dozen member banks in the Twelfth District that enter this market often enough to be included in the Federal Reserve sample survey begun in 1959. Given the size and sophistication of West Coast banks, their participation in this market is no surprise, but their role as net *suppliers* of federal funds to the rest of the country is surprising. During the fifteen months from September 1959 to November 1960, for example, Twelfth District member banks were net sellers of federal funds to other parts of the nation in every month but January and February 1960.[8] During those two months they experienced heavy and surprise reserve losses because of a shift from savings deposits into new Treasury securities offering higher yields. This was also the first time in at least a decade that free reserves had become negative at country banks in the region. It was obviously a time of unusually severe pressure.

Within the group of West Coast banks there could be individual banks which relied heavily on the federal-funds market. So long as their needs were supplied by other banks in the region, such borrowing banks would in fact be relatively illiquid but would not stand out from the group in the figures just noted. This does not appear, however, to be the case. From various reports of close observers, the large accommodating banks in the District seem to be net sellers of federal funds. They buy large quantities to accommodate their correspondents, but for the most part they resell not only these but also additional amounts drawn from their own excess reserves. In general, it appears that when California banks participate in this market on their own account, it is

---

[8] "The Role of Twelfth District Banks in the Federal Funds Market," Federal Reserve Bank of San Francisco, *Monthly Review,* June 1961, p. 115.

typically to invest idle funds and not to relieve their own liquidity pressures.

It is important to realize the profound implications of these patterns for the liquidity positions of banks in this region. If these banks have little need to supplement their reserves by borrowing from the Federal Reserve, and if they have enough excess reserves to permit frequent and large investment in the federal funds market, then California banking must be characterized by special features which allow a more efficient management of reserves than is possible in other regions. Otherwise, the comparatively tight position of these banks suggested by all the standard liquidity measures would force them to more frequent borrowing, and make such frequent lending unlikely. By the same token the existence of these special characteristics makes it clear that California banks cannot be judged by the common standards. Special weight must be attached to their *appearing* to be close to the line of illiquidity when in fact they may not be any closer than other banks are.

c. The special character of California banks

What might be those peculiar features of California banks? Four possibilities come to mind. There may be other candidates as well, but these four are certainly among the most important.

The first three are structural characteristics of banks in the region— their large size, the unusual incidence of branch banking, and the high ratio of time deposits to demand deposits. The fourth influence is of a somewhat different nature, being apparently less deeply imbedded in the structure of California banking, and consequently less certain to persist indefinitely—it is the large net inflow of reserves from the rest of the country, especially the contribution of the federal government.

(1) *The large size of banking units.*—A direct comparison of average sizes makes the point at once. In total assets the average for California banks in 1962 was $24.4 million, whereas in the United States as a whole it was $20.7 million. In total deposits the averages were $22.0 million for California banks and $18.5 million for the country at large. By either measure California banks stand almost one-fifth higher than the national average.

To avoid possible distorting effects of a few very large banks, we should look also at the size distribution of California banks as they compare with others. This is done in Table 8, which shows the 1962 distribution of California banks by total resources and the correspond ing distribution for banks in the country as a whole. The California banks are obviously much more numerous in the larger-size classifica tions.

A large bank can run a leaner liquidity position because of its greater opportunities for specialization. It can have at least one man devoted to close management of its day-to-day reserve position, making fore casts of reserve inflows and outflows. It can make profitable use of the federal funds market, partly because it is large enough to provide or absorb the minimum lot-sizes in which federal funds are traded. The secondary reserves of a large bank also can be managed with greater

TABLE 8

NUMBER OF UNITED STATES AND CALIFORNIA BANKS BY SIZE OF BANK, 1962

Size of bank in total resources (millions of dollars)	Number of banks		Percent of total banks	
	United States	California	United States	California
Less than 1.................	949	4	6.8	3.1
1–2.5.....................	3,292	10	23.7	7.8
2.5–5....................	3,454	17	24.8	13.3
5–15.....................	3,834	39	27.6	30.5
15–25....................	927	17	6.7	13.3
25–50....................	678	12	4.9	9.4
50 and over..............	779	29	5.6	22.6
Totals.................	13,913	128	100.1	100.0

ᵃ Some banks did not report total resources: 4 in California; 76 in the United States.
SOURCE: Rand McNally, *Banker's Directory, 1962.*

efficiency. Repurchase agreements with securities dealers become a realistic possibility, and these can be tailored closely to the bank's impending reserve needs. Weekly decisions can be made about participation in the Treasury bill auction.

Size also offers advantages in the management of earning assets. One of these advantages is the greater opportunity to spread the risk among a variety of borrowers. The ability to analyze special propositions in greater depth is also a potential function of size.

(2) *The unusual incidence of branch banking.*—The uniqueness of the California system of branch banking needs little documentation. The implications of the system for liquidity needs, however, are perhaps less obvious.

We may note, to begin with, that the large-scale study of banking structure over the country by Schweiger and McGee found a strong correlation between loan-asset ratios and the incidence of branching systems.[9] Correlation is not causation, but there is good reason to assume

[9] Irving Schweiger and John S. McGee, "Chicago Banking," *The Journal of Business,* July 1961, pp. 203–367.

that branching makes possible a more efficient use of a given liquidity position as stated by the standard measures.

In part, branch systems are simply another facet of relative size in a banking population. If an area of any size had only one bank, it would of course be a large branch system. A further contribution to liquidity made by branches, independent of the advantages for size alone, is the wide geographical net thrown by such a system, a net making it more probable that deposit transfers will not be attended by the need to transfer reserves. California banks enjoy this advantage to an unusual degree. The privilege of state-wide branching in, say, Rhode Island, would give a bank not so much a net as a sieve with great holes in it through which funds would surge back and forth to and from Boston and New Bedford in Massachusetts and New London in Connecticut. Indeed, the longest stretch between these New England towns, spread over three states, is about the distance from Oakland to Sacramento. By contrast, the state boundaries of California encompass a number of major trading areas. There is a much greater chance that deposits withdrawn from one part of the state will move only to another part of the state. There is no certainty, of course, that they will land in the same branch system from which they were withdrawn, but the chances are certainly greater than if the funds were moved out of the geographical limits entirely.

(3) *The high ratio of time deposits to demand deposits.*—Time and savings deposits, long prominent in the liabilities of California banks, now almost equal demand deposits. Except for the largest banks, in fact, demand deposits are less than half the total (see Morrissey, this volume) . The importance of this pattern for liquidity needs is familiar. Time and savings deposits are, by definition, much less subject to surprise withdrawal. Their rate of turnover is only a fraction of the rate for demand deposits.

In the particular circumstances of California banking, however, two more points of significance are noteworthy. First is the surprising strength of commercial banks as savings depositories in the face of dazzling competition from nonbank intermediaries in the area. Over a number of years West Coast savings and loan associations have lured enormous annual volumes of money imports. Despite this pulling power, an important fact of life to counting houses a continent away, the California banks nevertheless maintain and increase the high ratio of time to demand deposits. Member banks apparently offer the highest permissible rates under Regulation Q to achieve this result, but the long experience of success has developed an understandable confidence that they will continue to enjoy the low volatility of deposits associated with such a high ratio. Against such a history they seem justified in holding their liquidity ratios to lower levels than banks in other regions.

The second additional point is the changing character of time and savings deposits, resulting from the recent sharp growth in negotiable time certificates of deposit. These certificates were issued in some volume before 1961, and the West Coast banks were among the larger issuers. But the great burst after early 1961 came with the acquisition of certificates by large nonfinancial corporations—as a short-term liquid investment—and the volume of certificates issued by the West Coast banks did not grow at anything like the rate experienced in the Federal Reserve System as a whole. Moreover, of the volume outstanding near the end of December 1962, the proportion initially issued to corporations was much lower than in the country at large.[10] California banks, as more limited issuers of this new kind of time deposit relative to their total time and savings liabilities, are much less likely to suffer the liquidity drains expected at other banks at cyclical turning points, or at times when other short-term market rates rise above the Regulation Q ceilings, and the monetary authorities decide not to raise those ceilings.[11]

All things taken together, the time and savings deposit patterns of California banks seem greatly to reduce their liquidity needs.

(4) *The secular inflow of reserves from other regions.*—Our information on the interregional flow of funds is much too sparse to support an extended analysis. It appears from Professor Minsky's research, however, that California received large net inflows over a decade or more. Probably, though less certainly, the inflows were relatively steady. At least they seem not to have been concentrated in just a few years of the period.

The impact of these inflows on the liquidity positions of California banks is even more speculative. It seems a possibility, for example, that the heavy and continuing inflows of reserves from other regions might swamp normal seasonal and cyclical outflows from California banks, reflecting different patterns of trade and the uneven geographical progress of business recessions and recoveries. On the other hand, it is

---

[10] "Twelfth District Participation in the Expanding Secondary Market for Negotiable CD's," Federal Reserve Bank of San Francisco, *Monthly Review*, June 1963, pp. 82–91. See also Robert Lindsay, "Negotiable Time Certificates of Deposit," *Federal Reserve Bulletin*, April 1963, pp. 458–468.

[11] The failure of the San Francisco National Bank is perhaps a case in point. Whatever else may have been involved, trouble came when the bank was unable to redeem its time certificates of deposit at maturity, and not as a result of heavy withdrawals of demand deposits.

also possible that the existence of these special reserve inflows heightens the normal swings of seasonal and cyclical outflow. Treasury tax collections, for example, are seasonal, and so are their expenditures to some degree, but the transfer of Treasury cash balances from one region to another may have yet a different pattern, depending on the geographical incidence of debt management activity, or the nature of the expenditure of any number of other influences.

Still another interpretation is that the inflows have accounted for all the evidence of apparent liquidity. Perhaps the reason California banks have borrowed so little from the Federal Reserve, and loaned so much in the Federal funds market, is that they could not act fast enough to place these steady inflows into more permanent investments. This view would help explain the curious "U-shape" of their liquidity structure—with high levels of both the most liquid and the least liquid assets, and with low levels of the assets in between.

In sum, we may assume that the secular inflows had some part in easing liquidity pressures on California banks. But without a great deal more study we only can guess either at the magnitude of this influence or the patterns it followed. We can only say that it probably did not work against the other special features of California banking.

3. A LOOK AHEAD

Bank liquidity, we should remember, also can be thought of as the capacity to extend further credit. It is assurance to the banker that he will be ready to lend when customers of special importance come to borrow. In the longer-run setting, however, this reason for bank liquidity drops out of consideration. It applies essentially to capacity held in reserve during slack periods, to be utilized fully as business recovery turns into expansion. Thus, for periods longer than the business cycle, this liquidity need becomes a question of the appropriate rate of growth for the reserve base of California banks. It is no longer a liquidity problem. Our concern focuses entirely on liquidity as a buffer against reserve losses.

Our free-hand sketch of developments over the past decade suggests that the relatively low liquidity of California banks, as measured by conventional ratios, is the consequence of the region's unusual banking structure. It does not stem, it would seem, from less prudent management than is practiced in other states. In looking ahead, however, one must ask whether these special features will continue to develop in the same direction. If this seems likely, the liquidity ratios of California banks could fall still lower without necessarily indicating a weakening in the defenses against trouble.

For the first three special features discussed above, the future promises further improvement in the efficiency of reserve management. Unless a marked reversal occurs in public policy, the average bank size can be expected to increase rather than diminish. Similarily, we may anticipate growth, not decline, in the incidence of branch banking, again barring a sharp turn in regulatory policy. The rise of several large branch systems complicates the outlook, but it seems a reasonable guess that this development will at most only slow the tide, not turn it back. The ratio of time deposits to demand deposits of course has an upper limit, but that limit is a long way off, and the ratio has shown no tendency to decline for many years. Finally, the new technologies in managing the payments mechanism (as discussed elsewhere in this volume) are still spreading through the banking community, and other new technologies lie ahead. Altogether, these considerations forecast a further decline in liquidity ratios without increase in vulnerability.

California's balance-of-payments outlook is another matter. The consequences of a decline or reversal in strategic elements of reserve inflows to California are discussed by Minsky in this volume. A shift to net outflow in one of these strategic sources of reserves, or even a slowing down in the rate of inflow, may have serious secondary effects, stopping off the inflow of reserves from other sources as well.

In assessing the implications of these possible events for California bank liquidity, we may distinguish three kinds of problems:

(1) Suppose important inflows of reserves thin down or end altogether, for whatever initial reasons. This might uncover outflows of a seasonal or cyclical nature which had operated all along and would have led to temporary reserve losses at California banks, had not the funds come in so steadily over the years from federal and other sources. That is to say, without the special outside sources, the reserve base of California banks might enter a pattern of rising and falling, instead of rising continuously, sometimes rapidly and sometimes slowly, but always moving up.

If this were the outcome of a changed balance of payments, California banks might have to restructure their liquidity positions. They might have to borrow more in seasons of outflow. They might have to liquidate more secondary reserves in times of cyclical drain, when the reflux of funds could not be anticipated at an early date. For both these actions they would need to push their liquidity ratios higher than otherwise, and probably higher than they are now.

Moving to more liquid positions as a permanent strategy, however, would not have to be done all in one blow. California banks, although less liquid than earlier and less liquid than their counterparts in other regions, are nonetheless not illiquid. They hold large quantities of government securities, and could meet even a sudden onset of these new cyclical and seasonal patterns of outflow. They would have ample time to restructure their asset positions, without panic and without turning suddenly stringent as suppliers of credit to California borrowers.

(2) If the net inflows were reversed, turning into net outflows of magnitude in and out of season, the liquidity position of California banks would come under more serious pressure. No more than this can be said, however, without specifying how large the outflow was and how rapidly it developed. The reserve base would rise and fall over seasons and over cycles, but the falls would remove more than the rises restored. The banks would then be party to all the problems of a declining region. Their liquidity positions were not designed to meet such a problem if it arose suddenly. They could meet it only if they were 100 percent liquid—held nothing but marketable assets of a totally risk-free nature. As matters stand, their income would decline, and their ability to extend credit would slowly wither, but they would not become completely illiquid unless reserves were leaving the region in panic proportions.

(3) The banks' debtors may suffer major reverses if their continued prosperity depends on the large net inflow of capital and reserves to California, and the banks may suffer with them. A variety of direct and indirect dependencies in these inflows is explored in this volume by Minsky; but the special trouble that banks might experience is the shrinkage of their own assets. If debtors fail to meet their commitments to banks, the banks, in meeting their own commitments, have to sell off liquid assets. If they do not possess enough of these—i.e. if their liquidity ratios are too low—they will be in trouble of their own and fall under the shadow of insolvency. The shadow will darken if too few of the liquid assets are national, as distinct from regional. Bank failures, of course, ramify through the community in disastrous ways, leading to other failures. Alternatively, and partly to stave off illiquidity and insolvency, banks could tighten up their lending standards sharply. This too could lead to slack and failure elsewhere in the community.

It must be stated again that we cannot define an adequate liquidity position. We know only past positions and positions in other parts of the country. If there is general collapse in a region, normal and prudent risks turn out to be imprudent. When collapse comes, it is a mistake to have loaned anything to anyone. In a mild stagnation, however, one can guess that California banks have sufficient secondary reserves to sustain a considerable round of reverses. For in addition to their secondary liquidity provision, the banks hold sizable amounts of investments—long-term Treasuries and (mainly California) municipal securities—for which there is a gradually expanding national market. The banks also possess large, though not appreciably growing, amounts of government-backed mortgages which also are national assets to some extent. It is necessary that sufficient time be available to turn these assets into cash, however, for their degree of marketability varies with the current state of total credit demand.

Two final points should be added.

First is the possibility that California's time of trouble, if it comes at all, might strike at the worst possible stage of the business cycle. It might catch California banks with their liquidity defenses at lowest ebb—i.e. somewhere around the upper turning point of the national business cycle. It is especially pertinent to recall that both the downturns in 1953 and 1957 were accompanied by, if not triggered by, cutbacks in federal defense spending. If a future decline in these outlays in California were to come as a part of a national reduction, then California banks might begin to suffer reserve losses at the cycle stage at which they were already nearest to being illiquid. And if the turn in the cycle should be led by a change in the level or composition of federal spending, California banks might find themselves exposed to reserve losses while market opportunities for liquidating their remaining secondary reserves and investments were least favorable. The downturn might start in California while credit markets were still tight in the rest of the country.

The second point is the need for vigilance by public bodies. The banks must, of course, manage their own liquidity positions. As individual businesses they must also have the freedom to seek profits where they see the chance. This includes freedom to make mistakes and run losses. But given the very leanness of California bank liquidity by conventional standards, the potential of illiquidity must be kept actively on the agenda. In particular it must be remembered that the chief evidence of sufficient liquidity is the combination of large lending of federal funds and small borrowing from the Federal Reserve. The possibility that this pattern is a byproduct of large continuous inflows to the region cannot be refuted firmly. Should these inflows fall away, they might carry the evidence of ample liquidity down with them, leaving the banks much less liquid than they now appear to be.

CHAPTER III

COMMERCIAL BANKING AS AN INDUSTRY

California Banking and Competition

DAVID A. ALHADEFF

THE PARTICIPATION of California banks in the growth and development
of the State is part of the broader market process by which the savings
of the community are mobilized and allocated among competing uses.
In this process, all financial institutions, banks and nonbanks alike,
act as intermediaries between ultimate suppliers of and demanders of
funds. It is the purpose of this chapter to examine California bank
markets and some of the major factors which influence their structure
and performance.

1. PROFILE OF CALIFORNIA BANKING, 1951–1962

The number of California banks fell from 201 in 1951 to a 1959 low
of 115 and rose to 129 by 1962 (Table 1). For the period as a whole the
total number of banks was reduced by 72. However, the number of
branch banks increased from 50 in 1951 to 66 by 1962, whereas the unit
banks declined from 151 to 63, or by 88. During the same period the
number of branch offices almost doubled (from 1,004 to 1,923).

Table 2 shows the change in the (asset) size of distribution of California banks between 1951 and 1962. In 1951 the modal size group,
containing almost 30 percent of California's banks was $2 to $5 million.
By 1962 the modal size group contained 26 percent of California's
banks and had grown to $10 to $25 million.[1] Almost two-thirds of the
banks in 1951 were in the $10 million-or-less size class, but only 41.2
percent by 1962. At the other end of the scale, in the $50 million-or-
more size class, the percentage changed from 10.1 to 22.7.

Table 3 shows the growth (of assets) of the 76 banks continuing in
existence from 1951 through 1962. The modal growth of the survivors
was between 51 and 100 percent, and slightly more than half grew
between 51 and 150 percent. However, Figure I shows no relation be-

[1] The size categories used in this and other tables are based on FDIC categories for
recent years. The FDIC size categories are based on deposits; the tables in the text
are based on assets.

159

TABLE 1

NUMBER OF BANKS AND BANKING OFFICES IN CALIFORNIA, 1951–62

Year (December 31)	All banks	Unit banks	Branch banks	Branch offices[a]	All offices
1951.............	201	151	50	1,004	1,205
1952.............	199	147	52	1,001	1,200
1953.............	206	148	58	1,023	1,229
1954.............	171	118	53	1,085	1,256
1955.............	149	96	53	1,174	1,323
1956.............	139	85	54	1,266	1,405
1957.............	128	74	54	1,348	1,476
1958.............	124	69	55	1,427	1,551
1959.............	115	57	58	1,515	1,630
1960.............	117	55	62	1,633	1,750
1961.............	122	57	65	1,747	1,869
1962.............	129	63	66	1,923	2,052

[a] Branch offices do not include "banking facilities."
SOURCE: *Federal Reserve Bulletins.*

TABLE 2

NUMBER OF CALIFORNIA BANKS, BY SIZE OF BANK, 1951 AND 1962

Size of bank (Total resources in millions of dollars)	Number of banks		Percent of total banks	
	1951	1962	1951	1962
Less than 1....................	3	2	1.6	1.7
1–2.........................	21	4	11.2	3.4
2–5.........................	56	18	29.9	15.1
5–10........................	43	25	23.0	21.0
10–25.......................	33	31	17.6	26.0
25–50.......................	12	12	6.4	10.0
50–100......................	4	10	2.1	8.4
100–500.....................	10	8	5.3	6.7
Over 500....................	5	9	2.7	7.6
Total....................	187	119	99.8[a]	99.9[a]

[a] Totals do not add to 100.0 percent because of rounding.
SOURCE: Compiled from *Bankers Directory*, Rand McNally, 1951, and 1962. The number of banks in California in Table 1 is larger than in Table 2 because: (1) nondeposit trust companies are excluded in Table 2, (2) two banks in the same town and with the same set of officers were counted as only one bank in Table 2, and (3) year-end figures are used in Table 1 and mid-year figures in Table 2.

tween size of bank in 1951 and its growth between 1951 and 1962.[2] These growth patterns include the effects of the many mergers in California during this period.

[2] For the 76 continuing banks, the rank correlation between size of bank in 1951 and growth of bank from 1951 to 1962 was zero.

2. NONBANK COMPETITION FACED BY CALIFORNIA BANKS

Market boundaries are imprecise; typically they are zones rather than sharply demarcated lines. As a first approximation, the limits of an economic market can be defined in terms of the identifying characteristics of the product or service which is traded between the buyers and sellers. This first approximation definition of a market is often inadequate to define precisely the boundaries of specific markets for it does not convey a sense of the interdependence that often exists among sellers of nonidentical products (or services). (Hereafter, "service" may be substituted for "product" where appropriate.)

Economic substitutability also is insufficient to define precisely the boundaries of banking markets because substitutability is a matter of degree. Where services offered by different sellers are highly substitutable in consumers' minds, no significant price difference can prevail in the common market where the services are offered. Lesser substitutability permits a greater price difference. To appraise the amount of possible nonbank competition in the market for any particular bank service, it must be determined if nonbank substitutes exist, if they are good, and if they are important. Since banks are multiproduct firms, they deal in a number of markets. It is convenient for analytical purposes to divide these into deposit markets, where banks act as mobilizers of the community's funds, and loan and investment markets, where they act as disbursers of those funds to a variety of users. This division is an expository simplification which ignores the relationship which sometimes exists between loan and deposit markets. For convenience, too, the markets in which banks operate often are called "banking markets" even though nonbank suppliers are active and important in some of those markets.

a. Deposit markets

Reserves are the most important raw material for the banking system, but demand and time deposits are the most important raw materials for an individual bank. Although capital is indispensable in extending credit, it is not per se an important source of funds for credit extension. In attracting demand deposits, the banks' possible competition differs in different submarkets. The two main submarkets for demand deposits —and the line between the two is clearly not hard and fast—correspond to the two main reasons for holding demand deposits, namely, for transactions purposes and as a liquid reserve. Although the deposits

FIGURE I
Bank Size in 1951 and Bank Growth Between 1951 and 1962

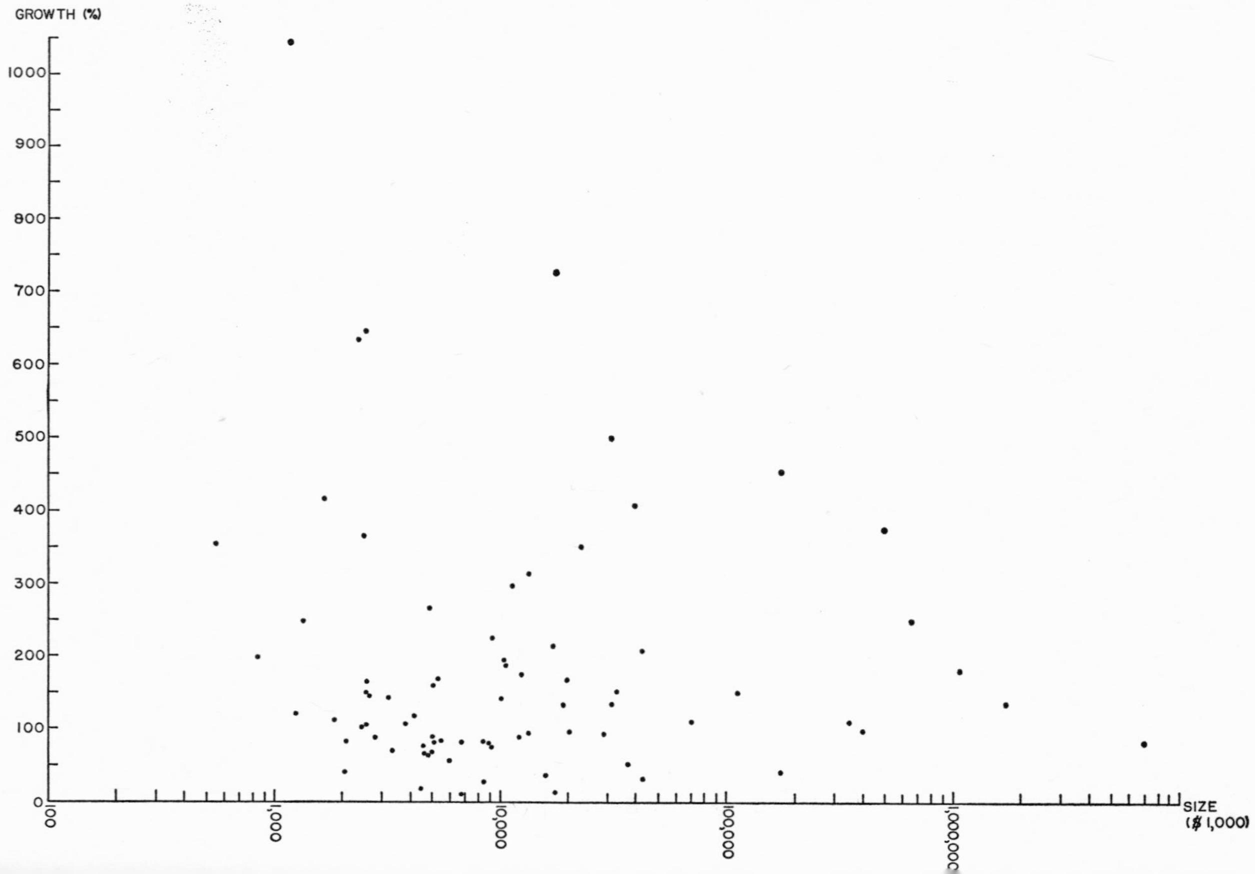

maintained for these two purposes may be held in a common account, the possible competitive forces are quite different.

Demand deposits held for transactions purposes come very close to being unique, i.e. only very limited substitution is possible. A different situation prevails for demand deposits held as a liquid reserve. These funds are held as a buffer to smooth out irregularities in receipts and expenditure flows, as a reserve for unexpected contingencies, as a tem-

TABLE 3

CALIFORNIA BANKS IN CONTINUED EXISTENCE BETWEEN 1951 AND 1962
(by growth of assets)

Growth (in percent)	Number of banks	Percentage of continuing banks
Negative	0	0
0–50	7	9.2
51–100	23	30.3
101–150	16	21.0
151–200	10	13.2
201–300	7	9.2
301–400	5	6.6
401–500	4	5.3
501–1,000	3	3.9
More than 1,000	1	1.3

SOURCE: Compiled from *Bankers Directory*, Rand McNally, 1951 and 1962.

porary repository of liquid assets pending their more favorable disposal, and as a repository for sums not transferred to some other form because of neglect or because it is not worthwhile. This submarket for demand deposits is not a commercial bank private preserve. Alternatives to a demand deposit held as a liquid reserve include cash, a commercial bank time or savings account, a savings and loan association share account, a credit union deposit, a U. S. Treasury bill, open-market commercial paper, and other highly liquid short-term assets. In this submarket, therefore, California commercial banks face possible competition not only from each other but also from nonbank financial institutions, from business firms, and from the government.

Commercial banks also seek to attract the public's funds as time and savings deposits. These deposits are liquid, safe, and carry a return, and they must compete with a variety of other short-term assets which are also liquid, safe, and carry a return. In general, the list of possible substitutes is much the same as for demand deposits held as liquid reserves. The importance of one of these alternatives in California is indicated by the large volume of share accounts of the California savings

164   DAVID A. ALHADEFF

and loan associations—in recent years, about the same as time and savings deposits at California commercial banks.[3] In short, since there are numerous nonbank suppliers of substitutes for commercial bank time and savings deposits, California banks as a group face a great deal of possible nonbank competition in this market.

b. Loan and investment markets

In the markets for securities, commercial banks are important suppliers of funds to federal, state, and local governments, and to private corporations. In 1963 California banks held almost $6 billion of U. S. government obligations and an additional $3 billion of other securities.[4] When California banks enter the markets for securities, they face possible competition from insurance companies, savings and loan associations, mutual savings banks, pension funds, mutual funds, private individuals, nonfinancial corporations, nonprofit institutions, foreigners, and other commercial banks outside of the state. Thus, while California banks held almost $6 billion of U. S. government obligations in 1963, commercial banks in other states held $49 billion, mutual savings banks $5.5 billion, insurance companies $9.2 billion, nonfinancial corporations $10.4 billion, savings and loan associations $3.3 billion, state and local governments $12.5 billion, and all others $66.3 billion.[5]

In the consumer loan market, California commercial banks confront possible competition from consumer and sales finance companies, credit unions, and numerous retail outlets. There are no figures to show the size of these nonbank suppliers in California. In the U. S. as a whole, however, commercial banks at the end of 1963 held 40.2 percent of total installment credit and 31.3 percent of noninstallment credit.[6] Some nonbank suppliers depend on the banks for part of their funds, but others secure large amounts from their own equity capital and from the money and capital markets. Consumer borrowers recently have turned to suppliers in mortgage markets to secure funds for purposes traditionally financed by consumer loans. Moreover, some lenders have actively encouraged homeowners to use mortgage credit for non-real estate expenses.[7] There are no accurate figures on the amount of mortgage credit thus diverted. However, if the practice becomes more important, California's banks will face competition in the consumer loan market from such nontraditional consumer lenders as life insurance

[3] For example, cf. *Savings and Loan Fact Book*, 1964, p. 14, and Federal Deposit Insurance Corporation, *Annual Report for 1963*, p. 146.
[4] Federal Deposit Insurance Corporation, *Annual Report for 1963*, p. 146.
[5] *Federal Reserve Bulletin*, August 1964, p. 1053.
[6] *Federal Reserve Bulletin*, February 1964, pp. 218–219.
[7] Cf., "Homes in Hock," *Wall Street Journal*, July 24, 1963, p. 1.

companies and savings and loan associations as well as from the more customary nonbank suppliers of consumer credit.

California commercial banks are important but not the sole lenders in the mortgage markets. Nonbank competitors sharing this market include life insurance companies, mutual savings banks, savings and loan associations, pension funds, various state and federal lending agencies, and private individuals. In 1963 nonfarm mortgage recordings in California were $9.8 billion, of which commercial banks originated only 15.6 percent. By comparison, savings and loan associations originated only 15.6 percent. By comparison, savings and loan associations originated 52.8 percent, individuals 13.3 percent, insurance companies 2.3 percent, and others 16.1 percent.[8]

Commercial banks in California also face possible competition from nonbanks in supplying medium-and longer-term business credit. Intermediate- or longer-term business credit from a bank is commonly provided in the form of a term loan. As an alternative to this, large borrowers may arrange a private placement with an insurance company or a security market flotation; smaller companies do not have access to these nonbank sources, but they are sometimes able to secure the necessary funds from SBIC's.

The commercial banks in California are the most important but not the only institutional suppliers of short-term business credit. Other suppliers include commercial finance companies, various government agencies, and nonfinancial corporations (in the form of trade credit). These provide substitutes, but not perfect substitutes. Commercial finance companies commonly concentrate on marginal borrowers who have difficulty securing normal bank accommodation. Moreover, the high rates typical in commercial finance companies reduce their attractiveness as alternatives for the short-term borrower eligible for a bank loan. Credit from various government lending agencies is usually available under restrictive conditions and, in the ordinary course of business, most borrowers cannot resort to government agencies as an effective alternative to a bank. Trade credit is doubtless an important source of funds for many, especially for smaller business firms but is available only for limited periods and purposes.

3. REGULATORY BARRIERS TO COMPETITION

a. Price controls

The character and extent of regulatory controls condition the competitive capacity of banks and nonbanks. Some regulatory controls paralyze part of the price mechanism pertinent to commercial bank

---

[8] *Savings and Loan Fact Book,* 1964, p. 52.

operations. Specifically, regulatory authorities have completely prevented the price mechanism from operating by proscribing interest payments on demand deposits.[9] In addition, they have restricted the free play of market forces for time and savings deposits by setting a ceiling rate for interest payments on those deposits.

The prohibition of interest payments on demand deposits was imposed as part of the monetary reform legislation of the early 1930's. The intent in the Banking Act of 1933 was to prevent the large New York City banks from using interest payments to attract funds from the rest of the country for use in speculative activity on the securities exchanges.[10] At present, a more important reason for prohibiting interest payments on demand deposits is to prevent large city banks from draining funds away from interior banks to the detriment of the drained areas.[11] This argument is reminiscent of the localism argument of the "twenties" which held that a bank's first duty is to serve the customers in its local area without reference to the attractiveness of alternative outlets in other areas. Under a policy of localism, considerations other than efficiency and productivity are introduced into the allocation of funds. In any case, the argument that funds should not be employed away from local areas (towns or cities) where they were collected loses much of its force in California because the large branch banks can and do shift funds within the state to meet shifting demands.

The primary reason for continuing to prohibit interest payments on demand deposits is the belief that bank safety requires limits on deposit competition. In practice, however, the effect is not always to limit competition but to deflect it into other channels. For example, instead of paying for deposits explicitly, banks adjust the service charges of their depositors according to their balances, and negotiate loan terms for business borrowers with reference to the size of the borrowers' balances. Moreover, the regulation does not have the same significance for all banks. As is shown later, the demand deposit market is composed of submarkets with different market structures. Banks operating in the submarkets with the least competitive structures least need any protection which the regulation could offer and in the submarket with the most competitive structure, deposit competition is muffled rather than suppressed.

[9] The regulation also proscribes payments in any other form. Cf., *Federal Reserve Act*, Sec. 19, par. 13.
[10] Cf., *Report of the Committee on Financial Institutions to the President of the United States,* April 1963, p. 19.
[11] Cf., *Ibid.,* p. 20.

The ceiling rate on time and savings deposits, applicable to both national and state-chartered banks in California, is also intended to limit competition on the grounds that a free market for time and savings accounts would lead to a dangerous increase in bank costs and would force banks into unsound portfolio acquisitions in an attempt to cover those higher costs. However, in some of the submarkets for time and savings deposits, there is strong competition from nonbank suppliers (of substitutes for time and savings deposits). Thus, while the ceiling rate regulation limits banks' freedom to compete, it does not protect commercial banks against nonbank competition. On balance some banks consider the regulation to be a competitive handicap and have urged the authorities to provide relief from the unwanted "protection." In recent years, the Federal Reserve authorized its member banks to pay higher rates on time and/or savings deposits on January 1, 1957,[12] January 1, 1962, July 17, 1963, and November 24, 1964.[13]

Although competitive pressures both from banks and nonbanks are less intense in other submarkets, the use of a ceiling rate sometimes brought about the very situation it was designed to avoid, for some members of the public interpreted the higher ceiling rate authorized in 1962 as an official rate which the banks should be able to pay.[14] As a result, some banks had to raise their deposit rates when competitive pressures alone would not have had that result.

It has often been said that a free market for deposits would lead bankers to undertake unsound risks (in the form of excessive maturities, excessive risks, unbalanced diversification, etc.) to pay higher deposit rates. However, as long as entry into the banking business continues to be strictly regulated to screen out those unwilling to respect the fiduciary nature of their business or to abide by the restraints which that relationship imposes, the fears that greater freedom would make bankers irresponsible seem exaggerated. In any case, a provision for standby controls could prevent rates from being raised to unsound levels if price controls were dropped.

It should be stressed that, even if the fears of unsound banking are well founded, price controls are not a reliable means to prevent un-

---

[12] One economist observed that "The Board [of Governors of the Federal Reserve System] itself concedes that no sooner do the limits which it has set become effective (i.e. begin to hold down rates on time deposits below what they would otherwise be), than it is inclined to raise them!" Joseph Aschheim, *Techniques of Monetary Control* (Baltimore, 1961), p. 145.

[13] Cf., *Federal Reserve Bulletin*, December 1956, p. 1301; December 1961, p. 1404; August 1963, p. 1068; and December 1964, p. 1520.

[14] Cf., *National Banks and the Future: A Report of the Advisory Committee on Banking to the Comptroller of the Currency*, 1962, p. 117.

sound portfolio practices. Price controls can hold some competitive pressures in check, can suppress a bank's ability to respond by price action, but cannot prevent a banker from violating the standards of sound portfolio management. The only sure way to prevent unsound portfolio practices, including the assumption of unwarranted risks, is by a fully effective system of bank supervision. With or without price controls, the public interest in bank safety requires a program of effective supervision to prevent unsound practices whether induced by too much competition, by incompetence, by cupidity, by fraud, by the pressure of excessive funds, or by any other influence. Thus, further study of ways to increase the effectiveness of bank supervision would serve the public interest both in bank safety and in competition.

b. Portfolio controls

Commercial banks in California presently compose their portfolios subject to numerous restrictions imposed by the regulatory authorities. Detailed regulations of the federal and state authorities, not always the same, seek to accomplish substantially the same goal, namely to ensure that the portfolio policy of the regulated banks is consistent with maintaining the liquidity and solvency of the banks. Of the many regulatory restrictions, some merely reinforce the banks' own self-imposed restrictions, others add to them. The most important portfolio controls seek to limit the total amount of risk in the portfolio—by insisting on a particular relation between a bank's capital and the total volume of its earning assets, by prohibiting certain classes of assets entirely, by forcing a minimum amount of diversification, and so on.

In composing his portfolio, a banker seeks to balance the need for liquidity and solvency against the need for profit. In regulating bank portfolios, the authorities seek to balance the need for bank safety against the need for portfolio flexibility to promote mobility of funds and competition which in turn lead to a better allocation of financial resources and greater economic growth. In a dynamic economy, any structure of controls must be reviewed periodically to determine if the balance between safety and flexibility is appropriate to present needs and circumstances. Where it is possible to remove or to liberalize existing restrictions on bank portfolios without impairing bank safety, relaxation of the restrictions permits banks to contribute more effectively to economic growth and to a more efficient allocation of resources.

Although the appropriate relaxation of portfolio restrictions would serve both public and bank interests, increased portfolio flexibility by itself can make only a limited contribution to greater economic growth.

In part this is because rigidities imposed on banks by portfolio controls do not always produce corresponding rigidities in the flow of funds. For example, although banks are prevented by restrictions against bank purchase of equity securities from supplying funds to their customers by purchasing equities directly, they can do so indirectly by making loans for the purchase of securities to individuals, brokers, and others. In addition, many customers are flexible enough to tailor their needs to accommodate the legal restrictions of banks and of other important institutional savings repositories as well. The rigidity has also been moderated by the banks which developed forms of credit (e.g. the term loan) which do not violate the legal restrictions and are acceptable substitutes at least for some customers. Finally, some customers who cannot be accommodated at a bank have met their needs through other lenders and other channels.

Another reason why relaxing portfolio restrictions by itself can make only a limited contribution to greater economic growth is that it frees a bank to move into higher risk levels but does not by itself enlarge a bank's capacity to undertake the higher risks. The total loss a bank can sustain is limited by its capital (including reserves) and it is doubtful that the legal restraints have been as important for several years as the capacity restraint in inhibiting banks from taking greater risks. Under these circumstances, if riskier assets are not compensated by larger capital (including reserves), a banker who reaches out for a high-yield, high-risk asset will want to balance it with a low-yield, low-risk asset to leave unchanged the total risk level in the total portfolio. A step forward would thus be compensated by a step backward, and the net progress might well be zero. For increased portfolio flexibility to make its greatest contribution to economic growth, greater *freedom* for banks to assume risk must be combined with a greater *capacity* to bear risk. In its study of the financial structure, the Commission on Money and Credit suggested various incentives to enhance the banks' capacity and willingness to assume risks, including tax incentives to promote retention of earnings, FDIC insurance premiums related to the ratio of risks assets to capital and reserves, issue of debentures subordinated to claims of depositors, and issue of preferred stock.[15]

c. Differential regulations

Bank competition is conditioned not only by the existence of regulatory controls but also by the fact that different kinds of controls are imposed on banks and other financial—especially deposit—institutions.

---

[15] Cf., *Report of the Commission on Money and Credit*, 1961, pp. 171–174, *passim*.

There are many such differences but, in recent years, the most widely mentioned differences have been the different regulations with respect to interest payments on savings deposits, to reserve requirements, and to loss reserves. Although these regulations affect the competitive balance between banks and nonbanks, they were not designed for that purpose and their competitive impact is largely a by-product of pursuing other goals.

Competition among the firms *in a given financial structure* will direct the flow of funds to each in accord with the operating efficiency and productivity of the different institutions. Differences in efficiency and productivity are partly inherent in the different institutional charters and in the relevant legislation defining their legal powers. Given the inherent differences in the legal powers of different kinds of financial institutions, the competitive efficiency and productivity of any firm depends on the competence and energy of its staff and management, its capital equipment, its organization, and so on.

The differential regulations between banks and nonbanks affect this flow of funds by their particular effect on the competitive balance among different firms. Thus, the different treatment with respect to reserve requirements or loss reserves acts like a subsidy for some firms and a cost (or earnings) handicap for others; and the differential regulation about ceiling rates on deposits may prevent some but not other firms from bidding as much for deposits as they feel their operating efficiency and ability to employ the funds productively justifies. As a result of differential regulation, the competitive flow of funds in a given financial structure may not be the same as it would if these particular regulatory differences did not exist. Similarly the flow may be affected by other institutional differences which affect the competitive interrelations among financial firms. However, the effects of particular differential regulations on an optimal flow of funds cannot be fully assessed within the framework of a given financial structure, i.e. one in which we take as given the existence of different kinds of financial institutions with particular sets of legal powers, the number and size distribution of each kind at any moment of time, and the prevailing policy concerning entry conditions for each kind. If the particular way in which competition channels the flow of funds among the firms of an existing financial structure is to be optimal, the financial structure also must be optimal.

In principle, it is possible to depend solely on the workings of competition to evolve an optimal financial structure in terms of the number, size, and kind of financial firm. However, sole reliance on competition to accomplish that goal would oblige the authorities to make charters readily available for different kinds of financial institutions and to accept the decisions of a competitive market with respect to the number, kinds, and sizes of firms. In practice, for reasons of safety and stability, public policy does not permit free entry of financial institutions. To this extent, competition within a given financial structure cannot by itself ensure an optimal allocation of resources.

Since it is public policy not to depend entirely on the market mechanism to determine the composition of the financial structure, that function must be performed in part by the chartering authorities. In a dynamic growth economy like that of California, it is particularly important to make a periodic review of public policy with respect to the number, kind, and legal powers of the financial institutions to be authorized. In a constantly changing economic environment, there is a danger that the financial structure which may have served well the needs of one day will not be optimally adapted to the different needs of another day, and the allocation of resources may suffer for it.

4. MARKET SEGMENTATION AND BANK COMPETITION

California banks collectively face a wide array of possible competitors in many of their activities. However, due to market segmentation, California banks are not equally exposed to the full extent of this possible competition in all of their operations. For a variety of reasons both the deposit and the loan and investment markets in which banks operate are shot through with both supplier and demander immobilities. Because of these immobilities, many of the markets described in Section 2 are fragmented into submarkets with varying degrees of insulation from each other. These submarkets differ not only in their degree of autonomy but also in size and number of participants (both on the demand and supply side). As a result of these different market conditions, the intensity of competition varies widely in the different markets and submarkets in which California's banks participate.

In principle, it is necessary to define a market for each borrower or depositor depending on his mobility. In practice, it is meaningful to define banking markets for borrowers of high, low, and intermediate mobility because many borrowers (or depositors) have basically similar mobility.

a. Deposit markets

(1) *Demand deposits (for transaction purposes).*—Commercial banks come close to having a unique product in demand deposits for transaction purposes (see next section for discussion as liquidity reserves).

This product is available at any bank in the country and the total number of banks is more than sufficient to ensure full and effective competition if all banks participated in a common national market for demand deposits. In practice, the market for demand deposits is national only for some and local for most depositors.

Because of their widespread operations, national companies are able to compare demand deposit terms countrywide and to place their several accounts most favorably. As a consequence of their wide-ranging mobility, these depositors pull diffusely located banks into a common demand deposit market.

The situation is quite different for the typical individual depositor of small means who prefers to deal with a local or even an immediate-neighborhood bank. It is possible for a small depositor to live in (say) Berkeley, California, and to maintain a deposit account at a bank in a distant state, but it is inconvenient because of delays in doing business by mail, the possible difficulty in paying local merchants with checks on an out-of-town bank, the inability to transact deposit business while in the bank on other business, and so on. Because of these barriers to long-distance banking, the typical small depositor does not even investigate the terms on which demand deposits are available at nonlocal banks, and he is in no position to enforce competition between his local bank and an outside bank.

Between the extremes of the very large firm operating in a national market for demand deposits and the typical small depositor operating in a local market, there are intermediate-size depositors who transact their deposit business in an area larger than the local area but smaller than the entire country.

(2) *Time and savings deposits.*—The substitutes for demand deposits as a liquid reserve are substantially similar to the substitutes for time and savings deposits. Hence, both kinds of deposits can be dealt with as part of a common market.[16]

Large depositors find it both feasible and worthwhile to compare the deposit terms offered by local and nonlocal banks. In addition, many compare the returns which can be earned in different kinds of short-term money market paper. On occasion some even compare the returns available at foreign banks or in foreign money markets. These large depositors include large business firms, state and local governments, and foreign commercial banks and official institutions.[17] None of these

---

[16] For a discussion of the implicit deposit rate on demand deposits, cf., J. Gurley and E. Shaw, *Money as a Theory of Finance* (Washington, D.C., 1960), pp. 151–153.

[17] "Interest Rates on Time Deposits, Mid-1963," *Federal Reserve Bulletin,* June 1963, p. 769.

groups is eligible to hold passbook savings accounts; but they can hold time deposits in the form of negotiable time certificates of deposits. The deposits of foreign governments and international institutions are particularly sensitive to differentials in interest rates.[18] To permit commercial banks to compete more effectively for the deposits of these particularly mobile depositors, the Federal Reserve removed the ceilings (for a period of three years after October 15, 1962) on the interest rates that member banks may pay on time deposits of foreign governments, central banks, and certain international institutions.[19] Thus, when a California bank solicits the accounts of these large, mobile depositors, it competes with banks elsewhere in the country, with open market paper (including Treasury bills) and, in some cases, with foreign banks and money markets.

At the opposite extreme, the typical small depositor is comparatively immobile and his choice is limited to local bank and nonbank suppliers. He may be unaware of the terms available from banks and nonbanks in other parts of the state or the country, or if aware, may feel it not worth the expense or inconvenience of dealing with a distant institution. The difference in the amount of interest received on a small account cannot be large in absolute terms even when the rate differential is comparatively large. Thus, although there are no publicly available figures on this matter, it is doubtful that small depositors account for a significant part of the substantial sums that some California institutions have attracted from other parts of the country. The small depositor also is not likely to be informed about open market alternatives. In any case, a combination of the technical impediments to dealing in those markets and the small size of his account precludes these as realistic alternatives.

Intermediate-size depositors, whose deposits are large enough to make it worthwhile to note any growing differences between local and outside rates but not large enough to warrant "sharp pencil" operations, are also not large enough to deal in U. S. Treasury bills, open market commercial paper, and (possibly) time certificates of deposit. Thus, while the alternatives available to this intermediate mobility group extend beyond those available in local areas, they fall short of those open to very large depositors.

The significance of the mobility of the intermediate-size depositors can extend beyond their own operations. The major institutional suppliers of savings accounts, commercial banks, and savings and loan associations, lacking a mechanism for separating small and medium-size

[18] *Ibid.*, p. 772.
[19] Cf., *idem.*

accounts, offer the same terms to both. In any particular situation the local savings institutions must decide whether it is worthwhile to raise rates for both small and medium-size depositors in order to attract the more mobile medium-size depositors.

b. Loan and investment markets

(1) *Security markets.*—California banks face different degrees of competition in security markets, ranging from markets in which local banks are dominant to those (like U. S. government securities) in which competition approximates the possible competition described earlier. Every bank which participates in the latter market is in direct competition with other banks, nonbanks, business firms, private individuals, and so on. No single bank has a position of market power in that market, i.e. no single bank can significantly affect market price by its own action. The same is generally true of the market for the securities of highly-rated state and local governments and national corporations.

The market is thinner for the securities of business corporations or local governments whose credit ratings are less well-known to potential investors in all parts of the country or not as highly regarded as those of prime issuers. These securities tend to be sold to local investors either familiar enough with local conditions to appraise the risks involved, or perhaps motivated by local loyalty[20] or by a concern for customer relations. According to the Federal Reserve Bank of San Francisco, "One large bank in California has a policy of bidding on all California municipal issues that are eligible for bank investment. The policy of that bank assures issuers of eligible bonds of at least one bid except in cases where the issue may be unacceptable to the bank for technical or legal reasons."[21] For issuers whose mobility is thus restricted, the potential number of suppliers is clearly far smaller than it is for the prime issuers. Indeed, the market in which the less mobile issuers must operate has more of the characteristics of the customer loan market than of an impersonal open market.[22]

(2) *Consumer loans.*—The market for consumer loans includes well-defined submarkets for automobile, other consumer durables, repair and modernization, and personal loans. Because consumer loans are

[20] Cf., R. I. Robinson, *Postwar Market for State and Local Government Securities* (Princeton, 1960), pp. 86–87. In this connection, it is interesting to note that the largest bank in California limits its underwriting activities to securities issued by the state of California or of its local government units. *Ibid.*, p. 104.

[21] Federal Reserve Bank of San Francisco, "The Twelfth District Municipal Securities Market," *Monthly Review*, March 1957, p. 60.

[22] *Ibid.*, pp. 86–87, 104.

made to small borrowers, the market for each type of consumer loan is fragmented into numerous local submarkets. Both bank and nonbank suppliers operate in these submarkets. Because of various market imperfections, loan terms are not always uniform within a particular submarket. Borrowers do not always bother to compare the terms offered by different lenders, and many who do bother may find it difficult to balance the numerous dimensions other than explicit rate in the loan package offered by different lenders.

Lender immobilities also contribute to market segmentation. Some lenders choose to concentrate on a certain range of the risk spectrum of consumer loans. Banks commonly cater to better risk borrowers and leave the higher risk loans to nonbank lenders. Different risk specialization by bank and nonbank lenders moderates the direct rivalry between them.

(3) *Mortgage loans.*—Both borrower and lender immobilities fragment the market for mortgage funds into submarkets with varying degrees of insulation. Borrower immobilities are most pronounced for the typical private-home buyer who characteristically must seek a mortgage from suppliers represented in his local area (e.g. town or city). These may include non-California lenders, but the bulk of these funds probably is supplied by California-based financial institutions and individuals.

At the opposite end of the scale, large borrowers for commercial purposes (e.g. some large-tract builders) may seek funds in much wider geographical areas. The size of their potential borrowings and the scope and nature of their operations are sufficient to be "visible" in centers geographically removed from their base of operations. Accordingly, even though a large commercial and a private-home borrower are located in the same town or city, they have direct access to a different number of alternative suppliers in markets with different geographical spread.

Some segmentation of the mortgage market stems from lender immobilities which arise, in part, from the difficulties of doing business over a wide area. Thus, it might not be feasible for (say) a New York-based pension fund to establish representation in numerous California communities in order to compete directly with local lenders. Other lender immobilities are imposed by law. For example, commercial banks may not lend as much on a given noninsured residential mortgage as the savings and loan associations may lend, nor (except for insured mortgages) for as long a maturity. In addition, some lenders have been limited to a 50-mile radius. Mortgage market immobilities produce a spectrum of submarkets with different market characteristics. We need to know a good deal more about different classes of mortgage-seekers in California, the structure of the markets in which they operate, any differences in market results, and extent of linkage (or insulation) between the submarkets.

(4) *Business loans.*—In seeking short-term business loans, some borrowers have access to any bank in the country and some even to foreign banks; some are limited to local alternatives; and the others fall between these extremes. The differences in mobility of different borrowers are related to their differences in size and scope of operations, but more fundamentally to their credit standing and how readily it can be appraised by prospective lenders.

Lenders in local areas are the natural suppliers of small borrowers by virtue of their comparative advantage over a distant bank not only in appraising a local loan, but also in negotiating, supervising, and collecting it. Improvements in transportation and communication which integrate nearby localities into a larger economic unit enhance the mobility of the small borrowers by extending the area within which the small borrower's credit standing is visible. At the other extreme, very large borrowers are highly mobile not because it is inconvenient for them to negotiate with distant banks but, more fundamentally, because of an excellent credit standing which lenders in any part of the country can readily appraise.

5. MARKET CHARACTERISTICS UNDER STATEWIDE BRANCH BANKING

a. Pressures for uniformity

The large branch-banking systems in California add special dimensions to the analysis of banking competition. Statewide branch banking tends to break down the insulation of local markets within the state. Due to statewide branch banking there is pressure for similar terms to be offered in the more competitively structured local markets of the major cities and in the less competitively structured local markets of smaller towns. It is easy for consumers to compare the terms offered on standardized services (e.g. service charges for individuals' checking accounts, or interest rate on individuals' savings accounts) in different parts of the state by local branches of a statewide system. Since any adverse discriminatory treatment in a particular small town local market could be identified readily, the large branch systems are under strong pressure as a matter of sound public relations to offer the same terms to their smaller-town and larger-city customers.

These pressures are not likely to work in reverse. Thus in a few instances, the customers in a small town local market may be treated more favorably than their major city counterparts. This has happened occasionally when a branch bank took over a unit bank committed to a particularly generous policy with respect to (say) service charges. In that event, the pressure for uniformity did not spread from the small to the major community. This is partly because small town terms are usually unknown to major city customers and partly because the pattern in a particular small town is not sufficiently important to excite major city public opinion.

There is less customer pressure for uniformity on less standardized services (e.g. business loans) among different branches of a large branch bank because the terms are negotiated individually and privately. On the other hand, there is pressure for uniformity from the internal organizational needs of a large branch bank. As a result, there is a tendency, even for these less standardized services, for the terms in the more competitively structured local markets of the major cities to be offered as well in the less competitively structured local markets of the smaller town. Thus, statewide branch banking tends to pull together the different local markets in the state.

Under statewide branch banking, small customers in smaller California towns benefit from the more competitive pressures in major city local markets. On the other hand, the competitive pressures in the latter are affected by the fact that there are fewer independent banking alternatives in California's major cities than in comparable cities in states where branch banking is limited or prohibited. There is no way of knowing on a priori grounds or from published data how these pressures balance out in terms (say) of the rate charged to immobile borrowers in the small local markets of California.

Although the large branch banks operate in both national and local markets, they are not under the same pressure in each to equalize the terms offered to customers. It is possible, then, for yields to be higher on time than on savings deposits or for loan rates on short-term commercial loans to be lower on the national than in local markets without necessarily incurring local customer dissatisfaction. The public relations pressures for uniform treatment of all customers are less effective in these cases because small local market customers generally consider large customers who operate in the national markets to be outside their orbits of comparison. There is also less pressure for uniform treatment from internal organization needs for the important business of major customers usually is concentrated either in the head office or in a small number of major branch offices.

178 DAVID A. ALHADEFF

b. Product differentiation

When economic substitutability is taken into account, the market boundaries for many bank services must be expanded to include non-bank substitutes. Conversely, imperfect substitutability can fragment the market for a bank service even when all of the suppliers of the service are commercial banks. Anything which differentiates the service of one bank from that of another impairs their mutual substitutability.

Product differentiating elements often are deliberately fostered by banks in order to develop customer loyalty to a particular bank. Thus, bankers put great emphasis on service, and competition in terms of service is often a substitute for competition in terms of price. Successful product differentiation engenders customer loyalty, and customer loyalty to a bank, like brand loyalty to a product, introduces considerations other than price into the customer's decisions. Where the differentiating elements are weak, the price differences among competing banks must be small; where they are strong, price differences can be greater.

Different forms of product differentiation appeal to different customers. For example, large borrowers generally prefer to deal with large banks which can provide large loans from their own resources and this preference gives large banks a competitive edge over small banks in competing for the business of large borrowers. At the opposite extreme, many small borrowers prefer to deal with small banks because they believe their needs receive more sympathetic and personalized attention. Small borrowers and depositors also put a high premium on the proximity of a bank.

Product differentiation is important because of the implications for market boundaries. Where product differentiating elements are weak, all producers of the same general product or service can be considered to operate in a common market. As product differentiating elements become stronger, they progressively impair substitutability. When substitutability becomes highly attenuated, product differentiation causes the original market to be divided into submarkets.

In California, product differentiation can take a special form. Statewide branch banking makes it possible for some banks to offer statewide banking facilities through a network of branch offices located in all parts of the state. If bank customers mobile enough to operate on the state market[23] strongly prefer statewide facilities, banks otherwise in a

---

[23] As explained later, the term "state market" is intended as a suggestive rather than as a precise description of the geographical range of borrowers and depositors of intermediate mobility. The kind of empirical investigation which would be required to identify geographical market boundaries with precision is beyond the scope of this study.

common market are separated into two submarkets consisting of those which can and those which cannot provide statewide facilities. If the bank customers in the state market are indifferent or only mildly prefer statewide facilities, this separation does not occur. This point has an important bearing on the analysis of the market effects of certain bank mergers. For purposes of public (especially merger) policy, it is important to have more information about the views of bank customers in the state market in California toward this particular form of product differentiation, i.e. do most or only a few prefer it, and are their preferences marked or moderate?

c. Interbranch mobility of funds and competition

It is often noted that branch banks can shift funds from local areas of excess supply to local areas of shortage. To assess the competitive implications of this fact, it should be noted that interbranch mobility of funds does not increase the number of suppliers available to the immobile local borrower; it simply increases the total supply of funds available in the local market. To illustrate the market consequences of this distinction, consider the hypothetical case of a seller with a monopoly position in two separated markets and with a different elasticity of demand in both markets. To maximize profits, the firm would price discriminate in both markets and shift output to equate marginal revenue in both markets to marginal cost. The shifting of output would not lead to identical prices in both markets but only to identical marginal revenues and to monopoly prices. If this hypothetical seller held a monopoly position in one market but a completely competitive position in the other, he might shift output from the competitive to the monopoly market to maximize profits, but the price in the monopoly market would still be a monopoly price. Thus, interbranch mobility of funds per se does not enhance competition in local markets.

Interbranch mobility of funds could affect competition indirectly if it led to a significant change in concentration in the local market. In a local market containing only large branch banks, interbranch mobility of funds would not lead to any significant change in concentration in the local market. Interbranch mobility could bring about a change in concentration in a rapidly growing community which required a net import of outside funds if one bank (or more) in the local market was either a unit or small branch bank and one (or more) was a large branch bank—but the change would probably be an increase in concentration. Aside from any effects on concentration, interbranch mobility might indirectly affect market behavior via a cost effect, i.e. if imported funds had a lower marginal cost than funds secured locally.

6. BANK MERGERS

The future extent of both bank and market concentration in California will be affected by the number and kind of mergers which occur and by the number and kinds of entry. Public policy can have an important influence on both. For expository convenience, this discussion of the market impact of bank mergers is limited to their effects in markets where nonbank financial institutions are least important, i.e. the markets for demand deposits (for transactions purposes) and those for short-term business loans.

a. Market effects

Analysis of the effects of mergers on market structure is complex because mergers have different effects in different markets. Thus, the elimination of one bank by a merger between two California banks which served the market of the most mobile depositors and borrowers would not significantly affect either the number of banks available or the extent of concentration in that market. This market position is not inherently immune to the cumulative effects of mergers but it is supported by the prevailing prohibition against interstate branch banking and limitations on expension by bank holding companies. By contrast, the elimination of one bank by a merger between two California banks in one of the markets consisting of the least—or the intermediately— mobile depositors and borrowers could have a measurable impact on the number of alternatives and the level of concentration in that market because each of those markets is served by a comparatively small number of banks.

The market effects of mergers are not always straightforward. Although all mergers eliminate a bank, not all eliminate an alternative source of supply. A merger between two banks which operated in the same local market would reduce the number of alternatives in that market. On the other hand, if one bank acquires another and converts it into a branch in a local market in which the acquiring bank had not formerly been represented, the merger would not reduce the number of independent alternatives in the market even though it would eliminate one bank.

Some mergers affect more than one market, but not symmetrically. Thus, a merger of local banks could have repercussions in the state market, but the market effects would depend upon the particular circumstances of the merger. If the merger took the form of uniting several small banks, each serving a different local market, the merger would not affect the number of independent alternatives in each of the local markets. Alternatively, if some were in the same local markets, the merger would raise concentration in those markets. At the same time a merger which brought banks too small to be effective alternatives in the state market within the orbit of comparison of borrowers and depositors in the state market would increase the number of alternatives in that market. In a different case, a merger of (say) two banks might not affect the premerger level of concentration in local markets but it would increase concentration in the state market if both banks had individually participated in that market before the merger.

The possibility of statewide branch banking in California introduces a special complication in analyzing the market concentration effects of some mergers. Consider the merger of two banks, each a participant in the state market, but neither with statewide facilities. If their merger created a new bank with statewide facilities, it would endow the combined bank with an element of product differentiation which neither bank had before the merger. Such a merger has a different effect on the market concentration faced by different subgroups of borrowers and depositors. This form of product differentiation shades gradually from an element which may only slightly impair the unity of the state market to one which can split it into virtually independent and separated parts.

The analysis of mergers has been expressed in terms of their effects on market *structures*. An analysis of their effects on market *behavior* is complicated by the fact that correspondence is not unique between the intensity of rivalry and the particular number of banks in a market in which any bank could measurably affect market price by its own action. Vigorous competitive behavior is *possible* in a market with (say) two or three banks, and cannot be ruled out entirely in a one-bank town. Other things being equal, however, competitive behavior is more *probable* with a large rather than a small number of suppliers. Hence, it is reasonable to suppose that a merger which reduces the number of banks in an oligopoly market will, other things being equal, reduce the chances for competitive behavior.

A merger could affect market behavior even if the number of banks in the market did not change. This would happen whenever a merger replaced a less with a more aggressive bank, or vice versa. In addition, in California a merger which replaced a small bank (or branch of a small branch bank) by a branch of a large branch bank might alter market behavior in a small-town local market because of the pressures for uniformity associated with widespread branch bank systems. This result is not certain, however, because a "pressure for uniformity" is not tantamount to a guarantee of uniformity.

b. Banking factors

Mergers can affect not only the number of banks but also the banking factors: the financial history and condition of each bank, the adequacy of its management, and the convenience and needs of the community to be served.[24] A merger which enhanced the banking factors with no adverse effect on the structure of banking markets presents no conflict of goals for public policy. In other cases, a conflict is more apparent than real. For example, a merger which eliminated a bank threatened with failure does not really alter, but rather anticipates a change in, the market structure.

More difficult decisions are raised by mergers which affect the market structure adversely while enhancing the banking factors. Regulatory authorities can sometimes resolve the conflict in a manner which preserves the benefit to the banking factors without sacrificing the competitive structure, e.g. by preferring as the acquiring bank one which would not impair the competitive structure over one which would damage it. In other cases public policy can avoid conflicts by anticipating problems and taking present steps to reduce the chances of future conflicts. For example, if lack of management succession is a factor in mergers, a public policy which promotes a greater supply of well-trained bankers will gradually diminish the succession problem and thereby relieve the pressure for mergers which would impair the competitive structure of banking markets. In still other cases regulatory authorities can resolve the conflict between competition and banking factors by distinguishing between private and social gains to the banking factors from a proposed merger. Consider a merger which enhances the banking factors by (say) extending the loan limits of the two banks. If (to illustrate the point) the only (or major) effect of the enhanced lending limits were to enhance the merging bank's ability to compete for the business of the most mobile California borrowers, the private would be greater than the social gain. The reason, of course, is that the intended beneficiaries of the merger already enjoy access to bank credit on reasonably competitive terms, and one more or one less supplier would not affect them significantly.

In short, although it may not be possible by these approaches to resolve all cases of conflict between the banking factors and competitive factors, it should be possible to reduce their number significantly.

---

[24] Cf., "Amendment to Federal Deposit Insurance Act," *Federal Reserve Bulletin*, June 1960, p. 611.

c. California mergers, 1951–1962

The record of mergers among California banks during the years 1951–1962 is shown in Table 4. The number ranged from a 1951 low of two mergers to a 1954 high of 39 mergers which included twenty-three banks merged together to form a new branch system. For the period as a whole

TABLE 4

NUMBER OF CALIFORNIA BANKS ABSORBED IN MERGERS, 1951–1962

Years	Number of absorbed banks	Percent of total California banks, end of year
1951............................	2	1.00
1952............................	5	2.51
1953............................	3	1.46
1954............................	39	22.81
1955............................	29	19.46
1956............................	12	8.63
1957............................	15	11.72
1958............................	3	2.42
1959............................	11	9.56
1960............................	3	2.56
1961............................	6	4.92
1962............................	5	3.88
Total............................	133	

SOURCE: Data supplied by the Federal Reserve Bank of San Francisco.

133 banks were eliminated by merger. The number of banks eliminated annually by merger, as a percentage of the total number of banks in California during the same year, ranged from 1 percent in 1951 to 22.8 percent in 1954. Mergers wiped out more than 10 percent of total California banks in each of three years; during five years, more than 8.5 percent were eliminated.

Table 5 shows the size distribution of the absorbed banks which were in existence in 1951. Almost 60 percent of the banks in California in 1951 were absorbed by merger before 1963. The resources of these absorbed banks were 16.38 percent of the California banks total in 1951. However, 62.8 percent of the assets of the absorbed banks came from only five banks in the size-group of $100–500 million. In general, therefore, although most mergers during the period eliminated smaller banks, the few mergers of larger banks absorbed a greater volume of resources than the combined mergers of smaller banks.

TABLE 5

Size Distribution in 1951 of California Banks Absorbed in
Mergers Between 1951 and 1962

Size-class[a] (total resources in millions of dollars)	Number of absorbed banks	Absorbed banks as percent of total 1951:	
		Number of banks	Resources of banks
Less than 1	1	.5	.01
1–2	16	8.6	.15
2–5	34	18.2	.76
5–10	31	16.6	1.42
10–25	17	9.1	1.67
25–50	4	2.1	.87
50–100	3	1.6	1.29
100–500	5	2.7	10.42
Over 500	0	0	0
Total	111[b]	59.4	16.59

[a] In all mergers, the larger (or largest) bank in 1951 was counted as the absorbing bank even if the charter of the smaller bank was retained after the merger.
[b] The smaller number of mergers shown in Table 5 than in Table 4 is largely accounted for by the sixteen banks chartered after 1951 which were absorbed by merger before 1962.
SOURCE: Compiled from *Bankers Directory*, Rand McNally, 1951 and 1962.

7. BANK ENTRY

a. Entry barriers

The conditions of entry into banking affect competition in two ways: where entry is not blocked nor excessively difficult, situations of entrenched market power are less likely to develop; where market concentration exists, it is less likely to be associated with noncompetitive behavior. In spite of these considerations, free entry is not permitted in banking, and those already engaged in banking, bound as they are in a fiduciary relationship with their customers, are not permitted full freedom in conducting their business. Before they will issue a new charter, the chartering authorities carefully check the background, character, and competence of the organizers and prospective management of a new bank. In this way, they try to prevent entry by people unwilling to respect the public-trust nature of banking or not competent to run a bank. To provide depositors with at least a minimum of protection against losses, the authorities require a minimum amount of capital as a condition of entry. To protect banks against unsound or excessively risky undertakings, each new entrant also is required to agree to numerous restrictions on his freedom to compose his portfolio. To ensure compliance with those regulations, each bank must agree to submit to periodic supervision and examinations by appropriate regulatory authorities. Although there may be disagreement about specific details of this broad complex of bank restrictions, there is no disagreement in general about the need to restrict entry to those who can raise sufficient capital and who are qualified by character, experience, and ability, to conduct a sound banking business.

Barriers (such as those above) which prevent entry by banks which are unsoundly financed, incompetently managed, and frivolously or fraudulently conceived, enhance the public interest in bank safety without impairing the public interest in bank competition. After the banking crisis of the thirties, bank entry was also restricted on a "need" basis with a view to limiting competition and avoiding unsound portfolio practices which might be stimulated by a greater degree of bank rivalry. However, the need barrier is not a reliable means to control either the amount of competition which banks face or unsound portfolio practices.[25]

Entry would not be equally easy in all markets even if a need barrier did not exist. It is impossible for a wholly new bank to enter in a meaningful way into the market where California's largest borrowers secure their funds. Deposits are the overwhelming part of any bank's loanable funds and, under the best of circumstances, it would take years for a wholly new bank to grow enough to become a meaningful supplier in that market. Merger can provide a way to gain entry into this market but, as we have seen, additional entry would not significantly affect those California customers sufficiently mobile to deal on a national market.

In the state as in the national market, entry is not possible for wholly new firms and is facilitated by some mergers. However, entry via merger may have different market effects in the state than in the national market for the state market is dominated by a few large banks.

Minimum capital requirements are not serious obstacles to entry into local markets. More effective hurdles in past years have been the chartering policies of state and national banking authorities. Moreover, by contrast with the national market, entry into local markets could significantly affect their structure. However, it is doubtful that entry barriers are responsible for the small number of banks or banking offices in most local California markets served by one or a few banks. Many local markets are simply too small to support a large number of banks or branches, and easier entry conditions would not change this basic fact.

---

[25] For a fuller discussion of this point, cf. D. Alhadeff, "A Reconsideration of Restrictions on Bank Entry," *Quarterly Journal of Economics* (LXXVI, May 1962), pp. 246–263.

DAVID A. ALHADEFF

On the other hand, the *potential* for easier entry could have an effect on market behavior similar to actual entry. To forestall new entrants, the firms already in the local market would be under constant pressure to charge low loan rates to borrowers, pay high rates to time and savings depositors, improve the kind and quality of their services, and reduce costs. In short, to forestall entry, the existing banks would have to anticipate those things which an enterprising entrant might do.

b. Market effects under branch banking

The analysis of the market effects of entry has more dimensions in California than in a unit bank state. In a unit banking state the opening of a unit bank qualifies as effective entry for it increases the number of independent alternatives in a given market. In California, by contrast, the opening of a branch office, even a de novo office, is not per se evidence of effective entry. A de novo branch qualifies as effective entry into a local market only when the parent bank has no other branches in the same local market.[26] When a branch bank opens a de novo branch in a local market in which it is already represented, the de novo office increases the number of banking offices, but not the number of independent alternatives. Indeed, the new entrant may lead to greater concentration within the local market. At a minimum, it will not reduce concentration as it would if the entrant were a unit or branch bank not already represented in that particular market.

When a branch bank enters a local market by acquiring an existing bank and converting it into a branch, that does not constitute effective entry even if the branch bank had no previous branches in the market. A branch bank office would be substituted for a unit (or other branch) bank office, but there would be no change in the number of independent alternatives.

Another complication in analyzing the effects of entry by branch banks into local markets stems from the fact that the resources available to a branch bank in a particular local market are not limited to the deposits which it can attract in that market. As a result, under some circumstances, a branch bank entry may change the concentration in a local market even when is does not change the number of independent alternatives. Consider a rapidly growing community which requires a net import of outside funds to meet its expanding demands for credit.

---

[26] This accords with the view of the Federal Reserve Bank of San Francisco that "In determining whether there were two or more competing banks in an area, branches of the same bank were not considered to be separate banks." Joint Committee on the Economic Report, *Monetary Policy and the Management of the Public Debt*, Senate Document 123, Part 2, p. 780.

Suppose that the local market of such a community was shared equally by (say) two unit banks. If a large branch bank entered the local market by acquiring one of the unit banks and converting it into a branch, the entry would probably increase market concentration. On the other hand, if the community was served by a unit or small branch bank and also by an office of a large branch bank, the entry of a second large branch by acquiring the unit or small branch bank and converting it into a branch would probably reduce concentration.

The analysis of entry is also complicated (especially in a branch bank state like California) because a given entry may have different (and perhaps conflicting) effects in different markets. For example, an effective entry by a branch bank into a local market increases the number of alternatives and thereby reduces concentration in that market. If the branch bank is small, its entry into local markets also may reduce concentration in the state market by accelerating the overall growth of the small branch bank and thereby facilitating its entry (or an expansion of its activities) in the state market. On the other hand, if the branch bank was already large enough to operate in the state market, the entry which reduced concentration in the local market might actually lead to an increase in concentration in the state market. At the same time, however, if the entry helped the bank to achieve more expanded network of banking facilities, it could reduce concentration in that submarket of the state market consisting of customers with a strong preference for banks with statewide banking facilities.

c. Size of bank and effectiveness of entry

In view of the presence of large branch banks in California, an important practical question is whether entry by a large branch bank leads to more effective competition in a local market, both at entry and thereafter, than entry by a small branch or unit bank. The answer to this question is moot pending further investigation. First, there is very little firm information about the comparative market behavior of large and small banks in the same local markets in California either at the time of entry or thereafter. Second, there is no information about the comparative costs of the different-size banks in California in terms relevant for this discussion, i.e. there is not enough information to judge their comparative *capacity* to compete even if they were disposed to engage in unbridled competition.

Although various studies of bank costs have shown that small banks have higher unit costs than large banks, the available evidence does not answer the question of economies of scale in terms pertinent to the decision about branch or unit bank entry. We still need to learn how the costs of different size banks compare *on identical output.* A small bank is not just a miniature large bank. Banks of different size differ in important ways, and a particularly important difference between them is their different size-mix for both loans and investments. However, we do not yet have enough evidence to know whether the lower unit costs of large banks are due to bona fide economies of scale. This question has important policy implications and is a particularly fruitful area for further research.

In the absence of pertinent cost data, certain points are worth noting. First, despite different cost levels, banks of vastly different sizes do in fact exist side by side in the same areas and in some of the same markets. Second, between 1951 and 1962, 63 banks entered the California market in spite of the presence of banking giants. Third, banks are going through a technological revolution in handling their internal operations. Hence, whatever past costs may have been, conclusions based on those data may be fallible guides to the emerging cost patterns. Perhaps banks too small to install their own electronic data-processing equipment will suffer serious cost disabilities. On the other hand, they may be able to secure the cost advantages of electronic equipment without attaining the minimum requisite size by leasing some of the excess capacity of the larger banks, or by pooling the requirements and sharing the costs of the equipment among a group of smaller banks. This, too, is a fruitful area for further research.

d. Branch and unit bank entry in California, 1951–1962

The comparative record of branch and unit bank entry is set forth in Table 6. Sixty-three new banks were opened in California between 1951 and 1962, equal to 31.5 percent of the total number of California banks at the beginning of 1951. For the period as a whole, an average of five new banks opened each year. In 1961 the number of new entrants jumped to eleven and remained at that level during 1962. For the entire period, 1,000 branch offices were opened—more than doubling the total number of branch offices. Converted branches reached a peak number of 39 in 1954 and declined to an average level of 4 per year during 1960 through 1962. By contrast, the number of de novo branches, which averaged 72 per year for the entire period, rose dramatically during the last three years of the period to an average of 135, or almost double the average rate for the period as a whole. As noted above, the number of effective entrants is not necessarily equal to the number of branches opened during the period nor even to the total number of de novo branches.

TABLE 6

Number of New Banks and Branches in California, 1951–62

Year	New banks	Branches	
		De Novo	Converted
1951................	1	25	2
1952................	4	17	5
1953................	11	20	3
1954................	5	27	39
1955................	8	63	29
1956................	2	83	12
1957................	4	69	15
1958................		79	4
1959................	1	80	10
1960................	5	118	3
1961................	11	115	5
1962................	11	173	4
Total..............	63	869	131

Source: Compiled for the author by Research Department, Federal Reserve Bank of San Francisco.

8. CONCENTRATION IN CALIFORNIA BANKING MARKETS, 1951–1962

In many phases of their business California banks compete with non-banks as well as with each other, but the markets for transaction balances and for short-term business loans are restricted primarily to bank suppliers. How has the high level of bank concentration in California affected market concentration in these primarily bank markets?

a. Limitations of the data

The tables in this section can provide only an approximation of the changes in the structures of both the state and local markets because the necessary information is not available. For example, to calculate concentration in a particular local loan market by the usual measure of market shares of leading firms, we need both the total volume of loans made to the borrowers limited to that market and the volume of loans which each bank supplied to that market. We cannot calculate the total volume of loans made in any particular local market because we lack information to identify the borrowers limited to that local market. Some borrowers who deal with local banks have sufficient mobility to have access to banks in entirely different areas, and it would be meaningless to include their loans in the figures for the local market simply because they chose to deal with local banks. The measurement problem is further complicated in California because published branch bank loan figures are not available for individual branch offices.

Since the information necessary to calculate market shares is lacking, concentration in local borrower and depositor markets was measured by the number of bank alternatives available in each town or city having a bank in 1951 and again in 1962. However, even this calculation involves an approximation, for no survey ever has been made to determine the geographical boundaries of bank markets in the state. In the absence of information about boundaries for specific small customer markets, each town or city is treated as if it were the effective limits of the market for all small borrowers and depositors within its boundaries.

The concentration calculations for the state market must also be an approximation because the information required to calculate concentration in the state market in terms of market shares is not available. Briefly, no public survey ever has been made to identify the characteristics of the California borrowers with state mobility. Hence, it is impossible to calculate the total volume of business loans made to such borrowers nor, of course, to determine what percentage of these loans was made by the leading lenders in the state market. In the absence of this information, an approximate notion of concentration can be derived by calculating the loans made by the leading California banks as a percentage of total loans of all California banks.

b. Concentration in local markets

Table 7 shows how the number of banks in California towns and cities changed between 1951 and 1962. In this table a "bank" refers either to a unit bank or to a banking office of a branch bank. Multiple offices of the same bank in one town or city were counted as one "bank." The towns in which the number of banks was the same in 1962 as in 1951 lie along the diagonal in Table 7; those in which the number was smaller in 1962 than in 1951 lie to the right, and larger to the left, of the diagonal. In 1962, 242 towns had the same number of banks as in 1951; only nine towns had one less bank; 118 towns had one additional, 51 towns had two additional, and 28 towns had at least three additional banks. Thus, concentration was lower in 44 percent of the 448 California towns which had banks in 1951. This reduction in concentration was due to the net effective entry during the period. There were 932 entrants into local markets between 1951 and 1962 (Table 6) but it is apparent from Table 7 that only 471 were net effective entrants, i.e. only 471 entrants actually increased the number of "banks" in the markets where the entry occurred (as compared with their number in 1951). Indeed, the reduction in concentration described above was due to effective entry by 332 "banks" because 139 of the 471 net effective entrants were in towns that were bankless (or did not exist as towns) in 1951.

TABLE 7

CROSS-CLASSIFICATION OF CALIFORNIA TOWNS, BY NUMBER OF "BANKS" IN TOWN, 1951 AND 1962

Number of "banks" in town	Number of towns in 1951										
	0ab	1	2	3	4	5	6	7	8	9	10c
0b		5									
1	77	175	1								
2	19	68	49	1							
3	5	19	38	11	1						
4	1	4	21	9	5						
5	1	2	7	5	1	1	1				
6		1	3		5						
7				3	1						
8			2	1				1			
9					1				1	1	
10c					1	1					2

(Left axis label: Number of towns in 1962)

a In some of these cases, the town did not exist in 1951.
b Bankless.
c Signifies "more than nine."
SOURCE: Compiled from Bankers Directory, Rand McNally, 1951 and 1962.

Table 8, summarizing the distribution in Table 7, shows the number of "banks" in each of the local markets in California in 1951 and 1962. The majority (61.2 percent) of local markets in California was served by only one "bank" in 1951, and 94 percent by three "banks" or fewer. Only 1 percent of the markets had 7 or more "banks," 2 percent 5 or more; and 6 percent 4 or more "banks." By comparison, in 1949 (the closest year for which comparable figures were already computed elsewhere), 75.5 percent of the local markets in the United States as a whole had only one "bank"; 97.2 percent had three or fewer; and only 2.8 percent had four or more "banks."[27]

[27] The figures for the U.S. are taken from D. Alhadeff, Monopoly and Competition in Banking (Berkeley, 1954), p. 46.

TABLE 8

DISTRIBUTION OF CALIFORNIA TOWNS, 1951 AND 1962,
BY NUMBER OF "BANKS" IN TOWN

Number of "banks" in town	1951		1962	
	Number of towns	Percent of total	Number of towns	Percent of total
1..................	274	61.2	254	46.4
2..................	119	26.6	137	25.0
3..................	28	6.2	74	13.5
4..................	18	4.0	40	7.3
5..................	3	.7	18	3.3
6..................	1	.2	9	1.6
7..................	1	.2	4	.7
8..................	1	.2	4	.7
9..................	1	.2	3	.5
More than 9........	2	.4	4	.7
Total..........	448	99.9ᵃ	547	99.7ᵃ

ᵃ Totals do not add to 100.0 because of rounding.
SOURCE: Compiled from *Bankers Directory*, Rand McNally, 1951 and 1962.

Between 1951 and 1962, the percentage of one-bank towns in California declined from 61.2 to 46.4; the percentage of two-bank towns remained approximately unchanged. Hence, there was a general increase in the percentage of bank-towns in the higher bank-town categories. For the local markets in California as a whole, concentration (as measured by the number of "bank" alternatives in local markets) declined during the period under study. This development in California's local market contrasts strikingly with that for the United States as a whole during a roughly comparable period. Between 1949 and 1960, the percentage of one-bank towns in U. S. local markets declined from 75.5 to 74.1; of local markets with three or fewer banks was virtually constant at 97.6 in 1960 versus 97.2 in 1949; and of local markets with four or more "banks" declined from 2.8 to 2.4.[28]

c. Concentration in state markets

California borrowers with mobility at the state level had a reasonably large number of alternatives available within the state: 187 banks in 1951 and 119 in 1962. However, the loan resources of all California banks are overwhelmingly concentrated in a few large banks. Moreover, most borrowers with sufficient mobility to deal with any of the banks in the state prefer to deal with the larger banks, both branch and unit.

[28] The figures for the U.S. are taken from D. Alhadeff, "Bank Mergers: Competition versus Banking Factors," *Southern Economic Journal* (XXIX, January 1963), p. 225.

Table 9 lists the California suppliers of 1 percent or more of all loans made by California banks. In 1951 one bank transacted more than half of the loan business of California banks; two banks each accounted for $7\frac{1}{2}$ to 8 percent; another supplied $4\frac{1}{4}$ percent; and the balance of the large banks each supplied between 1 and $2\frac{1}{2}$ percent. In 1962 the level of loan concentration was still high, but the pattern had changed. Eleven banks each supplied 1 percent or more of all loans of California banks

TABLE 9

LOANS HELD BY CALIFORNIA BANKS WITH ONE PERCENT OR MORE OF
TOTAL LOANS OF ALL CALIFORNIA BANKS, 1951 AND 1962

Rank of bank (based on loans)	As percent of total loans held by all California banks		Cumulative percentage of loans held	
	1951	1962	1951	1962
1.............	53.86	44.19	53.86	44.19
2.............	7.80	10.86	61.66	55.05
3.............	7.46	9.22	69.12	64.27
4.............	4.27	8.20	73.39	72.47
5.............	2.58	6.94	75.97	79.41
6.............	2.27	3.05	78.24	82.46
7.............	2.26	2.14	80.50	84.60
8.............	1.83	2.07	82.33	86.67
9.............	1.63	1.86	83.96	88.53
10.............	1.46	a	85.42	
11.............	1.07	a	86.49	

ᵃ Less than 1 percent.

in 1951, but only nine banks each supplied 1 percent or more in 1962. At the same time, the percentage of loans of California banks made by the largest bank declined from almost 54 to 44. Even though the next three banks increased their share of total loans, the percentage of total bank loans held by the top four banks was slightly smaller in 1962 than in 1951. On the other hand, the cumulative percentages held by successive groupings of the other large banks were larger in 1962 than in 1951. Indeed, whereas it took eleven banks to reach 86.5 percent of total loans in 1951, eight banks reached the same figure in 1962.

A somewhat different picture emerges if concentration in the state market is measured in terms of total assets (Table 10) instead of total loans. Most of the large banks held a greater percentage of the total resources of California banks than of loans. However, due to the striking exception of the 1951 figure for the largest bank, concentration in 1951, as measured by the cumulative percentages held by successive groupings of large banks, was higher in terms of loan than of asset holdings; for 1962, both measures gave very similar results.

These figures suggest that concentration was high in the state market both at the beginning and end of the period. Concentration increased in some ways and decreased in others. Thus, the share of the loan market held by eleven banks in 1951 was held by only eight banks in 1962. On the other hand, the market share of the largest bank fell sharply during the period.

TABLE 10

ASSETS HELD BY CALIFORNIA BANKS WITH ONE PERCENT OR MORE
OF TOTAL ASSETS OF ALL CALIFORNIA BANKS, 1951 AND 1962

Rank of bank (based on total assets)	As percent of total assets of all California banks		Cumulative percentage of total assets	
	1951	1962	1951	1962
1	45.12	41.41	45.12	41.41
2	11.13	13.24	56.25	54.65
3	6.91	9.78	63.16	64.43
4	4.18	7.81	67.34	72.24
5	3.24	7.32	70.58	79.56
6	3.12	3.15	73.70	82.71
7	2.58	2.56	76.28	85.27
8	2.33	2.43	78.61	87.70
9	2.30	1.97	80.91	89.67
10	2.07	a	82.98	
11	1.96	a	84.94	
12	1.13	a	86.07	
13	1.12	a	87.19	

a Less than 1 percent.

Two submarkets should be distinguished in examining the changes in concentration in the state market. One submarket consists of those customers in the state market who prefer to deal with the larger banks instead of with the small banks in the state but who do not make a sharp distinction between banks which can and cannot provide state-wide banking facilities. Tables 9 and 10 show how market concentration has changed for this group. The other submarket consists of those customers in the state market who not only prefer to deal with large banks but who strongly prefer those which can offer statewide banking facilities. This group had more alternatives in 1962, when there were three statewide branch systems, than in 1951, when there was one. No statistics are available to answer the question of how important this submarket of the state market is at the present time. This, too, would be a most useful area for further research.

The Allocation of Funds by The Commercial Banks in the California Economy, 1946-1975[1]

FREDERIC P. MORRISSEY

1. INTRODUCTION

THE PRIMARY FUNCTION of the commercial banks is twofold. First, they facilitate a payments mechanism through the receipt of deposits, their safekeeping, and their general transferability. This function requires a substantial degree of liquidity in the assets of a commercial bank which is provided through vault cash, reserves or deposits with the Federal Reserve and other banks, short-term government securities, and other assets which it is hoped can be converted on short notice, without substantial loss, into cash and equivalent assets. The second principal function is the provision of credit necessary for the smooth conduct of personal and corporate transactions in the economy.

The focus of this study is directed primarily to the allocation of loans and investments by the commercial banks—that is, to the left-hand side of the balance sheet. A major determinant of the allocation of investment funds by any financial institution—the assets in which the institution invests—is the structure of the claims against the institution. In the case of commercial banks there are the demand deposits, time and savings deposits, and the capital account. Inasmuch as Mr. Towey's paper in this volume deals with liquidity analysis, and Mr. Schaaf's with mortgage investments, it appears that three other specific areas of bank investments call for attention here: commercial and industrial loans, consumer and personal loans, and government securities.

---

[1] Acknowledgment is made of the exceptional contribution of Mrs. Patricia Bragg and of the cooperation of the Federal Reserve Bank of San Francisco.

195

2. THE LEGAL AND SIZE STRUCTURE OF CALIFORNIA BANKING

Although California commercial banks can be classified for analytical purposes in many ways, it seems appropriate here to differentiate on the basis of state or federal charter and on the basis of membership in the Federal Reserve System. Thus there are national banks, all of which are members of the Federal Reserve System, and state banks which may or may not be members of the system. Were it possible, it would be convenient to state that the source of the charter and membership (or nonmembership) in the Federal Reserve System is closely related to size— a relevant determinant of lending power, services, specialization of function, and so on. Yet in fact it appears that although all national banks are members of the Federal Reserve System, many California national banks are fairly small or local banks. Similarly, state-chartered banks vary in size as well as in membership in the Federal Reserve System. Therefore it seems appropriate to establish study classifications for national (54 banks with assets of $24 billion in 1963), state member (16 banks with assets of $8.1 billion in 1963), state nonmember (79 banks with $2.3 billion assets in 1963), plus a special group of national and state banks (7 in 1963 with deposits in excess of $275 million). This last segment, which makes up about 85 percent of total assets over the period, is composed of the large branch banks so prominent in the California economy. On the other hand, an approximation to a sample of the small banks can be obtained by looking at the state nonmember banks as a group (this category contains the First Western chain). Of course the latter class does not comprise all of the state's small banks by any means. Specific data have been collected and analyzed for 1946, 1951, 1956, 1958, 1959, 1960, 1961, 1962, and, where available, 1963. Generally, the assets and deposits reflect year-end data as contained in publications from the Federal Deposit Insurance Corporation, Federal Reserve System, State of California, State Banking Department, and Comptroller of the Currency. The rates of growth are computed on a compound basis and, in some cases, are approximations.

a. A comparison of selected growth rates—California and the United States

The rate of growth in assets and deposits of California banks has exceeded that of United States banks as a whole (see Table 1). Starting with a slightly lower growth rate of total deposits in the five-year period 1946 to 1951 (California 3 percent; United States 3.5 percent), total de-

TABLE 1
GROWTH RATES[a] PER YEAR—CALIFORNIA AND THE U. S.
(in percent)

Years	California			All insured California banks[b]				All U. S. banks	
						Deposits			
	Population	Personal income	Total assets	Loans	Total	Demand	Time	Total deposits	Total assets
1946–1951	3⅛	7	3½	15¼	3	2⅞	3⅜	3½	3¾
1951–1956	4¼	8	5¾	10	5½	5⅛	5¾	4⅛	4¼
1956–1961	3⅝	6½	6¾	7½	6¾	4¾	9	4¾	5
1961–1963	3.4	7.1	8.1	14.2	6.9	2.5	11.7	4.5	5.1
1946–1963	3.6	7.2	5.6	11.1	5.2	4.0	6.7	4.2	5.3

[a] Growth rates have been rounded.
[b] Includes only commercial banks.
SOURCES: Department of Commerce, Bureau of Census, *Current Population Reports*, Series P-25, 229, 238, 239, and 301.
Federal Deposit Insurance Corporation, *Assets, Liabilities, and Capital Accounts*, 1946, 1951, 1956, 1961, and 1963.
U. S. Department of Commerce, Office of Business Economics, *Survey of Current Business*, August 1964.

198

posits have accelerated in each succeeding five-year period: rate of growth in percent, California to United States, 1951–1956, 5.5 to 4.12; 1956–1961, 6.75 to 4.75; 1961–1963, 6.9 to 4.5. Thus, the accelerating rate of growth in deposits for the nation as a whole is magnified greatly for California banks. There is an accelerating rate of growth in total assets both for California and United States banks, and the same relative pattern exists as for deposits. California bank assets grew at a lower rate relative to the nation at large from 1946 to 1951, 3.5 versus 3.75 percent, increasing to 5.75 against 4.25 from 1951 to 1956, 6.75 against 5 percent from 1956 to 1961, and reaching 8.1 as opposed to 5.1 from 1961 to 1963.

The causes of the higher growth rates for California appear to be a reflection of in-migration to California and of the high levels of capital investment accompanying the rising population and increased economic activity in the state.[2]

It is worth noting that California banks had a differential rate of growth in demand and time deposits—with the latter in the vanguard in each time period. Although the rate of increase of California demand deposits roughly paralleled that of total deposits in the United States (in percent: 2.87 versus 3.5; 5.12 versus 4.12; 4.75 versus 4.75; and 2.5 versus 4.5, with a seventeen-year average of 4.0 versus 4.2), the increase in time deposits has been much greater, reaching 11.7 percent in the last two-year period and an average annual increase of 6.7 percent over the whole period.

It may be noted that total deposits in California have outpaced population rates of growth, 5.2 versus 3.6 percent for the seventeen-year period. Conversely, compare the high growth rate of personal income for the state with that of total deposits, where the latter is much lower over the whole period (5.2 percent for deposits versus 7.2 percent for personal income), yet the differential narrows in the later periods as deposits increase at rates of 6.75 and 6.9 in 1956–1961 and 1961–1963, respectively, while the growth of personal income declines to 6.5 and 7.1 percent during the same periods. The rapid acceleration in the growth rate for time deposits is the reverse of the growth rate pattern for personal income, yet for the whole period the personal income growth rate is higher than that for time deposits (7.2 percent for personal income compared with 6.7 percent for time deposits).

The final statistic to be emphasized from Table 1 is the unusually high rate of growth in total loans. The 15.25 percent growth rate for the initial five-year period reflects the ability in the early post-World War

---

[2] See also *Monthly Review—Federal Reserve Bank of San Francisco,* July 1962, pp. 140–141.

II period to translate public securities into loans and the high corporate and personal demands, but the 10 and 7.5 percent rates in the second and third periods again suggest strong interests in commercial, industrial, and personal lending by California banks. This conclusion is substantiated in Table 2 where loan/deposit ratios of all banks in Illinois, New York, and California are presented. A striking difference is shown between California and New York on the one hand, and the unit banking system of Illinois on the other.

b. The trend in deposits

It is well known that California banks have had a higher ratio of time to total deposits that other banks in the nation. Nationally, time deposits constituted about 20 percent of total deposits compared with almost 38 percent for California banks in 1946. The rising importance of time deposits shows in the recent figures of about 30 percent nationally, but 46 percent in California. Thus, the growing bank liabilities in California currently are distributed almost equally between time and demand deposits (Figure I). There is a difference in the relative importance of time and demand deposits, based on the size of the banks considered. For the smaller banks of the state, identified here with the nonmember state banks, Figure IVa shows that time deposits constitute a much larger, though narrowing, percentage of total deposits. (Those banks represented in Figure III also may be considered small by California standards.)

The large banks in California had a predominance of demand deposits until recently; now, however, there is a rough equality in the two types of deposits (Figure II). The evidence in Figure III, comprising all California banks less the largest member banks, wherein time deposits exceed demand deposits, presents an anomaly. For this group, the differential in time and demand deposits is fairly stable and presumably reflects a composition of somewhat larger banks than in the nonmember state group. It may be concluded that demand deposits have exceeded time deposits in the large California banks until recently when the proportions have become equal. For the smaller banks, time deposits continue to exceed demand deposits, but the margin is narrowing.

c. Implications for investment and loan policy

That time and savings deposits have a greater characteristic of permanence or stability, at least in the short run, needs little emphasis. It has been suggested that California banks have been able to use this feature to carry a high ratio of loans to deposits. Table 2 shows that all Cali-

TABLE 2

LOANS AS A PERCENT OF TOTAL DEPOSITS

Year	All banks	National	California banks[a]					New York	Illinois
			State members	State nonmembers	Eighth[b] largest	All California less 8 largest			
1946.........	25.5	26.1	23.4	24.4	25.9	23.5		25.4	20.2
1951.........	43.6	45.1	37.9	42.7	43.9	38.8		41.4	29.2
1956.........	53.9	54.7	51.5	52.6	54.0	49.1		55.3	40.4
1961.........	56.0	56.1	56.2	53.5	55.3	52.6		55.4	46.6
1962.........	59.6	58.9	62.4	57.8	58.9	57.0		57.9	49.8
1963.........	63.8	62.5	67.7	63.6	55.7	88.3[c]		62.7	53.7

[a] Figures are of Insured Commercial Banks.
[b] Member banks with average deposits in excess of $275 million from 1946–1962 (Union bank had less than $275 million in 1946, but deposits exceeded that amount from 1951 to date so it was also included in 1946).
[c] This figure may be overstated due to the inclusion of discounts in total loans of the largest banks.
NOTE: Figures as of December of each year; loan figures are the gross amount except for the eight largest—these later figures are net.
SOURCE: Federal Deposit Insurance Corporation, Assets, Liabilities, and Capital Accounts of Insured Commercial Banks, 1946, 1951, 1956, and 1961–63.

Time and Demand Deposits as a Percent of Total Assets:
All Insured California Banks

% of Total Assets

$ 34,860,000,000

$ 32,343,000,000

$ 29,845,000,000

$ 26,888,000,000

$ 26,061,000,000

$ 24,859,000,000

$ 21,548,000,000

$ 16,310,000,000

$ 13,753,000,000

——— Time
– – – Demand
  * Total Assets

100
80
60
40
20

1950   1955   1960

SOURCE: Federal Deposit Insurance Corp., *Assets, Liabilities and Capital Accounts,*
1946, 1951, 1956, and 1958–1963.

FIGURE II

Time and Demand Deposits as a Percent of Total Assets: Eight Largest California Member Banks

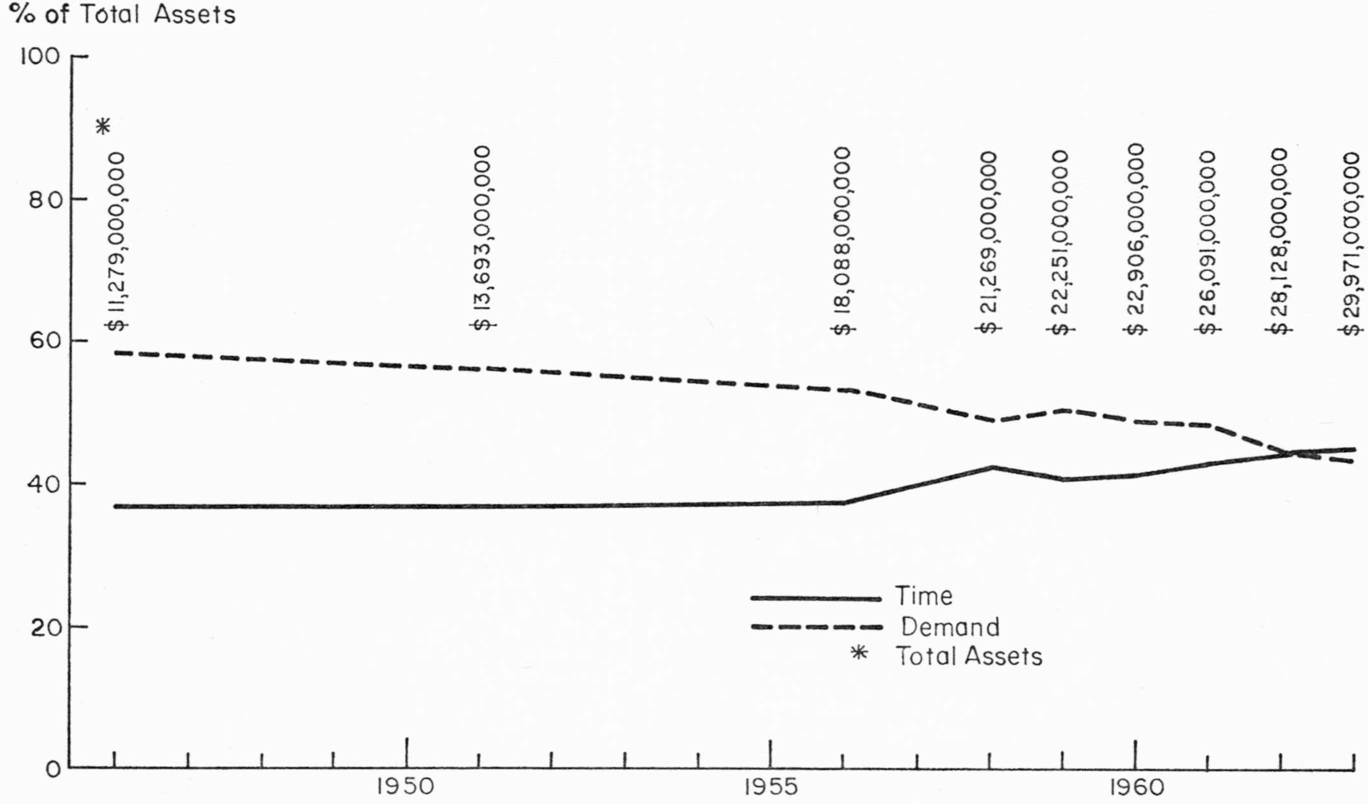

SOURCE: Federal Reserve Bank of San Francisco, correspondence during 1962.

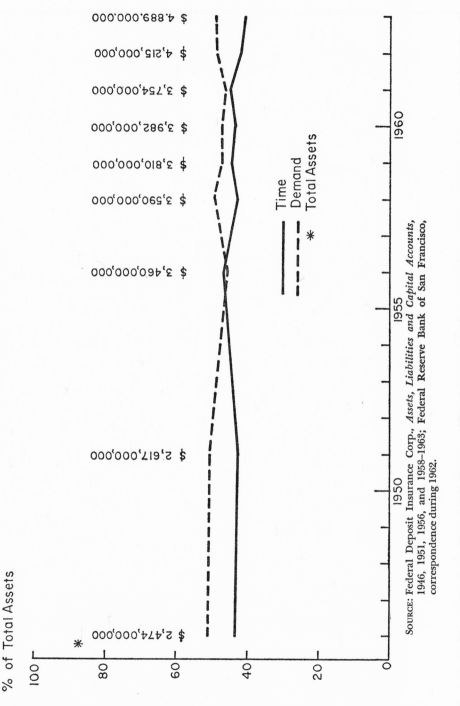

Time and Demand Deposits as a Percent of Total Assets:
All California Banks, Less Eight Largest

% of Total Assets

Time
Demand
∗ Total Assets

Source: Federal Deposit Insurance Corp., *Assets, Liabilities and Capital Accounts*, 1946, 1951, 1956, and 1958–1963; Federal Reserve Bank of San Francisco, correspondence during 1962.

$ 2,474,000,000
$ 2,617,000,000
$ 3,460,000,000
$ 3,590,000,000
$ 3,810,000,000
$ 3,982,000,000
$ 3,754,000,000
$ 4,215,000,000
$ 4,889,000,000

1950   1955   1960

100   80   60   40   20   0

FIGURE IV
Time and Demand Deposits as a Percent of Total Assets:
California National and State Member Banks, Less Eight Largest

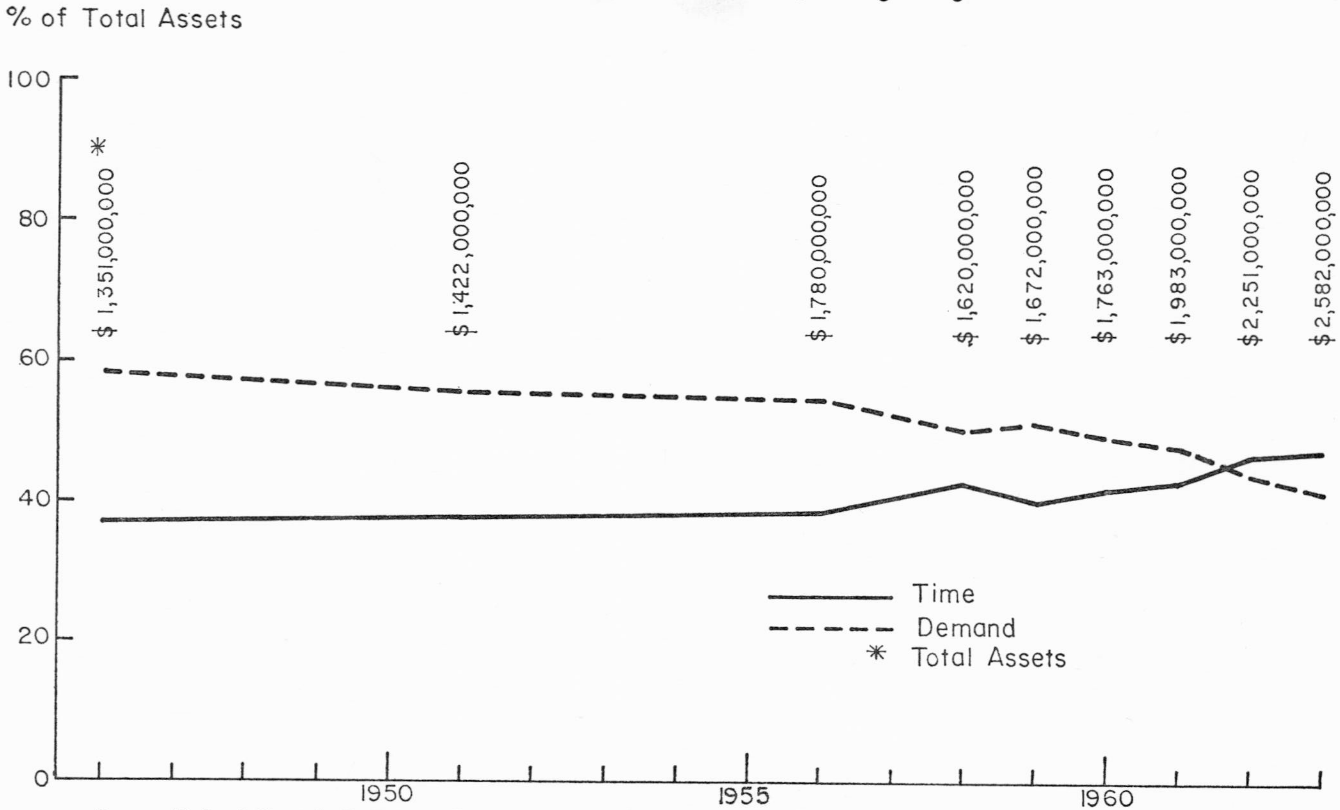

% of Total Assets

$2,582,000,000
$2,251,000,000
$1,983,000,000
$1,763,000,000
$1,672,000,000
$1,620,000,000
$1,780,000,000
$1,422,000,000
$1,351,000,000

Time
Demand
* Total Assets

100
80
60
40
20
0

1950   1955   1960

SOURCE: Federal Deposit Insurance Corp., *Assets, Liabilities and Capital Accounts,*

Time and Demand Deposits as a Percent of Total Assets:
California Nonmember State Banks

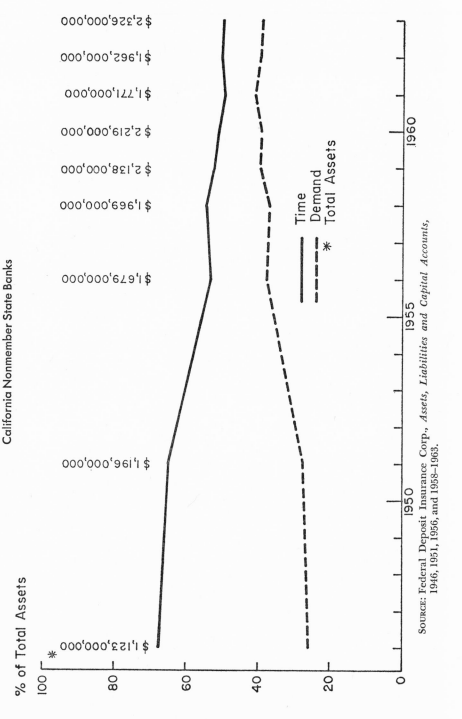

SOURCE: Federal Deposit Insurance Corp., *Assets, Liabilities and Capital Accounts*, 1946, 1951, 1956, and 1958–1963.

TABLE 3

Composition of Total Assets for Selected Areas and Years: Operating Insured Commercial Banks
(in percent)

| | Cash and balances with other banks | | | | | | | | Obligations of the U. S. Government | | | | | | | |
| | | | | California | | | | | | | | California | | | |
	U. S.ª	New York	Illinois	All	National	State member	State non member	Largestᵇ	U. S.ª	New York	Illinois	All	National	State member	State non member	Largestᵇ
1946..	22.9	21.8	23.7	19.6	20.0	21.6	12.3	20.2	49.9	49.6	51.0	49.6	48.4	52.1	34.5	48.9
1951..	24.9	26.6	25.0	19.0	18.6	23.6	11.8	19.4	34.2	28.4	40.0	32.2	31.0	34.9	37.2	31.2
1956..	22.4	24.0	21.8	18.2	18.1	21.3	11.8	18.9	26.8	19.8	32.7	24.3	23.6	24.8	29.4	23.2
1958..	20.6	23.0	20.2	16.5	16.6	18.7	10.0	17.1	27.7	21.8	34.1	26.5	25.7	28.5	29.5	26.1
1959..	20.2	22.9	19.0	17.4	17.4	20.5	10.8	18.1	24.0	16.1	30.1	21.0	19.8	22.6	27.3	20.0
1960..	20.2	23.3	19.0	16.7	17.0	18.2	10.6	17.3	23.6	18.6	28.4	20.7	19.6	22.6	26.0	19.9
1961..	20.3	23.1	21.3	17.4	17.6	18.3	11.0	17.9	23.8	19.1	25.7	22.1	21.4	22.9	27.0	21.5

Year																
1946	5.3	4.4	5.7	5.6	5.8	3.0	9.5	5.4	20.9	23.0	19.0	24.1	24.7	22.4	22.8	24.6
1951	7.4	7.1	7.5	7.5	7.7	5.1	11.2	7.3	32.3	36.2	26.9	39.9	41.2	35.1	38.6	40.6
1956	7.4	5.9	8.2	7.1	7.2	5.6	9.7	6.8	41.7	47.8	36.6	48.5	49.1	46.8	47.2	49.2
1958	8.5	7.4	9.0	8.4	8.5	6.5	12.4	7.9	41.3	45.0	35.7	46.3	46.8	44.7	45.7	46.6
1959	8.3	7.2	9.2	7.4	7.4	6.0	11.2	7.0	45.5	50.6	40.7	51.9	52.9	49.4	48.4	52.6
1960	8.0	6.8	9.0	7.3	7.3	5.9	10.6	6.9	45.9	47.5	42.3	52.4	53.0	51.3	49.7	52.9
1961	8.5	7.6	9.8	7.8	8.1	5.9	11.6	7.5	45.0	46.1	41.7	49.9	50.0	50.1	47.8	50.2
1962	9.8	9.7	11.9	9.1	9.7	6.5	11.3	8.9	47.3	48.5	43.4	52.6	52.0	54.7	51.3	52.8
1963	10.3	12.0	13.6	9.6	10.3	7.2	11.2	9.5	53.9	52.7	47.9	56.7	55.8	59.4	56.2	49.5

Other assets[d]

Year								
1946	1.0	1.2	.6	1.1	1.1	.9	.9	1.1
1951	1.2	1.7	.6	1.4	1.5	1.3	1.2	1.4
1956	1.7	2.5	.7	1.9	2.0	1.5	1.9	1.8
1958	1.9	2.8	1.0	2.3	2.4	1.6	2.4	2.3
1959	2.0	3.2	1.0	2.3	2.5	1.5	2.3	2.3
1960	2.3	3.8	1.3	2.9	3.1	2.0	3.1	2.9
1961	2.4	4.1	1.5	2.8	2.9	2.8	2.6	2.8
1962	2.4	3.9	1.5	3.1	3.2	3.0	3.0	3.1
1963	2.4	2.8	.3	2.2	2.3	1.7	2.3	9.6[e]

a Includes possessions or "other areas."

b With one exception, all banks included had average deposits during 1946 and each succeeding year in excess of $275 million.

c Loans are gross except for the "Largest," California banks.

d Includes bank premises, furniture and fixtures, real estate and miscellaneous assets.

e This is overstated by a reclassification of the data.

SOURCE: Federal Deposit Insurance Corporation, *Assets and Liabilities of Operating Insured Commercial Banks*, 1946, 1951, 1956, and 1958-1963.

FIGURE V

Composition of Assets: All Insured California Banks

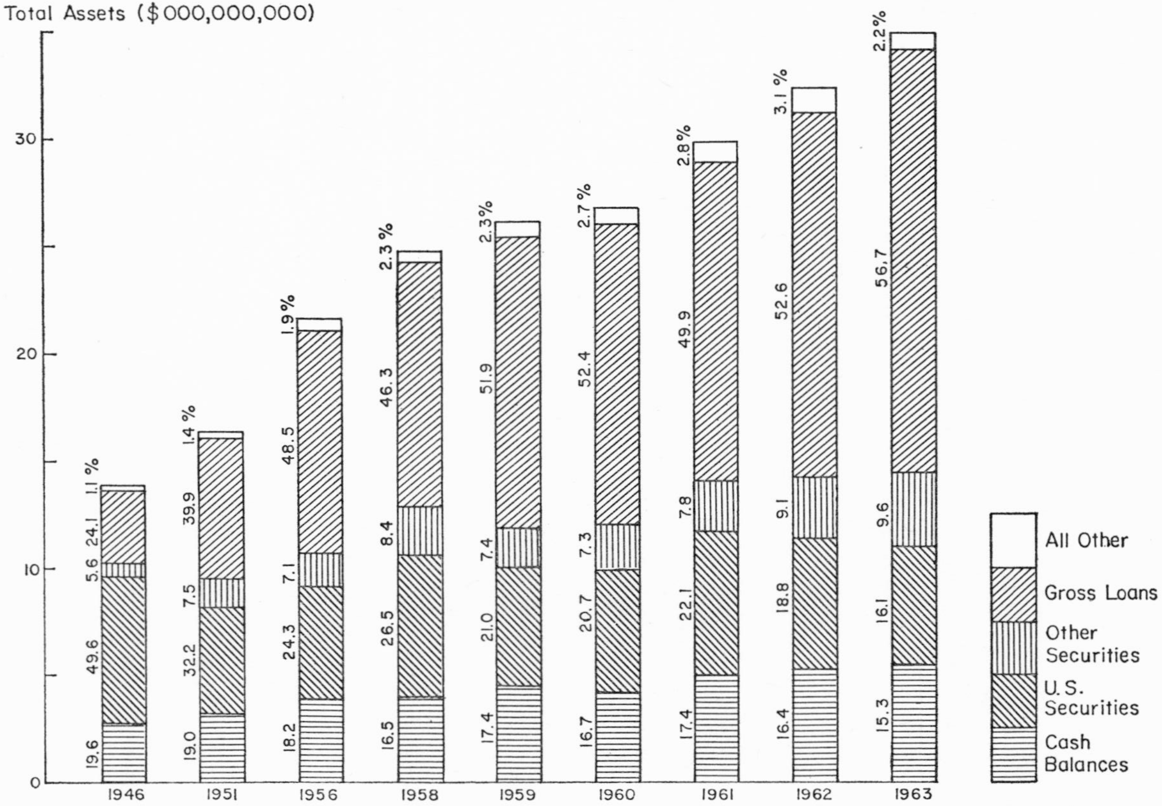

Total Assets ($000,000,000)

Legend:
- All Other
- Gross Loans
- Other Securities
- U.S. Securities
- Cash Balances

Year	All Other	Gross Loans	Other Securities	U.S. Securities	Cash Balances
1946	1.1%	49.6	5.6	24.1	19.6
1951	1.4%	39.9	7.5	32.2	19.0
1956	1.9%	48.5	7.1	24.3	18.2
1958	2.3%	46.3	8.4	26.5	16.5
1959	2.3%	51.9	7.4	21.0	17.4
1960	2.7%	52.4	7.3	20.7	16.7
1961	2.8%	49.9	7.8	22.1	17.4
1962	3.1%	52.6	9.1	18.8	16.4
1963	2.2%	56.7	9.6	16.1	15.3

Source: Federal Deposit Insurance Corp. Assets, Liabilities and Capital Accounts

FIGURE Va

Composition of Assets: All United States Insured Commercial Banks

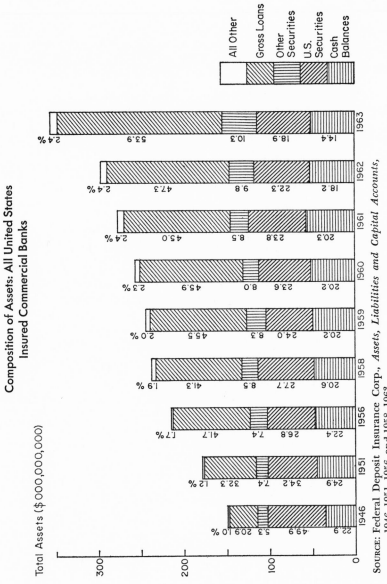

Total Assets ($000,000,000)

Legend:
- All Other
- Gross Loans
- Other Securities
- U.S. Securities
- Cash Balances

1963: 2.4% | 53.9 | 10.3 | 18.9 | 14.4

1962: 2.4% | 47.3 | 9.8 | 22.3 | 18.2

1961: 2.4% | 45.0 | 8.5 | 23.8 | 20.3

1960: 2.3% | 45.9 | 8.0 | 23.6 | 20.2

1959: 2.0% | 45.5 | 8.3 | 24.0 | 20.2

1958: 1.9% | 41.3 | 8.5 | 27.7 | 20.6

1956: 1.7% | 41.7 | 7.4 | 26.8 | 22.4

1951: 1.2% | 32.3 | 7.4 | 34.2 | 24.9

1946: 1.0% | 20.9 | 5.3 | 49.9 | 22.9

Source: Federal Deposit Insurance Corp., *Assets, Liabilities and Capital Accounts,* 1946, 1951, 1956, and 1958-1963.

FIGURE Vb

Composition of Assets: All New York State
Insured Commercial Banks

Total Assets ($ 000,000,000)

	All Other
	Gross Loans
	Other Securities
	U.S. Securities
	Cash Balances

1963: 2.8% / 52.7 / 12.0 / 14.7 / 17.8
1962: 3.9% / 48.5 / 9.7 / 16.7 / 21.2
1961: 4.1% / 46.1 / 7.6 / 19.1 / 23.1
1960: 3.8% / 47.5 / 6.8 / 18.6 / 23.3
1959: 3.2% / 50.6 / 7.2 / 16.1 / 22.9
1958: 2.8% / 45.0 / 7.4 / 21.8 / 23.0
1956: 2.5% / 47.8 / 5.9 / 19.8 / 24.0
1951: 1.7% / 36.2 / 7.1 / 28.4 / 26.6
1946: 1.2% / 23.0 / 4.4 / 49.6 / 21.8

Source: Federal Deposit Insurance Corp., *Assets, Liabilities and Capital Accounts*, 1946, 1951, 1956, and 1958–1963.

FIGURE Vc
Composition of Assets: All Illinois
Insured Commercial Banks

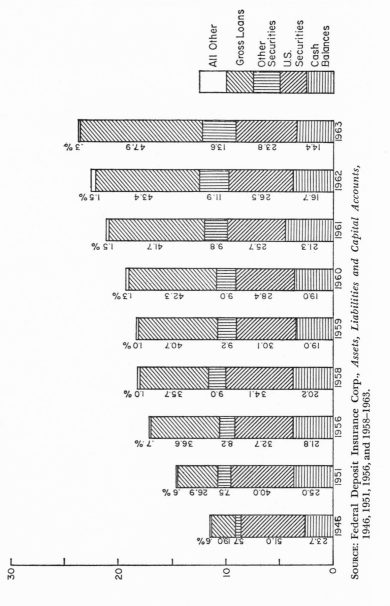

Total Assets ($ 000,000,000)

	Gross Loans	Other Securities	U.S. Securities	Cash Balances	All Other

1963 — 47.9 | 13.6 | 23.8 | 14.4 | .3 %

1962 — 43.4 | 11.9 | 26.5 | 16.7 | 1.5 %

1961 — 41.7 | 9.8 | 25.7 | 21.3 | 1.5 %

1960 — 42.3 | 9.0 | 28.4 | 19.0 | 1.3 %

1959 — 40.7 | 9.2 | 30.1 | 19.0 | 1.0 %

1958 — 35.7 | 9.0 | 34.1 | 20.2 | 1.0 %

1956 — 36.6 | 8.2 | 32.7 | 21.8 | .7 %

1951 — 26.9 | 7.5 | 40.0 | 25.0 | .6 %

1946 — 19.0 | 5.7 | 51.0 | 23.7 | .6 %

Source: Federal Deposit Insurance Corp., *Assets, Liabilities and Capital Accounts*, 1946, 1951, 1956, and 1958–1963.

fornia banks have kept pace with the traditionally high loan/deposit ratios of New York banks, and Table 3 verifies that California has a higher proportion of total assets in loans than do New York banks. It should be noted that there exists a considerable degree of uniformity among the various California bank classifications and that size alone has little impact. On the other hand, the State of Illinois data show somewhat lower loan/deposit ratios in each year (Table 2).

3. THE ALLOCATION OF ASSETS

The average annual compound rate of growth in total assets for California banks has been reported at 5.6 percent (Table 1), a rate which has more than doubled the total assets claimed by the California banks, approximately $14 billion in 1946 and $35 billion in 1963. There has been a differential impact of this increase in total assets among the various assets which the banks hold. A graphic summary of these changes is available in Figure V. In brief, two major changes are noted—a decline in the proportion of assets invested in United States government securities and a major increase in the proportion invested in the broad category of loans and discounts. On the other hand, the proportions of cash balances, collections, and miscellaneous assets have been relatively stable, and the final classification of assets—other securities—has tended to increase slightly.

Figures Va, b, and c portray the asset composition of all insured banks in the United States, New York State, and Illinois. Although all groups have similar portfolios, United States banks have a higher proportion of assets in cash items and an almost proportionately smaller amount in loans and discounts. The New York banks follow the countrywide pattern closely, but the Illinois banks show a greater preference for federal government securities.

The pattern over time of asset composition for the California banks is almost precisely duplicated when the national banks in California are segregated (Figure VI). When all state member banks of the Federal Reserve System in California are grouped (Figure VIa), the same general pattern exists, except that a slightly higher proportion of assets is reflected in cash balances and collections. Their proportion of assets in United States government securities is close to that of the industry as a whole. Yet members of the Federal Reserve System group tend to allocate a smaller portion of their assets to loans and discounts. The comparison of the predominantly small state nonmembers of the Federal Reserve System (Figure VIb) and the eight largest California banks (Figure VIc) bears out the importance of size in asset allocation. Al-

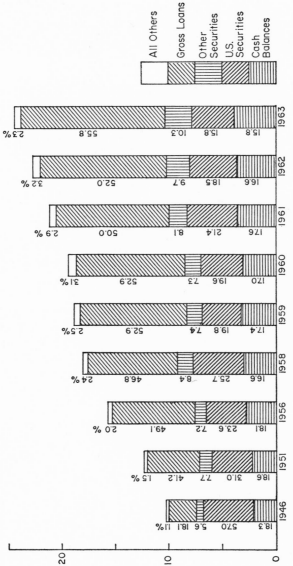

FIGURE VI

Composition of Assets: California National Banks

Total Assets ($ 000,000,000)

All Others
Gross Loans
Other Securities
U.S. Securities
Cash Balances

1946: 18.3%, 57.0, 5.6, 18.1, 1.1%
1951: 18.6%, 31.0, 7.7, 41.2, 1.5%
1956: 18.1, 23.6, 7.2, 49.1, 2.0%
1958: 16.6, 25.7, 8.4, 46.8, 2.4%
1959: 17.4, 19.8, 7.4, 52.9, 2.5%
1960: 17.0, 19.6, 7.3, 52.9, 3.1%
1961: 17.6, 21.4, 8.1, 50.0, 2.9%
1962: 16.6, 18.5, 9.7, 52.0, 3.2%
1963: 15.8, 15.8, 10.3, 55.8, 2.3%

SOURCE: Federal Deposit Insurance Corp., *Assets, Liabilities and Capital Accounts*, 1946, 1951, 1956, and 1958–1963.

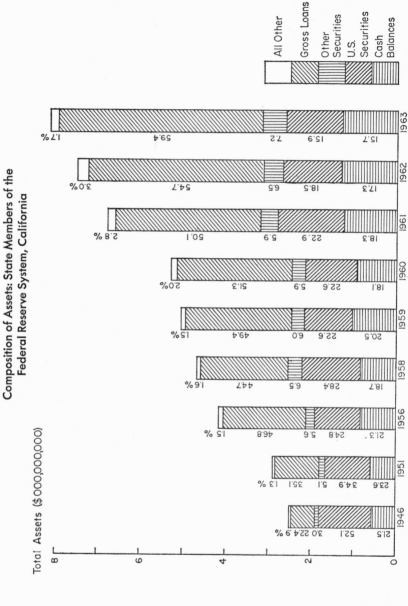

FIGURE VIa

Composition of Assets: State Members of the
Federal Reserve System, California

All Other
Gross Loans
Other Securities
U.S. Securities
Cash Balances

Total Assets ($000,000,000)

1946
21.5 52.1 3.0 22.4 0.9%

1951
23.6 34.9 5.1 35.1 1.3%

1956
21.3 24.8 5.6 46.8 1.5%

1958
18.7 28.4 6.5 44.7 1.6%

1959
20.5 22.6 6.0 49.4 1.5%

1960
18.1 22.6 5.9 51.3 2.0%

1961
18.3 22.9 5.9 50.1 2.8%

1962
17.3 18.5 6.5 54.7 3.0%

1963
15.7 15.9 7.2 59.4 1.7%

SOURCE: Federal Deposit Insurance Corp., *Assets, Liabilities and Capital Accounts,*

FIGURE VIb

Composition of Assets: State Nonmembers of the Federal Reserve System, California

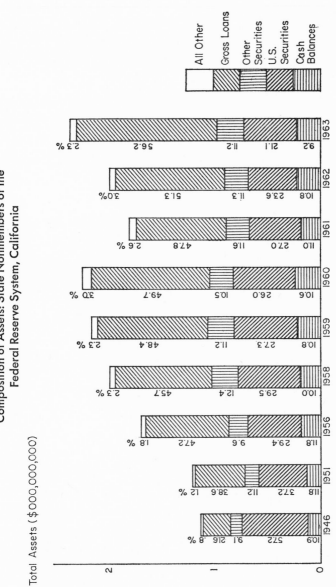

Total Assets ($000,000,000)

Legend:
- All Other
- Gross Loans
- Other Securities
- U.S. Securities
- Cash Balances

1963: 2.3%, 56.2, 11.2, 21.1, 9.2
1962: 3.0%, 51.3, 11.3, 23.6, 10.8
1961: 2.6%, 47.8, 11.6, 27.0, 11.0
1960: 3.0%, 49.7, 10.5, 26.0, 10.6
1959: 2.3%, 48.4, 11.2, 27.3, 10.8
1958: 2.3%, 45.7, 12.4, 29.5, 10.0
1956: 1.8%, 47.2, 9.6, 29.4, 11.8
1951: 1.2%, 38.6, 11.2, 37.2, 11.8
1946: .8%, 21.6, 9.1, 57.2, 10.9

SOURCE: Federal Deposit Insurance Corp., *Assets, Liabilities and Capital Accounts,* 1946, 1951, 1956, and 1958–1963.

FIGURE VIc

Composition of Assets: Eight Largest California Commercial Banks

Total Assets ($000,000,000)

Legend: All Other · Gross Loans · Other Securities · U.S. Securities · Cash Balances

Year	(bottom to top, %)
1946	20.2 / 48.9 / 5.4 / 24.6 / 1.1%
1951	19.4 / 40.6 / 7.3 / 31.2 / 1.4%
1956	18.9 / 49.2 / 6.8 / 23.2 / 1.8%
1958	12.1 / 46.6 / 7.9 / 26.1 / 2.3%
1959	18.1 / 52.6 / 7.0 / 20.0 / 2.3%
1960	17.3 / 52.9 / 6.9 / 19.9 / 2.9%
1961	17.9 / 50.2 / 7.5 / 21.5 / 2.8%
1962	16.8 / 52.8 / 8.9 / 18.2 / 3.1%
1963	16.1 / 49.5 / 9.5 / 15.3 / 9.6%

SOURCE: Federal Reserve Bank of San Francisco, correspondence during 1962.

though these two groups show the same general pattern—the relative decline of United States government obligations and the increasing proportion of assets in loans and discounts—the nonmember state banks have a substantially smaller proportion of assets classified as cash balances and collections, a percentage approximately one-half of that for the large banks in California. Another distinction is the greater reliance on securities, both United States government and other, as an offset to the lower proportion of cash balances and collections for the nonmember group. The investment in the broad category of loans and discounts appears to parallel fairly closely that of the three other groups. The large banks have been less prone to invest in all types of securities and have devoted a larger proportion of their assets to loans.

In summary, the pattern of change in assets held by commercial banks in California has been much like that of the rest of the United States. The initial period, 1946, reflected the end of wartime restriction on private lending and compulsory investment in United States government securities. As new investment and lending opportunities became available, the California banks steadily decreased the proportion of assets invested in United States government securities, and simultaneously increased their absolute and relative investment in loans. This same general pattern is applicable to the large and small banks alike, with some differences in degree.

a. The pattern of loan composition

The broad changes in the composition of loans by all California banks is demonstrated in Figure VII, which reports loans as a percentage of total assets for all California banks. The rapid growth in total loans from 1946–1951, as reported in Table 1 (over 15 percent annual rate of growth), is also reflected (Figures XI–XV) in the relatively steep slope of the graph for loans to real estate, commercial and industrial, and individual categories. Again, the lesser slopes for the five-year interval, 1951–1956, reflects the lower growth rate (10 percent) for total loans as reported in Table 1, and the practically horizontal segment, 1956–1961, again reflects the still lower (7.5 percent) annual growth rate for total loans of Table 1. It should be noted that although 7.5 percent annual growth rate is high, it is almost equalled by the 6.75 percent annual growth rate of total assets in the same period, hence the nearly equivalent growth rates of the numerator and denominator of Figure VII cause the apparent absence of growth from 1956 to 1961.

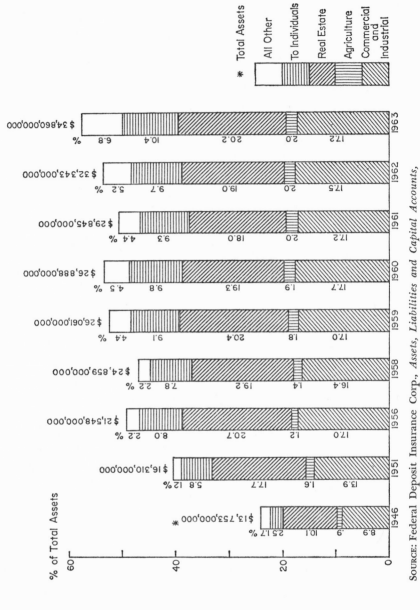

FIGURE VII

Loan Categories as a Percent of Total Assets:
All California Insured Commercial Banks

Total Assets *

All Other

To Individuals

Real Estate

Agriculture

Commercial
and
Industrial

% of Total Assets

$34,860,000,000
% 8.8 6.8 10.4 20.2 2.0 17.2 1963

$32,343,000,000
% 5.2 5.7 9.7 19.0 2.0 17.5 1962

$29,845,000,000
% 4.4 9.3 9.3 18.0 2.0 17.2 1961

$26,888,000,000
% 4.5 9.8 19.3 1.9 17.7 1960

$26,061,000,000
% 4.4 9.1 20.4 1.8 17.0 1959

$24,859,000,000
% 2.2 7.8 19.2 1.4 16.4 1958

$21,548,000,000
% 2.2 8.0 20.7 1.2 17.0 1956

$16,310,000,000
% 12 5.8 17.7 1.6 13.9 1951

$13,753,000,000 *
% 1.7 2.5 10.1 .9 8.9 1946

60

40

20

0

Source: Federal Deposit Insurance Corp., *Assets, Liabilities and Capital Accounts,*

Analysis of Figure VII, all California banks, demonstrates that real estate loans presently are the largest classification, followed closely by loans to commerce and industry, with loans to individuals comprising about 10 percent of total assets or a little more than one-half the dollar value of real estate and of business loans. During the period 1946–1951, the proportion of assets allocated to real estate loans not only was larger than that for commercial and industrial purposes, but increased at a more rapid rate. In the 1951–1956 period, the proportion of assets allocated to the three most important categories continued to increase at roughly the same rates. Accordingly, by 1956 real estate loans commanded over 20 percent of total assets, with commercial and industrial loans accounting for 17 percent and loans to individuals some 8 percent of bank assets. Since 1956, however, total assets have increased at about the same rate as real estate loans. Consequently, by 1963 the latter still represented about 20 percent of total assets, whereas continued commercial and industrial lending increased to 17 percent and loans to individuals reached 10 percent of total assets.

Therefore, it can be concluded that the transition to loans and discounts after 1946 is reflected in the increasing demands of real estate, commercial and industrial, and individual credit requirements. Real estate loans have not increased relatively since 1956, but the increasing needs of commerce and industry and of individuals have been accommodated.

The category of loans called agricultural may be misleading. In an economy where agriculture is as important as it is in California (about 7 percent of gross product in 1957 and 5.7 percent of total civilian employment), a substantially greater emphasis on loans in this category could be expected. The $120 million in this classification increased to $635 million by the end of 1962, with a predominance apparently in the larger banks. A problem arises out of the use of December data which may eliminate many seasonal loans to agriculture. In addition, it is quite certain that much agricultural lending appears under business lending to California Parking, DiGiorgio, Kern County Land, and so on, who in turn finance many growers and processors. Accordingly, the accuracy of the segregation of agricultural loans is open to doubt and the aggregate figures may be grossly understated.

The final category, all other loans, includes a polyglot of uses and recipients, such as loans to commercial and foreign banks, to brokers and security dealers, as well as loans for the purpose of purchase and carrying of securities and for meeting bank overdrafts. The increasing importance of this category, 4.5 percent of assets in 1960–1962, suggests

220 FREDERIC P. MORRISSEY

greater interest by the banks in accommodating other segments of the capital market, although the increase in 1958 represents a reclassification of loans by regulatory agencies.

(1) *Variations in loan patterns among different bank classifications.*— The examination of the subgroups of California banks—the eight largest member, national, state member, and state nonmember—suggests some striking differences in the allocation of assets among various loan components. Starting with the similarities, Figure VIIa for the eight largest, and Figure VIII for national banks in California, have the same general pattern of asset distribution among the various types of loans as is seen for all California banks. Yet, historically, a greater proportion of assets appears in commercial and industrial loans for both the largest eight and the national banks than for all California banks.

Figure IX, detailing loans to asset composition for state member banks, follows the same general pattern. Here, however, commercial and industrial loans have constituted a higher percentage of total assets (1 to 2 percentage points) and real estate loans were less significant (1 to 3 percentage points) when compared with all California banks. In fact, real estate loans accounted for a smaller percentage of assets than did commercial and industrial loans—the only category of banks with this distinction. As with national banks, in 1961 and 1962 these two major differences from the industry as a whole were virtually eliminated. Also, note the major increase in assets devoted to the category all other loans—a reclassification which would tend to reduce loans in the commercial and industrial classification.

Finally, as indicated in Figure X for state nonmember banks, a group of banks which has not experienced the same growth rates in assets as the others, major variations from the industry pattern occur. Throughout the period, state nonmember banks have been much more interested in real estate loans—in fact, these reached 30 percent of total assets in 1951 and 1956, but have subsequently declined to 22 percent of total assets, a ratio more akin to that of the banking industry as a whole. Again, loans to commerce and industry were much lower than those of the rest of the industry (lower by 2.5 percent of total assets) in 1946 and 1951, but since that time a steady increase in this category has raised the proportion to 15 percent, a level still below that of the industry as a whole. Finally, the pattern for this group of banks agrees closely with that for the all-bank pattern with respect to agricultural loans and the all other loan category.

FIGURE VIIa

Loan Categories as a Percent of Total Assets: Eight Largest Member Banks

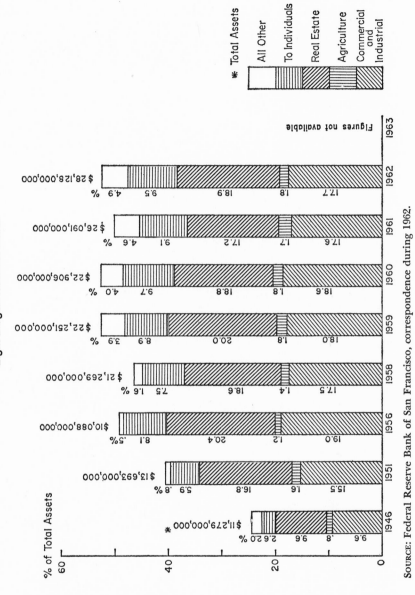

SOURCE: Federal Reserve Bank of San Francisco, correspondence during 1962.

FIGURE VIII
Loan Categories as a Percent of Total Assets:
California National Banks

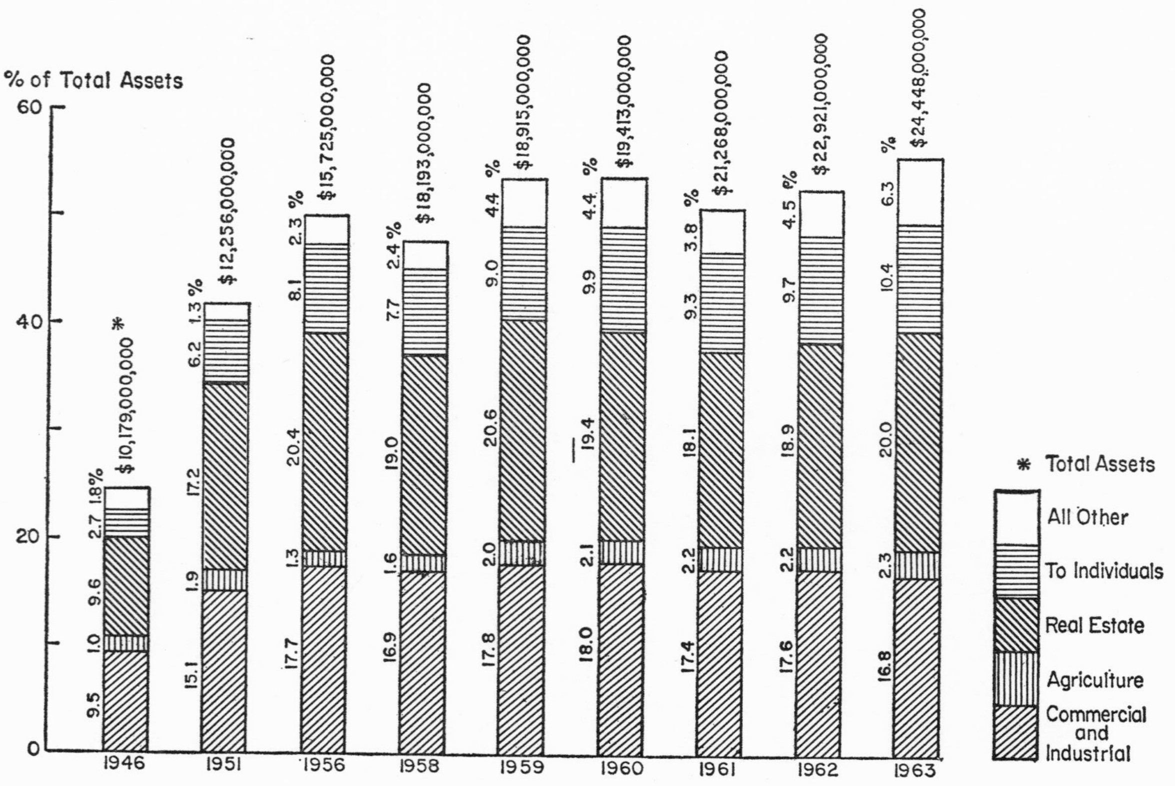

* Total Assets
All Other
To Individuals
Real Estate
Agriculture
Commercial and Industrial

SOURCE: Federal Deposit Insurance Corp., *Assets, Liabilities and Capital Accounts*, 1946, 1951, 1956, and 1958–1963.

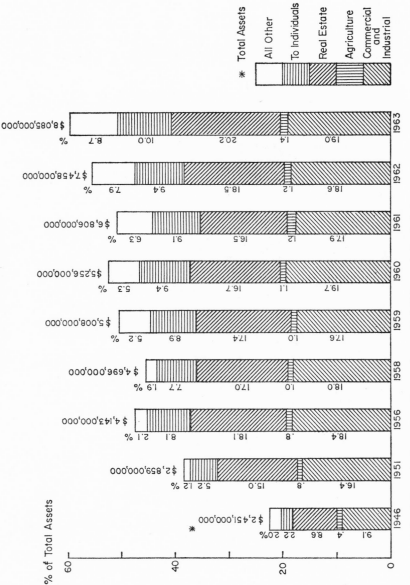

Loan Categories as a Percent of Total Assets: California State Member Banks

SOURCE: *Federal Deposit Insurance Corp., Assets, Liabilities and Capital Accounts,* 1946, 1951, 1956, and 1958–1963.

FIGURE X

Loan Categories as a Percent of Total Assets: State Nonmember California Banks

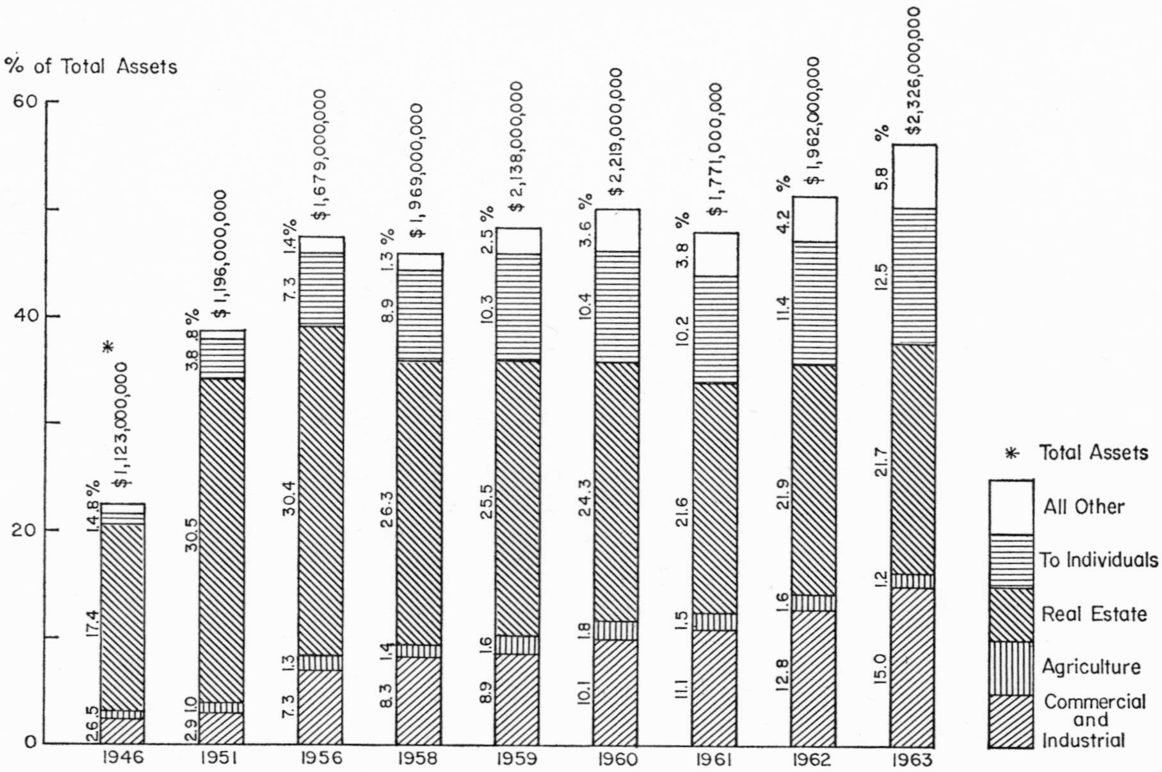

% of Total Assets

* Total Assets
All Other
To Individuals
Real Estate
Agriculture
Commercial and Industrial

$2,326,000,000
1963
5.8 % 12.5 21.7 1.2 15.0

$1,962,000,000
1962
4.2 % 11.4 21.9 1.6 12.8

$1,771,000,000
1961
3.8 % 10.2 21.6 1.5 11.1

$2,219,000,000
1960
3.6 % 10.4 24.3 1.8 10.1

$2,138,000,000
1959
2.5 % 10.3 25.5 1.6 8.9

$1,969,000,000
1958
1.3 % 8.9 26.3 1.4 8.3

$1,679,000,000
1956
1.4 % 7.3 30.4 1.3 7.3

$1,196,000,000
1951
3.8 % 30.5 2910

$1,123,000,000
1946
1.4 % 17.4 26.5

60
40
20
0

Source: Federal Deposit Insurance Corp. Assets, Liabilities and Capital Accounts

Comparison of Figures VIIa and X gives some indication of the diversity between the loan policies of the largest and the small banks. The predominant role of real estate loans for the small bank group, offset by the lesser asset proportion in commercial and industrial loans, and the rough equivalence of asset proportions devoted to loans to individuals, are the outstanding comparative features of the size comparison.

The major differences and similarities in the loan portfolios of the various classifications of banks can be portrayed in another manner. Figures XI through XV provide a quick summary of the percentage of assets allocated to (1) real estate, (2) commercial and industrial, (3) agricultural, (4) individuals, and (5) "all other" loans, by the bank classifications used above. The major variations, as noted earlier, include (a) the greater importance of real estate loans to state nonmember banks, and the lesser reliance on commercial and industrial loans by the same group; (b) the relative lack of importance of agricultural loans, with the national banks devoting about twice as large a proportion of assets to agricultural loans as the state member banks; (c) the consistent increase and uniform pattern of assets devoted to loans to individuals; and (d) the relative importance of commercial and industrial loans to all groups with the exception of the state nonmember banks.

In summary, analysis of the loan patterns in different bank categories shows that the national banks in California compare very closely with the industry as a whole, with somewhat greater accommodation to commercial and industrial loans. State member banks also have emphasized commercial and industrial loans and have devoted less of their resources to real estate loans. The nonmember state banks have shown a distinct preference for real estate loans until 1956, and since have more nearly followed the industry pattern. Throughout the subclassifications, lending to individuals and to commerce and industry has tended to increase absolutely and relatively to total assets. It may be concluded that the banking industry has responded to changes in the loan requirements in California and has devoted relatively higher proportions of their assets to loans than is reported for commercial banks throughout the United States, New York State, or Illinois (see Table 3).

(2) *Loans to commercial and industrial borrowers.*—It is apparent from Figure VII that the commercial and industrial loans of California banks have grown very rapidly and constitute a proportion of assets exceeded only slightly by real estate loans. This growth reflects the business development in California and the ability of California banks to convert other assets, especially United States government

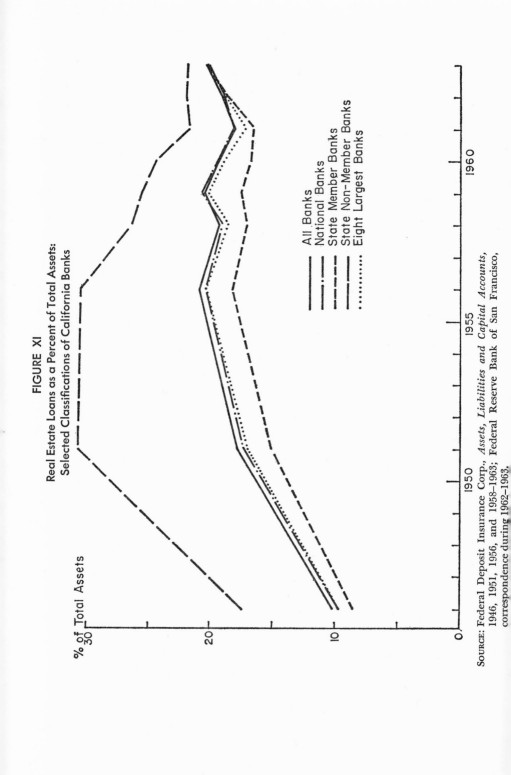

FIGURE XI

Real Estate Loans as a Percent of Total Assets:
Selected Classifications of California Banks

All Banks
National Banks
State Member Banks
State Non-Member Banks
Eight Largest Banks

% of Total Assets

SOURCE: Federal Deposit Insurance Corp., *Assets, Liabilities and Capital Accounts*, 1946, 1951, 1956, and 1958–1963; Federal Reserve Bank of San Francisco, correspondence during 1962–1963.

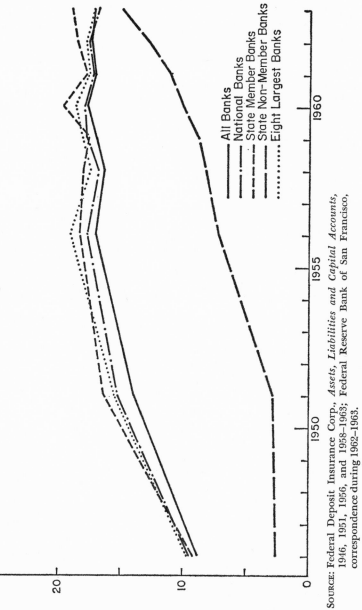

FIGURE XII

Commercial and Industrial Loans as a Percent of Total Assets:
Selected Classifications of California Banks

% of Total Assets

— All Banks
—·— National Banks
—·· State Member Banks
— — State Non-Member Banks
········ Eight Largest Banks

20

10

0

1950   1955   1960

SOURCE: Federal Deposit Insurance Corp., *Assets, Liabilities and Capital Accounts,*
1946, 1951, 1956, and 1958–1963; Federal Reserve Bank of San Francisco,
correspondence during 1962–1963.

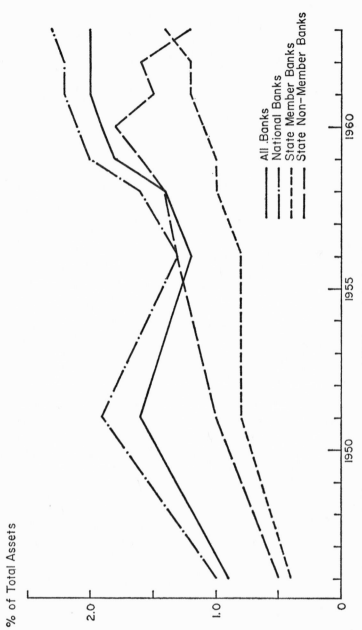

FIGURE XIII

Agricultural Loans as a Percent of Total Assets:
Selected Classifications of California Banks

% of Total Assets

2.0

1.0

0

1950   1955   1960

——— All Banks
—·—·— National Banks
———— State Member Banks
———— State Non–Member Banks

SOURCE: Federal Deposit Insurance Corp., *Assets, Liabilities and Capital Accounts,*
1946, 1951, 1956, and 1958–1963.

Selected Classifications of California Banks

% of Total Assets

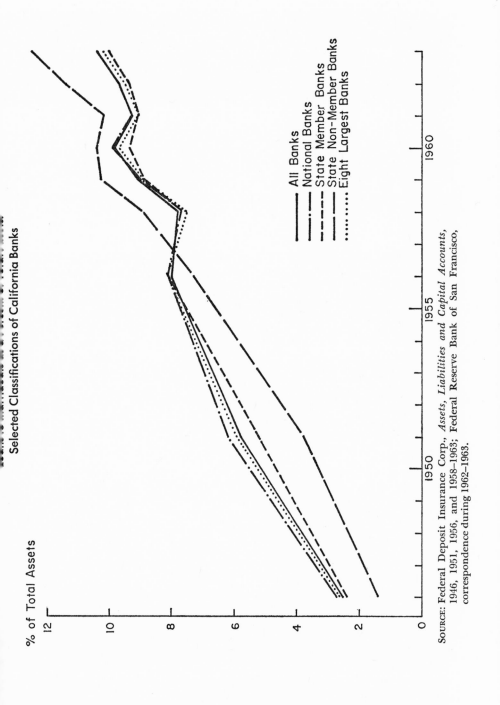

All Banks
National Banks
State Member Banks
State Non-Member Banks
Eight Largest Banks

1950   1955   1960

SOURCE: Federal Deposit Insurance Corp., *Assets, Liabilities and Capital Accounts,* 1946, 1951, 1956, and 1958–1963; Federal Reserve Bank of San Francisco, correspondence during 1962–1963.

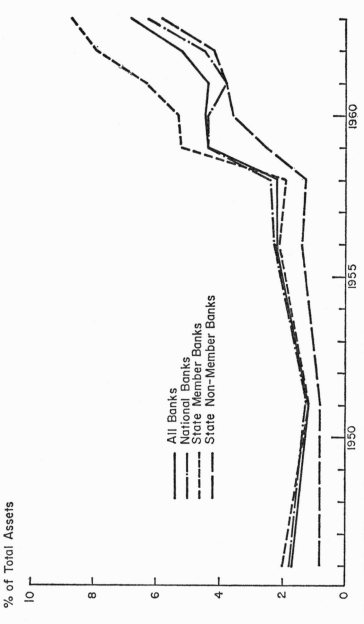

FIGURE XV

All Other Loans as a Percent of Total Assets:
Selected Classifications of California Banks

% of Total Assets

All Banks
National Banks
State Member Banks
State Non-Member Banks

SOURCE: Federal Deposit Insurance Corp., *Assets, Liabilities and Capital Accounts,*
1946, 1951, 1956, and 1958–1963.

securities, into this type of loan. The positive influences of bank size,[3] the extent of branching, and the high proportion of time deposits, are additional factors which contribute somewhat greater stability of assets and access to borrowers. On the other hand, the uniformly high loan/ deposit ratios of the various categories of California banks (Table 2) cast some doubt on the role of sheer size in furthering a proclivity to greater commercial and industrial lending.

It is surprising that so little information is available on the loan policies of banks—not only for California, but for the nation as a whole. Most of the collected data concern the cyclical availability of credit in the aggregate, and little attention seems to have been paid to bank functions in the operating level. Even the most recent survey of credit supply conditions for business and industry, completed in 1957, does not treat California discretely, but refers to the Twelfth Federal Reserve District of which California is the largest portion. The 1957 survey reported in the *Federal Reserve Bulletin,* April, 1959, was a sequel to similar studies in 1946 and 1955. These surveys, together with analysis of data for nineteen leading cities on short-term business loans for the United States, including the Twelfth District, provide some basis for comment on lending policies of California banks.[4]

Analysis of these data indicates: (1) California banks tend to loan to intermediate-size firms, i.e. that large group of borrowers with assets between $50,000 and $25 million; (2) both in 1955 and 1957 western banks, on the average, dealt with smaller-sized borrowers than the large eastern banks; (3) absolute loan size was not small because over half of all business loans were in excess of $500,000. The relatively smaller-size loan is attributed to the smaller size of domestic firms in California, whereas the larger domestic firms and the parent companies of western branches tend to have greater access to the eastern financial markets. Moreover, it appears that the large western banks lend more than large eastern banks to small firms. This is evidenced by the fact that the percentage increases in loans to all sizes of borrowers for the western banks from 1955 to 1957 compared very favorably with that of the rest of the nation, whereas large eastern banks increased their loans principally to large firms.

---

[3] See Irving Schweiger and John McGee, "Chicago Banking," *Journal of Business,* July 1961.

[4] Loan survey for 19 leading cities in the United States for the first 15 days of each quarter. Business loans made by 24 bank offices in five leading cities of the 12th District for the first 15 days of each quarter, 1959–1963.

The loan surveys of the five major cities of the Twelfth District suggest that 80 to 85 percent of loans made in the period 1959 to 1963 were under a line-of-credit arrangement. About 40 percent of these line-of-credit loans had a maturity of three months and one-fourth were repayable on demand. Loans maturing in one and one half years or more made up about 6 percent of the total dollar amount in September 1959, and September 1962, but much less at other times. Such maturities (one and one half years and more) accounted for about 2 percent of the total number of line-of-credit loans in the 1959 to 1963 surveys.

Average interest rates for all line-of-credit loans appeared low, ranging from 4.75 percent in March 1959, to 5.56 percent in March 1960, with an approximate average of 5.3 percent for all periods.

Loans made under arrangements other than a line of credit, about 15 percent of the total, carried the same general maturity pattern— demand and three months maturities most popular. Approximately 2 percent exceeded one and one half years. These loans, however, generally carried a higher interest rate, about .2 to .5 percentage points, particularly when maturity was less than one year.

The term loan (maturity greater than one year) tends to be significant among California banks. Borrowers under these agreements are in industries with traditionally heavy fixed-capital requirements—metals, petroleum, coal, chemical, rubber, and public utilities. In 1957 banks with deposits of $1 billion or more held more than half the dollar volume of term loans outstanding in the United States, with the Twelfth District banks holding 13.8 percent of the amount of term loans outstanding and 18.6 percent of the total number. This concentration increased substantially during the 1955 to 1957 period.

Little comment is necessary on the observation that the surveys show that interest costs tend to have an inverse relationship to size of loan, and that interest costs have risen for all borrowers during the postwar period. However, whereas small borrowers have had to pay more for their loans, the increase appears relatively smaller than for the largest borrowers. The higher interest cost for small firms reflects risk differentials, collateral supervision, and greater credit investigation expense per dollar of loan. On the other hand, that interest rates charged the small borrower have not increased proportionately to those charged the large borrower suggests that basic interest cost is only one factor in the cost of a loan and that costs of supervision, investigation, and so on may have been relatively fixed in the postwar period.

There is also some evidence in the surveys that interest rates have a degree of flexibility from one quarter to the next, but that western borrowers experience more rigidity in this respect than eastern borrowers. Also observable is the substantial variability in interest charged in the same size loan category at any given time, and again this variability is more pronounced for the western lenders.[5] For example, under the loan classification $200,000 and over, for the five cities in the Twelfth District the single interest rate category where the largest percentage of loans are made was 4 percent and 4.5 percent in the first and second

TABLE 4

PERCENTAGE OF LOANS BY SIZE

Size of loan	United States			Twelfth District		
	March 1959	March 1960	Average thereafter	March 1959	March 1960	Average thereafter
5½ percent and above						
$10,000–99,999..........	34	81	61	53	92	82
$100,000–999,999..........	21	59[a]	40	36	79	62
6 percent and above						
$10,000–99,999..........	21	44	37[b]	29	67	60[b]
$100,000–999,999..........	10	26[c]	22[b]	17	46[d]	37[b]

[a] Peak here was in December 1959 at 61 percent.
[b] Approximate.
[c] Peak here was in December 1959 at 29 percent.
[d] Peak here was in December 1959 at 47 percent.
SOURCE: Federal Reserve Bank of San Francisco, communications during 1962.

quarters of 1959, respectively, and 5 percent for the remainder of 1959 and the first half of 1960. For the subsequent periods the most prevalent rate is 4.5 percent. However, for any of the above periods the percentage of loans made at any one interest rate is never larger than 42 percent (compared to 66 percent for the nineteen cities) and in most cases the percentage loaned out at 6 percent is nearly as high. Thus, there seems to be greater variability in interest rates charged western borrowers in the same size loan category than for all borrowers.

Furthermore, interest costs are higher at western banks for almost any category of loans than for the nation as a whole. This relationship can be seen by comparing at various times the percentage of loans by size category outstanding at 5.5 percent and up in the Twelfth District and at 6 percent and up in the country as a whole (Table 4).

---

[5] Such differentials in interest rates would be expected in view of the lack of homogeneity of risk, collateral, bargaining power of borrower, etc.

The higher interest rates charged by western banks might be attributed to differences in risk, collateral, and the like at any given time. Yet the differential pattern seems to have existed throughout the postwar period. The surveys suggest that on large loans of $200,000 and more, western banks charge .25 to .5 percent more than do eastern banks, and this differential continues even today. Of course, it may be that such a premium must be paid for loans in a capital importing region such as California, but this persisting differential connotes an imperfection in the monetary mechanism in the country, or that western firms are continually subject to greater risks. There clearly is no available evidence of the latter and, on an a priori basis, a conclusion of greater risks in a rapidly growing area seems unlikely. In a truly competitive money market, very small differentials in interest rates should be expected to cause funds to flow to the high-rate area and tend to eliminate the differential.

It seems clear, however, that interest costs are higher to western borrowers at western banks, and that this situation continues to persist except, perhaps, in periods of monetary restraint when eastern rates approximate western rates. Certainly there is no evidence that western banks have attempted to restrict loans; in fact, the high loan/deposit ratios (Table 2) suggest the opposite.

This interest rate differential may make little difference to California corporations in their decision to invest in additional inventory, plant, and so forth. Profit expectations of corporations in a growing region such as California may be higher than those elsewhere. Hence, as long as financial accommodation is available, variations in the cost may be of little significance. It may be argued that since interest is a deductible expense for tax purposes, the federal government pays half the cost. Thus, insofar as the higher interest rates do attract more capital to a region and so provide a greater degree of loan accommodation, the continued differential may be more of a blessing than a handicap to western borrowers.

The other relevant question for the future is whether the interest rate differential is likely to persist. If a greater approximation to a perfect monetary mechanism is anticipated, the differential should tend to be eliminated or reduced. Williams' projected slowdown in the rate of growth of California's economy, and Towey's discussion of technical changes improving communications and liquidity suggest the possibility of a narrowing of the differential in the future.

In any forecast of business lending it would be useful to know which industries rely most heavily on bank credit and then to determine, as

Williams attempts to do, whether these industries will expand more rapidly or more slowly until 1975. In this way some indication of the expansion or contraction of business lending could be achieved. Unfortunately, information on lending by industry classification is virtually nonexistent. The Federal Reserve Bank of San Francisco collects and publishes a statement, by general industry classification, of the weekly changes in loans reported by banks in the Twelfth District. Table 5 provides a summary of these data on a yearly basis from December 26, 1951 to July 1, 1959, when loans to nonbank financial institutions were reclassified. Table 5a provides the same data with revised industrial reclassifications from July 1959, to September 27, 1961. Again, beginning September 27, 1961, further revisions took place in the industrial classifications, particularly to provide data (Table 5b) on durable and nondurable industry classifications. Therefore, there is limited continuous data for loans to various industries. Moreover, the change in reported loans is observed to be a small proportion of total loans and discounts outstanding in the Twelfth District. Accordingly, some doubt about how representative the data are must be expressed. Further limitations on the usefulness of these data arise out of the initial and concluding dates used in the tables. For example, 1951 would reflect activity influenced by the Korean conflict, and July 1, 1959 might introduce seasonal factors (as would August 27, 1963) not accounted for in the initial December date. Accordingly, the value of these data is somewhat restricted for this analysis.

With these caveats it might be inferred from Table 5 that major increases have occurred in the use of bank credit by the industrial classifications of metal and metal products, petroleum and chemical, and, to a lesser extent, by textiles, apparel, and leather. Major decreases were recorded by the food, liquor, and tobacco manufacturing industries, and by commodity dealers. In trade and related areas, the public utilities, construction, and wholesale and retail groups all were responsible for increases of major magnitudes. Generally speaking, those industries responsible for the major increases in bank lending are predicted to be those to increase their proportion of employment in California in 1976 (see Williams, Table 5). Similarly, comparisons with the distribution of gross product by major industry in 1976 (Williams, Table 8) suggest that the segments which have used increasing amounts of bank credit will make the major contribution to California's output in 1976. For example, manufacturing, construction, and the services will expand their contribution; public utilities will hold constant; whereas agriculture and mining, it is predicted, will decline relatively.

TABLE 5
COMMERCIAL AND INDUSTRIAL LOANS: CHANGES IN LOANS BY INDUSTRY
WEEKLY REPORTING MEMBER BANKS OF THE TWELFTH FEDERAL RESERVE DISTRICT
(millions of dollars)

Borrower	Dec. 26 '51 to Dec. 26 '52	Dec. 26 '52 to Dec. 30 '53	Dec. 30 '53 to Dec. 29 '54	Dec. 29 '54 to Dec. 28 '55	Dec. 28 '55 to Dec. 26 '56	Dec. 26 '56 to Dec. 25 '57	Dec. 25 '57 to Dec. 31 '58	Dec. 31 '58 to July 1 '59	Net change Dec. 26 '51 to July 1 '59
Manufacturing and mining									
Food, liquor and tobacco	−150.7	−9.6	−35.4	−11.6	101.0	11.4	−30.4	−101.2	−226.5
Lumber and forest products	−9.9	−13.2	−1.6	33.0	57.7	−18.6	−21.6	−7.3	18.5
Textiles, apparel and leather	−3.9	.1	−3.6	9.5	−2.3	−2.7	−2.1	−7.7	2.7
Metal and metal products (including machinery and trans. equip.)	141.8	31.7	−82.0	18.5	106.4	35.9	−4.0	72.9	329.2
Petroleum, coal, chemical and rubber	35.3	−14.8	−5.8	30.8	45.6	22.3	−4.6	−10.5	109.9
Other manufacturing and mining	−54.3	−7.3	−10.8	11.5	28.5	29.5	−18.4	16.9	10.2
Trade									
Wholesale	−22.1	−9.8	−3.6	42.1	16.1	−6.0	−5.2	39.0	50.5
Retail	−5.5	−12.3	−35.7	77.7	37.6	22.7	−70.8	41.5	79.8
Commodity dealers	−29.6	−39.5	−20.5	.2	42.0	−17.9	−14.4	−55.7	−135.4
Sales finance companies	34.7	−37.0	7.9	113.9	−50.6	48.7	9.5	29.4	137.5
Public utilities (including transportation)	−39.6	−46.4	8.9	−37.5	43.3	54.2	−22.7	51.9	104.9
Construction	−34.9	−4.6	1.4	51.4	18.8	−6.7	6.5	14.3	55.4
All other types of business	−6.0	−10.7	57.8	59.1	91.5	35.7	105.2	71.1	403.7
Classified changes[a]	−144.7	−32.2	−111.4	398.6	535.6	208.5	−84.0	170.0	940.4
Unclassified changes[b]	297.0	45.2	141.4	205.4	206.4	87.5	70.0	214.0	1,266.9
Net change in commercial and industrial loans	152.3	13.0	30.0	604.0	742.0	296.0	−14.0	384.0	2,207.3
Total loans and discounts of member banks in 12th District[c]		9,220	9,418	11,124	12,613	13,178	13,812	16,537	
Net change in industrial and commercial loans as a percent of total loans[d]		0.14	0.32	5.43	5.88	2.25	0.10	2.32	

a Net change of the above categories.
b Net change in the above areas for banks not reporting or changes in other categories not listed above.
c Net change in 12th District.
d As of last Wednesday in December.

TABLE 5a

COMMERCIAL AND INDUSTRIAL LOANS: CHANGES IN LOANS BY INDUSTRY
WEEKLY REPORTING MEMBER BANKS OF THE TWELFTH FEDERAL RESERVE DISTRICT
(millions of dollars)

Borrower	July 1 '59 to Dec. 30 '59	Dec. 30 '59 to Dec. 30 '60	Dec. 30 '60 to Sept. 27 '61	Net change July 1 '59 to Sept. 27 '61
Manufacturing and Mining				
Food, liquor and tobacco......	131.9	− 6.2	− 36.4	89.3
Lumber and forest products....	34.4	2.0	− .2	36.2
Textiles, apparel and leather...	1.9	4.5	13.5	19.9
Metal and metal products (including machinery and transportation equip.)...........	− 33.9	20.9	7.1	− 5.9
Petroleum, coal, chemicals and rubber....................	12.7	− 8.9	− 30.6	− 26.8
Other manufacturing and mining	− 27.1	9.3	26.4	8.6
Trade				
Wholesale....................	23.4	24.6	− 18.2	29.8
Retail......................	− 12.7	24.5	− 33.4	− 21.6
Commodity dealers.............	97.6	− 32.7	− 55.1	9.8
Public utilities (including transportation)....................	− 18.2	52.2	38.7	− 4.7
Construction.................	25.7	15.4	− 4.8	36.3
All other types of business.......	− 87.9	90.4	66.5	69.0
Classified changes[a]...........	147.8	196.0	−103.9	239.9
Unclassified changes[b].........	306.2	80.0	91.9	478.1
Net changes in commercial and industrial loans...............	454.0	276.0	− 12.0	718.0
Loans and discounts of member banks in 12th District[c]........	16,537	17,139	18,499	
Net change in commercial and industrial loans as a percent of total loans[d]..................	2.74	1.61	0.06	

a Net change of the above categories.
b Net change in the above areas for banks not reporting or changes in other categories not listed above.
c As of year end of the last date on the column heading and not adjusted for seasonal variation.
d As of last Wednesday in December.
NOTE: At the end of the week of July 1, 1959, loans to finance companies, mortgage loan companies, and other nonbank financial institutions were removed from commercial and industrial loans to be reported separately. Also loans to sales finance companies and those to other nonbank financial institutions from "all other" types of business; other reclassifications occurred and consequently these data are not comparable to past years.
SOURCE: Federal Reserve Bank of San Francisco, *Monthly Review*, 12th Federal Reserve District, April-May, 1963.

TABLE 5b

COMMERCIAL AND INDUSTRIAL LOANS: CHANGES IN LOANS BY INDUSTRY
WEEKLY REPORTING MEMBER BANKS OF THE TWELFTH FEDERAL RESERVE DISTRICT
(millions of dollars)

Borrower	Sept. 27 '61 to Dec. 27 '61	Dec. 27 '61 to Dec. 26 '62	Dec. 26 '62 to Aug. 28 '63	Net change Sept. 27 '61 to Aug. 28 '63
Durable goods—manufacturing (total)................	−11.7	20.6	−46.6	−37.7
Primary metals..............	− 5.7	− 1.6	8.0	.7
Machinery..................	2.1	1.8	5.0	8.9
Transportation equipment.....	8.7	32.5	−56.5	−15.3
Other fabricated metal products	−12.9	−13.1	− 8.3	−34.3
Other durable goods..........	− 3.9	1.0	5.2	2.3
Nondurable goods, mfg. (total)..	57.5	11.0	−75.0	− 6.5
Food, liquor and tobacco......	42.7	24.3	−98.5	−31.5
Textiles, apparel and leather...	− 7.9	4.6	18.6	15.3
Petroleum..................	17.5	−16.6	3.4	4.3
Chemicals and rubber.........	7.3	−13.2	3.0	− 2.9
Other nondurables............	− 2.1	11.9	− 1.5	8.3
Mining.......................	22.3	24.7	3.0	50.0
Trade Commodity dealers...........	30.0	18.0	−37.5	10.5
Other wholesale..............	12.6	3.4	15.0	31.0
Retail......................	16.4	4.9	23.7	45.0
Transportation, communication and other public utilities	61.0	1.3	6.4	68.7
Construction...................	.7	32.0	14.5	47.2
All other types (mainly services).	70.5	50.5	58.8	179.8
Classified changes[a]...........	259.3	166.4	−37.7	388.0
Unclassified changes[b].........	76.7	301.6	118.7	497.0
Net changes in commercial and industrial loans..............	336.0	468.0	81.0	885.0
Total loans and discounts of member banks in 12th District[c]....	18,499	21,102[d]		
Change in commercial and industrial loans as a percent of total loans[d]......................	1.82	2.22		

See notes page 239

If the indicated trends in these far from complete data are reliable, a tentative conclusion could be reached that industrial and commercial lending might be maintained. Certainly it would be too optimistic to expect increases comparable to those of 1946 to 1956 (see Figure VII), but the maintenance of current proportions of assets in this loan category (almost 16 percent—Figure VII) would be not unduly optimistic. There are, however, some good reasons for believing that the early 1950's explosive increase of loans will not recur. First, a slightly slower growth rate is expected in California's economy. Second, and equally important, the somewhat disappointing performance of business loans in the current business recovery is indicative of a lack of demand. There is no agreement on the cause of this lack of demand, but it may be attributed to the development of the so-called "second banking system" —large corporations offering direct competition in performing one of the major functions of commercial banks.

Large national manufacturing corporations have been experiencing heavy cash flows, augmented in the past few years by liberalized depreciation policies which permit deferral (or forgiveness) of taxes. In addition, the improved corporate earnings have permitted larger retention of earnings. Coupled with these internal sources, many nonfinancial corporations with very strong credit positions have been able to tap open market sources of funds that are developing through direct placement of term loans, debentures, and commercial paper. Thus, through these devices, many business units appear able to circumvent bank borrowing and, in fact, even may be eliminating or reducing the need of other potential borrowers by more generous trade credit to smaller companies. The "second banking system" would appear then to be a direct competitive threat to the most profitable of commercial bank operations.

It is difficult to determine the breadth and pervasiveness of this type of bank circumvention—and equally difficult to forecast the banking system's response. It is felt by many that the commercial banks will have to develop a new flexibility and dynamism to counter these developments successfully. In view of these competitive factors, the increase in business loans will tend to parallel the general economic growth of the region. The $5 billion investment in commercial and industrial loans

a Net change of the above categories.
b Net change in the above areas for banks not reporting or changes in other categories not listed above.
c As of year end of the last date on the column heading and not adjusted for seasonal variation.
d As of last Wednesday in December.
NOTE: Beginning with the date September 27, 1961, the industry classifications have been revised to give a breakdown for manufacturing industries by durable and nondurable goods and to furnish added detail to sub-classifications. Due to rather extensive reclassifications of loans reported in other industry categories as well, the outstandings on which week-to-week changes are computed are not comparable with those that served as a basis for earlier changes.
SOURCE: Federal Reserve Bank of San Francisco, *Monthly Review*, 12th Federal Reserve District, April-May, 1963.

TABLE 6

Selected Loan Categories as a Percent of Total Assets:
California Member Banks With Total Average Deposits of $275 Million

	1946	1951	1956	1958	1959	1960	1961	1962	1963
Real estate loans—total	9.6	16.8	20.4	18.6	20.0	18.8	17.7	18.9	20.1
Other loans to farmers	.8	1.6	1.2	1.4	1.8	1.8	1.7	1.8	1.9
Commercial and industrial	9.6	15.5	19.0	17.5	18.0	18.6	17.6	17.7	17.2
Loans to individuals—total	2.6	5.9	8.1	7.5	8.9	9.7	9.1	9.5	10.2
Auto installment	.6	2.4	4.0	3.6	3.9	4.0	3.8	4.1	N.A
Other retail consumer goods—installment	.5	1.0	.8	.6	.9	.9	.9	.8	N.A
Repair and modernization—installment	.3	.8	.8	.7	.8	.8	.7	.8	N.A
Other installment	.6	.8	1.0	1.1	1.4	1.6	1.4	1.4	N.A
Single payment	.7	.8	1.5	1.5	1.8	2.3	2.3	2.4	N.A
Total loans as a percent of total assets	24.6	40.6	49.2	46.6	52.6	52.9	50.2	52.8	49.5
Total assets (billions of dollars)	11	14	18	21	22	23	26	28	30

Figures may not add due to rounding.
Source: Federal Reserve Bank of San Francisco, communications during 1962.

of California banks, therefore, can be expected to increase to approximately $10 billion by 1975 if bank assets expand at a 5 percent per year rate as predicted.

(3) *Loans to individuals.*—Slight differences exist among the various categories of California banks in the proportion of total assets invested in loans to individuals (Figure XIV). A fairly continuous growth of loans to individuals appears—increasing from 2 to 10 percent of total assets in 1963. As might be expected, installment loans constitute almost three-fourths of these, and single-payment loans make up the remainder (Table 6). The auto installment loan, representing 4 percent of total bank assets, is the largest single component. Installment loans for retail consumer goods, and for home repair and modernization, constitute 8 percent each, with other installment loans making up the balance. The continued public interest in consumers' durable goods, home modernization, and other purchases financed through installment loans, point to substantial growth in this category. The competition of financial subsidiaries, personal finance companies, and other lending agencies may be formidable, but banking institutions appear to have a priority claim on quality loans to individuals. On balance, continued growth in this area of lending by the commercial banking industry should occur.

b. The pattern of investment in securities

It was noted that California banks were devoting a smaller percentage of their assets to obligations of the United States government and to other securities (see Figure V). Some details of these security holdings are provided in Table 7. The California banks have reduced the proportion of their assets in securities from 55 percent, as of December 31, 1946, to approximately 28 percent by 1959, and it has remained at roughly this proportion through 1962. In 1963 the proportion declined to about 26 percent. The major drop occurred between 1946 and 1951 and since then has tapered off. As the proportion of assets invested in securities has declined, the proportion of United States governments has decreased fairly consistently. Obligations of the federal government in 1946 equalled 90 percent of total securities held, with long-term maturities predominating. By 1963 the proportion of United States governments declined to 62.5 percent, and the long-term maturities (5 years and more) comprised 15 percent of total securities.

Another important aspect of change in security holdings is the increasing quantity of state and local government securities held by the banks. There has been a continuous increase in the proportion of state

TABLE 7

SELECTED CATEGORIES AS A PERCENT OF TOTAL SECURITIES: CALIFORNIA OPERATING INSURED COMMERCIAL BANKS

	December 31, 1946				December 31, 1951			
	All banks	National	State members	State non-members	All banks	National	State members	State non-members
Obligations of the U. S. Government	89.8	89.3	94.4	85.1	81.0	80.0	87.1	77.0
Treasury bills, certificates of indebtedness and notes	33.2	24.7	39.1	16.8	34.4	34.0	43.1	19.6
Other bonds maturing in 5 yrs. or less	15.2	13.3	24.6	12.2	32.3	34.0	32.5	18.0
Other bonds maturing in 5 to 10 yrs	31.4	33.8	27.5	20.0	5.5	4.6	8.5	6.9
Other bonds maturing in over 10 yrs	9.8	8.2	3.0	34.6	7.2	8.0	1.7	28.2
Other securities	10.2	10.7	5.6	14.9	18.9	20.0	12.9	23.2
Obligations of states and political subdivisions	7.7	8.3	3.0	12.4	12.5	12.7	8.6	18.8
Total securities as a percent of total assets	55.2	54.2	55.2	64.0	39.7	38.7	40.0	48.3

	December 31, 1956				December 31, 1958			
	All banks	National	State members	State non-members	All banks	National	State members	State non-members
Obligations of U. S. Government direct	77.4	76.6	81.7	75.2	76.0	75.3	81.4	70.3
Treasury bills, certificates of indebtedness and notes	21.3	18.8	30.9	21.5	28.4	25.4	39.8	28.8
Other bonds maturing in 5 yrs. or less	29.3	30.0	29.9	22.2	27.8	30.1	23.5	19.5
Other bonds maturing in 5 to 10 yrs	13.8	14.5	12.2	11.7	15.5	15.7	15.9	12.7
Other bonds maturing after 10 yrs	11.4	11.6	7.6	17.7	3.9	3.9	2.0	2.1
Other securities—total	22.5	23.4	18.3	24.8	24.0	24.7	18.6	29.7
Obligations of states and political subdivisions	18.4	19.2	14.0	21.2	19.3	19.4	15.8	25.2
Total securities as a percent of total assets	31.4	30.8	30.3	39.1	34.9	34.1	34.9	41.9

	December 31, 1959				December 31, 1960			
	All banks	National	State members	State non-members	All banks	National	State members	State non-members
Obligations of the U. S. Government direct	73.8	72.8	79.0	70.9	73.9	72.8	79.1	71.0
Treasury bills, certificates of indebtedness and								

...maturing in 5 yrs. or less (row cut off)								
Other bonds maturing in 5 to 10 yrs.	16.4	17.7	12.8	14.8	9.8	8.9	10.0	14.7
Bonds maturing after 10 yrs.	2.2	1.5	3.5	4.2	1.8	1.2	3.1	3.1
Other securities—total	26.2	27.2	21.0	29.1	26.1	27.2	20.6	29.0
Obligations of states and political subdivisions	22.0	22.3	19.0	25.6	22.3	22.6	18.8	26.9
Total securities as a percent of total assets	28.4	28.3	28.6	38.6	28.0	26.9	28.5	36.5

	December 30, 1961				December 28, 1962			
Obligations of U. S. Government	73.8	72.4	79.4	69.9	67.5	65.7	73.9	67.6
Treasury bills, certificates of indebtedness and notes maturing in 1 yr. or less	22.7	22.7	20.1	29.2	17.6	17.2	17.2	22.7
Treasury notes after 1 yr.	20.7	22.0	20.6	9.0	17.7	18.4	15.6	17.0
Other bonds in 5 yrs. or less	21.5	19.6	28.2	19.4	17.8	16.4	25.0	10.6
Other bonds in 5 to 10 yrs.	7.5	7.0	8.2	9.8	13.7	13.0	15.6	15.6
Other bonds after 10 yrs.	1.2	.8	2.0	1.9	.4	.3	.3	1.4
Other securities—total	26.2	27.5	20.5	30.1	32.5	34.3	26.1	32.4
Obligations of states and political subdivisions	22.9	23.6	19.1	27.5	28.1	29.1	24.2	29.3
Total securities as a percent of total assets	29.9	29.5	28.8	38.6	27.9	28.2	24.7	35.0

	December 1963			
Obligations of U. S. Government	62.6	60.4	68.9	65.3
Treasury bills, certificates of indebtedness and notes	28.5	27.0	31.0	36.2
Other bonds maturing in 5 yrs. or less	18.4	17.0	26.2	11.2
Other bonds maturing in 5 to 10 yrs.	14.1	14.7	10.8	16.6
Other bonds maturing in over 10 yrs.	1.2	1.3	.5	1.2
Other securities	37.5	39.6	31.1	34.8
Obligations of states and political subdivisions	32.8	34.4	28.2	30.0
Total securities as a percent of total assets	25.7	26.1	23.1	32.3

SOURCES: F.D.I.C., *Assets and Liabilities of Insured Operating Commercial Banks.* Federal Deposit Insurance Corporation, *Assets, Liabilities, and Capital Accounts of Insured Commercial Banks,* 1946, 1951, 1956, and 1958–1963.

and local bonds held by the California banks—from 7.7 percent in 1946 to 33 percent of total securities by the end of 1962. This category alone reflects an investment of almost three billion dollars—or an increase of a little less than $2.2 billion from 1946 to 1962. The decade 1946–1956 witnessed a twofold increase in these state and local government bonds, and during the subsequent nine years this category more than doubled. The investment aspects of these holdings, of course, reflect the outpouring from California governmental units as well as the tax advantage carried by this type of security.

Several differences in the security investment by the various categories of banks in California deserve brief comment. The state nonmember banks have carried a higher percentage of their assets in securities, starting in 1946 with nearly two-thirds so invested compared with over half for all California banks. In each of the years under study this differential has been maintained, so that in December 1963 the nonmember state banks had 32 percent whereas all California banks had roughly 26 percent of their assets in securities. Also these state nonmember banks invested more heavily in state and local issues, although the differential was virtually eliminated by 1963. The state member banks, however, have consistently held a smaller percentage of total securities in the issues of state and local jurisdictions, and a higher percentage in United States governments—68.8 percent in 1963 compared with 62.5 percent for all California banks. The final comment regarding intergroup variation concerns the substantial volatility in the proportion of assets of the national banks invested in short-term governments. Although the published data do not give a continuous picture of investment in securities with less than one year to maturity, by implication the holdings of Treasury bills, notes, and certificates of indebtedness point to this volatility on the part of the national banks in California. It might be observed also that securities not accounted for in federal, state, and local issues, are consistently less than 5 percent of the total.

As to the future, there seems to be little doubt that the role of United States government securities will continue to be first that of the provision of liquidity, and second that of investment for return with limited risk. The provision of liquidity is a requirement of the banking system. The investment in United States governments for a return will depend on the availability of other investment opportunities with higher profit potential. The projected outpouring of state and local government issues probably will continue to attract California banks in view of the yields and tax provisions accompanying them. If the proportion of total assets represented by state and local issues is continued as at present (10 percent approximately), then California banks could be expected to invest $5.94 billion in these issues—or an approximate 100 percent increase over the present holdings. It is quite possible that the proportion may be higher if opportunities for investment in real estate mortgages and commercial and industrial loans do not materialize as they did in the decade of the fifties.

4. PROJECTIONS—1975

Reporting and interpreting the past is much easier and safer than projecting into the future. This is particularly true since no neat or precise relationship appears among economic indicators in California and particular segments of bank assets. Robbins and Terleckyj[6] reported a close relationship between percentage increases in assets of commercial banks and in personal income by states from 1947 to 1956—a relationship not apparent for California over the 1946 to 1961 period. Personal income in California rose at a 7 percent rate, total bank assets at 5.6 percent. This holds for the five-year periods also: 1946–1951 personal income increased at a 7 percent rate, total bank assets at one-half this rate. Again in 1951–1956, personal income grew at 8 percent per year, total assets at 5.75 percent; and in 1961–1963, 7.1 percent as opposed to 8.1 percent. In the five years 1956–1961, the rate of increase in personal incomes was 6.5 percent against 6.75 percent for total assets. Accordingly, except for this five-year period, there is no close relationship appropriate for a twelve-year projection.

It seems appropriate, however, to conclude that the role of California banks in financing the California economy will continue large. When Williams' Table 1A projections in this volume are considered, suggesting only a very slight decrease in California population growth rates, 3.65 percent (1947–1963) versus 2.91 percent (1963–1975), and in gross product originating, 5.42 percent (1947–1963) versus 5.50 percent (1963–1975), certainly it seems reasonable to expect that total bank assets will continue to expand at a rate only slightly below that of the 5.6 percent for the 1946–1963 period. Thus, if a future annual growth rate of 5 percent is agreed upon, about $63 billion total assets will accrue by 1975. It must be recognized that bank assets are determined in part by the volume of reserves available, and reserves are subject to determination by federal monetary policy. Accordingly, bank assets are not merely a function of regional economic development but are dependent, at least

---

[6] Sidney M. Robbins and Nestor E. Terleckyj, *Money Metropolis* (Cambridge, 1960), p. 171.

in part, upon national economic policy. Yet this approximate doubling of assets reflected by a 5 percent growth rate compares with the growth rate of gross earnings for California commercial banks of about 5.2 percent determined independently by Wendt (this volume).

In a separate study, Bogen and Krooss concluded that time deposits of commercial banks will continue to increase more rapidly than demand deposits and will account for over 60 percent of total commercial bank deposits nationally by 1975.[7] This ratio appears optimistic for California, but accepted as a first estimate, it means approximately $34.0 billion in time deposits in California banks in 1975 and $22.5 billion in demand deposits, assuming total bank assets of $63 billion. These approximations compare with Wendt's conclusions that time deposits will be $31.6 billion and demand deposits $21.8 billion in 1975 if postwar growth rates for each are continued. The Wendt estimates of deposits appear to support total assets of $60 billion for all California banks to compete with other financial intermediaries for the savings of individuals and business. Current holdings of deposits reflect a rough equality—50 percent each for demand and time deposits in California—or $28 billion in each category for 1975, assuming total assets of $63 billion. If commercial banks are free to compete for savings accounts without artificial interest rate ceilings, the achievement in 1975 of $28 to $30 billion of time deposits is not unrealistic. The major assumption in achieving a forecast of bank assets, then, is the continuation of a competitive position for the commercial banks in their bid for savings deposits coupled with an economic growth rate only slightly below recent levels.

What will the asset structure of the California banks' balance sheet look like in 1975, assuming $63 billion of assets? The largest single class of total bank assets, exceeding 50 percent will continue to be loans and discounts. After all, this type of investment is the chief function of the commercial bank and no change in the economy is in sight to alter this function. Loan/deposit ratios approximating 60 percent may continue if time deposits continue to be important to California banks. Accordingly, loans of $32 to $34 billion may be anticipated. Commercial and industrial loans will be the major component, surpassing real estate mortgages as California's industrialization continues and competition forces a retreat by commercial banks from the mortgage market. Hence commercial and industrial loans may reach or exceed $10.8 to $11 billion in 1975 if the competitive threat of the "second banking system" is met by the banks. In addition real estate mortgages will be less signifi-

---

[7] Jules I. Bogen and Herman E. Krooss, *Savings and Other Time Deposits in Commercial Banks—New York* (The Authors, 1962), p. 12.

cant. The extension of credit to individuals will continue to be an important outlet for banks and nothing indicates that the proportion of assets allocated for individual loans will decrease below the present 10 percent level; in fact, the rise of consumer durables in individual budgets suggests greater individual reliance on bank financing. Therefore, at least $6.5 billion of loans to individuals can be anticipated, with the agricultural and other-loans categories utilizing the balance of the $32 to $34 billion of loan assets.

In the absence of revolutionary changes in business and individual demands for liquidity and payment practices, the requirements for cash balances (and their equivalents) will not change drastically. Perhaps cash balances and United States governments should be combined, particularly for the near maturities of the latter. The liquidity requirements may well continue to consume 3 percent of total assets, with continued waning interest in intermediate- and long-term governments. As indicated earlier, the securities of state and local governments will continue in substantial supply and will provide attractive outlets for California bank funds. Bank holdings of state and local obligations may reach $5.5 to $6.0 billion, or more, as the proposed mammoth state and local capital improvements are financed.

In summary, total assets of California banks may reach $63 billion by 1975. Loans will be the largest component—at least 50 percent of the total. In view of the increased role of manufacturing, finance, insurance, and construction in California's gross product (Williams, Table 8), commercial and industrial loans can be expected to become dominant. The areas of relative decline—agriculture and the extractive industries—have not been large users of bank credit. Consequently, it may be anticipated that the commercial bank role will continue to be enlarged through loan accommodations to the expanding areas. Again, the rising importance of loans to individuals probably will continue as households expand their purchase of consumer durables. The one question mark, of course, is if the relative decline in real estate loans will continue and if loan expansion in other areas will offset this possible decline. The projected trends in the California economy, as outlined by Williams, suggest that the trend of recent postwar changes in bank asset allocation should continue if California banks are going to facilitate the economic growth of the West.

The Savings Function and Mortgage Investment by California Banks and Financial Institutions

ALBERT H. SCHAAF

1. INTRODUCTION AND SUMMARY

THE CENTRAL FOCUS of this study is on the role of commercial banks in the savings and mortgage markets of California. It is divided into three main sections. The first examines the operations and changing roles of commercial banks in various types of real estate financing activities during the period 1945–1963. The second seeks to analyze and explain the reasons for the postwar developments and changes that have taken place. In the third section we use these findings to make projections and evaluations of future developments in the state's mortgage and savings markets and the roles that commercial banks may play. We will be concerned with both the future volume of state mortgage credit needs and the manner in which financial resources are allocated to meet these needs.

The main conclusions of the study may be summarized as follows:

1. The position of commercial banks in California's savings and mortgage markets declined substantially from 1945 to 1963. In the early postwar years banks held around 50 percent of the state's institutionally-held mortgage debt, and their time deposits exceeded the savings accounts of savings and loan associations tenfold. By the end of 1963 the bank debt share was about 20 percent and savings and loan accounts were slightly larger than time deposits.

2. The permanent mortgage investment activity of banks fluctuated widely, marked by a shift from a heavy concentration in federally-underwritten residential loans to a concentration in conventional residential and nonresidential mortgages. Fragmentary evidence indicates that banks played only a minor role in the vast importation of mortgage funds into the state.

249

3. Banks remained relatively more active in short-term mortgage financing, especially construction lending, although savings and loan associations greatly increased their construction lending as part of their general expansion. In other real estate financing activities banks supply probably all of the debt financing used by mortgage companies and dominate the home-improvement loan market. In view of these activities as well as the volume of long-term mortgages required to maintain, and increase, banks' portfolios it is well not to overemphasize the decline in the importance of bank credit in California's real estate markets. The decline of commercial bank activity is most pronounced when viewed in terms of relative shares rather than absolute amounts.

4. These developments appear as logical results of several legal and economic factors operative in savings and mortgage markets. Legally, banks cannot offer as liberal terms on conventional mortgages as other lenders, especially savings and loan associations, and yield problems in tight money periods reduce the effectiveness of federally-underwritten loans as a competitive device for banks. Banks also are prevented legally from offering savings deposit rates as high as savings and loan associations while public acceptance of associations as close substitutes for banks as savings depositories is growing. Concurrently, associations are restricted largely to mortgage investment. Insurance companies and mutual savings banks, making particular use of FHA and VA loans, also expanded their activities in California's postwar mortgage markets. Faced with so much competition in the mortgage market and enjoying certain shelters (particularly from savings and loan associations) in their position in various nonmortgage lending areas, it is understandable that commercial banks would increase their relative activity in the lucrative fields of business and consumer lending and regard mortgage investment as more of a residual.

5. We estimate that about $80 billion in mortgage debt will be outstanding in California in 1975, roughly a 100 percent increase over 1963's estimated total of $41 billion. This estimate assumes continuing unchanged relationships between the growth of personal income and mortgage debt. Although over one-third of the postwar mortgage credit needs of the state were met with out-of-state funds, the problems of assuring an ample supply of future mortgage credit do not appear acute. Savings accounts in commercial banks and savings and loan associations have grown spectacularly. Mortgage credit shortages might be more of a problem if these deposits prove not entirely stable and if savings and loan associations are empowered to penetrate nonmortgage lending fields. Should these developments reduce local mortgage credit supplies,

there is good reason to believe that future relatively easy money conditions will permit the secondary market to operate at least as well as it did in the early and middle 1950's to bring sufficient funds into the state. This could be done through traditional mechanisms employing federally-underwritten mortgages or through new private secondary-market developments of various types.

6. As long as the legal and economic reasons for the compartmentalization of the state's financial markets exist there is little reason to expect much change in the status quo. The status quo developed strong lending institutions and techniques and was reasonably efficient in providing the mortgage credit needed for California's enormous postwar growth. The status quo may be criticized, however, on the grounds that it can lead to an inefficient and unsound misallocation of total financial resources and that it may reduce the level of competition in the mortgage market. Placing commercial banks and savings and loan associations on more nearly equal footings in all savings and credit markets should improve the operation of both the total credit market and the mortgage market. At the same time such a move does not appear likely to diminish seriously the total supply of mortgage funds. Actions along these lines include tighter controls of savings and loan association lending, elimination of differential tax treatment, liberalization of the maximum terms allowed on bank conventional mortgages, permission for savings and loan associations to engage in nonmortgage lending, and decontrol of interest rates on federally-underwritten mortgages.

2. COMMERCIAL BANK ACTIVITY SINCE WORLD WAR II

How important is the real estate market to banks? How important are banks to the real estate market? These questions are examined in both relative and absolute terms, with specific reference to the 1945–1963 period. Neither question can be answered with certainty. Data are scarce and, when available, are not always in the most useful categories. Four types of bank real estate financing activity may be distinguished.

First, banks invest funds in long-term "permanent" mortgage loans. These are usually to allow purchase of real estate, most often property already improved or to be improved with the proceeds of the loan. Some permanent mortgage loans, however, are obtained for nonreal estate purposes. Unfortunately these cannot be isolated, hence are treated as part of total bank real estate financing activity.

In addition to long-term mortgages banks also provide short-term loans to finance the construction of land improvements. These so-called "construction loans," repaid when building is completed, usually take the form of mortgage loans secured by the partially improved property. Banks may also finance construction by making regular business loans to builders. These cannot be identified in available data.

A third type of real estate financing by banks consists of so-called "interim financing" of mortgage companies. These loans, not mortgages although sometimes secured by mortgages, are business loans to mortgage companies. They have come to play an important role in the mortgage brokerage operations so vital to the supply of real estate credit in California.

Finally, banks finance residential construction activity by making "home improvement" loans, classified as consumer loans rather than mortgages, for the repair and modernization of existing improvements. Thus we find that bank real estate lending varies by legal form, by purpose of loan, and by length of maturity.

In addition to these four types of real estate lending, banks assist in the provision of real estate credit by other lenders by selling seasoned mortgages out of their portfolios or, more often, mortgages originated expressly for the purpose of immediate resale. By these activities banks import mortgage funds into California markets, usually from institutional investors in the northeastern United States.

The two principal types of available data concerning bank real estate financing are statistics on bank mortgage holdings and recordings. Neither of these bears directly on any of the five types of real estate financing described above; they reflect changes in all types of mortgage lending activity and do not include any nonmortgage loans. By examining the few data available on certain of the specific types of activities, as well as the series on holdings and recordings, it is possible to draw at least some general inferences concerning the answers to our two questions.

a. Mortgage holdings

California commercial banks traditionally have been among the most active in the nation in permanent mortgage lending. The absence of mutual savings banks, the widespread use of branch banking, the importance of time deposits, and the relative intensity of the demand for mortgage credit have contributed to this result. In the post-World War II period, the importance of mortgages to California commercial banks has lessened; the degree to which California banks differ from the average nationwide picture has diminished; and the decline in the relative importance of commercial banks in the provision of long-term credit to California real estate markets has been profound.

(1) *Bank mortgage holdings, 1945–1963.*—The data in Table 1 summarize the mortage investment activity of California commercial banks in the postwar period. They show the net flow of funds into mortgages, the relative importance of these investments to banks, and the changing composition of the real estate loan portfolio.

TABLE 1

REAL ESTATE LOANS HELD BY INSURED COMMERCIAL BANKS IN CALIFORNIA AT YEAR-END, 1945-1963

Year-end	Real estate loans outstanding				As percentage of real estate loans			
	Amount (millions)	As percentage of			Conventional residential	FHA	VA	Non residential
		Assets	Loans	Time deposits				
1945.....	$ 950	6.9	43.3	19.8	....	....	....	18.8
1946.....	1,389	10.1	41.8	25.9	....	....	....	18.3
1947.....	2,052	14.7	46.1	36.8	....	....	....	14.6
1948.....	2,370	17.0	46.7	41.7	....	....	....	14.7
1949.....	2,468	17.5	49.2	42.2	....	....	....	14.2
1950.....	2,723	18.0	46.3	46.3	....	....	....	13.4
1951.....	2,896	17.8	43.9	45.8	24.3	33.7	28.3	13.6
1952.....	3,127	17.7	42.5	45.4	25.0	36.7	24.4	13.9
1953.....	3,341	18.4	43.7	45.9	21.5	39.8	24.9	13.2
1954.....	3,574	18.3	46.1	45.1	25.9	39.8	20.4	13.9
1955.....	3,993	19.2	43.2	48.9	26.1	40.8	18.3	14.8
1956.....	4,463	20.7	42.1	53.1	25.7	41.6	17.8	14.8
1957.....	4,410	19.4	39.4	46.4	25.8	41.0	16.3	16.8
1958.....	4,776	19.2	40.8	44.5	28.0	40.4	13.4	18.1
1959.....	5,317	20.4	38.7	48.9	29.5	41.2	10.6	18.6
1960.....	5,181	19.3	36.2	45.5	31.4	39.2	9.3	20.1
1961.....	5,358	17.9	35.4	41.7	34.4	36.9	7.8	20.9
1962.....	6,153	19.0	35.5	42.2	37.2	33.3	6.0	23.6
1963.....	7,027	20.2	35.6	43.8	38.8	30.0	5.0	26.2

SOURCE: Federal Deposit Insurance Corporation.

The net volume of bank mortgage lending generally followed the expansions and contractions in commercial bank activity during the postwar years. Rather wide fluctuations in activity made banks the most unstable supplier of mortgage funds among the various institutional lenders in California mortgage markets.

The immediate postwar period witnessed a substantial increase in bank mortgage portfolios. This resulted in a rise in the percentages that mortgages represented as a share of bank assets and time deposits but not of total loans. The relative increase in mortgage holdings was accompanied by a corresponding rise in other private loans, both financed largely by a decline in bank holdings of Treasury bonds.

The major part of this portfolio readjustment was over by the end of 1947. Since then bank mortgage holdings have occupied a fairly stable relationship to bank assets and time deposits although some annual fluctuations have been sharp. The expansion in bank mortgage holdings was most rapid in 1955–1956, 1958–59, and 1962. Bank mortgage portfolios actually decreased in 1957 and again in 1960. Lagged and cumulative responses to changes in monetary policy are evidenced by these fluctuations as well as by the increased rate of time deposit growth following the 1957 and 1962 increases in deposit-rate ceilings.

A rather different pattern from that exhibited by mortgage-asset ratios shows up in the relationship of mortgages to other loans. Recent mortgage-total loan ratios show a substantial decline. For example, the years 1962 and 1963 each witnessed almost twice as large a net mortgage portfolio increase as any other postwar year, but despite this activity the share of mortgages in total loans was unchanged. Mortgages as a percentage of total loans declined steadily from 1954 to 1961 except for a slight upturn in 1958. From 1945 through 1956 the ratio of mortgages to total loans fluctuated within a range of 42 to 49 percent. In 1961, 1962, and 1963 it was 35 percent.

The composition of commercial bank mortgage loan portfolios also underwent some interesting shifts. Most pronounced was the steady decline in FHA-VA holdings from their 1953 high of 65 percent of all real estate loans to 35 percent at the end of 1963. Most of this was in VA loans which declined from 28 percent of total real estate loans in 1951 to 5 percent in 1963. In the early and middle 1950's FHA loans rose from 34 to 42 percent of mortgage holdings, partly offsetting the decline in the VA portfolio. FHA also declined in recent years, however, falling from 41 percent in 1959 to 30 percent in 1963. Accompanying these declines were increases both in conventional residential and nonresidential mortgage lending. Between the mid-1950's and the end of 1963 the former advanced from 21 to 39 percent and the latter from 13 to 26 percent of mortgage holdings. All of the latter increase was in *nonfarm* nonresidential lending. Farm mortgage loans did not exceed 3 percent of total mortgage holdings at any time.

(2) *Interbank comparisons.*—California banks' relative movement away from mortgage investments in recent years is in direct contrast to the average behavior of all United States commercial banks outside of California. In the immediate postwar expansion—1945 to

1948—the experience was similar. For California banks real estate loans
rose from 6.9 to 17.0 percent of total assets and from 43.3 to 46.7 percent
of total loans; for all other U. S. commercial banks mortgages went from
2.6 to 6.0 percent of total assets and from 15.8 to 22.2 percent of total
loans. From 1948 through 1963, however, California bank mortgage
holdings changed very little as a percentage of total assets while, as a
percentage of total loans, mortgages fell by almost one-fourth. For all

TABLE 2

REAL ESTATE LOANS HELD AS A PERCENTAGE OF ASSETS AND LOANS,
CALIFORNIA AND ALL OTHER U. S. INSURED COMMERCIAL BANKS

Real estate loans as a percentage of:	End of selected years			
	1945	1948	1956	1963
Total assets				
California banks	6.9	16.9	20.7	20.2
Other U. S. banks	2.6	6.0	9.3	11.6
Total loans				
California banks	43.3	46.7	42.1	35.6
Other U. S. banks	15.8	22.2	22.2	23.0

SOURCE: Federal Deposit Insurance Corporation.

other U. S. banks mortgages rose from 6.0 percent of total assets in 1948
to 10.7 percent at year-end 1962 and remained a virtually unchanged
share of total loans.

In short, all United States banks have accelerated their lending activity recently, but in California, unlike the average picture elsewhere,
real estate lending has not increased as much as nonmortgage lending.
As a result the mortgage–total assets and mortgage–total loans ratios
of California banks exceed the national averages by a margin considerably smaller today than traditionally. As shown in Table 2, the most
significant part of the relative shift away from mortgages by California
banks has occurred in the years since 1956.

(3) *Bank share in the permanent mortgage market.*—Although mortgages have declined somewhat in importance to California commercial banks, particularly compared to nonmortgage loans, the importance of banks in the California mortgage market has declined far
more. Table 3 shows the debt held on California real estate by the major
institutional lenders at selected intervals during the postwar period.
The totals represent about 80 percent of the total mortgage debt outstanding on California property. The only private type of holder of

256 ALBERT H. SCHAAF

any importance not included in the data is the "individuals" category, a group whose share has probably remained fairly constant at 10–15 percent during the period. For our purposes the changing market shares of the "Big Four" institutional lenders is the point of interest. The years shown in Table 3 are those for which data on all four lenders are available.

TABLE 3

MORTGAGE DEBT HELD BY THE FOUR MAJOR INSTITUTIONAL
LENDERS ON CALIFORNIA REAL ESTATE

Mortgage debt held by:	End of selected years				
	1950	1954	1957	1960	1963
Commercial banks					
Amount in millions	$2,723	$3,574	$4,410	$5,181	$7,027
Percentage of total	47.2	35.1	29.2	24.2	20.5
Savings and loan associations					
Amount in millions	1,227	2,835	5,068	9,141	17,652
Percentage of total	21.3	27.8	33.6	42.7	51.8
Insurance companies					
Amount in millions	1,701	3,386	4,540	5,458	6,697
Percentage of total	29.6	33.3	30.1	25.5	20.1
Mutual savings banks					
Amount in millions	100	384	1,064	1,621	2,635[a]
Percentage of total	1.7	3.8	7.1	7.6	7.6

[a] Estimated by increasing the known 1962 total ($2,196,000,000) by 20 percent, the amount of increase in *total* out-of-state mortgage holdings in 1963 reported by mutual savings banks. National Association of Mutual Savings Banks, *Mutual Savings Banking Annual Report, 1964*, p. 38.
SOURCES: Federal Deposit Insurance Corporation, California Savings and Loan League (from Federal Home Loan Bank Board), Institute of Life Insurance, and National Association of Mutual Savings Banks.

The traditional dominance of commercial banks in California mortgage markets is exemplified clearly by the figures for 1950. In the following thirteen years the bank share fell by over 50 percent. Equally striking is the rise of over 100 percent in the share held by savings and loan associations. By the end of 1963 associations and banks roughly had traded places.

The comparison of banks and savings and loan associations is particularly important since, in many ways, they are quite similar. They are local lenders, operating largely with local funds, and have the local knowledge and personal contact that enables them to invest in heterogeneous and illiquid conventional mortgages. Insurance companies and mutual savings banks, both out-of-state or "interregional" lenders, operate in the FHA-VA markets or, in the case of insurance companies, in very high-grade conventional mortgages secured both by residential and nonresidential properties. The market share of insurance companies, after early 1950's expansion, fell by more than one-third. Much of this decline was matched by the expanding share of the mutual savings banks, virtual unknowns in California mortgage markets before the 1950's.

In absolute terms, however, by far the most substantial change has been the enormous growth of savings and loan association portfolios. All institutional lenders have increased their net holdings of mortgages significantly. The marked declines in the market shares of commercial banks and insurance companies are due largely to the much greater increase in the holdings of savings and loan associations.

b. Mortgage recordings

Data on mortgage recordings indicate the actual volume of lending activity by banks. They are only a rough indication since the published data are limited to loans under $20,000, and sometimes several recordings are made in the process of originating a single loan. Also, the data are not classified as to type of loan, especially maturity, and we cannot know the extent to which the originating bank retains the mortgages as permanent portfolio investments. Thus recordings and holdings may differ widely and the latter are the better measure of bank mortgage *investment* activity. But recordings do provide some measure of the number and amount of real estate loans the bank is making. This is particularly important in that many mortgage loans, particularly construction loans, are very short-term and changes in activity in them tend to be hidden by figures on portfolio changes.

In Table 4 the recordings by California commercial banks of mortgages under $20,000 are compared with those of savings and loan associations and with all other lenders combined. Again we find a decline in the relative volume of commercial bank activity over the postwar period, roughly matched by an increased share of savings and loan association recordings. Similarity between postwar changes in the percentage shares of the two lenders in holdings and recordings should not be overemphasized since the more appropriate comparison is between recordings and *changes* in holdings. Also, since the recordings data refer only to mortgages of less than $20,000, the more relevant comparison is between recordings and changes in the *residential* portfolios of banks. About 90 percent of the holdings of savings and loan associations are residential mortgages.

Examination of recordings and changes in residential holdings shows that the relative activity of banks has declined somewhat less in the case of recordings. For example, during the five-year period from 1957 through 1961 bank residential mortgage portfolios increased by only $500 million but they recorded $5 billion in mortgages. In these same five years savings and loan holdings increased by $7 billion, fourteen times the increase registered by banks, while their recordings totaled

TABLE 4

NONFARM MORTGAGES UNDER $20,000 RECORDED IN CALIFORNIA
BY SELECTED TYPES OF LENDERS, 1946–1963

Year	Nonfarm mortgages under $20,000 recorded by:					
	Commercial banks		Savings associations		All others[a]	
	Amount (millions)	Percentage of total	Amount (millions)	Percentage of total	Amount (millions)	Percentage of total
1946	$ 740	42.1	$ 274	15.6	$ 745	42.3
1947	889	45.2	334	17.0	742	41.8
1948	663	37.1	338	18.9	747	35.9
1949	498	30.6	414	25.4	715	44.0
1950	653	27.3	666	27.8	1,073	44.9
1951	626	25.5	655	26.7	1,174	47.8
1952	647	24.6	854	32.4	1,132	43.0
1953	671	22.3	940	31.3	1,394	46.4
1954	796	23.1	1,046	30.4	1,594	46.5
1955	1,250	26.2	1,497	31.3	2,029	42.5
1956	1,325	26.8	1,517	30.6	2,110	42.6
1957	856	18.8	1,634	35.9	2,059	45.3
1958	1,214	24.0	1,775	35.2	2,056	40.8
1959	1,446	21.9	2,641	39.9	2,526	38.2
1960	714	11.9	2,573	43.0	2,700	45.1
1961	983	14.3	3,368	48.9	2,540	36.8
1962	1,413	17.2	4,024	49.1	2,731	33.7
1963	1,524	15.6	5,175	52.8	3,108	31.6

[a] Category consists largely of individuals, mortgage companies, and insurance companies. Mortgage company recordings represent almost entirely loans by insurance companies, mutual savings banks, and the Federal National Mortgage Association.
SOURCE: California Savings and Loan League (from Federal Home Loan Bank Board).

$11 billion, slightly more than double the bank figure. Over the entire period from 1945 through 1963 the net increase in savings and loan mortgage portfolios was over three and one-half times that of banks ($18 billion compared to $5 billion) while savings and loan recordings were less than twice those of banks ($29 billion compared to $16 billion). In short, commercial banks are considerably more active as mortgage *lenders* in California than the examination of their mortgage holdings indicates.

Three explanations for the apparent differences between bank recording and investing activity may be advanced. The first, a certainty, is simply a matter of arithmetic. The pay-off of the long-term mortgage portfolios of banks requires a very large volume of recordings just to keep portfolios constant. There is always some run-off, and only loans made in excess of that figure add to holdings. Thus we would expect that the greater recordings of savings and loans would have a magnified effect upon increasing their holdings since it is the extra or marginal recordings that swell portfolios. A second possibility is that banks have sold a large volume of loans, either seasoned ones out of existing port-folios or newly-recorded ones never intended to be retained as per-manent investments. A third possibility is that bank mortgages have a much higher pay-off rate than savings and loans holdings. We shall con-clude from the following discussions of bank construction lending and mortgage brokerage that, of these two latter possible reasons, the third is the more important.

c. Construction lending by banks

As a short-term loan to finance production, usually less than a year in duration, construction loans often are popular with banks even in cases where the bank is not interested in permanent mortgage lending. Generally they are quite profitable and in line with the concept of the banks' primary role as that of business financing. Firms in the residential construction industry often are short of working capital, and construc-tion financing is of great importance to the building process. Many lenders, of course, also regard construction lending as a way to obtain the permanent loans. Especially in California, commercial banks often have taken this position. At other times, however, they have limited their operations to construction financing alone, regarding it as a source of profitable short-term business loans while leaving the permanent mortgage investment for other lenders.

No systematic data are available on the volume or sources of con-struction mortgage funds, either nationally or in California. Evidence indicates, however, that the decline in the relative importance of banks as permanent mortgage lenders is not matched by as extensive a decline in their activities as construction lenders. Local studies of the Los Angeles and San Francisco mortgage markets in the early postwar years suggest that commercial banks were very active in construction lending, particularly in northern California.[1] Maisel estimates that banks pro-vided construction financing for 90 percent of the tract housing erected

---

[1] James Gillies and Clayton Curtis, *Institutional Residential Mortgage Lending in Los Angeles County, 1946–51* (Los Angeles: Real Estate Research Program, University of California, 1956), Ch. V. Paul F. Wendt and Daniel B. Rathbun, *The San Francisco Bay Area Residential Mortgage Market* (Berkeley: Real Estate Research Program, University of California, 1952), p. 18.

in the Bay Area in the late 1940's.[2] In a study of large-volume house-builders in northern California (firms building over 100 houses per year), Herzog finds that commercial banks provided about half of the institutionally-supplied construction financing from 1950 through 1960, with some decline over the period. The only other institutional construction lenders of any importance were savings and loan associations, whose activity increased somewhat during the later years of the decade.[3] Interviews with several leading banks operating both statewide and in northern California indicate that commercial banks have continued construction lending even in periods when their permanent mortgage lending dwindled to almost nothing.

Analysis of data on bank mortgage recordings, holdings, pay-offs, and sales result in an estimate of about $700 million as the average annual volume of new construction financed by commercial banks in California in the 1956 to 1959 period. Total bank mortgage recordings under $20,000 totaled $4,800 million in the 1956 to 1959 period. In these same years banks increased their residential mortgage holdings by $900 million and required $1,600 million in acquisitions to replace pay-offs at an assumed rate of 10 percent of their outstanding portfolio (which averaged about $4,000 million in residential loans). As discussed in the next section, banks sold about $650 million in mortgages during the period. The residual $1,650 million in mortgage recordings provides the basis for an estimated volume of roughly $400 million per year in short-term construction loans (maturities of less than one year). If we assume that 45 percent of gross portfolio additions represent *long-term* mortgages used to finance the purchase (and construction) of new housing (as is the case with savings and loan associations), we would add $300 million per year (roughly one-fourth of 45 percent or $2,500 million) to our estimate for a total of $700 million as the average annual volume of residential construction financed by bank credit in California from 1956 to 1959.

The increased lending activity of savings and loan associations extends to construction lending, and the indications are that especially in southern California their gains are considerable relative to commercial banks in this field. Savings and loan new construction mortgages in California rose from $734 million in 1956 to $1,298 million in 1959, the period in which we estimated bank lending as $700 million

[2] Sherman J. Maisel, *Housebuilding in Transition* (Berkeley: University of California Press, 1953), p. 158.

[3] John P. Herzog, *The Dynamics of Large-Scale Housebuilding* (Berkeley: Real Estate Research Program, University of California, 1963), Ch. III.

annually. In the 1945 to 1949 period, years of alleged commercial bank dominance in construction lending, savings and loan association construction lending averaged about $150 million annually. In 1963 associations recorded $2,485 million in construction loans. The conclusion seems warranted that commercial bank credit for financing residential construction, although always available in significant amounts, has become relatively less important in recent years and that this decline has been more than offset by increased activity of savings and loan associations. This is not surprising since associations have had more permanent loan funds available and ordinarily seek to finance the construction process as well as the permanent loan, often as a package deal.

d. Bank mortgage sales

As California is a capital-deficit area, commercial banks might be expected to engage rather heavily in the importation of funds by selling mortgages to out-of-state investors. Such sales in the secondary mortgage market, including sales by mortgage companies to institutions committed to purchase prior to origination, are the chief transmission belt of interregional mortgage funds. No systematic data are available on mortgage sales by banks. Scattered evidence indicates, however, that in general California banks have not been very active in this regard. Interviews with several leading banks and perusal of several annual reports lead, with one exception, to the same general conclusion.

Availability of statewide FHA and northern California VA data for the years 1956 through 1959 makes some estimate of bank sales possible.[4] Due to economic and legal limitations, virtually all commercial bank mortgage sales consist of transactions involving insured (FHA) or guaranteed (VA) mortgages. Commercial banks originated insured mortgages of $1,450 million in the four years 1956 through 1959. On the basis of northern California experience their statewide guaranteed lending may be estimated at $400 million during the same four years. (Commercial banks recorded about $100 million in guaranteed mortgages in the nine-county Bay Area during the period and, on the basis of population ratios, a statewide estimate requires increasing this amount fourfold.) Commercial bank FHA-VA holdings increased by $400 million from year-end 1955 ($2,350 million outstanding) to year-end 1959 ($2,750 million outstanding) while another $800 million was needed to meet pay-offs at the national average annual rate of about

---

[4] These data are reported in A. H. Schaaf, *The Supply of Residential Mortgage Funds in the San Francisco Bay Area, 1950–1960* (Berkeley: Real Estate Research Program, University of California, 1962), Ch. V.

8 percent during those years.[5] The difference between total recordings of $1,850 million and total portfolio needs of $1,200 million furnishes us with the estimate that banks sold $650 million in FHA-VA mortgages in the 1956 to 1959 period.

This averages out to a trifling $160 million annually during a period when California money and real estate markets were producing large demands for additional mortgage money. The major role in the importing of mortgage funds into California in the postwar years was played by mortgage companies, with a significant amount provided recently by various activities of savings and loan associations. The volume of those imports is suggested by the estimate that out-of-state funds were supporting over one-third of the total mortgage debt outstanding in California at the end of 1963.

e. Nonmortgage real estate financing by banks

Bank credit supports some real estate market activities through non-mortgage lending comprised mainly of small business and consumer loans. Two such activities are mentioned here since they are so closely related in purpose and functional effect to many bank mortgages. They are loans to mortgage companies and home improvement loans.

There are no statewide data on bank loans to other participants on the supply side of the mortgage market. Nationally, a special FDIC survey in 1950 revealed that total credit outstanding to mortgage lenders by commercial banks was $404 million and periodic surveys by the Federal Reserve Board between 1954 and 1959 reported amounts varying from $517 to $1,305 million.[6] About 80 percent of these loans went to mortgage companies and, in California, this percentage probably would be substantially higher. Northern California mortgage companies reported in 1960 that banks were the sole suppliers of their debt financing which equaled about 7 percent of the total mortgage debt they were servicing.[7] Typically, mortgages held by the mortgage company serve as collateral for these loans. Short-term financing, often called "mortgage warehousing," is required particularly if the mortgage company has closed the permanent mortgage without a firm commitment or with an extended advanced commitment since the company has to disburse the loan funds to the property seller and may have to hold the mortgages for quite a period before receiving cash from the permanent

---

[5] For yearly pay-off rates see Schaaf, *op. cit.*, p. 51.

[6] U.S., Federal Deposit Insurance Corporation, *Operating and Insured Commercial and Mutual Savings Banks, Assets and Liabilities*, Report No. 33, June 30, 1950; Board of Governors, Federal Reserve System, *Federal Reserve Bulletin*, September 1955, December 1956, March 1958, March 1959.

[7] Schaaf, *op. cit.*, p. 35.

mortgagee. Sometimes the bank making the short-term loan may agree to retain the permanent mortgage pledged as security at the conclusion of the warehousing loan period at a reservation or "stand-by commitment" price. Undoubtedly these arrangements facilitate the important catalytic role played by mortgage companies in the mortgage market. Most companies are small-scale and in need of working capital. Interim financing also allows companies without commitments more time to seek out buyers and hence improves market performance.

Commercial banks traditionally have been very active in the home improvement loan field. They have originated over 80 percent of all loans insured under the FHA Title I program.[8] Their share of the Federal Reserve Board's series on holdings of consumer installment credit for repair and modernization loans has remained at or above the 75 percent level throughout the postwar years.[9] Although not technically mortgage credit, these funds are of significant importance to the residential construction industry. Repair and modernization of existing structures accounted for better than one-fifth of total residential construction expenditures in the postwar years.

Note, however, that savings and loan associations also are active in this field. Their loans are in the form of conventional mortgages and thus are not included either in Title I or consumer loan totals. Repair and modernization loans by associations have not been published separately since 1953, at which time they were nationally far below commercial bank levels. But the category in which they are included has risen sharply in recent years.

f. Summary of commercial bank postwar mortgage lending experience

Although the data presented above are incomplete and often constitute only the roughest of estimates, they are probably sufficient to permit general observations regarding the role of commercial banks in California's postwar mortgage markets. The main conclusions may be summarized briefly as follows:

(1) Probably the outstanding feature has been the decline in the relative share of debt held by commercial banks vis-à-vis the market share of savings and loan associations.

(2) Commercial bank mortgage lending has been fitful, varying annually between amounts barely sufficient to cover short-term construction loans and pay-offs of long-term holdings to amounts sufficient to increase portfolios by almost $1 billion.

---

[8] U.S., Housing and Home Finance Agency, *Annual Reports.*
[9] Board of Governors, Federal Reserve System, *Federal Reserve Bulletins.*

(3) After the mid-1950's banks generally shifted away from FHA-VA lending into conventional residential and nonresidential markets.

(4) Banks have in all years continued to extend a sizable volume of construction financing, often without retaining the permanent financing, but their share in financing total building activity in the state has declined substantially compared to that of savings and loan associations.

(5) Banks have been relatively unimportant as a transmission belt for the importation of mortgage funds into the state.

(6) Finally, banks have played an important role in providing debt financing for mortgage companies, and they have continued to be very active in the field of repair and modernization loans, although savings and loan associations have substantially increased their activities in the latter field in recent years.

3. CAUSES OF POSTWAR CHANGES IN THE ROLE OF BANKS

In brief our thesis is that the postwar changes in the role of commercial banks in California mortgage and savings markets are the logical result of certain legal and economic factors. These have combined to place banks at positions of both advantage and disadvantage in different financial markets. Naturally the banks have operated in consequence so as best to enhance their own interests.

a. Legal disadvantages of banks in conventional mortgage markets

Commercial banks are disadvantaged by their inability to offer loan terms as liberal as those offered by other institutional lenders, especially savings and loan associations, in conventional mortgage lending. National and state bank controls differ slightly, but in the main all banks in California are forbidden to extend mortgage credit in excess of 75 percent of the appraised value of the property, or for maturities greater than 20 years, and their mortgage portfolio cannot exceed 60 percent of their time deposits. Savings and loan associations, at the other extreme, can lend up to 80 percent, or under certain conditions up to 90 percent, of appraised value and for 25 years. Individuals and life insurance companies also may offer more liberal conventional mortgage terms than commercial banks. Insurance companies, however, are hampered in many conventional market areas by lack of local knowledge and presence. Consequently they favor either FHA and VA loans or very high-grade residential and nonresidential conventional loans. Mutual savings banks can invest only in FHA and VA loans in California.

b. The declining role of FHA-VA loans

Bank disadvantages in conventional mortgage markets were offset by the mid-1930's FHA emergence. Restrictions on conventional mortgage terms and portfolio sizes did not apply to insured loans and, after the Veterans' Readjustment Act of 1944, to guaranteed loans. Since these loans have extremely liberal terms banks could compete effectively with savings and loan associations in local markets. The greatly improved liquidity and safety of the loans were the rationale for exempting them from conventional mortgage controls and for encouraging many banks to alter institutional policies against mortgage lending—policies which actually made the legal limitations quite unnecessary.

California commercial banks invested heavily in insured and guaranteed mortgages. Earlier figures are not available, but at the close of 1951, 62 percent of their total mortgage portfolio and 72 percent of their residential holdings were insured or guaranteed. This was at a time when banks accounted for almost half of the state's institutionally-held mortgage debt. In more recent years, however, the availability of federal mortgage underwriting lost much of its importance as a device to improve banks' market position in the competition for borrowers.

The most commonly cited reason for this was a decline in the investment attractiveness of FHA and VA loans, particularly for commercial banks. Maximum chargeable interest rates and loan fees, controlled on these loans, have not been adjusted frequently and adequately to match higher alternative investment yields. For a number of institutional and economic reasons, secondary market discounting has been of limited usefulness as a means of increasing effective yields, especially for local lenders such as banks who ordinarily do business directly with the borrower. Various congressional and administrative actions of recent years also have tended to restrict the general usefulness of mortgage insurance, inclining to employ the device more as a means of implementing special housing programs. The VA loan program, of course, has declined as the number of eligible veterans has decreased.

Coupled with these developments has been increasing conventional loan term liberalization by savings and loan associations and willingness to originate mortgages that might not meet federal underwriting standards. Often these loans have been combined with a junior mortgage and may well require less down payment than an insured or guaranteed loan. Compared with FHA-VA loans, conventional loan processing is usually much faster; there is no insurance premium to be paid; and the lender is not hampered by the FHA-VA limitations on the maximum amount per loan. As builders have shifted to producing larger and more costly housing in recent years, it probably is correct to assert that savings and loan association conventional loans often have been a considerably better house-marketing aid than federally-underwritten loans—even in periods when the latter have been available without a substantial seller discount.

A final reason for diminished importance of the FHA and VA programs to commercial banks has to do with the effectiveness of these programs rather than their shortcomings. The liquidity, safety, and legality of FHA and VA mortgages as investments for out-of-state institutions have induced a widespread flow of funds into California mortgage markets. Insurance companies have invested heavily in these mortgages and federal underwriting is wholly responsible for the entrance of mutual savings banks into California mortgage markets. Thus while the FHA and VA programs tended to increase the competitive position of banks vis-à-vis savings and loan associations in local mortgage markets, they also induced a substantial additional competition for loans through their effects on interregional flows.

c. Bank disadvantages in savings markets

Banks have been handicapped in recent years in competing for savings deposits, with savings and loan associations once again providing the intensive competition. This is particularly important since banks traditionally have geared their mortgage lending activity to the growth of their time deposits, and the volume of time deposits serves as one of the legal limitations on bank conventional mortgage lending activity. These policies are based on the assumption that time deposits are more stable than demand deposits and that mortgages are long-term and illiquid. A bank's obligation to meet instantly all requests for withdrawal of demand deposits gives rise in turn to the concentration of bank investments in short-term, liquid assets. According to this line of reasoning it follows that only time deposits can be placed safely in mortgages.

Unquestionably there are errors and oversights in these institutional rules of thumb and time-honored legal regulations. Nevertheless the relationship between time deposits and mortgages is important, and any factor which affects a bank's time deposit position adversely also inhibits its mortgage lending activity. It is no accident that the historic proclivity of California banks to mortgage loans was matched by their unusually large holdings of time deposits.

Relative to savings and loan associations, however, the time deposits of California commercial banks have grown very slowly. From the end of 1945 to the end of 1963 statewide time deposits increased from $4,799 million to $16,042 million, about three and one-half times. Over the same period association savings accounts rose from $460 million to $16,-534 million, about 36 times. With associations placing more than this amount of funds in mortgages it is little wonder that they have completely outpaced commercial banks in the mortgage market.

Several factors account for the California commercial banks' decline in local savings markets. Probably most important are Federal Reserve Board controls over the interest rates paid on time deposits. These controls have placed banks' rates as much as 35 percent below those available from associations. Coupled with this is the increasing confidence of the public in the safety provided associations' accounts by the Federal Savings and Loan Insurance Corporation. This insurance and aggressive promotional and locational policies by associations have gone far to eliminate much of the nonprice differentiation undoubtedly once possessed by bank time deposits in local savings markets. The importance of price competition in these markets is attested to not only by the rapid growth of association accounts but also by the very sizable increases in time deposits following the boosts in time deposit rates in 1957 and 1962.

An additional factor in the rapid growth of association-held savings is the *economic* ability of the associations to pay high rates. Mortgage loans probably are not the most profitable items in a bank's total portfolio but they certainly earn much higher returns than many bank assets. The high returns on mortgages during a major real estate boom and certain income tax advantages give savings and loan associations both the ability and the incentive to offer very attractive rates to depositors. With legal and institutional requirements forcing banks to keep a good portion of their assets in lower-yielding investments, legal controls on time deposit rates cannot be blamed solely for the banks' failure to meet fully association competition for local savings.

d. Bank disadvantages in mortgage brokerage

The apparently modest role played by banks in importing funds through mortgage sales may seem surprising. Certainly banks can and do sell some mortgages from their permanent portfolios to meet current lending needs and to readjust the composition of their earning assets. It might seem logical, however, for banks to endeavor to develop a mortgage brokerage and servicing volume in view of their experience in mortgage lending and servicing, their correspondent relationships with other banks, and their familiarity with national money markets. This is to be expected especially in a capital-deficit area such as California where banks have experienced particular difficulties in meeting local demands for credit, notably in tight money periods. We have noted that banks provide most of the funds for mortgage company operations, and mortgage servicing is a very profitable business. Banks also provide stand-by commitments and construction financing. It might seem logical and efficient for banks to take over the entire operation, including mortgage origination for resale and continued servicing. Their failure to do this has several possible explanations. In part it may be simply a case of failing to exploit a profitable new area; perhaps some uncertainty as to the true costs and net returns involved in an expanded mortgage servicing business; or possibly due to certain relative advantages of mortgage companies in the performance of mortgage brokerage operations.

Mortgage company advantages are several. The brokerage function is important, and if done properly requires skills and time allotments which may be beyond the specialties and interests of commercial banking. The chief secondary market purchasers—insurance companies and mutual savings banks—may find certain disadvantages in doing business with a competing lender. It is understandable that banks put their own portfolio needs first and offer to sell good-quality loans only when their own funds are exhausted. Mortgage companies originate loans only to sell and devote all of their time to brokerage and servicing activity. Builders, the chief secondary-market mortgage sellers, also cannot be expected to welcome the resultant reduced competition for their business if local mortgage companies disappeared from the scene. Although California banks might be strong enough to overcome these obstacles, most specifically by denying financing to mortgage companies, the struggle would not be easy and in the long run might do more harm than good to the overall position of banks in California's financial markets.

e. Advantages of banks in nonmortgage lending

The relative disadvantages of banks in competing for mortgage loans and personal savings should not be overemphasized. Conventional loan terms of 20 years and 75 percent of value are sufficient to service many borrowers, and few California banks ever have come very close to the ceiling mortgage-time deposit ratios. Insured mortgages still offer certain attractions for both borrowers and lenders, especially in easy money periods. Through their many branches California banks can tap local savings markets in extensive and minute detail, and the wide range of services offered by large banks is still an important attraction for holders of savings accounts.

Recognition of these points leads to somewhat different conclusions as between bank policies in savings markets and in mortgage markets. Despite somewhat lower rates on time deposits, other advantages are sufficient to maintain the banks' competitive position in savings markets. Assuming a continuing greater freedom to raise rates, banks undoubtedly will pursue their aggressive competition for savings, with concomitant time deposit growth. Even with the higher interest costs, these funds usually can be made to show a profit with intelligent loan and investment management. Thus the lag in bank time-deposit growth probably is due largely to aggressive competition from savings and loan associations and legal restrictions on banks.

The decline in bank mortgage lending, however, may be due as much to bank advantages in nonmortgage loan markets as to bank disadvantages in mortgage lending. Three main factors could be responsible for channeling bank funds into nonmortgage lending areas. These relate to efficiency, profitability, and market shelters.

Traditionally the principal lending function of a commercial bank is short-term business loans, and it is in this field that the banks' greatest familiarity and expertise lie. Even in California, where "department store" banking always has been practiced widely, banks have been the most important source of credit to business including, in the mortgage market, loans to builders and mortgage companies. Closely allied to business loans are short-term loans to finance consumer purchases—loans in which California banks have been outstanding. Although mortgage lending has been relatively more important to California banks than to others, this is mainly a reflection of the wide range of credit services offered by the giant branch banks of California. This range itself may be due in part to the greater past use of eastern credit sources by larger California business borrowers. Substantiating data are not available, but it is possible that some of the relative decline in bank mortgage lending is due to these firms turning more to California banks for financing and their demands being met by reducing the share of bank funds tied up in long-term mortgages. If so, the residual nature of mortgage investments for banks becomes increasingly apparent.

Banks probably find mortgage loans somewhat less profitable than many business and consumer loans. Systematic data are not available on yields of individual parts of bank portfolios. However, the effective yield of the typical fully amortized, conventional, long-term mortgage, with interest paid on the declining balance, generally is not as high as the effective yields on consumer loans (usually amortizing but with interest on the original balance) or on unamortized business loans in which the full interest is deducted from the initial amount advanced. Lower mortgage costs have also been an objective of many programs of federal government assistance to the mortgage market. The profitability of mortgages for banks has been emphasized recently within the banking industry, but the yield comparisons usually have been between mortgages and bonds. This comparison is not inappropriate, particularly if the mortgages are insured or guaranteed, but mortgages are not among the most profitable items in the *loan* portfolio.

A final reason for banks to eschew mortgage lending lies in the legal market shelter that they enjoy in nonmortgage markets by virtue of the prohibition on nonmortgage lending by savings and loan associations. This prohibition has a double effect. It intensifies competition in the mortgage market by forcing the savings and loan associations to channel all of their rapidly-growing funds into mortgages. And it keeps the association out of other banking areas apart from those that they can invade by means of mortgage lending for nonreal estate purposes.

f. Conclusions on reasons for bank performance

It seems apparent that the relative withdrawal of banks from permanent mortgage lending in California is expectable. The unusually strong position of commercial banks in California mortgage markets was perhaps somewhat of an historical accident; a combined result of branch banking, the absence of mutual savings banks, large time deposits, and relatively fewer business credit demands. The growth of savings and loan associations and the inflow of out-of-state funds provide increased competition for banks in the mortgage market. At the same time banks are faced with increased demands for business and consumer loans, usually strongest in periods of pinch due to restrictive federal monetary policies. Faced with a need for greater selectivity, it is understandable that banks turn to areas of less competition and greater profits. Mortgage lending is, after all, the special business of savings and loan associations and mortgage companies and is more the business of insurance companies and mutual savings banks than it is of commercial banks.

4. PROJECTIONS AND EVALUATIONS OF FUTURE DEVELOPMENTS

The following discussion of possible future changes in the commercial bank role in California savings and mortgage markets, and the evaluation of some of the implications of such changes, makes no pretense of being either exhaustive or definitive.

The future *volume* of California's mortgage credit and the future *structure* of the mortgage lending industry in the state are primary concerns. Throughout the discussion of both issues attention is directed to the implications of two future alternatives. One possibility is a continuation of the status quo with regard to the legal and institutional advantages and disadvantages of the various types of lenders in savings, mortgage, and nonmortgage markets—a situation that we will describe as a "compartmentalization" of these financial markets. The other possibility is that legal and institutional changes will enable the various institutions to compete more freely and equally in savings and lending markets. Possible developments in this direction include tighter public controls of the appraisal and lending practices of savings and loan associations, permission for savings and loan associations to expand into some nonmortgage lending fields, legal changes to allow banks to offer more liberal mortgage terms and higher savings deposit rates, and decontrol of interest rates on federally-underwritten mortgages.

a. The future volume of mortgage credit

In examining California's future mortgage credit needs and the chances of meeting them, the situation extant at the end of 1963 must be appraised before an attempt can be made to form some idea of future needs. Are the sources and market techniques responsible for the existing supply adequate for the future, and what changes, if any, may be desirable?

(1) *The existing situation.*—At the end of 1963 the situation in California regarding the supply of mortgage credit may be summed up as follows: The total volume of credit supplied in the postwar years was sufficient to finance an unprecedented growth and to provide a disproportionately large amount of credit outstanding in California as compared with other regions. Over one-third of the total mortgage debt outstanding was financed by out-of-state funds. California's borrowers continued to pay relatively high costs for their mortgage funds, but the cost differential seemed not overly important, particularly in view of the enormous amount of mortgage credit supplied to borrowers in the state.

(a) California's relative debt position.—In a monograph prepared for the study of housing in California by the Governor's Advisory Commission on Housing Problems, UCLA professors Leo Grebler and James Gillies state that "On the whole, it would be difficult . . . to make a case for any severe lack of funds to California borrowers."[10] General support for this conclusion is found in the relative housing position of the state's

---

[10] Governor's Advisory Commission on Housing Problems, *Housing in California: Appendix* (The Commission, 1963), p. 391.

residents and their relative use of debt when compared with the country as a whole. Housing production from 1945 to 1963 has about doubled the standing stock in California. According to the 1960 Census, 13.5 percent of the state's dwelling units was "substandard" as compared with 26.8 percent of the U. S. total. The Census also revealed that 73 percent and 66 percent of the housing stock in the Los Angeles and San Francisco SMSA's, respectively, was mortgaged compared with 63 percent for all U. S. SMSA's and debt-value ratios were 56 percent in the two California SMSA's compared with 54 percent of all U. S. SMSA's.

(b) California's dependence on imported funds.—Although the exact amount and holders of the total mortgage debt outstanding in the state are not known, an estimate that one-third of the total represents out-of-state funds appears conservative. The four institutions shown in Table 3 hold nationally about 80 percent of all mortgage debt. Among these four institutions in California, all of the mutual savings bank total, about 80 percent of the insurance company total, and about 25 percent of the savings and loan association total represent outside funds. The life insurance company percentage (80 percent) is roughly the same as the percentage of total U. S. life insurance in force held by non-Californians in companies not domiciled in California. The savings and loan percentage (25 percent) consists of Federal Home Loan Bank advances ($1.4 billion outstanding in California at the end of 1963), the estimated out-of-state deposits in California associations (reported to comprise about 15 percent of total deposits in 1960 in a survey by the Stanford Research Institute), and funds invested by out-of-state savings and loan associations in loan participations sold by California associations. From the start of the participation loan program in 1957 to the end of 1963, sales in the 12th FHLB district totaled $1.9 billion while purchases amounted to $500 million. There is some reason to believe, however, that almost all of the district purchases were made by associations in the Pacific Northwest from California associations. The savings and loan holdings of out-of-state funds are all scaled down in varying amounts to account for funds not placed in mortgages and for FHLB advances that represent California money. The techniques used were those employed by Grebler and Gillies.[11]

The foregoing means that about $13.3 billion out of the $33.8 billion shown in Table 3 represents out-of-state funds, approximately 37 percent. A large part of the estimated $7 billion in debt not accounted for in Table 3 is held by individuals, assumedly mostly Californians. But the

---

[11] See Governor's Advisory Commission on Housing Problems, *op. cit.*, pp. 279–280.

$7 billion also includes about $1 billion in holdings of the Federal National Mortgage Association, some pension fund money, out-of-state holdings of Cal-Vet bonds, and other external sources. If these sources comprise 25 percent of the $7 billion (probably a conservative estimate), the share of external funds in the total volume of California mortgage debt would amount to 35 percent.

(c) Differential costs of mortgage credit in California.—The substantial augmentation of the supply of funds available to California mortgage borrowers has not eliminated the historic differentials between mortgage credit costs in California (and the southern and western parts of the United States generally) and the northeastern part of the country. Census data on conventional first-mortgage interest rates, FHLB data on both rates and loan fees, and secondary market prices of insured and guaranteed loans all tell the same story. The typical California mortgage borrower pays about 20 percent more for his credit than his counterpart in New York, Massachusetts, and other of the more urbanized states of the northeast and, in somewhat lesser degree, the midwest. This difference undoubtedly was greater before the advent of the federal mortgage programs in the 1930's, but it has changed little in the postwar period.[12] It has varied somewhat with recent changes in monetary policy, widening in tight money periods and narrowing when credit supplies were more plentiful.

Although this cost differential is commonly and justifiably lamented, two points should be emphasized. First, obviously it has provided a strong attraction for outside funds. In addition to extra costs attributable to distance and differences in risks, some stimulus is necessary to induce an interregional flow of funds. The more perfect the market the less such a differential need be. The interregional mortgage market is notoriously imperfect and in the conventional sector almost nonexistent. On the savings side, geographic variations in per capita savings have obtained for decades. In view of the vast flow of mortgage funds into California during the postwar years perhaps the surprising aspect is that the required differential has not been larger.

Second, we should consider the impact of the differential on the borrower's costs. Grebler and Gilles provide the following comparison of monthly housing costs with a 5 percent and a 6 percent loan, assuming an initial loan amount of $20,000, a 25-year term, level-payment amortization, and an estimate of 3 percent of the initial loan amount annually for taxes, insurance, heat, water, and maintenance:[13]

---

[12] Governor's Advisory Commission on Housing Problems, *op. cit.*, pp. 384–388.
[13] *Ibid.*, p. 389.

	5 percent loan	6 percent loan
Debt Service	$117.00	$128.80
Other Housing Expense	50.00	50.00
	$167.00	$178.80

The increase in interest costs of 20 percent involves, in the case of a fairly substantial and long-term loan, an increased outlay of $11.80 per month. The increase in total monthly housing costs is 7.3 percent. Any judgment must be arbitrary since we really have no standard for comparison or evaluation. While such extra financial costs might not seem to be very great, they require an extra $60 monthly income at a housing expense-income ratio of 20 percent. If we expect a continuation of the enormous capital imports that have been required to meet the demands, however, the more important question for the future seems to revolve around maintaining the inflow of funds rather than cutting the cost differentials, desirable as the latter objective might be.

(2) Future prospects.—In assessing the future situation with regard to mortgage credit needs in California, two factors stand out: (1) It is not unreasonable to expect that outstanding mortgage debt will continue to grow at the same rate that it has since World War II. (2) The prospects for a continued ample supply of funds through existing channels appear bright, but the answer depends in part upon assumptions as to the future levels of prices, savings, and employment in the national economy generally and resulting federal monetary and housing credit policies.

(a) Future needs.—Our estimate that the amount of mortgage debt outstanding in California in 1975 will total around $80 billion rests upon two key assumptions. The first is that personal income in the state will increase by $48 billion between 1963 and 1975, rising from $52 to $100 billion. This assumption derives from the known total of $52 billion in 1963 and the 1975 estimate of $100 billion provided by Williams (this volume). The second assumption is that the relationship between the growth of personal income and that of mortgage debt will continue unchanged from its level in the immediately prior period of the same time span. In the twelve years from 1950 to 1962 California's personal income rose by $29 billion while its mortgage debt increased by $23 billion.[14] Thus for every one dollar increase in personal income, mort-

---

[14] This represents an estimated mortgage debt increase of 200 percent and is based upon the increase in the residential debt reported by the 1950 and 1960 Censuses for the combined Los Angeles–Long Beach and San Francisco–Oakland SMSA's. This increase was 180 percent, and in the two additional years it probably increased by more than the remaining 20 percent of our total estimate. However, the two metro-

gage debt rose by about 80 cents. If the same relationship holds in the twelve years from 1963 to 1975, the expected increase of $48 billion of personal income will mean an increase in outstanding mortgage debt of $39 billion, i.e. from our estimated 1963 figure of $41 billion to $80 billion in 1975.

The assumption that the income-debt growth relationship will remain the same, although by no means foolproof, is not unwarranted. The two key determinants of the growth of mortgage credit are the volume of new construction and the amount of additional borrowing on the security of existing properties. Williams (Table 3) expects the average annual rate of population growth in California to fall from 4.0 percent in the 1950's to 3.3 percent in the 1960's and to 2.7 percent in the 1970's. This would presage some decline in the rate of growth of real estate improvements and thus in the rate of growth of mortgage debt. On the other hand it is quite possible that there may be an increase in the rate at which Californians borrow against their mounting equities in existing properties.

(b) Reasons for pessimism.—Were California's future needs considered in terms of the volume and sources of domestic and imported mortgage funds during the 1950's, the prospects might not appear too bright.[15] The major concern lies with the federal programs. About 40 percent of the $15 billion in out-of-state funds previously estimated as outstanding in California at the end of 1963 either were insured or guaranteed. However, in the six years from 1957 through 1962 the combined FHA-VA loan volume was about 18 percent of the total amount of recorded California mortgages under $20,000; the corresponding figure for the seven years from 1950 through 1956 was 27 percent. The continuing inflow of mutual savings bank funds, all to insured or guaranteed mortgages, has prevented this decrease from being much larger. But this is likely to taper off. Mutual savings banks had virtually no mortgage holdings on California properties in 1950. From this position they have built up rapidly, but their total resources are growing slowly and there are home-state pressures against their investing too large a percentage of funds in foreign markets.

(c) Reasons for optimism.—For three reasons future problems in meeting state mortgage credit needs appear far less formidable than they do when forecasts are arrived at by simply projecting past situations and

politan areas have probably witnessed a faster rate of mortgage debt increase than the state as a whole. There are no comparable data for other years or for non-residential debt.

[15] Cf. Leo Grebler, "California's Dependence on Capital Imports for Mortgage Investment," *California Management Review* (Vol. V, Spring 1963), pp. 47–54.

market techniques. Each of these three possible future developments presages an ample future supply of mortgage credit in California, and only one involves any increase in commercial bank lending or importing activity. The three factors overlap and influence one another, but it is illuminating to consider them separately.

(1) The growth of state savings deposits.—In the first place the phenomenal growth in state savings deposits in very recent years may signal some lessening in the capital-importing character of California. In 1960, although second in per capita personal income, California ranked seventh among the states in per capita combined commercial bank time deposits, mutual savings bank savings deposits, and savings accounts in savings and loan associations.[16] From 1960 to 1963, however, the volume of time deposits and savings accounts in California rose from approximately $1,150 to $1,850 per capita, an increase of over 60 percent in three years, while the corresponding national increase, including time deposits in mutual savings banks, was only about 30 percent. These trends reflect increases in personal savings (but not in the propensity to save) as well as shifts of funds from other forms of liquid assets, one of which is demand deposits. An unknown amount of California's growth also is accounted for by a movement of outside funds into California deposits, probably mostly into savings and loan association accounts. Thus part of the California increase represents external funds and, furthermore, the increased time deposits have no necessary effect on the supply of mortgage money. However, the great rise in state savings deposits, particularly those in savings and loan associations, undoubtedly signifies an increase in the volume of local funds seeking mortgage investments.

(2) The prevalence of easier money conditions in the future compared with the 1950's.—There are good reasons to expect that the capital importing facilities developed in the 1950's may operate more dependably and adequately in the future. The growing flood of money seeking investment outlets in the United States bears directly on this second factor also, particularly with regard to the FHA. Borrowers' periodic difficulties in obtaining FHA and VA loans in California in the first postwar decade were due almost entirely to restrictive monetary policies and rising money yields coupled with the relatively inflexible yields on insured and guaranteed mortgages. When credit was plentiful and monetary policy easy, the federal programs boomed. In more recent years these same monetary factors were at work, but added to them was the increasing competition of the conventional lending of the savings and loan associations which has resulted in large part from the enormous

---

[16] Grebler, *op. cit.*, pp. 52–53.

increase in association savings accounts, some of it representing imported funds.

Thus the conclusion appears warranted that as long as the supply of loanable funds is plentiful one or both of two conditions prevails. Either the federal programs work well to bring funds in, or they are not needed due to a plethora of local money or money imported through other channels. Notable among the latter are interregional savings deposit flows, participation lending, and FHLB borrowing by savings and loan associations; life insurance company conventional lending; and state borrowing for Cal-Vet bonds (state mortgage insurance also has been proposed). All of these possibilities have important ramifications for the affected institutions, intermediaries such as mortgage companies, the housing and mortgage markets, the future of various federal programs, and the like. For our purposes, however, their importance lies in the fact that commercial banks played a minor role in these developments and, as long as these sources provide an ample and competitive supply of funds in the state, there is neither a need nor an attraction for a step-up in commercial bank lending or importing activities. It is possible that commercial bank mortgage lending may stay at its recent high levels, of course, since the growth of time deposits is part of the overall picture.

The *sine qua non* in the rather optimistic view portrayed above is the postulation of a continued condition of high savings flows and easy money conditions. A thorough analysis and defense of such a projection would carry us far beyond the scope of this paper. However, we have been in this type of situation since 1960, and strong arguments may be advanced to indicate a continuation for an indefinite period. At the very least, it seems defensible to argue that monetary conditions will be no more stringent than they were during the 1950's when the supply of local and imported mortgage credit in California was enormous. Tight money conditions reflect a national shortage of real resources, and it is necessary and proper that all areas, California included, be forced to reduce their levels of economic activity in such periods. Thus tight money credit shortages are not really something to be circumvented or overcome.

Expectations of generally easy money conditions in the future are based on forecasts of future economic activity. True, there will be a rise in household formation with its stimulating effect on many consumer and capital markets. Yet the same underlying population factor means an increase in the labor force which, with continuing automation, provides enormous productive capacity. The postwar capital boom, following the lean years of the depression and World War II, was over essentially by 1957. Since that time we have witnessed a prosperous economy, but one with little inflation, fairly high unemployment, and ample financial resources. Although there are and will be many unmet needs, particularly in the public and low-income private sectors, it seems realistic to argue that conditions of some economic slack may occur persistently, particularly in view of the private-enterprise orientation of the political and economic system. Such a forecast is not one of depression or stagnation; rather it is the economy of abundance which modern technology can provide. In the financial climate associated with such an economy, however, problems of regional mortgage credit shortages tend to be less acute. The FHA-VA experiences during the easy money periods of the postwar years may serve as one example of such a financial climate. The more recent years of plentiful supplies of local and inter-regional conventional funds are another.

(3) The possible development of new capital-importing facilities.—A third possibility for meeting future mortgage credit needs is the development of new importation techniques. Here the commercial banks could play an expanded role. Certainly the existing avenues are not perfect, and future needs for imported funds will remain. It seems most unlikely that domestic savings could rise by enough to provide all the mortgage money needed in California in the coming decade or so, and, regardless of how easy monetary conditions are nationally, the importation of mortgage credit will require positive action. Thus it is not inconceivable that existing market processes may be supplanted, and various proposals and schemes advanced in recent years have this aim. Their general objective is to provide conventional mortgages with improved standardization, liquidity, and safety.

Insofar as these schemes improve the general secondary market in conventional mortgages it is possible that they could lead to an expanded role for commercial banks as mortgage credit importers. However, another possible result is a firmer, broader, and more permanent position for mortgage companies freed of dependence on government programs. They might well turn into key "market-makers," establishing prices and trading in mortgages with uncommitted inventories. Today's larger mortgage companies, by reason of experience and specialization, are suited logically to assume this role. Although they have capitalization problems not faced by commercial banks, such problems may not be insurmountable.

An increased rate of bank activity is envisioned in proposals to establish an intra-industry mutual organization to insure bank conventional mortgages. The insurance, among other things, would enable and encourage banks to trade in mortgages among themselves and possibly with other institutional investors. Banks in capital-deficit regions thus could be expected to increase their mortgage credit importing activity through the secondary market resale method. Such a development is always possible, of course, particularly if the FHA becomes increasingly restricted to implementing special purpose programs of direct public concern. However, the economic feasibility of private mortgage insurance is still to be demonstrated and, among the banks themselves, there is by no means a universal interest in or agreement with the proposition to establish an industry-owned mortgage insurance facility.

b. Structural developments

It probably is not an exaggeration to argue that the future actions of savings and loan associations are the key determinants of the role that commercial banks will play in California savings and mortgage markets. Two general possibilities present themselves: there may be little change in the existing situation; or there may be some movement towards freer institutional participation in various financial markets.

(1) The future role of banks assuming continued compartmentalization.—The most important single feature of the existing situation is the compartmentalization of the state's credit and savings markets. We have seen that banks operate under certain disadvantages in mortgage and savings markets while possessing advantages in many nonmortgage lending fields. As long as the savings and loan associations are locked into the mortgage market, and the major interregional lenders remain active, it seems improbable that commercial banks will find it advantageous to treat permanent mortgage lending as more than a residual activity.

In this case either of two possibilities seems likely. One is that banks will proceed about as they have in recent years. They will come in and out of the permanent mortgage market; the "residual" can be quite substantial, as it often has been for California banks, when business and consumer credit demands slacken or time deposits rise sharply. On a more steady basis, banks will finance mortgage companies and home improvements. Banks also will compete for construction loans, and here they are at a disadvantage when the permanent financing is supplied by savings and loan associations which want and can obtain the construction financing too. Finally, in the main, banks will limit their secondary market activities to adjustments in their own portfolios and to meeting changed liquidity needs; they will not actively import funds into the state through mortgage brokerage, and they will not seek to develop a servicing business.

The most uncertain part of this prognostication, still assuming a compartmentalized financial market, lies in the last point mentioned. It is conceivable that commercial banks could expand their mortgage brokerage and servicing activities. Certain advantages and efficiencies lie in this direction since banks now supply the short-term credit and stand-by commitments necessary for the mortgage companies' operations, and they actively seek construction loans. It might appear logical for the banks to take over the entire operation.

Three counter arguments should be noted, however. First, the only major income advantage for banks would lie in the expansion of their servicing operations. They already realize income from the financing and stand-by commitments they provide the mortgage companies, and they are in a good position to obtain the construction financing business as part of the package. Second, we have noted the reservations with which outside permanent investors may view a bank take-over. Quite possibly a *quid pro quo* would require that banks largely discontinue the permanent mortgage lending activity. In view of the apparent, even if sporadic, interest of California banks in adding to their permanent mortgage portfolios, such a development does not seem likely. Third, we have noted the possibility of a diminution in the amount of future importing activity through traditional secondary market resale techniques. Certainly a bank's estimation of the future of such activities would have to be somewhat optimistic before it would undertake the difficult task of assuming the role now played by well-established mortgage companies.

(2) *Evaluation of the "compartmentalization" case.*—We may conclude that as long as the present compartmentalization of state financial markets persists, there seem to be strong and logical economic reasons for continuing the status quo. In evaluating the status quo it is well to bear in mind that it results from a natural economic evolution and has provided an abundance of mortgage financing for California's enormous postwar development. Serious questions can be raised, however. Those discussed here do not pretend to constitute a complete list. They deal with problems of the allocation of total financial resources and of competition on the supply side of the mortgage market.

(a) Effects on the allocation of total financial resources.—It is hard to justify any compartmentalization of markets on traditional market theory grounds, and the present instance is no exception. The publicly imposed advantages enjoyed by savings and loan associations in savings markets, notably deposit insurance and differential deposit rates, together with their legal obligation to restrict their investments to mortgage loans, are obvious blueprints for misallocation of financial resources.

It is beyond the scope of the present undertaking to attempt to measure and assess the nature, dangers, and actual present degree of such misallocation. However, the recent spectacular growth of association savings accounts and the knowledge that these funds must be and are being converted into mortgage obligations are at least grounds for uneasiness regarding the effects on mortgage lending standards and possible overbuilding in some segments of state real estate markets. Further, as many of these funds probably represent diversions from other sections of the capital market, this could lead to credit shortages for sound, needed, and worthwhile ventures in those areas.

On the other hand, it should be recognized that some advocate policies favoring the residential mortgage market. Many of today's policies result from conscious governmental attempts to channel funds into the housing market in an effort to reduce the costs of mortgage credit and increase the production of housing.

(b) Effects on the level of competition in mortgage lending.—A second problem is competition, or the lack of it, in mortgage lending. The advantages enjoyed by savings and loan associations, coupled with their powerful position in savings markets and their inability to enter other markets, naturally tend to drive other institutional lenders out of the mortgage market.

Obvious dangers result. Savings and loan associations traditionally charge borrowers more than other institutional lenders, reflecting in part their willingness to accept poorer quality loans. But it also undoubtedly reflects some degree of monopoly power in local mortgage markets which will certainly not diminish if other institutions reduce the scope of their mortgage lending activity.

Although legally protected geographical barriers do exist, several competing associations are available to borrowers in most urban areas. However, mergers and holding companies may continue to reduce such competition. Also, collusion of independent firms is always easier if they are of a common type, joined together in a trade association, with the same legal controls, costs, and managerial problems. Mortgage lending is mainly a small-scale, personal-service business probably with few of the offsetting gains in efficiency that so often partly justify concentration in other industries. In short, a diminution of interinstitutional competition in mortgage lending is not welcome.

(3) *Projections and evaluations assuming decompartmentalization.*— Moves towards decompartmentalization of mortgage and savings mar-

kets could take at least four forms. First, stronger federal and state regulations, tighter enforcement of present controls and mortgage risk evaluations, and removal of present differential shelters from income tax liabilities would limit the ability of savings and loan associations to offer such liberal conventional mortgage terms and to compete so aggressively for savings. Second, associations could be permitted to make specified nonmortgage loans and to hold a higher percentage of nonresidential and nonsingle family mortgages. Already nonreal estate lending by associations is undoubtedly increasing in the form of property owners borrowing against their existing real estate equities to finance consumption and business expenditures. Third, commercial banks could be permitted to offer more liberal conventional mortgage terms and to make more rapid upward adjustments in time deposit rates. Fourth, interest rates on insured and guaranteed loans could be decontrolled.

Changes along these lines would lead to rather different projections from those derived under the compartmentalization assumption. Savings and loan associations would lose some of their competitive edge in mortgage markets and would turn more to nonmortgage lending fields. Both of these developments would induce commercial banks to exploit every possible credit market including mortgage finance, and to step up their permanent mortgage lending activity. Impetus also might be given to the formation of a private insurance device for conventional mortgages, increased secondary market activities, and attempts to build their mortgage servicing accounts. But banks would also feel increased competition from associations in these and related areas, such as the financing of mortgage companies. Mortgage companies also might achieve increased vigor. If our earlier prognostications about future monetary policies are correct, a decline of savings and loan competition in mortgage lending and decontrol of FHA interest rates would be accompanied by expanded FHA operations and interregional flows through traditional secondary market channels.

These changes have many ramifications and implications, particularly for the general theory and practice of commercial banking as well as the established principles of savings and loan association practices and specializations. A discussion of these is impossible here. However, from the standpoint of the issues considered in Section (2), a move toward decompartmentalization would appear to be good. The possibility of a dangerous imbalance in credit flows would be eliminated; a better allocation of total financial resources would be realized; and the level of competition in all affected markets would be raised. The abundance of future mortgage credit supplies might be reduced somewhat if savings and loan associations were no longer limited to mortgage lending. However, the supply of funds should remain ample, with a large volume of imports through either established or newly-developed market channels, as long as future monetary conditions are no tighter than those that prevailed in the 1950's.

CHAPTER IV

COMMERCIAL BANKING AS A BUSINESS

Earnings and Capital Problems of California Banks, 1946–1975

PAUL F. WENDT

1. INTRODUCTION

AN ADEQUATE SUPPLY of bank capital is in the long-run interests both of the public and the stockholders. Bank capital has important implications for the safety of bank deposits and for earnings growth. Although the short-run interests of bank stockholders may be to operate with the smallest possible amount of capital to profit from leverage, adequate capital is necessary to maintain the confidence of corporate depositors and to support growth in earning assets and profits.

Bank profitability is one key to the adequacy of present and future capital. This report (1) reviews the profitability of the banking industry in California since World War II, (2) considers the outlook for earnings of banks, and (3) estimates their ability to raise the necessary capital.

The conclusion of this study is that California banks probably will maintain a relatively high rate of growth in operating income and profits during the next decade (4 percent), although the growth rate may be lower than that achieved during 1946 to 1962. Future levels of federal and state income taxation, patterns of government regulation, and the degree to which California banks are able and willing to finance new capital requirements through capital note issues, will have important influence upon profits growth and upon the availability of capital to California banks. Present indications are that capital notes will provide an attractive substitute for new equity capital issues as a means of financing the future growth of commercial banking in California.

2. POST-WORLD WAR II PROFITABILITY

High rates of population and economic growth in California since World War II resulted in a more rapid expansion in bank assets and earnings in the state than for the nation as a whole.

287

California banks, in common with all commercial banks in the nation, expanded holdings of United States government securities rapidly during World War II, and, as a result, government and state bonds accounted for a preponderant portion of bank assets in 1946. They were thus in a highly favorable position to expand loans during the postwar years.

From 1946 to 1963, the assets of all insured banks in California increased by a multiple of 2.41; loans increased 6.76 times; capital accounts increased 3.57 times, while net profits after taxes increased 2.68 times. For commercial banks in the United States during this period, assets increased by 1.97 times; loans increased by 5.22; capital accounts by 2.70, and net profits after taxes increased by a multiple of 2.38.[1]

Growth of banking was undergirded by population and income expansion in California far surpassing that for the nation. The ratio of California's population to that of the entire nation has increased in each decennial census from 2.0 percent in 1900 to 7.0 percent in 1950 and 8.9 percent in 1960. California's population increased by 48.5 percent, while the United States' population increased by 18.5 percent.[2] Total personal incomes in California increased by 36.0 percent from 1950 to 1962, and average per capita personal incomes in California of $2,871 in 1962 were among the highest in the nation.[3]

Total deposits of insured commercial banks in California more than doubled between 1946 and 1963. During this same period, deposits of all insured commercial banks in the United States rose more slowly (1.9 times). It can be noted (Table 1) that the percentage increase in demand deposits of California banks exceeded that of all commercial banks by a substantial margin. The rate of increase in time deposits was about the same for California and the nation during the postwar period. Time and savings deposits, however, accounted for substantially higher proportions of total deposits for insured California banks than for all insured commercial banks. This is an important factor influencing earnings trends.

The growth in California banking has been accompanied by a decline in the number of insured commercial banks in the state from 187 in 1946 to 149 as of December 31, 1963. This decline in the number of banks was accompanied by an approximate doubling in the total num-

---

[1] *Annual Reports,* 1946–1963, Federal Deposit Insurance Corporation.

[2] *United States Census of Population 1960,* United States Summary Number of Inhabitants, PC(1) IA U.S., U.S. Department of Commerce, Bureau of the Census, 1961, Table 9.

[3] U.S. Department of Commerce, *Survey of Current Business,* April 1963, p. 9.

ber of bank offices from 1,004 in 1951 to 1,923 in 1962.[4] By the end of 1963, eight California banks were among the fifty largest banks in the nation (ranked by deposit size), compared with eleven banks in the New York Reserve District and four in the Chicago District. The substantial

TABLE 1

MEASURES OF POST-WORLD WAR II GROWTH, INSURED COMMERCIAL BANKS
CALIFORNIA AND THE UNITED STATES

(billions of dollars)

All insured commercial banks	Average for year 1946	Average for year 1963	1963 ÷ 1946 (in percent)
California:			
Number of banks, December 31...	(187)	(149)	0.80
Total assets..................	$13.727	$33.066	2.41
Total loans...................	2.667	18.020	6.76
Total deposits................	13.026	29.611	2.27
Time deposits..............	5.086	15.306	3.01
Demand deposits...........	7.940	14.305	1.80
Capital accounts..............	.615	2.195	3.57
Net profit after taxes.........	.072	.193	2.68
Percent net profits to capital			
accounts....................	.1171	.0879	.75
United States:			
Number of banks, December 31...	(13,354)	(13,291)	.99
Total assets..................	$151.857	$298.941	1.97
Total loans...................	27.763	145.028	5.22
Total deposits................	141.792	264.069	1.86
Time deposits..............	31.920	104.508	3.27
Demand deposits...........	109.872	159.562	1.45
Capital accounts..............	9.008	24.284	2.70
Net profits after taxes.........	0.902	2.152	2.38
Percent net profits to capital			
accounts....................	0.1002	0.0883	.88

SOURCE: Annual Reports Federal Deposit Insurance Corporation: 1946, Table 120; 1963, Tables 112. 120.

number of large banks in California and in the Twelfth District reflects the high rate of deposit growth and loan expansion in the West, as well as the fact that the laws of the Twelfth District states permit branch banking on a wider scale than those of most other states.

The capital accounts of insured commercial banks in California in 1963 were over 3 times as great as in 1946, representing a substantially larger percentage rise than for all insured commercial banks.

[4] David A. Alhadeff, *Monopoly and Competition in Banking*, Berkeley, University of California Press, 1954.

FIGURE I

Comparison of Earnings and Expenses of California and United States Insured Commercial Banks, 1946–1962

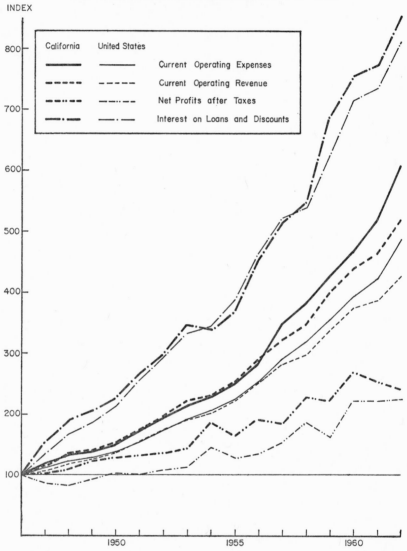

SOURCE: Federal Deposit Insurance Corporation, *Annual Reports,* 1946–1962.

The net profits of California banks increased 2.68 times from 1946 to 1963, exceeding the increase of 2.38 times for all insured commercial banks in the Unted States (Table 1). The percentage of net profits after taxes to capital accounts was somewhat higher for California banks until 1961, but has narrowed since, due in large measure to the influence of the increasing cost of time deposits.

Profits after taxes increased at a higher rate during the post-World War II period for insured commercial banks in California than for all insured United States banks. This was so because expansion in interest on loans and discounts and total operating revenues has more than offset a larger percentage increase in current operating expenses. A somewhat more rapid increase in operating expenses for California insured banks in 1962 accounts for the decline in profits shown in Figure I for that year.

The hypothesis that high rates of economic growth in the state have sustained rapid growth in commercial bank assets and high profit levels for banks seems to follow from the above.

a. Earnings and expenses of California banks, 1946 to 1963

Table 2 shows the long-term earnings trend for California insured commercial banks since 1946. The dominant factor contributing to the increase in operating revenues was the expansion in income from loans. Service charges on loans and deposits accounted for most of the remaining earnings gain over the period. Increases in employment costs and interest paid on time and savings deposits accounted for approximately 75 percent of the total increase in current operating expenses between 1946 and 1963. Although net income before taxes rose from less than $100 million in 1946 to $340 million in 1963, increases in federal and state income taxes absorbed over one-half of the gain. The very large percentage increase in occupancy costs is particularly notable and reflects, of course, the substantial increase in the number of bank offices since World War II.

b. Analysis of earnings by size of bank

Attention has already been drawn to the persistent decline in the number of insured commercial banks in California during the postwar period and to the expanding role of the large branch banks. It is of some significance, therefore, to review the rates of earnings growth for the large branch banks in comparison with all other insured commercial banks in California.

PAUL F. WENDT

TABLE 2

INCOME AND EXPENSES: ALL INSURED COMMERCIAL BANKS IN CALIFORNIA
1946, 1951, 1956, 1961, 1962
(millions of dollars)

	1946	1951	1956	1961	1962
Current operating revenue—					
Total	$284.8	$487.2	$811.1	$1,321.7	$1,476.1
Interest on U. S. government obligations	106.3	83.2	126.1	180.3	194.5
Interest and dividends on other securities	16.7	24.3	35.5	57.1	73.2
Interest and discounts on loans	113.7	300.1	512.8	878.5	970.5
Service charges and fees on loans	2.4	7.6	19.5	25.3	34.6
Service charges on deposit accounts	13.4	30.2	57.8	97.8	105.2
Other charges, commissions, fees, revenues	21.5	27.5	34.9	41.8	51.0
Trust department	10.7	14.3	24.5	40.9	46.9
Current operating expenses—					
Total	$182.3	$311.0	$512.8	$944.4	$1,110.4
Salaries—officers	25.1	39.6	60.9	97.6	108.3
Salaries and wages—other employees	62.4	101.4	166.2	245.8	256.9
Officers and employee benefits				37.6	45.5
Fees paid to directors and commissioners	.6	.8	1.0	1.2	1.3
Interest paid on time and savings deposits	43.0	90.9	146.0	346.6	468.8
Interest on borrowed money	.0	1.2	4.2	4.6	8.0
Occupancy expense—bank premises	3.6	5.9	10.9	57.1	64.5
Furniture and equipment				28.9	37.1
Other current operating expenses	41.3	58.9	104.2	125.0	119.9
Taxes other than net income	6.3	12.2	19.3		
Recoveries, transfers from reserves, profits	28.4	16.7	17.7	74.3	32.6
Losses, charge-offs, transfers to reserves	33.8	34.0	67.5	109.0	88.0
Net income before taxes	97.1	158.9	248.5	342.7	310.2
Federal taxes	22.1	58.5	102.4	137.8	104.6
State taxes	3.1	5.2	8.1	21.2	31.8
Net income after taxes	71.9	95.1	137.9	183.7	173.8

SOURCE: Federal Deposit Insurance Corporation, *Annual Reports*, 1946, 1951, 1956, 1961, 1962.

The indices in Table 3 reveal relatively greater percentage increases in gross earnings and net profits before and after income taxes over the period from 1946 to 1963 for California's largest banks than for the smaller banks. Generalization from these data is made difficult by the fact that the Bank of America accounts for approximately 40 percent of the total resources of California's larger banks. It can be noted that the percentage expansion in earnings on loans for the larger bank group was almost twice that for all other insured commercial banks in California. Similarly, interest on securities rose at more rapid rates for the larger banks. It is only with respect to service charges on deposit accounts that California's smaller banks showed the largest percentage rise over the period.

Closer examination of the trends (see Figure II and Table 3) indicates that the differences in rates of expansion between California's large and small banks appear to have narrowed for some categories of income in more recent years. Since 1959 the rate of expansion in loan income and service charges on deposit accounts has, for example, been approximately the same for the largest banks as for all other California insured banks. At the same time, the relative expansion in salaries and wages, and interest on time and savings deposits, continues to be more rapid for California's largest banks. As a result of these trends, the rate of increase of net profits before and after taxes has been somewhat more rapid for all other insured California banks than for the largest banks since 1961. As will be seen below, however, this may be viewed as a temporary phenomenon.

The relative rates of increase in earnings, expenses and net profits for different segments of time are reflected in the slopes for the variables shown in Figure II. The narrowing in the relative rates of expansion in earnings by size of bank referred to above is apparent in more recent years. It can be seen that the increase in interest paid on time deposits had a particular impact on the 1961 and 1962 earnings of the larger banks, which assume a major role in this sector. It might be expected that higher interest charges paid on time deposits would be offset over any period of time by higher loan charges, particularly on the real estate mortgages. For this reason the apparent unfavorable effect on bank profits of higher interest paid on time deposits may be temporary. This conclusion is affirmed in bank earnings figures for the first half of 1963.

Table 4 shows the rising trend in the importance of California's banks with deposits of $275 million or more. It can be seen that by 1963, California's eight largest banks accounted for 85.4 percent of

FIGURE II
Rates of Change of Total Earnings and Expenses and Net Profits
After Taxes. California Member Banks with Total Deposits
of $275 Million or More and All Other
Insured Commercial Banks, 1946–1962

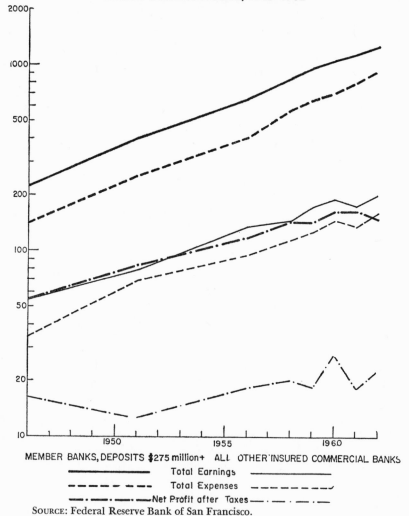

MEMBER BANKS, DEPOSITS $275 million+   ALL OTHER INSURED COMMERCIAL BANKS
━━━━━━━━━━━━━━ Total Earnings ━━━━━━━━
━ ━ ━ ━ ━ ━ ━ Total Expenses ━ ━ ━ ━ ━ ━ ━
━・━━・━━・━Net Profit after Taxes ━・━━・━━・━

Source: Federal Reserve Bank of San Francisco.

total earnings and for 86.7 percent of earnings on loans by California insured commercial banks. The percentages of total earnings accounted for by California's large banks rose consistently from 1946 to 1962 but declined somewhat in 1963. Although the ratio of total expenses accounted for by the larger banks also rose during the post-World War II period, the rate of increase was less rapid with the exception of interest on time deposits. As a result, it can be seen that the larger banks accounted for over 90 percent of total net profits after taxes in 1961 and for over 86 percent in 1962 and 1963. The implications of these trends will be considered in more detail in the analysis of operating ratios.

c. Analysis of operating ratios, 1946 to 1963

The annual operating ratios for member banks in the Twelfth District provide a basis for viewing the post-World War II earning record in more detail. The ratios shown in Table 5 are unweighted arithmetic averages for individual banks and understandably obscure differences in individual bank performance. It can be noted that California bank earnings, expressed as a percentage of total capital accounts before and after federal income taxes, declined sharply since 1961 from the postwar peak reached in 1960. Rising employee costs and interest on time deposits were the principal factors accounting for the decline in earnings. However, it can also be seen that a rising rate of return in recent years, particularly on loan portfolios, was an important offsetting influence. As a result, Table 5 shows that net profits after taxes as a percentage of total assets have remained relatively stable during the postwar years. The decline in net profits expressed as a percentage of capital accounts from 1946 to 1951 reflects the substantial additions made to capital by California banks during that period.

Table 6 reveals that net income before and after income taxes has varied considerably since World War II for large and small California banks as a percentage of total assets and of capital accounts. In more recent years profits appear to have been somewhat higher as a percent of capital accounts for the banks with deposits exceeding $50 million but there is no clear indication that profitability is directly related to bank size. It can also be observed that net current operating earnings and the rate of dividend payments have been substantially higher for California's large banks. The latter trend can be attributed in part to the fact that the larger banks have been growing rapidly, and that higher dividends have been used as a basis for making their capital stocks attractive to investors. The impact of rising interest rates over

TABLE 3

ANALYSIS OF EARNINGS AND EXPENSES OF INSURED COMMERCIAL BANKS IN CALIFORNIA BY SIZE OF BANK, SELECTED YEARS 1946, 1951, 1956, 1961, 1962

(millions of dollars)

	1946	1951		1956		1961		1962	
	Millions of dollars	Index 1946 = 100	Millions of dollars	Index 1946 = 100	Millions of dollars	Index 1946 = 100	Millions of dollars	Index 1946 = 100	Millions of dollars
Member banks in Calif. with avg. total deposits of $275 million or more									
Total Earnings:	227.7	179.2	408.0	295.1	673.5	503.3	1,145.6	557.2	1,274.4
Government securities[a]	84.8	78.6	66.2	125.4	102.3	185.6	153.2	192.9	164.0
Other securities[a]	12.6	153.2	19.3	228.6	28.8	369.8	46.6	484.1	61.1
Earnings on loans	92.9	279.9	260.0	480.6	446.5	851.3	790.9	941.1	874.3
Service charges	11.5	226.1	26.0	420.9	48.4	717.4	82.5	775.6	89.2
Trust department	9.1	131.9	12.0	244.0	22.2	409.9	37.3	469.2	42.7
All other earnings	16.8	128.0	21.5	150.6	25.3	208.3	35.0	256.5	43.1
Total Expenses:	145.9	172.5	251.7	285.9	417.7	554.3	808.8	652.4	951.8
Salaries and wages	73.3	160.8	117.9	255.0	186.9	446.4	327.2	480.5	352.2
Interest on deposits	30.8	228.2	70.3	383.8	118.2	969.5	298.6	1,316.9	405.6
All other expenses	41.8	151.9	63.5	269.4	112.6	437.8	183.0	464.1	194.0
Net current earnings	81.8	187.4	153.3	312.7	255.8	411.6	336.7	394.3	322.6
Total net losses (−) or recoveries (+)					−25.2		+13.4		−11.4

Net profits after taxes	55.4	148.4	82.2	215.5	119.4	298.6	165.4	271.8	150.6
Number of banks	11		11		9		8		8

All other banks in Calif.

Total Earnings:	57.1	138.7	79.2	241.0	137.6	308.4	176.1	353.2	201.7
Government securities[a]	21.5	79.1	17.0	110.7	23.8	126.0	27.1	141.9	30.5
Other securities[a]	4.1	121.9	5.0	163.4	6.7	256.1	10.5	295.1	12.1
Earnings on loans	20.8	192.8	40.1	318.7	66.3	421.1	87.6	462.5	96.2
Charges on deposit accounts	1.9	221.0	4.2	494.7	9.4	805.3	15.3	842.1	16.0
Trust department	1.6	143.7	2.3	143.7	2.3	225.0	3.6	237.5	3.8
All other earnings	7.2	147.2	10.6	404.2	29.1	444.4	32.0	598.6	43.1
Total Expenses:	36.4	162.9	59.3	261.3	95.1	372.5	135.6	435.7	158.6
Salaries and wages	14.2	162.7	23.1	283.1	40.2	378.9	53.8	412.0	58.5
Time and savings deposits[b]	12.2	168.8	20.6	227.9	27.8	393.4	48.0	518.0	63.2
All other expenses	10.0	156.0	15.6	271.0	27.1	338.0	33.8	369.0	36.9
Net current earnings[c]	20.7	96.7	19.9	205.3	42.5	195.6	40.5	208.2	43.1
Net profits before taxes	21.2	99.1	21.0	152.8	32.4	156.1	33.1	178.8	37.9
Taxes on net income	4.7	170.2	8.0	293.6	13.8	312.8	14.7	314.9	14.8
Net profits after taxes	16.5	78.2	12.9	112.1	18.5	110.9	18.3	140.6	23.2
Number of banks	176		179		123		109		115

a Interest and dividends.
b Interest.
c There are no losses or recoveries for the years considered.
SOURCE: Federal Reserve Bank of San Francisco.

TABLE 4

ANALYSIS OF EARNINGS AND EXPENSES OF INSURED COMMERCIAL BANKS IN CALIFORNIA BY SIZE OF BANK
(PERCENTAGE OF TOTAL EARNINGS AND EXPENSES AND RELATIVES, 1946 = 100)
SELECTED YEARS 1946–1962

	1946		1951		1956		1961		1962	
	Index 1946 = 100	Percent of total	Index 1946 = 100	Percent of total	Index 1946 = 100	Percent of total	Index 1946 = 100	Percent of total	Index 1946 = 100	Percent of total
Member banks in California with average total deposits of $275 million or more										
Total earnings:	100.0	79.9	104.7	83.7	103.9	83.0	108.5	86.7	108.0	86.3
Interest and dividends on government securities	100.0	79.8	99.7	79.6	101.6	81.1	106.5	85.0	105.6	84.3
Interest and dividends on other securities	100.0	75.4	105.3	79.4	107.6	81.1	118.6	89.4	110.7	83.5
Earnings on loans	100.0	81.7	106.0	86.6	106.6	87.1	110.2	90.0	110.3	90.1
Service charges on deposit accounts	100.0	85.8	100.3	86.1	97.5	83.7	98.3	84.4	98.7	84.8
Trust department	100.0	85.0	98.7	83.9	106.6	90.6	107.3	91.2	107.1	91.0
All other earnings	100.0	70.3	87.1	61.2	66.0	46.4	74.1	52.1	71.6	50.3
Total expenses:	100.0	80.0	101.1	80.9	101.7	81.4	107.0	85.6	107.1	85.7
Salaries and wages	100.0	83.8	99.9	83.1	98.6	82.0	102.9	85.6	102.8	85.5
Interest on time and savings deposits	100.0	71.6	108.0	77.3	113.1	81.0	120.2	86.1	120.8	86.5

Net profits before income taxes	100.0	78.2	110.0	86.8	111.2	87.0	115.5	90.3	112.3	87.8
Taxes on net income	100.0	81.3	107.5	87.4	107.6	87.5	111.6	90.7	109.6	89.1
Net profits after taxes	100.0	77.0	112.2	86.4	112.5	86.6	116.9	90.0	112.5	86.6
Number of banks		11		11		9		8		8

All other banks

Total earnings:	100.0	21.1	77.2	16.3	80.6	17.0	63.0	13.3	64.4	13.6
Interest and dividends on government securities	100.0	20.2	101.0	20.4	93.6	18.9	74.3	15.0	77.7	15.7
Interest and dividends on other securities	100.0	24.6	83.7	20.6	76.8	18.9	43.1	10.6	67.1	16.5
Earnings on loans	100.0	18.3	73.2	13.4	70.5	12.9	54.6	10.0	54.1	9.9
Service charges on deposit accounts	100.0	14.2	97.9	13.9	114.8	16.3	109.8	15.6	107.0	15.2
Trust department	100.0	15.0	93.2	16.1	62.7	9.4	58.7	8.8	60.0	9.0
All other earnings	100.0	29.7	130.6	38.8	180.5	53.6	161.3	47.9	167.3	49.7
Total expenses:	100.0	20.0	95.5	19.1	93.0	18.6	72.0	14.4	71.5	14.3
Salaries and wages	100.0	16.2	100.6	16.9	107.1	18.0	85.7	14.4	86.3	14.5
Interest on time and savings deposits	100.0	28.4	79.9	22.7	66.9	19.0	48.9	13.9	47.5	13.5
All other expenses	100.0	18.4	96.2	17.7	102.2	18.8	82.1	15.1	84.2	15.5
Net current earnings	100.0	20.2	64.4	13.0	70.8	14.3	53.5	10.8	58.4	11.8
Profits before income taxes	100.0	21.8	60.5	13.2	59.6	13.0	44.5	9.7	50.0	10.9
Taxes on net income	100.0	23.0	54.8	12.6	54.3	12.5	43.5	10.0	58.3	13.4
Net profits after income taxes	100.0	23.0	59.1	13.6	58.3	13.4	43.5	10.0	58.3	13.4

SOURCE: Federal Reserve Bank of San Francisco, communications during 1962. Percentage calculations by the author.

TABLE 5

Operating Ratios, California Member Banks
Selected Years, 1946–1962

All California member banks	1946 Trend ratio 1946=100	1946 Percent	1951 Trend ratio 1946=100	1951 Percent	1956 Trend ratio 1946=100	1956 Percent	1961 Trend ratio 1946=100	1961 Percent	1962ᵃ Trend ratio 1946=100	1962ᵃ Percent	Percentage change 1946–1962
Percentage of total earnings:											
Interest on U. S. government securities	100.	41.5	51.3	21.3	48.7	20.2	43.1	17.9	43.1	17.9	− 56.9
Interest and dividends on other securities	100.	4.7	74.5	3.5	83.0	3.9	95.7	4.5	97.9	4.6	− 02.1
Earnings on loans	100.	37.0	154.3	57.1	156.5	57.9	167.0	61.8	169.4	62.7	+ 69.5
Service charges on deposit accounts	100.	5.1	147.1	7.5	188.2	9.6	184.3	9.4	172.5	8.8	+ 72.5
All other earnings	100.	11.9	89.1	10.6	70.6	8.4	53.8	6.4	50.4	6.0	− 48.7
Total earnings	100.	100.0		100.0		100.0		100.0		100.0	
Office and employee benefits								2.9		3.0	
Salaries and wages	100.	30.8	109.1	33.6	105.5	32.5	95.1	29.3	90.3	27.8	− 9.7
Interest on time deposits	100.	13.4	122.4	16.4	121.0	16.2	182.8	24.5	216.4	29.0	+116.4
All other expenses	100.	14.9	103.5	20.6	102.0	20.3	97.5	19.4	93.5	18.6ᵇ	− 6.5
Total expenses	100	64.1	110.1	70.6	107.6	69.0	118.7	76.1	122.3	78.4	+ 22.3

Net recovery and profits (or losses)		+1.4		−3.6		−4.7		0.6		−0.3	
Net increase (or decrease) valuation reserves						−2.7		−2.7		−2.4	
Taxes on net income	100.	9.0	103.3	9.3	95.5	8.6	110.0	9.9	78.9	7.1	− 21.1
Net profits	100.	28.3	58.3	16.5	53.0	15.0	42.0	11.9	41.7	11.8	− 58.3
Percentage of total capital accounts											
Net current earnings before taxes	100.	17.5	84.6	14.8	118.3	20.7	98.3	17.2	88.0	15.4	− 12.3
Profits before income taxes	100.	17.6	72.7	12.8	87.5	15.4	89.2	15.7	77.8	13.7	− 22.2
Net profits	100.	13.2	61.4	8.1	72.7	9.6	65.1	8.6	63.6	8.4	− 33.3
Cash dividends declared	100.	2.9	100.0	2.9	103.4	3.0	110.3	3.2	103.4	3.0	3.4
Percentage of total assets											
Total earnings	100.	2.1	170.0	3.57	201.9	4.24	244.3	5.13	247.6	5.20	+147.6
Net current earnings before taxes	100.	0.8	133.7	1.07	162.5	1.30	152.5	1.22	138.7	1.11	3.7
Net profits	100.	0.6	93.3	0.56	103.3	0.62	100.0	0.60	100.0	0.60	....
Rates of return on: U. S. government securities	100.	1.4	114.3	1.6	170.0	2.38	222.1	3.11	230.0	3.22	+128.6
Other securities	100.	3.3	81.8	2.7	77.6	2.56	97.3	3.21	100.0	3.30	....
Net recoveries and profits and losses on securities		0		0		−0.34		0.41		0.20	....
Earnings on loans	100.	6.6	89.4	5.9	96.8	6.39	106.7	7.04	106.8	7.05	+ 6.1
Number of banks		111		117		82		58		58	

a Includes Hawaii.
b Includes net occupancy of bank premises 4.5 percent. All other expenses 14.1 percent.
SOURCE: Federal Reserve Bank of San Francisco, *Operating Ratios of Member Banks*, Twelfth Federal Reserve District, Selected Years, 1946-1962.

AVERAGE OPERATING RATIOS FOR CALIFORNIA MEMBE)

	California, 1946				
	Banks with total deposits (thousands of dollars)				
	Under 2,000	2,000 to 5,000	5,000 to 15,000	15,000 to 50,000	50,000 to 150,000	275,000 and over[a]

	Under 2,000	2,000 to 5,000	5,000 to 15,000	15,000 to 50,000	50,000 to 150,000	275,000 and over[a]
Number of banks	5	41	36	14	5	10
Summary ratios						
Percentage of total capital accounts						
1. Net current operating earnings	10.5	17.6	18.7	16.0	25.3	14.4
2. Net income before related taxes	11.0	17.8	19.3	15.6	21.5	14.5
3. Net income (after taxes)	8.8	13.8	14.5	11.2	15.7	10.3
4. Total dividends declared	2.2	2.4	3.0	3.4	3.7	4.3
Percentage of total assets						
5. Total current operating revenue	2.1	2.1	2.1	2.1	2.2	1.8
6. Net current operating earnings	0.6	0.8	0.8	0.7	1.0	0.6
7. Net income (after taxes)	0.5	0.6	0.6	0.5	0.6	0.5
Sources and disposition of earnings						
Percentage of total earnings						
8. Interest on United States government obligations	37.9	41.1	42.2	38.8	32.2	50.7
9. Interest and dividends on other securities	4.5	5.0	4.7	4.6	4.6	3.4
10. Interest, discount, service charges, and other fees on loans	32.3	37.1	37.7	38.7	46.7	29.7
11. Service charges on deposit accounts	8.5	5.9	4.8	3.7	3.4	3.9
12. All other operating revenue	16.8	10.9	10.6	14.2	13.1	12.3
13. Total current operating revenue	100.0	100.0	100.0	100.0	100.0	100.0
14. Salaries and wages	37.1	31.9	29.2	30.4	25.3	32.9
15. Officer and employee benefits						
16. Interest on time and savings deposits	9.0	13.3	13.5	15.6	13.6	12.5
17. Net occupancy expense of bank premises						
18. All other operating expenses	24.2	19.7	19.6	20.8	16.8	19.6
19. Total current operating expenses	70.3	64.9	62.3	66.8	55.7	65.0
20. Net current operating earnings	29.7	35.1	37.7	33.2	44.3	35.0
21. Net recoveries and profits (or losses—)[b]	+2.5	+1.3	+3.0	0.5	5.1	+1.2
22. Net increase—(or decrease) in valuation reserves[c]						
23. Taxes on net income	6.3	7.7	10.2	9.2	10.8	10.1
24. Net income (after taxes)	25.9	28.7	30.5	23.5	28.4	26.1
Rates of return on securities and loans						
Return on securities						
25. Interest on United States government obligations	1.3	1.4	1.4	1.4	1.3	1.4
26. Interest and dividends on other securities	3.3	3.4	3.3	2.8	3.6	3.3
27. Net recoveries and profits (or losses—) on total securities[d]	0	0	+0.1	+0.1	0.1	0.1
Return on loans (net)						
28. Interest, discount, service charges, and other fees on loans	6.0	5.9	5.5	4.6	5.0	3.8
29. Net recoveries (or losses—) on loans[d]	0.6	0.1	0	0	0.1	+0.7
Distribution of assets						
Percentage of total assets						
30. United States government obligations	55.5	56.3	58.9	55.7	53.6	61.9
31. Other securities	3.5	3.7	4.0	3.5	4.6	2.6
32. Loans and discounts (net)	12.0	14.5	15.4	17.2	21.2	14.0
33. Cash assets	27.4	24.7	21.0	22.5	19.8	20.6
34. Real estate assets	1.6	0.7	0.6	0.9	0.7	0.5
Capital and deposit ratios—in percentages						
35. Total capital accounts to total assets	6.9	4.7	4.7	4.4	4.0	4.5
36. Total capital accounts to total assets less United States government obligations and cash assets	45.9	31.7	36.2	22.5	15.2	30.0
37. Total capital accounts to total deposits	7.5	5.0	4.9	4.7	4.2	4.7
38. Total time and savings deposits to total deposits	27.6	32.4	35.8	36.8	34.5	30.0
39. Interest on time and savings deposits to total time and savings deposits	0.7	0.8	0.8	0.9	0.9	0.8

[a] No banks with total deposits of $150,000,000 to $275,000,000.
[b] Net recoveries or losses on loans, securities, and other assets excluding changes in valuation reserves on loans and securities for 1961 and 1962.
[c] On loans and securities for 1961 and 1962.

| | California, 1950 | | | | | | California, 1961 | | | | | California and Hawaii, 1962 | | | | |
| | Banks with total deposits (thousands of dollars) | | | | | | Banks with total deposits (thousands of dollars) | | | | | Banks with total deposits (thousands of dollars) | | | | |
Under 2,000	2,000 to 5,000	5,000 to 15,000	15,000 to 50,000	50,000 to 150,000	275,000 and over[a]	Under 5,000	5,000 to 15,000	15,000 to 50,000	50,000 to 275,000	275,000 and over	Under 5,000	5,000 to 15,000	15,000 to 50,000	50,000 to 275,000	275,000 and over
10	40	36	13	6	10	6	24	12	8	8	5	21	14	9	9
13.0	15.2	16.3	13.6	23.4	15.2	9.1	15.5	20.1	20.6	20.7	12.2	14.9	14.5	16.8	18.5
10.5	13.3	14.4	13.4	18.2	13.8	9.1	14.0	18.2	18.9	18.9	11.0	13.2	13.0	16.0	15.0
8.0	9.5	9.5	9.2	10.7	8.6	6.2	7.9	9.4	9.9	9.8	8.4	8.1	7.8	9.9	8.5
1.1	1.8	3.0	3.2	4.8	4.5	2.0	2.7	2.9	4.1	5.2	2.4	2.1	2.8	3.6	5.1
4.16	3.13	3.10	2.91	3.31	2.45	4.84	5.25	5.36	5.11	4.67	5.18	5.31	5.40	5.02	4.79
1.06	0.98	1.06	0.75	1.20	0.80	0.61	1.16	1.32	1.49	1.41	0.97	1.12	1.04	1.19	1.22
0.70	0.62	0.61	0.50	0.55	0.46	0.33	0.60	0.63	0.70	0.67	0.66	0.61	0.52	0.69	0.56
15.7	23.5	23.5	23.5	18.3	34.3	22.1	18.4	18.6	14.3	15.4	20.7	19.5	18.9	14.4	14.7
1.7	3.7	3.4	4.7	3.5	3.2	5.8	3.9	5.1	5.4	3.9	4.8	4.2	4.3	5.5	4.8
57.8	56.3	57.5	52.4	62.7	45.3	56.1	61.4	58.5	67.6	66.6	57.1	60.7	61.4	68.2	67.1
10.4	7.7	6.6	5.1	5.7	5.6	11.0	10.7	9.0	7.8	6.7	11.7	10.2	8.5	6.7	6.7
14.4	8.8	9.0	14.3	9.8	11.6	5.0	5.6	8.8	4.9	7.4	5.7	5.4	6.9	5.2	6.7
100.0	100.0	100.0	100.0	100.0	100.0	100.0	100.0	100.0	100.0	100.0	100.0	100.0	100.0	100.0	100.0
37.7	33.8	31.2	33.7	30.7	33.7	32.7	31.1	28.8	24.5	27.0	27.9	30.0	29.0	23.6	25.5
						2.4	3.2	2.8	2.7	2.9	1.8	3.3	2.7	2.7	3.6
6.8	14.1	15.4	16.3	13.9	13.1	28.7	23.3	24.3	25.7	23.8	32.9	26.5	29.1	32.8	29.1
						6.4	5.3	4.8	4.4	4.5	4.1	4.6	4.5	4.1	4.5
27.3	20.9	19.0	24.1	19.2	21.1	16.3	14.8	15.2	12.8	11.7	13.9	14.5	15.9	12.3	11.9
71.8	68.8	65.6	74.1	63.8	67.9	86.5	77.7	75.9	70.1	69.9	80.6	78.9	81.2	75.5	74.6
28.2	31.2	34.4	25.9	36.2	32.1	13.5	22.3	24.1	29.9	30.1	19.4	21.1	18.8	24.5	25.4
−3.5	−3.8	−3.4	−0.2	−7.7	−2.6	−2.5	0.6	1.0	0.5	2.1	0.6	−1.1	−0.4	2.4	−1.0
						1.3	−2.8	−2.6	−3.2	−4.7	−2.4	−1.2	−2.6	−3.6	−3.7
5.7	7.7	10.6	8.3	11.9	10.7	4.7	8.6	10.7	13.0	13.4	3.9	7.1	6.1	9.1	9.0
19.0	19.7	20.4	17.4	16.6	18.8	7.6	11.5	11.8	14.2	14.1	13.7	11.7	9.7	14.2	11.7
1.5	1.6	1.6	1.5	1.5	1.6	3.18	3.15	2.95	3.21	3.05	3.37	3.22	3.17	3.28	3.16
3.7	2.8	2.7	1.9	3.3	2.1	4.02	3.29	3.02	3.04	2.85	3.48	3.50	3.22	3.17	3.00
0	0	0	0	−0.1	0	0.17	0.39	0.26	0.56	0.71	0.10	0.08	0.29	0.53	0.07
7.5	6.1	5.8	5.2	5.7	4.3	7.52	7.09	7.45	6.72	6.19	7.20	7.27	7.37	6.57	6.47
−0.3	−0.2	−0.1	−0.1	−0.1	0	−0.56	−0.16	−0.13	−0.14	−0.17	−0.02	−0.17	−0.32	−0.15	−0.14
33.3	41.3	42.8	40.7	40.2	47.9	33.9	28.6	30.4	22.5	23.5	31.9	29.9	29.3	21.7	22.1
1.7	4.5	4.8	5.8	5.3	4.3	8.9	6.8	8.0	8.9	6.4	9.6	6.6	7.1	8.7	7.7
33.0	29.6	31.2	29.4	36.4	26.3	37.3	45.5	42.1	51.1	50.2	41.2	44.5	45.3	52.0	49.6
30.2	23.4	20.1	22.4	16.9	20.3	16.8	16.8	17.4	15.2	17.6	14.9	16.8	16.2	15.0	17.7
1.6	1.1	0.9	1.4	0.9	0.7	2.9	2.1	1.4	1.8	1.4	2.3	1.9	1.6	1.7	1.5
8.5	7.0	6.6	5.5	5.4	5.3	11.0	7.9	6.7	7.4	6.9	8.8	7.9	8.1	7.1	6.7
29.4	20.8	19.6	16.0	12.7	20.5	26.2	15.2	13.2	11.9	11.8	17.5	15.5	15.5	11.3	11.2
9.5	7.7	7.1	5.9	5.8	5.7	12.9	8.8	7.3	8.2	7.7	9.9	8.8	9.1	7.8	7.4
25.4	37.5	41.6	42.2	41.0	34.9	52.6	44.1	44.8	47.8	43.3	54.4	45.2	47.7	53.1	45.3
1.0	1.2	1.2	1.2	1.2	1.0	2.92	2.97	2.89	2.99	2.84	3.36	3.34	3.45	3.38	3.40

d Net recoveries or losses excluding changes in valuation reserves for 1961 and 1962.

NOTE: Balance sheet figures used as a basis for the ratios are averages of amounts. Reported for December 31 of the previous year and June and September and October for the year in question.

e Federal Reserve Bank of San Francisco, *Operating Ratios of Member Banks. Twelfth Federal Reserve District*, for the years 1946, 1950, 1961–1962.

most of the postwar period is seen in the gradual rise in the rate of return on securities and loans following the "accord" in 1950. The decline in the share of total earnings represented by earnings on securities is evident for all banks, but was a factor of particular importance for the banks in the largest asset category.

Table 6 shows that loan income more than doubled as a percentage of total income from 1946 to 1961 for the larger California banks, and increased substantially for all California insured commercial banks. In 1961 and 1962, loan income accounted for two-thirds of total earnings for California banks with deposits in excess of $50 million. Meanwhile, interest on securities represented less than 20 percent of total earnings for the larger banks in these years, as compared with 40–50 percent in 1946.

Service charges on deposit accounts were consistently higher as a percentage of total earnings for the smaller banks in California during the post-World War II period. Employment costs (including officer and employee benefits) also represented a larger share of total expenses for smaller than for larger California banks during the period, although the more rapid increase in officer and employee benefits for the larger banks has narrowed the spread in recent years.

The impact of income taxes appears to have been consistently more favorable for the smaller banks in California during the period since 1946. This is due in large part to the lower overall tax rate applicable to the income of smaller banks.[5]

Table 6 bears out the observation with respect to the more favorable tax position of the smaller banks. It can be observed that California banks with deposits under $2,000,000 reported taxes paid as a lower percentage of total expenses than for banks with deposits in excess of $2,000,000. It can also be noted that the average rate charged on loans was consistently higher for the smaller banks and it has already been seen that service charges were also higher as a percent of total earnings for these institutions.

It is somewhat surprising to observe that differences in the rates of return on securities among banks of various sizes are small for most

[5] Howard D. Crosse, *Management Policies for Commercial Banks* (Prentice-Hall Inc., Englewood Cliffs, New Jersey, 1962), p. 42. In discussing profitability of banks, Crosse says: "Small banks can still justify themselves in terms of profitability partly because their salary scales *are* low, partly because the interest rates they charge are somewhat higher than average, and partly because their net profits (to the extent that they do not exceed $25,000) are subject to a Federal income tax of only 30 percent as compared with the 52 percent tax on corporate profits in excess of $25,000." Based upon average operating ratios, he states that a bank would have to have deposits in excess of $2,300,000 before any of its operating earnings would be subject to taxes at the higher rate. Inclusion of tax-exempt income would increase this figure.

years shown in Table 6. In general, the smaller banks appear to have experienced a slightly higher return on both U. S. Government and other securities in recent years. This probably reflects a tendency for the smaller banks to invest in longer-term issues which generally have yielded higher returns. Higher capital-deposit ratios and, in recent years, higher ratios of investment in securities to total assets, offer further explanation for the higher returns from investments for smaller banks.

Attention must be called to the fact that the data in Table 6 represent a changing universe over the period. This, together with the fact that the ratios represent unweighted arithmetic averages of ratios for individual banks, suggests that the changes shown over time must be interpreted with considerable caution.[6]

d. Postwar changes in capital accounts

Table 7 summarizes the changes which have taken place since 1951 in the capital accounts of insured commercial banks in California and in the United States. Insured commercial banks in California added approximately $1.2 billion to capital accounts between 1951 and 1962. Approximately three-quarters of the total capital added resulted from retained profits, with the balance representing issuance of additional bank stock. Table 7 also indicates that retained earnings have accounted for somewhat higher percentages of new capital for California than for all banks in the United States over most of the period. Payout ratios have been notably higher for California insured banks during the postwar period, although this has been largely a reflection of a consistently high payout ratio for the Bank of America, which accounts for over 40 percent of total commercial bank capital and deposits in California.

It can be concluded from Table 7 and Figure III that California's commercial banks have enjoyed access to new capital through the securities markets on a par with all insured commercial banks in the nation. Further evidence of this trend is found in the fact that leading investment companies displayed a strong preference for California bank stocks in making additions to holdings in the banking industry in the quarter ended June 30, 1963.[7]

Confirmation of a favorable market for California bank issues is found in the observation that issues of leading California banks have

---

[6] The use of unweighted arithmetic averages of bank operating ratios tends to understate the importance of larger banks and to give exaggerated weight to the operations of the smaller banks.

[7] *Barron's,* August 5, 1963, p. 5, "Caution to the Winds."

TABLE 7

SOURCES OF CAPITAL AND PAY-OUT RATIOS
INSURED COMMERCIAL BANKS IN CALIFORNIA AND IN THE UNITED STATES
SELECTED YEARS, 1951–1962
(millions of dollars)

	1951	1960	1961	1962	Totals
Sources of capital:					
Insured commercial banks in California:					
New bank stock issues[a]	9.6	16.9	73.8	20.5	$ 310
Additions to capital from undivided profits, surplus and reserves[b]	63.2	103.0	181.1	95.4	$ 947
Increase in capital accounts[c]	72.8	119.8	254.9	115.9	$ 1,257
Insured commercial banks in the United States:					
New bank stock issues[a]	180.9	346.6	413.8	315.8	$ 3,418
Additions to capital from undivided profits, surplus, and reserves[b]	461.0	1,080.2	1,050.9	1,313.6	$ 5,012
Increase in capital accounts[c]	641.9	1,426.8	1,464.7	1,629.4	$12,430
Sources of capital as a percentage of all capital and pay-out ratios:	Percent	Percent	Percent	Percent	Totals as percents
California insured commercial banks:					
New bank stock issues	13.2	7.1	34.6	17.7	24.6
Undivided profits, etc.	86.8	92.9	65.4	82.3	75.4
Pay-out ratios[d]	61.0	50.0	55.4	63.7	
United States insured commercial banks:					
New bank stock issues	28.2	24.3	28.2	19.4	27.2
Undivided profits, etc.	71.8	75.7	72.8	80.6	72.8
Pay-out ratios[d]	46.1	41.5	44.8	47.0	

SOURCES:
  [a] Federal Deposit Insurance Corporation, *Assets, Liabilities, and Capital Accounts*, 1951–1962, year end accounts used.
  [b] *Ibid.*
  [c] *Ibid.*
  [d] Federal Deposit Insurance Corporation, *Annual Reports*, 1951–1962. The pay-out ratio represents dividends and interest on capital as a percent of net income after taxes.

consistently enjoyed favorable price-earnings and price-dividend ratios in comparison with other commercial banks in the United States.[8]

e. Comparative rates of return

Net profits after taxes have been consistently higher as a percentage of stockholders' equity for insured commercial banks than for all cor-

---

[8] Blyth and Co., Inc., *The Bank Stock Survey*, Mid-year 1962, 1963. See also, Moody's Investors Service, *Moody's Bank and Finance Manual*, 1962.

FIGURE III

Pay-Out Ratios and New Bank Stock Issues as a Percentage of
Total New Capital for United States and California
Insured Commercial Banks, 1951–1962

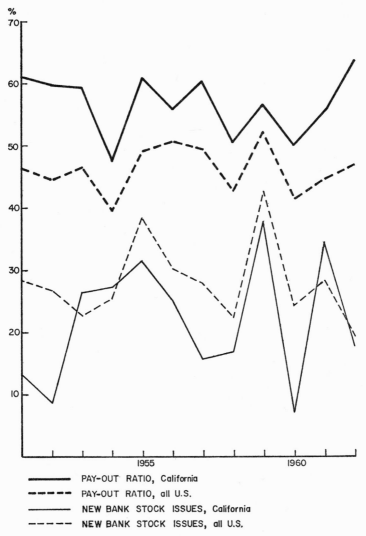

SOURCE: Federal Deposit Insurance Corporation, *Annual Reports,* 1951–1962.

TABLE 8

NET PROFITS AFTER TAXES AS A PERCENTAGE OF STOCKHOLDERS' EQUITY
ALL CORPORATIONS, LEADING MANUFACTURING CORPORATIONS AND INSURED COMMERCIAL BANKS
IN THE UNITED STATES AND IN CALIFORNIA
SELECTED YEARS 1946–1962

Net profits as a percentage of stockholders' equity for:[a]	1946	1951	1953	1954	1955	1956	1957	1958	1959	1960	1961	1962
All corporations[b]	8.1	9.7	7.5	7.1	8.5	7.9	7.1	5.5	6.5	7.2	N.A.	N.A.
Leading manufacturing corporations[c]	9.3	14.4	12.5	12.5	14.9	13.8	12.8	9.8	11.6	10.5	9.9	10.9
Insured commercial banks in the United States[d]	9.4	7.6	7.7	9.1	7.7	7.6	8.0	9.4	7.7	9.7	9.0	8.4
Insured commercial banks in California[d]	11.0	10.2	9.9	12.0	9.5	10.1	9.4	10.8	9.8	11.1	9.2	8.2

a Stockholders' Equity represents net worth.
b Includes all corporations reporting balance sheets. United States Treasury Department, Bureau of Internal Revenue, *Statistics of Income*, 1947, 1952, 1954–1961.
c First National City Bank. *Monthly Economic Letter*, April 1946, 1951, 1953–1962.
d Net profits after taxes from Federal Deposit Insurance Corporation, *Annual Reports*, 1946, 1951, 1953–1962. Net worth from Federal Deposit Insurance Corporation. *Assets, Liabilities, and Capital Accounts*, year end 1946, 1951, 1953–1962.

FIGURE IV

Rates of Return on Stockholders' Equity for all Corporations, Leading Manufacturing Corporations, California and United States, Insured Commercial Banks, 1953–1962

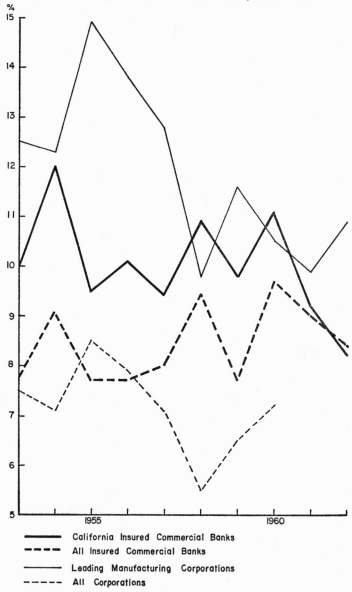

———— California Insured Commercial Banks

– – – – All Insured Commercial Banks

———— Leading Manufacturing Corporations

– – – – – All Corporations

SOURCE: See Table 8.

FIGURE V

Gross National Product and Gross Operating Earnings of All United States Insured Commercial Banks, 1937–1962

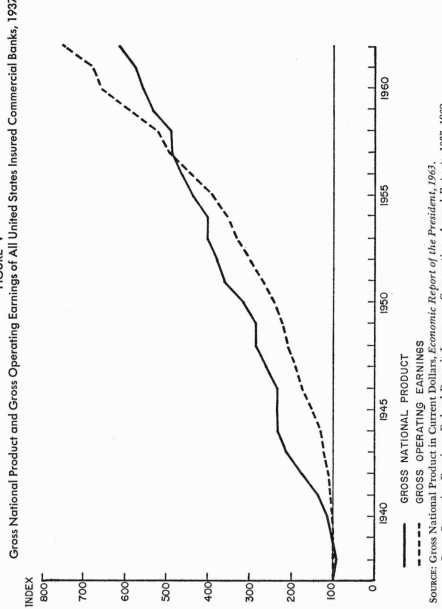

GROSS NATIONAL PRODUCT
GROSS OPERATING EARNINGS

SOURCE: Gross National Product in Current Dollars, *Economic Report of the President, 1963.*
Gross Operating Earnings, Federal Deposit Insurance Corporation, *Annual Reports,* 1937–1962.

porations in the postwar period. Furthermore, Table 8 shows that California insured commercial banks have consistently reported a higher ratio of net profits to stockholders' equity than have all insured banks in the United States. The apparent superior performance of California's banks is due in large measure to that fact that the ratio of stockholders' equity to deposits for the largest California banks is substantially below that for large banks in other areas. A lower stockholders' equity implies higher leverage and makes possible a higher ratio of net profits to stockholders' equity. Figure IV reveals that bank earnings have also been somewhat more stable as a percent of stockholders' equity than for all U. S. corporations.

The sharp decline in earnings as a percentage of equity for California banks in 1961 and 1962, shown in Figure IV, can be largely attributed to increases in interest paid on time deposits in those years. Although the maximum permitted interest rate on commercial time deposits was not increased until December, 1961, California banks adopted a policy of crediting interest from the date of deposit to date of withdrawal in the second quarter of 1961. As a result, California banks experienced a large increase in interest paid on time deposits in 1961. Because time deposits represent a substantially larger proportion of total deposits for California commercial banks, the impact of the permitted rate increase in 1962 was considerable.

3. OUTLOOK FOR EARNINGS

Profits of California's insured commercial banks have risen substantially during the post-World War II years, and commercial banking has produced higher rates of return than the average for all corporations in the United States and in California. Further, the rates of return on stockholders' equity have been higher and have shown greater stability in commercial banking than in many areas of manufacturing and trade. The ability of California's banking system to facilitate economic growth will depend upon the attraction of adequate capital resources to commercial banking which in turn will be influenced by the prospects for profits.

a. Relation of operating earnings to Gross National Product or personal income

Figure V shows the relation between gross operating earnings of all insured commercial banks in the United States and the Gross National Product from 1937 to 1962. Gross operating earnings of commercial

312   PAUL F. WENDT

FIGURE VI

Regression of Gross Operating Earnings of United States Insured Commercial
Banks on Gross National Product, 1937–1951 and 1952–1962
(billions of dollars)

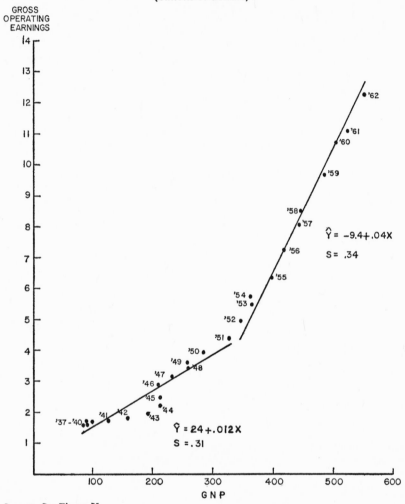

SOURCE: See Figure V.

FIGURE VII

Regression of Gross Operating Earnings of California Insured Commercial
Banks on California Personal Income, 1946–1962 (billions of dollars)

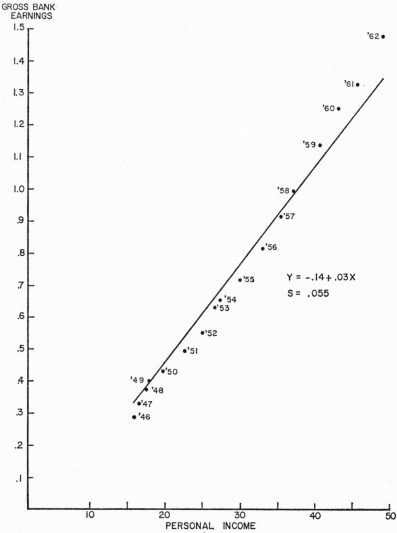

SOURCE: Gross Earnings, Federal Deposit Insurance Corporation, *Annual Reports,*
1946–1962.
Personal Incomes, *California Statistical Abstract,* 1962.

314   PAUL F. WENDT

banks have been closely related to changes in the Gross National Product. A comparison of Figures V and VI reveals that the relation between gross operating earnings of insured commercial banks and the Gross National Product has been much closer for the decade 1952 to 1962 than for the previous decade.

Historical data on the gross product by states are not available; however, a closely similar relation can be observed between gross earnings of California insured commercial banks and personal incomes in California (Figure VII).

The relation established between commercial bank gross earnings and personal incomes in California can serve as the basis for forecasting gross earnings. The equation $Y = -.14 + .03X$ states that from 1946 to 1962 a rise in personal incomes was usually accompanied by an increase in gross commercial bank earnings equal to approximately 3 percent of the amount of the increase in personal incomes. It is apparent from Figure VII that a higher regression coefficient for gross operating earnings than that shown (.03) would have resulted from a similar regression curve fitted for the past five years.

Personal incomes in California are expected to equal $100.3 billion by the year 1975. Based upon the above estimating equation, the gross earnings of California's insured commercial banks will equal approximately $2,869 million in 1975, which is 94.4 percent greater than reported gross earnings of $1,476 million in 1962. This represents an annual rate of increase of 5.2 percent, which compares with Williams' estimate of a gross product growth rate of 5.45 percent (see this volume).

This forecast rate of growth of approximately 5.2 percent per year is to be compared with the approximately 10.8 percent per year rate of growth over the sixteen-year period from 1946 to 1962 when bank operating revenues rose from $284.8 million to $1,476.1 million.

b. Receipts, expenses, and net earnings

The above estimating equation provides a measure of gross earnings rather than of net income before taxes. It is necessary to extend the model to make allowance for the probable impact of changes in expenses on commercial bank earnings in California if net earnings are to be forecasted.

The percentage change in California commercial bank net earnings before taxes over any period of time can be expressed as the difference between percentage changes in receipts and in expenses—that is:

$$\dot{E} = a\dot{I} - b\dot{X}$$

(1)

where: $\dot{E}$ = Percentage change in net earnings

$\dot{I}$ = Percentage changes in receipts

$\dot{X}$ = Percentage changes in expenses

a, b = Coefficients

Similarly, percentage changes in gross bank receipts from one period to the next may be represented as reflecting percentage changes in bank assets times the average rate of return on assets—that is:

$$I = a(A_{t+1}R_{t+1} - A_tR_t)/A_tR_t = a(\frac{A_{t+1}R_{t+1}}{A_tR_t} - 1)$$

(2)

where: A = Assets held by banks

R = Average rate of return earned on assets

t = Present

$t + 1$ = Some future time

a = Coefficient

Changes in bank expenses from one period to the next can be represented as a function of changes in wages paid and changes in interest paid on deposits, thus:

$$\dot{X} = f(\dot{W}, \dot{R}) = b\dot{W} + c\dot{R}_d$$

(3)

where: $\dot{W}$ = Percentage change in wages paid

$\dot{R}_d$ = Percentage change in interest paid on deposits

b, c = Coefficients

Substituting in Equation (1) above the representations of $\dot{I}$ and $\dot{X}$ shown in Equations (2) and (3), Equation (1) can be rewritten as follows:

(4)
$$\dot{E} = a(A_{t+1}R_{t+1} - A_tR_t/A_tR_t - (b\dot{W} + c\dot{R}_d)$$

$$= a(\frac{A_{t+1}R_{t+1}}{A_tR_t} - 1) - b\dot{W} - c\dot{R}_d$$

PAUL F. WENDT

FIGURE VIII

Comparison of Actual and Predicted Percentage Changes in Net Incomes
of California Insured Commercial Banks, 1946–1962

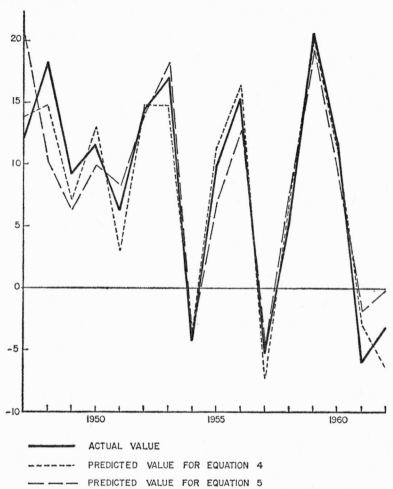

SOURCE: Federal Deposit Insurance Corporation, *Annual Reports*, 1946–1962. Calculations made by the author.

The relationship shown in Equation (4) was fitted over the period from 1946 to 1962 to determine the degree to which changes in the variables shown account for changes in the net current earnings before taxes of California insured commercial banks. Theoretically, of course, the variables shown in Equation (4) will not explain 100 percent of the change in net earnings of commercial banks over any period of time. However, changes in these independent variables over the period from 1946 to 1962 should explain a large percentage of the observed variation in commercial bank net earnings in California. Multiple regression analysis confirms this hypothesis.

Figure VIII shows the comparison of actual and estimated net incomes of California insured banks during the period from 1946–1962, using Equation (4). Note that the actual and estimated percentage changes in California bank net profits before taxes differ widely for the years 1948 and 1961–62, but that the fit is fairly good for the remaining years. Elements other than those considered were influential in affecting net profits in these years. Among the important factors not included in Equation (4) are occupancy expenses, including furniture and equipment, other current operating expenses and recoveries and losses, charge-offs and transfers to reserves. These items had a large combined influence on net profits before taxes of California insured commercial banks, particularly in recent years.

The values of the coefficients a, b, and c in Equation (4), the coefficients of multiple determination, the standard errors, F-level and student-T values are shown in Table 9. The value of the first variable in the equation, earnings on assets (AR_t), accounts for 67 percent of the total variance in net current earnings of California insured commercial banks over the period from 1946 to 1962. This and the third variable in the equation, interest paid on deposits (R_d), together account for 92.469 percent of the total variation in bank earnings during the period. In both cases high values for the F-level and student-T variables indicate that coefficients of these magnitudes are outside any probable ranges of sampling variability. During the period studied, changes in wages paid had little close statistical association with changes in bank earnings before taxes, as is indicated by the low addition to the coefficient of multiple determination and the small reduction in the value of the standard error of the dependent variable when the independent variable wages paid is added to the regression. This conclusion is confirmed by the low F-level and student-T value for this variable.

TABLE 9

COEFFICIENTS, COEFFICIENTS OF MULTIPLE DETERMINATION, STANDARD ERRORS, F LEVEL AND STUDENT-T TEST VALUES FOR REGRESSIONS OF PERCENTAGE CHANGES IN NET EARNINGS BEFORE TAXES ON PERCENTAGE CHANGES IN SELECTED INDEPENDENT VARIABLES, CALIFORNIA INSURED COMMERCIAL BANKS

Equation (4)

$$\dot{E} = \frac{a(A_{t+1}R_{t+1} - A_tR_t)}{A_tR_t} - (b\dot{W} + c\dot{R}_d)$$

where: $\dot{E}$ = percentage change in net earnings before taxes

$\frac{(A_{t+1}R_{t+1} - A_tR_t)}{A_tR_t}$ = percentage change in current operating revenue

$\dot{W}$ = percentage change in wages

$\dot{R}_d$ = percentage change in interest paid

Independent variables	Coefficients	Coefficients of multiple determination[a]	Standard Error	F level	Student T test
$\dfrac{(A_{t+1}R_{t+1} - A_tR_t)}{A_tR_t}$	1.668	.677	0.231	29.331	7.737
$\dot{W}$	−0.290	.688	0.217	42.775	−1.411
$\dot{R}_d$	−0.415	.935	0.060	1.933	−6.855
Standard error of $\dot{E}$ = 3.4770					

[a] The coefficients of multiple determination in column 2 represent the cumulative percentage of the variation in the dependent variable $\dot{E}$ explained by the independent variables. The differences in these percentages represent the amount of variation explained, in turn, by each independent variable.

The analysis in Equation (4) for the period 1946 to 1962 indicates that the net incomes of insured commercial banks in California can be predicted if the percentage changes likely to occur in gross earnings, wages, and interest paid can be estimated.

c. Estimating gross earnings

Independent forecasts of bank assets and applicable interest rates for 1975 were not made. The aggregate gross earnings-income relationship ($y = -.14 + .03X$) provides an estimate that gross earnings of California insured commercial banks can be expected to reach $2,869 million by 1975. This will be approximately double 1962 reputed gross earnings of $1,476 million.

d. Estimating wage and salary costs

The percentage increases in wages paid over the period 1962 to 1975 will depend upon changes in the number of employees and changes in average wage levels. During the period from 1950 to 1962, the average number of employees in California insured banks increased at an annual rate of 6 percent per year, while the average wage per employee increased at a rate of approximately $4\frac{1}{2}$ percent. As a result, the total wage bills increased at an average annual rate of approximately $10\frac{1}{2}$ percent from 1950 to 1962.

It would appear that wage and salary levels will continue their gradual rise in banking and other lines of endeavor in California between 1963 and 1975. The rate of growth in the number of employees in California insured banks has slowed somewhat in recent years, and automation of banking operations most likely will result in further reductions in the number of employees per dollar of gross earnings. Examination of Figure IX supports the hypothesis that wage bills of California insured commercial banks increase at approximately the same rate as has been estimated for gross bank earnings in the period from 1960 to 1975, namely, 5.2 percent.

e. Estimating interest cost

Changes in interest costs of California insured commercial banks will reflect changes in the volume of time deposits as well as changes in interest rates. The average interest rate paid on time deposits by California insured commercial banks has risen gradually over the past decade, and averaged 3.38 percent in 1962. The average interest rate paid on time deposits has followed trends in rates paid by competing savings institutions, which in turn have followed the course of long- and short-

FIGURE IX
Changes in Average Wages, Numbers of Employees, Total Wage Bills,
Taxes and Interest Paid on Deposits, and Gross Earnings of
Insured California Commercial Banks, 1946–1962

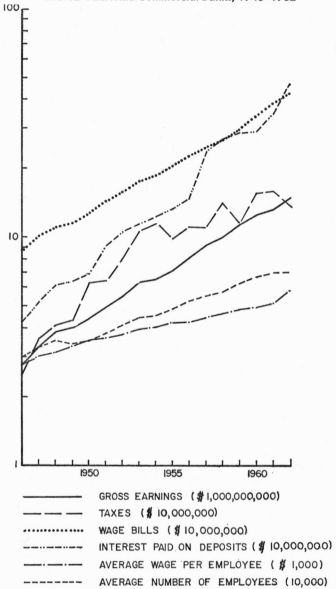

GROSS EARNINGS ($ 1,000,000,000)

TAXES ($ 10,000,000)

WAGE BILLS ($ 10,000,000)

INTEREST PAID ON DEPOSITS ($ 10,000,000)

AVERAGE WAGE PER EMPLOYEE ($ 1,000)

AVERAGE NUMBER OF EMPLOYEES (10,000)

SOURCE: Federal Deposit Insurance Corporation, *Annual Reports*, 1946–1962. Calculations made by the author.

term interest rates over the post-World War II period.[9] The rapid rise in interest rates paid on commercial bank time deposits since 1956 has reflected (1) the amendment of Regulation Q by the Board of Governors of the Federal Reserve System in 1957 and (2) the December 1961 rise in the interest rate ceiling on time deposits.[10] The probability of gradual relaxation and eventual removal of interest rate ceilings on time deposits makes it appear likely that market forces will predominate in the determination of interest rates paid on savings deposits in the 1970's.

In the light of these probable developments, forecasting the level of interest rates on time deposits in California insured commercial banks means forecasting trends in interest rates generally. Clendenin forecast that long-term money rates in the 1960's would swing widely in and about the 1958 range and would be accompanied by intermittent price-level inflation averaging about 1 percent per annum.[11] Drawing attention to the lag in personal saving in California in comparison with other leading states, Grebler views a prospect for continued high mortgage and other interest rates in California and continued dependence on capital imports.[12]

Assuming that the interest rate paid on time deposits will fluctuate around the present levels through the 1970's, it remains to estimate changes in the volume of commercial bank time deposits over the next decade. Bogen and Krooss as shown in Figure X conclude that time deposits of commercial banks will continue to increase more rapidly than demand deposits, and will account for over 60 percent of total commercial bank deposits nationally by 1975.[13] Time deposits represented approximately 48 percent of total deposits for California insured commercial banks as of December 31, 1962, as compared with 45 percent for all insured commercial banks in the United States. Barring any unforeseen statutory or other changes in the ability of California's insured commercial banks to compete with other savings institutions for time deposits, time deposits may be expected to continue to rise in the next decade at about the postwar rate for California insured commercial banks. Time deposits rose from approximately $4 billion in 1946 to $12.5 billion in 1962, which represented a compound annual rate of growth of 7.4 per-

[9] Jules I. Bogen and Herman E. Krooss, *Savings and Other Time Deposits in Commercial Banks,* A Banking Research Study by the Graduate School of Business Administration of New York University (New York: the authors, 1962), p. 56.

[10] *Ibid.,* p. 32.

[11] John C. Clendenin, "Price Level Variations and the Tenets of High Grade Investment," *Journal of Finance,* May 1959, p. 245.

[12] Leo Grebler, "California's Dependence on Capital Imports for Mortgage Investment," California Management Review, Spring 1963, Vol. V, No. 3, pp. 47–54.

[13] Bogen and Krooss, *op. cit.,* p. 12, Chart II.

FIGURE X

Projection of the 1945–1961 Deposit Trends of Commercial Banks

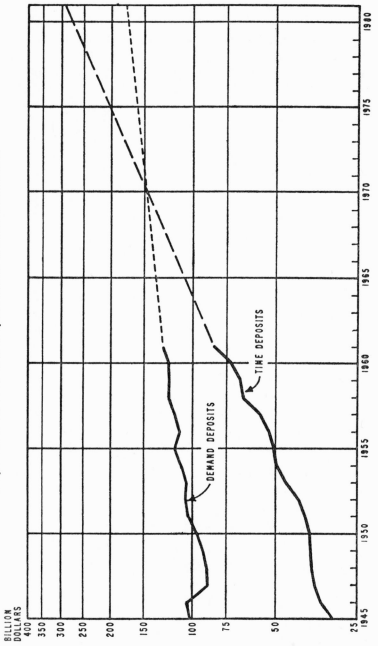

SOURCE: Jules I. Bogen and Herman E. Krooss, *Savings and Other Time Deposits in Commercial Banks*, Chart II, p. 12.

cent. During this same period demand deposits of California insured commercial banks approximately doubled from $6.5 billion to $12.6 billion, increasing at a compound rate of 4.3 percent per annum. If these relative rates of growth continue, total time deposits of California insured commercial banks may equal approximately $31.6 billion and demand deposits approximately $21.8 billion by 1975. Consideration of past and probable future competition from savings and loan institutions and the marked instability in short-term interest rates suggests that the actual growth achieved in time and demand deposits of California banks may vary considerably over the decade ahead from these projections.

f. Estimating net income

The foregoing estimates of the percentage growth in current operating revenues, wages, and interest paid over the period from 1962 to 1975 can be substituted in Equation (4) as a basis for estimating net income before taxes of California insured banks in 1975. Equation (4), with the parameters derived for the period 1946 to 1962 as shown in Table 9, is reproduced below:

(4) $\dot{E} = a(A_{t+1} R_{t+1} - A_t R_t / A_t R_t - (b\dot{W} + c\dot{R}_d)$

$\dot{E} = 1.67(A_{t+1} R_{t+1} - A_t R_t / A_t R_t - (.290\dot{W} + .415\dot{R}_d)$

The following percentage changes have been hypothesized for the independent variables over the period 1962 to 1975:

	Est. Percentage Change 1962 to 1975
Current Operating Revenues $(A_{t+1}R_{t+1} - A_t R_t / A_t R_t$	plus 95 percent
Wage and Salary Costs $(\dot{W})$	plus 95 percent
Interest Paid on Deposits $(\dot{R}_d)$	plus 153 percent

Assuming the above percentage changes in the independent variables and assuming that the same relationships apply in the period ahead as observed from 1946 to 1962, included in Equation (4), the percentage change expected in net income before taxes over this period (E) would be:

(4) $\dot{E} = 1.67\ (.95) - [.290\ (.95) + .415\ (1.53)]$

$\dot{E} = .6490$ or 64.9 percent

A 64.9 percent increase in net income before taxes for California insured banks over the thirteen-year period ending in 1975 yields a rate of growth of 3.9 percent per year. Annual earnings before taxes for 1975 are estimated to be approximately $516 million (1.65 percent of $310.2 million reported for 1962). This forecast growth rate of income before taxes compares with the 7.4 percent per year growth rate achieved in the time period 1946 to 1962.

g. Estimating future taxes

Taxes showed relatively little significant statistical association with changes in bank earnings before taxes in the period from 1946 to 1962. Consideration of expected behavior of income taxes is germane to an analysis of bank profitability.

Figure IX indicates that the rate of increase in taxes paid by California insured commercial banks during the period 1946 to 1962 was more unstable than for gross earnings and most of the important elements of expense. State income taxes tended to increase gradually over the period, while federal income taxes fluctuated more widely. State and federal income taxes averaged approximately 11 percent of total current operating revenues for California insured commercial banks for the years 1960 to 1962, and equaled 9 percent of gross revenues in 1962.

The 1964 tax bill lowered corporate taxes although the full benefit of the reduction will not be effective until 1969. During the intervening years the benefit is offset by provisions for acceleration of tax payments.[14] It appears realistic to anticipate that combined federal and state corporate income taxes will absorb moderately lower proportions of current operating revenues in 1975 than the 11 percent average of the past three years. Estimated current operating revenues of California insured commercial banks will be $2,869 million in 1975. If federal and state in-

---

[14] The American Enterprise Institute for Public Policy Research, *Special Analysis— Tax Proposals and the Federal Finances, Part III, Tax Issues of 1963*, 88th Congress, First Session, Report No. 7, July 30, 1963 (Washington, D.C.: American Enterprise Institute, 1963), pp. 19–20.

come taxes fall to 9 percent of current operating revenues, then taxes will be $246.6 million in 1975 or about 1.8 times the amount paid in 1962.

Assuming that in 1975 California insured commercial banks' annual earnings before taxes are approximately $518 million and that federal and state income taxes are approximately $246.6 million, earnings after income taxes would total approximately $271.4 million, as compared with $173.8 million in 1962. The indicated increase of 56.1 percent in net income after taxes over the thirteen-year period from 1962 to 1975 would represent a compound rate of growth of 3.5 percent per annum.

TABLE 10

ANNUAL RATE OF GROWTH OF EARNINGS, CALIFORNIA INSURED COMMERCIAL BANKS
REALIZED 1946–62 AND FORECAST 1962–75

	Realized 1946–62	Forecast 1962–75
Gross operating revenue..........................	10.8	5.2
Net income before taxes........................	7.4	3.9
Net income after taxes.........................	5.7	3.5

This estimate is based upon what many would consider a relatively pessimistic view of the outlook for bank income taxes in the state, and emphasizes the importance of this factor in affecting the ability of California insured banks to raise needed equity capital for future growth.

After-tax income increased from $71.9 million to $173.8 million in the sixteen-year period from 1946 to 1962, an annual rate of growth of 5.7 percent per year.

4. CAPITAL REQUIREMENTS AND AVAILABILITY

If the ratio of capital to deposits remains at present levels for California insured banks (7½ percent), then total bank capital requirements in the state would equal about $4 billion in 1975. Insured banks in California provided approximately three-fourths of their total new capital between 1946 and 1962 through retained earnings, and only one-fourth through new stock issues (Table 7).

The forecast rates of growth of various measures of bank earnings are consistently lower than the rates of growth observed in 1946 to 1962 (see Table 10). It therefore appears that retained earnings may not be as likely a source of addition to bank capital as they were in the recent past. Therefore, if the capital accounts of California banks are to grow as required by the growth of deposits, it may be expected that banks will

326 PAUL F. WENDT

pursue more aggressively "new ways" of raising capital through the sale of senior securities. Some issues associated with the use of senior securities by commercial banks are examined in the Appendix.

APPENDIX: THE USE OF SENIOR SECURITIES BY COMMERCIAL BANKS

Crosse has pointed out that "All the Federal supervisory authorities have consistently opposed the issuance of debt obligations by banks (except for the purpose of refinancing obligations due to the R.F.C.) on the grounds that bank capital should be permanent and not subject to retirement at the demand of the holders.[15] Despite the doubts and general disapproval of supervisory authorities, The Financial Institutions Act of 1957, as passed by the United States Senate, contained a provision permitting national banks to issue preferred stock, upon approval of the Comptroller of the Currency, when "it is the most practical method of obtaining desired and needed capital." The Act was not passed by the House of Representatives, and because of the great improvement in the market for bank common stock since 1957, the pressure for more direct authority to empower banks to issue preferred stock and/or debentures has not appeared until recently.

The 1962 Report of the Advisory Committee on Banking to the Comptroller of the Currency recommended that: "the use of preferred stock and debentures should no longer be regarded solely as emergency measures but should be recognized as normal methods for obtaining capital funds. The attitude of the Comptroller of the Currency should be liberalized. Flexibility should be afforded by permitting the use in appropriate cases of various features such as convertibility or subordination."[16]

Acting upon this recommendation, the Comptroller of the Currency announced regulatory changes in December, 1962, which permitted national banks to utilize preferred or debt securities as a normal means of raising capital.

Section 662 of the Financial Code of the State of California provides that state banks may issue notes or debentures upon securing the prior approval of the State Superintendent of Banks and of the majority of stockholders of the individual bank. Following approval, two state banks sold capital notes privately to institutional investors in 1963. The

---

[15] Howard D. Crosse, *Management Policies for Commercial Banks* (Englewood Cliffs, N. J., Prentice-Hall, Inc., 1962), p. 188.

[16] *National Banks and the Future,* Report of the Advisory Commission on Banking to the Comptroller of the Currency, Washington, September 17, 1962, pp. 77–83.

United California Bank sold $35 million of capital notes yielding 4.58 percent in mid-1963 and shortly thereafter, the Union Bank of Los Angeles completed the sale of a $25 million, 4½ percent issue. California's largest banks are reported to be studying the possibilities of debenture and note financing, but indications are that banks generally are "holding back waiting for action by the leaders."

The apparent reluctance of California's leading banks to employ debt capital on a wide scale can be explained in part by the fact that bank regulatory agencies do not appear in full agreement as to whether or not debentures and notes should be viewed as a part of bank capital in the legal sense.

Article 4 of Section 662 of the California State Banking Law states that: "Such capital notes or debentures shall not be deemed 'paid-up capital' or 'paid-in capital' as said terms are used in this banking law." Article 2, Section 1222 of the same law provides that loans to individual borrowers "should not exceed an amount equal to 10 percent of the combined capital and surplus of all departments of the bank." It would appear that some ambiguity might exist as to whether capital notes and debentures should be included as a part of capital for purposes of determination of loan limits to single borrowers. Although the Board of Governors of the Federal Reserve System has not made a formal ruling on the matter, it is reported that debentures and capital notes are not presently regarded as bank capital by the Board.

A further source of uncertainty arises from the limitation in Chapter 89 of the Banking Act of 1933 creating the Federal Deposit Insurance Corporation. This Act prohibits any reduction in the "capital" of insured banks without the prior approval of the Federal Deposit Insurance Corporation (12 U. S. Code, Sec. 1828c). If capital notes and debentures are construed as "capital" by the Federal Deposit Insurance Corporation, the above provision could serve to restrict banks in the future redemption of capital notes or debentures.

It is evident that clarification and joint agreement among bank regulatory agencies with respect to the inclusion or exclusion of notes and debentures in bank capital is needed in order to render the issuance of such obligations attractive to California banks on a large scale.

A further important question appears to be whether or not administrative approval of the issuance of preferred stock or debt securities will remove the "stigma" or "taint" associated with such financing as a result of the fact that preferred stock was used extensively under the provisions of the national Banking Emergency Relief Act of 1933. Corporate bank depositors and stockholders probably will continue to regard the issuance of senior securities as an indication of financial difficulty or weakness, *unless* these techniques of financing are used on a broad scale by banks generally. The prospects for this development will undoubtedly hinge upon the potential profitability of altering established bank capitalization standards. Charles M. Williams, in an article entitled "Senior Securities—Boon for Banks?," published in the *Harvard Business Review* for July-August 1963, concludes that:

1. If rates of bank profit, profit retention, and deposit increase hold near those of recent years, the average bank will be able to maintain its present capital/deposit ratio through capital accretion from internal sources—retained earnings and increases in bad debt reserves. That this will satisfy banking supervisors is indicated by their avowed satisfaction with the present level of capital in the banks generally.
2. Nevertheless, several hundred banks each year will seek new capital through the sale of securities. Interest in senior securities will be keenest in those banks where one or more of the following conditions exist:

Management and the board have a strong equity interest in the bank and for this or other reasons have a strong orientation toward the point of view of the stockholder. Since the major advantages of the use of senior capital accrue to the stockholders, a keen sensitivity to their interests will serve as a major motivation to its use.

Management willingness to innovate is high. Managements with strong traditionalist and conformist tendencies will doubtless stay with all-common structures.

Control aspects are important.

Rapid growth is accompanied by sharply rising costs and pressure on profits. This may well be the case of many banks whose rapid growth is in savings deposits as a result of aggressive interest-rate competition. If the net profit on the expanded savings deposits proves small, the attractions of lower-cost capital to support the low-return savings will be enhanced.
3. The use of senior capital will be greatly stimulated if and when several large, obviously prosperous, and highly regarded banks endorse the idea by example. Publicity regarding their use of senior capital would help greatly in getting senior securities better known among bankers, would provide ammunition in the form of case examples for investment bankers anxious to stimulate their own business with banks, and would encourage state supervisors to liberalize their views toward senior capital. Furthermore, by making the use of senior securities more completely respectable in the banking fraternity, their action would go a very long way to dispelling the depression-born stigma associated with the use of senior capital by banks. In fact, senior capital would be made more readily available in the future to those banks that may need to utilize it on a distress basis.
4. In the near term there will be considerable concern, on the part of both investors and bank managements, with sinking funds and other plans for early retirement of debentures. In time, debentures will be regarded more as truly long-term or semipermanent capital, long maturities will be used, and advanced refundings will become common.

5. Banker interest in senior securities will center in subordinated debentures rather than preferred stock. Large banks in time will show active interest in convertible securities.

6. Investor interest, particularly among institutions and pension funds, in bank senior securities will be keen. For some time to come, demand for these securities should exceed the supply.

7. The experience of banks generally with senior securities will prove favorable. Use of preferred stock and subordinated debentures over time will increase until they account for a very substantial portion of capital additions through sale of securities.[17]

Williams' analysis suggests that the potential profitability of the issuance of senior securities, particularly debentures, by banks is substantial, and that the prospects for large-scale issuance of such securities by banks are excellent.

Extensive use of preferred stock and debenture financing by California commercial banks would provide broader avenues leading to the nation's capital markets and make possible the introduction of greater leverage in bank capitalizations. Uncertainty as to the extent to which this departure from the conservative bank capitalization practices will or should occur heightens the difficulty of estimating future capital needs of California's commercial banks. At the same time, it suggests that alternatives to equity financing by banks will in all probability increase and hence that shortages of bank capital should not limit the state's growth in the period ahead.

---

[17] Charles M. Williams, "Senior Securities—Boon For Banks?" *Harvard Business Review,* July–August 1963, pp. 93–94.

An Evaluation of the Payments Mechanism in California, 1946–1975

RICHARD E. TOWEY

1. THE PAYMENTS MECHANISM: INTRODUCTION

COMMERCIAL BANKS are integrally involved in virtually all aspects of the payments mechanism. Not only do they administer the chief means of effecting payments—demand deposits—but also they are the source through which decisions are implemented by the general public to hold coin and currency as alternatives to demand deposits. Moreover, through their portfolio policies, banks play an important role in the mobilization of cash balances for transactions purposes, especially over the business cycle.

In performing these payments functions commercial banks have achieved an enviable position in the economy: their operations are largely taken for granted. It is widely assumed that difficulties of safety and acceptability of bank-issued payments media, to the extent they are traceable to the banks themselves, have long since been overcome. At least implicitly, the view is commonly held that administration costs of payments activity are borne mainly by the banks themselves as the price they pay for the ability to acquire earning assets. Therefore it is felt that banks have a sufficient incentive to seek low cost means of operating the payments system. Seldom are questions raised about the variety and suitability of present forms of making payments, the speed of effecting transactions, and the overall progressiveness of the industry.

The unquestioning attitude toward the performance of the commercial banks in their payments operations poses problems for this paper. The focus here is on developments in a subsector of the national economy: the State of California. It would be desirable to be able to discuss the operations of California banks in terms of how well they meet criteria of national payments efficiency. Yet this more general framework has not been systematically developed, and such a task is outside the scope of the present paper. Consequently, less ambitious analytical devices are adopted here. Changes in payments practices at California banks are traced over time, and developments in California are compared with those in the rest of the nation. The insights gained by these methods may suggest some of the results which would be achieved in a more general analysis.

2. DEVELOPMENTS IN THE CALIFORNIA PAYMENTS SYSTEM SINCE 1946

With the rapid growth in the California population and the broadening industrialization of the state, total demand deposit balances well nigh doubled between 1946 and 1963 (Table 1). A similar growth occurred in the more restricted segment representing balances held by individuals, partnerships, and corporations. Most of the rise in the latter category was accounted for by growth in the number of demand accounts, from about 3.1 million in 1946 to about 5.6 million in 1962. The average size of balance declined in the early postwar years, and since then has risen by only about 1 percent per year. Debits to demand accounts have risen even more sharply than balances. In sixteen of the larger financial centers in the state (including San Francisco and Los Angeles), debits exceeded $290 billion in 1963, compared with somewhat under $75 billion in 1946. Even with postwar price increases inflating the average size of check written, the volume of checks passing through California banks is now undoubtedly well over twice as large as that at the end of World War II. In their accounts of individuals, partnerships, and corporations, California banks indicate that they are currently processing "on us" checks and deposits at the rate of 1.5 billion items per year.

In the rest of the nation, growth in payments activity measures also has been impressive. For the United States as a whole, total demand balances increased by almost 60 percent between 1946 and 1963, and total debits rose nearly as rapidly as in California (Table 2). The overall national turnover rate of demand deposits, about 18 times per year in 1946, was about 44 times during 1963.

Data on the actual volume of checks circulating nationally each year are not available, but for 1952 it was estimated that about 8 billion checks were written for a total of $2 trillion. This compares with 3.5 billion checks written in 1939, the only other year for which data have been compiled. When the 1952 figures were published it was estimated

TABLE 1

MEASURES OF DEMAND DEPOSIT ACTIVITY AT CALIFORNIA BANKS, 1946–1963

Year	(1) Total demand deposits ($ billions)	(2) Demand deposits: individuals, partnerships, and corporations ($ billions)	(3) Estimated number of demand deposit accounts (millions)	(4) Approximate average size of balance ($)	(5) Debits to demand deposits, 16 Calif. cities ($ billions)	(6) "Deflated" debits to demand deposits, 16 Calif. cities ($ billions)
1946	$ 7.65	$ 6.27	3.1	$2,020	$ 75.39	$101
1948	7.45	6.05	3.3	1,830	88.78	100
1950	8.09	6.46	3.4	1,900	98.46	110
1952	9.45	7.59	4.0	1,900	116.76	119
1954	10.05	8.14	4.4	1,850	128.08	128
1956	11.25	9.29	4.6	2,020	157.92	151
1958	12.06	9.93	4.9	2,030	175.56	158
1960	12.95	10.59	5.1	2,080	210.03	184
1962	14.43	11.84	5.6	2,110	263.08	225
1963	14.94	12.42	...	.....	292.74	247

COLUMNS:

(1), (2) Total demand deposits and demand deposits of individuals, partnerships and corporations at insured banks, end of year. Source: Federal Deposit Insurance Corporation, *Call Reports*.

(3), (4) Estimates based on accounts held by the nine largest branch banks in California, end of year; estimates prepared by the author.

(5) Annual total for 16 California cities. Source: Federal Reserve Bank of San Francisco. Data prior to 1952 are for debits to total deposit accounts (including time deposits). The extent of over-estimate of demand debits for these years is approximately 3.30 percent, based on 1952 comparisons.

(6) Column (5) divided by implicit price deflator for GNP, 1954 = 100.

that 14 billion checks would be drawn by 1960 and 22 billion by 1970.[1] These estimates have become more or less the standard indicators of the growth of banking's "paper tiger"; in banking circles upwards of 14 billion presently-written checks is widely accepted as representing the general order of magnitude.

The check handling problem is much larger than even these figures indicate. In 1952 about 20 percent of all checks were drawn on the bank at which they were first presented, the other 80 percent being presented at other banks.[2] The average check deposited or cashed in a bank passed through a total of $2\frac{1}{3}$ banks (including the Federal Reserve) on the way to final collection. The American Bankers Association estimates that within each bank a transit check receives an average of two separate handlings, an "on us" check six, and a deposit four.

a. The impact of monetary policy on the payments mechanism

The significance of these developments in the banking system's payments handling may be placed more in focus if viewed in the context of national monetary policy. Monetary policy is assigned a major role in the attainment of the nation's economic goals, including full employment, growth, and price stability. In part these goals are pursued through varying the supply of demand balances. Total spending pressures in the postwar years tended periodically to become excessive, and the Federal Reserve sought to restrain these pressures through limiting the amount of reserves available for bank deposit expansion. The degree of pressure involved resulted in increases in the money supply averaging well under 2 percent per year for at least the past decade (Table 3). Even if all of this growth occurred in the realm of demand deposits, the gains for banks would have been modest, but the currency requirements of the general public also expanded in this period.

Business firms and households have learned to economize on the holding of cash balances, as with any scarce commodity, because of rises in the cost of holding money.[3] The rate at which a given amount of cash balances flows through the economy has increased sharply as the result of such practices as the placement of short-term cash balances in U. S. Treasury securities, negotiable time certificates of deposit, sales finance

---

[1] *Study of Check Collection System*, Report of Joint Committee on Check Collection to American Bankers Association, Association of Reserve City Bankers and Conference of Presidents of the Federal Reserve Banks, June 15, 1954, Chapter 1.

[2] *Ibid.*

[3] See Richard T. Selden, *The Postwar Rise in the Velocity of Money*, National Bureau of Economic Research Occasional Paper 78, New York, 1962, and particularly p. 532.

TABLE 2

MEASURES OF DEMAND DEPOSIT ACTIVITY AT UNITED STATES BANKS, 1946–1963

Year	(1) Total demand deposits ($ billions)	(2) Demand deposits individuals, partnerships and corporations ($ billions)	(3) Number of deposit accounts: individuals, partnerships, and corporations (millions)	(4) Approximate average size of balance ($)	(5) Debits to demand deposit accounts, 344 cities ($ billions)	(6) "Deflated" debit to demand deposit accounts, 344 cities ($ billions)	(7) Turnover rate of demand deposits 344 cities
1946	$103.42	$ 79.90	....	....	$1,017	$1,363	18
1948	105.15	81.70	....	....	1,128	1,387	20
1950	117.02	90.00	....	....	1,380	1,542	22
1952	129.99	98.90	....	....	1,643	1,675	24
1954	134.78	102.72	....	....	1,887	1,887	26
1956	144.38	110.40	52.2	$2,010	2,201	2,104	29
1958	149.49	114.64	54.4	1,970	2,440	2,202	31
1960	155.71	116.60	58.4	1,870	2,839	2,482	35
1962	163.21	123.30	....	....	3,436	2,944	41
1963	162.95	123.56	....	....	3,755	3,169	44

COLUMNS:
(1), (2) Total demand deposits and demand deposits of individuals, partnerships and corporations at insured end of year. Source: Federal Deposit Insurance Corporation, *Call Reports*.
(3), (4) As of end of January of the succeeding year. Source: Board of Governors of the Federal Reserve System, *Bulletin*, April 1961, page 406.
(5) Total of New York City, 6 other centers and 337 other centers. Source: Board of Governors of the Federal Reserve System, *Federal Reserve Bulletin*.
(6) Column (5) divided by Implicit Price Deflator for GNP, 1954 = 100.
(7) Average number of times per year. Source: same as column (5).
NOTE: ... indicates data not available.

company paper, repurchase agreements with government security dealers, and so on. The commercial banks themselves have contributed to this rise in the velocity of deposits in the process of adjusting their earning asset portfolios to changing market yields both over the business cycle and secularly. Yet improvements in the economizing of cash bal-

TABLE 3

MONEY SUPPLY IN THE UNITED STATES

AVERAGE OF DAILY FIGURES

(billions of dollars)

	Total money supply		Demand deposits		Coin and currency	
	Year average	Percent change	Year average	Percent change	Year average	Percent change
1947................	$111.8		$ 85.2		$26.6	
1948................	112.3	+0.4	86.2	+1.2	26.1	−1.9
1949................	111.2	−1.0	85.7	−0.6	25.5	−2.3
1950................	114.1	+2.6	89.1	+4.0	25.1	−1.6
1951................	119.2	+4.5	93.7	+5.2	25.6	+2.0
1952................	125.2	+5.0	98.5	+5.1	26.7	+4.3
1953................	128.3	+2.5	100.6	+2.1	27.7	+3.7
1954................	130.3	+1.6	102.8	+2.2	27.5	−0.7
1955................	134.4	+3.1	106.8	+3.9	27.6	+0.4
1956................	136.0	+1.2	108.0	+1.1	28.0	+1.4
1957................	136.7	+0.5	108.5	0.0	28.3	+1.1
1958................	138.4	+1.2	110.0	+1.4	28.4	+0.4
1959................	142.8	+3.2	113.9	+3.5	28.9	+1.8
1960................	140.9	−1.3	111.9	−1.8	29.0	+0.3
1961................	143.2	+1.6	113.5	+1.4	29.1	+0.3
1962................	146.0	+2.0	115.8	+2.0	30.1	+3.4
1963................	149.9	+2.7	118.4	+2.2	31.5	+4.6
Average annual increase 1952–1963....		+1.7		+1.7		+1.5

SOURCE: Board of Governors of the Federal Reserve System, Supplement to Banking and Monetary Statistics, Section 1, *Banks and the Monetary System*, Table 2 and *Federal Reserve Bulletin*.

ances by the banks or by the general public have a special impact on banks: they are required to process a greater volume of checks per dollar of demand deposits held. Thus the banks have been under increasing pressure to acquire additional earnings per dollar of assets and to cut unit costs of handling cash items to meet the expense of this mounting check volume.

b. The relative cost of demand deposit maintenance

The processing of demand deposit transactions—including teller, transit (check collection), and bookkeeping functions—accounts for a sizable part of bank operating expense and bank employment. In the sample of small-to-medium size banks included in the functional income and cost analyses of the Federal Reserve Banks of Boston and New York it was found that just over half of operating expenses other than interest on time deposits in recent years is allocable to payments functions.[4] About half of total employment at these banks stems from the performance of payments functions. Any change in these proportions from the earlier postwar period is unknown; loans have risen sharply relative to investments at banks since the end of World War II, and these tend to raise operating expenses and personnel requirements as well as income. Payments functions also may account for somewhat different proportions of total costs and employee requirements at larger-size banks.

No published studies are available to indicate their relative importance at the large branch banks in California. Undoubtedly demand account maintenance represents the greatest single use for staff at California banks, and with the probable exception of interest on time deposits, is their largest item of expense.

c. Staffing problems and salaries at banks

The rising volume of payments activity compounded the staffing problems at banks during the late 1940's and 1950's. Indeed, staff recruitment became an increasingly important stumbling block to banks essaying to meet the growing demand for their services. Nationwide, well over a quarter of a million new jobs opened at other than officer levels between 1946 and 1963, and more than one of every eight of these openings occurred in California (Table 4). With the relatively low salaries in the industry, the bulk of the bookkeeping and check collection positions were taken over by young women just out of school in the brief months or years before marriage and the rearing of families. Annual turnover rates in these positions often exceeded 100 percent at California banks. Turnover rates in teller and other clerical jobs also were uncomfortably high. To maintain minimum standards in all of these positions, many of the larger banks in the metropolitan areas found it necessary to operate special training schools on a continuous basis. The banks generally were unwilling or unable to raise salaries sufficiently to appeal to a different segment of the labor market, perhaps because the monotony of many banking routines made the requisite salary increases prohibitive. Even so, average annual salaries of bank employees have approximately doubled since 1946. In California the

---

[4] Federal Reserve Bank of Boston, *Functional Cost Analysis*, 1961 and 1962, and Federal Reserve Bank of New York, *Functional Analysis of Income and Expense*, 1962.

338

RICHARD E. TOWEY

TABLE 4
EMPLOYMENT AND AVERAGE SALARIES OF EMPLOYEES
INSURED BANKS IN CALIFORNIA AND REST OF THE UNITED STATES
1946–1963

Year	Number of employees	Average annual salary per employee[a]	Index of employment 1946 = 100	Index of average salary 1946 = 100	Salary differential California over rest of U. S.
California					
1946...........	27,520	$2,267	100	100	$384
1948...........	28,934	2,703	105	119	481
1950...........	30,873	2,867	112	126	497
1952...........	36,744	3,122	134	138	477
1954...........	39,039	3,446	142	152	556
1956...........	46,491	3,575	169	158	459
1958...........	48,756	3,878	177	171	487
1960...........	57,998	4,146	211	183	600
1962[b]...........	58,750	4,372	213	193	587
1963[b]...........	61,742	4,467	224	197	584
Rest of the United States					
1946...........	243,875	$1,883	100	100	
1948...........	263,081	2,222	108	118	
1950...........	281,451	2,370	115	126	
1952...........	321,581	2,645	132	140	
1954...........	347,586	2,890	143	153	
1956...........	387,072	3,116	159	165	
1958...........	408,267	3,391	167	180	
1960...........	448,598	3,546	184	188	
1962[b]...........	453,989	3,785	186	201	
1963[b]...........	470,078	3,883	193	206	

[a] Personnel other than officers.
[b] Personnel other than officers and building employees.
SOURCE: *Annual Reports*, Federal Deposit Insurance Corporation.

percentage increase has been fractionally less than in other parts of the nation, but the typical banking salary here has been $500 or more per year higher than elsewhere for most of the postwar period (Table 4).

d. Bank efforts to offset this cost squeeze

To meet the cost squeeze and maintain earnings, the banks have attempted to broaden the attractiveness of existing payments services, have sought markets for new services and methods for cutting operating costs. Service charges on deposit accounts have become a more important segment of bank earnings (Table 5). Yet until the recent introduction of high speed electronic data processing equipment, changes in banking practices affecting the payments mechanism occurred relatively slowly. Payments functions at banks remained highly labor-intensive. Improvements in such standard banking equipment as bookkeeping and proof machines still left the routines basically unchanged. Some banks introduced tabulating equipment for ancillary payments services such as pay-

TABLE 5

SERVICE CHARGES LEVIED ON DEPOSIT ACCOUNTS, INSURED BANKS
IN CALIFORNIA AND THE REST OF THE UNITED STATES, 1946–1963

Year	California			United States (other than California)		
	Service charges levied	Total current operating revenue	Service charges ÷ operating revenue *percent*	Service charges levied	Total operating revenue	Service charges ÷ operating revenue *percent*
1946.....	13.4	284.8	4.7	111.3	2,578.1	4.3
1948.....	20.4	275.9	5.4	153.4	3,127.7	4.9
1950.....	27.5	435.7	6.3	184.8	3,495.0	5.3
1952.....	33.0	551.4	6.0	211.7	4,380.3	4.8
1954.....	47.6	650.2	7.3	264.2	5,123.6	5.2
1956.....	57.8	811.1	7.1	328.1	6,420.8	5.1
1958.....	75.8	991.0	7.6	410.7	7,509.9	5.5
1960.....	93.0	1,252.4	7.4	497.0	9,471.1	5.2
1962.....	105.2	1,476.1	7.1	576.0	10,742.9	5.4
1963.....	115.3	1,652.6	7.0	613.6	11,857.1	5.2

SOURCE: *Annual Reports*, Federal Deposit Insurance Corporation.

roll preparation and account reconciliation, as well as for loan accounting and other purposes. Nevertheless, areas in which the banks met the challenge of changing conditions were concentrated more in the realm of credit extension than in their payments services.

Reserve pressures and the opportunity to improve earnings did stimulate the banks to modify their check collection procedures during the 1950's. Increasing use was made of correspondent banks rather than the Federal Reserve facilities for check collection. When sufficient volume (particularly, large dollar volume) was involved, a bank receiving checks drawn on out-of-city banks found it more profitable to send the checks directly to its correspondent in that city, where, because of the increased speed of air transportation, deposit credit was gained one or more days in advance of that called for under the Federal Reserve's deferral schedule. Also, where the volume warranted, authorities encouraged Reserve member banks to use direct intercity Reserve transactions rather than to go through the local Federal Reserve channels in collecting cash items drawn on out-of-city banks.

The change to direct check clearing is not without cost to the banks, of course; the more rapid credit for check collection given by a correspondent bank entails a service of check handling which is reflected in the size of the correspondent balance the sending bank must keep with the receiving bank. To banks elsewhere in the nation this requirement may not be burdensome because of their traditional holding of substantial amounts of "idle" correspondent balances. Even now the relative holding of correspondent balances by member banks outside of California is probably about the same as at the end of World War II, but with their available lending opportunities and cost pressures, according to bank officers, California member banks have drawn this type of balance down close to the minimum required for performance of the services they desire.[5] (Table 6)

3. AUTOMATION IN THE PAYMENTS SYSTEM

The rising postwar check volume, with the attendant cost pressures and staffing problems, has been largely responsible for the recent adaptation of high speed electronic data processing equipment to payments processing, in which the large California banks have been among the national leaders. One California bank is widely credited with having laid much of the groundwork for the introduction of automated equipment. For that bank, research into banking applications of computer technology goes back as far as 1950, and other banks were not slow in recognizing the potentialities. It may seem rather surprising, in view of apparent previous conservatism, that so much of the initiative should stem from the banking industry itself. In the early 1950's the equipment manufacturers were concentrating their efforts on other uses of computers, and the strength of banking's response to computer technology took them somewhat by surprise. The speed of response within this field may suggest also that at least a segment of the banking industry has a hitherto little-suspected propensity to innovate. It may be only that opportunities for innovation in the payments field were rather limited before the advent of automation.

---

[5] For present purposes, correspondent balance comparisons are most meaningful for member banks because nonmember correspondent balances may also be used in varying degrees to satisfy state legal reserve requirements. In California, for example, 6 percent of demand deposits must be held as cash in vault or deposits with the Federal Reserve, and the balance of the requirement may be satisfied with correspondent deposits.

Considerations of time and cost prevented a full-scale examination of the current progress of automation at all California banks. Tables 7 and 8, suggesting the extent to which this new equipment has affected bank practices and plans in California, are based on a special Federal Reserve survey conducted about mid-1962.[6] With more information about the potentialities of automation, and in view of the experience

TABLE 6

DEMAND BALANCES WITH OTHER BANKS IN THE UNITED STATES HELD BY MEMBER BANKS IN CALIFORNIA AND THE REST OF THE UNITED STATES, 1946–1963
(millions of dollars)

Year *End of December*	Member banks in California		Member banks in U. S. other than California	
	Amount of demand balances with banks in U. S.	As percent of total demand deposits less interbank *percent*	Amount of demand balances with banks in U. S.	As percent of total demand deposits less interbank *percent*
1946..........	$318.9	4.5	$5,580.7	7.6
1948..........	273.9	4.0	5,368.9	7.1
1950..........	299.0	4.0	6,540.6	7.8
1952..........	420.0	4.8	6,928.2	7.5
1954..........	364.8	4.0	7,217.9	7.5
1956..........	382.0	3.8	7,677.2	7.5
1958..........	321.3	2.9	7,615.9	7.3
1960..........	369.9	3.2	8,170.2	7.6
1962..........	318.9[a]	2.4[a]	7,383.2	6.5[a]
1963..........	303.9	2.2[a]	6,757.5	6.0[a]

[a] Because the *Call Report* date was earlier than usual in 1962 and 1963 some "windowdressing" through the use of inter-bank demand deposits was not possible; therefore the data for these years are probably lower than would otherwise have been expected.
SOURCE: *Call Reports*, Federal Deposit Insurance Corporation.

of the larger banks with equipment thus far installed, more smaller banks than are indicated in these tables have entered this field. Also some plans concerning the means of gaining access to the new technology have been modified in the interim. In this rapidly changing field, any survey becomes out of date quickly. But the tables still indicate that the initial impact of automation has been mainly at the larger banks, and that the percentage of banks automating tends to decline with size of bank. For a better understanding of the impact of automation on California banks, interviews for this study with officers of the

[6] Similar tables for the United States were published in the November 1962 issue of the *Federal Reserve Bulletin*, pages 1409 and 1411.

TABLE 7

AUTOMATION AT COMMERCIAL BANKS, BY SIZE OF BANK, STATE OF CALIFORNIA, MARCH 1962

Item	Total banks		Size of bank (total deposits, in millions of dollars)										
			1,000 and over		500–1,000		250–500		100–250		50–100		0–50	
	Number	Percent	Number	Percent	Number	Percent	Number	Percent	Number	Percent	Number	Percent	Number	Percent
Total banks reporting	112	100.0	5	100.0	4	100.0	3	100.0	6	100.0	6	100.0	88	100.0
Automating	29	25.9	5	100.0	4	100.0	1	33.3	3	50.0	2	33.3	14	15.9
Nonautomating	83	74.1	...	...	...	...	2	66.7	3	50.0	4	66.7	74	84.1
Status of computer														
Total banks	29	100.0	5	100.0	4	100.0	1	100.0	3	100.0	2	100.0	14	100.0
With computer systems:														
In operation	15	51.7	5	100.0	3	75.0	1	100.0	1	33.3	...	...	5	35.7
In process	4	13.8	...	...	...	...	...	...	...	...	...	...	4	28.6
Planned	10	34.5	...	...	1	25.0	...	...	2	66.7	2	100.0	5	35.7

Type of computer

	29	100.0	5	100.0	4	100.0	1	100.0	3	100.0	2	100.0	14	100.0
Total banks................	29	100.0	5	100.0	4	100.0	1	100.0	3	100.0	2	100.0	14	100.0
With general purpose computers:														
Large....................	2	6.9	2	40.0	...	...	...	...	...	...	...	...	1	7.1
Medium..................	4	13.8	1	20.0	...	...	...	...	1	33.3	1	50.0	7	50.0
Small...................	16	55.2	1	20.0	4	100.0	1	100.0	1	33.3	1	50.0	3	21.4
With special purpose computers................	3	10.3	...	...	...	...	...	...	...	...	...	...	1	7.1
Other....................	2	6.9	1	20.0	...	...	...	...	...	...	...	...	1	7.1
Unspecified..............	2	6.9	...	...	...	...	...	...	1	33.3	...	...	1	7.1

Arrangement for management of computer systems

	29	100.0	5	100.0	4	100.0	1	100.0	3	100.0	2	100.0	14	100.0
Total banks................	29	100.0	5	100.0	4	100.0	1	100.0	3	100.0	2	100.0	14	100.0
With arrangements to operate own computer:..	20	69.0	5	100.0	4	100.0	1	100.0	3	100.0	2	100.0	5	35.7
Single bank.............	19	65.5	5	100.0	4	100.0	1	100.0	2	66.7	2	100.0	5	35.7
Two or more banks co-operating.............	1	3.5	...	...	...	...	...	...	1	33.3	...	...	0	0.0
Contract for computer services................	8	27.6	...	...	...	...	...	...	...	...	...	...	8	57.1
Unspecified..............	1	3.5	...	...	...	...	...	...	...	...	...	...	1	7.1

SOURCE: Federal Reserve Bank of San Francisco.

TABLE 8

MICR Sorter Equipment at California Commercial Banks, March 1962

Item	Total banks		Size of bank (total deposits, in millions of dollars)										
			1,000 and over		500–1,000		250–500		100–250		50–100		0–50	
	Number	Percent	Number	Percent	Number	Percent	Number	Percent	Number	Percent	Number	Percent	Number	Percent
Total banks reporting........	112	100.0	5	100.0	4	100.0	3	100.0	6	100.0	6	100.0	88	100.0
							Status of sorter							
Banks with sorters:														
In operation.............	15	13.4	5	100.0	3	75.0	1	33.3	1	16.7	...	...	5	5.7
In process...............	1	.8	...	...	...	...	...	...	1	16.7	...	...	1	1.1
Planned.................	11	9.8	...	...	1	25.0	...	...	1	16.7	1	16.7	8	9.1
Banks not planning........	85	75.9	...	...	...	...	2	66.7	4	66.7	5	83.3	74	84.1
							Arrangements for management of sorter system							
Total banks.............	27	100.0	5	100.0	4	100.0	1	100.0	2	100.0	1	100.0	14	100.0
With arrangements to operate own sorter:														
Single banks...........	18	66.7	5	100.0	4	100.0	1	100.0	2	100.0	1	100.0	5	35.7
Contract for sorter services...............	6	22.2	...	...	...	...	...	...	...	...	...	...	6	42.9
Unspecified............	3	11.1	...	...	...	...	...	...	...	...	...	...	3	21.4

Source: Federal Reserve Bank of San Francisco.

state's nine large branch bank systems were conducted in mid-1963. (Through a merger, the nine banks became eight in late 1963.) For remarks in this section much is owed to the cooperation extended by these banks and their representatives.[7]

a. Automation of deposit accounting in California

As in most other parts of the nation, even the larger California banks generally are still in the process of converting their systems to the use of automated equipment. The primary use of computers and related equipment thus far has been in demand deposit bookkeeping.[8] Only after the completion of this mammoth task have most banks begun to seek other profitable applications of the new hardware.

The two largest banks in the state have set up a number of highly autonomous service centers strategically placed to accommodate their numerous and scattered branches. The other large banks, which in general have fewer and somewhat more geographically-concentrated branch systems, have established highly centralized service centers in Los Angeles and San Francisco. In some cases the computer system setups for demand deposit accounting of these banks are considerably more powerful than those used by the two largest banks. Also, among this latter group some intend to set up satellite service centers in outlying cities to feed taped information into their centralized systems. In both forms of organization it is necessary to operate elaborate transportation systems between and among branches and service centers to maintain "current day" bookkeeping schedules. Transportation time and the attendant costs have had a major influence on decisions by individual banks to adopt their respective systems of organization.

In most cases decisions on the scale of service centers also are influenced by the existence of economies and diseconomies of scale in aspects other than transportation. The cost of acquisition of computers tends to rise less than proportionately with the ability of the equipment to process data. Machine processing time lost during breakdowns can be catastrophic to operating procedures, and many large banks have foregone more elaborate computer setups in order to acquire sizable backup capacity through multiple purchases of less powerful computers. Similar considerations apply to other equipment such as sorters, printers, and the like. At or near rated capacity, a moderate-sized computer installa-

---

[7] Needless to say, the responsibility for the conclusions drawn from these interviews, as well as for any misstatement of fact, rests with the author alone.

[8] At some banks the initial uses of computers were outside the field of payments processing, but these are dwarfed by the magnitude of the bookkeeping use.

tion now involves approximately $1 of direct operating costs for $1 of equipment acquired. However, if transportation costs are excluded, the marginal cost of increasing output at a given installation appears to decline sharply for a substantial range of operations below rated capacity. That is to say, the short-run average variable cost for computerized deposit accounting has a pronounced U shape. On the other hand, most California banks appear to believe that in the range of their potential applications the long-run average cost curve for demand deposit accounting has at most only a moderate degree of downward curvature. There is the feeling that the more powerful the computer, the greater the cost economies in performing other banking services—ancillary payments services, internal accounting and reports, and so forth. In the payments field itself it is necessary to recognize that transportation costs rise rapidly with increased centralization of check processing and also that the most powerful computers adaptable to present methods of deposit accounting have a capacity well in excess of current needs for payments processing.

Although their statements permit these general observations to be made, most large California banks feel that their experience with computerized bookkeeping is insufficient to determine precisely their effect on costs. During the period of transition to computer operations the solution of programming and other problems necessitates below-optimal use of equipment. Moreover, in most cases the equipment is to be used jointly for demand deposit bookkeeping and other bank tasks, so the allocation of costs to present uses alone would distort the eventual calculations. For the bookkeeping application itself, the large California banks in general state they expect no substantial decline in their operating costs. Most of the banks expect their total cost outlays to rise somewhat less than proportionately with the future expansion in deposit activity. That is, the unit cost of servicing the present number of deposit accounts is expected to be lower, assuming that check volume per account remains roughly constant, but there will be offsets through growth in the number of accounts. Some banks state that sizable cost savings over manual systems have been experienced already, yet other banks expect even their unit cost to remain about the same.[9] Universally, the problem of bookkeeping staff turnover is expected to be alleviated.

In the light of these observations any generalizations about the eventual effect of automation on demand deposit processing costs must

---

[9] It has not been possible to compare present costs with the costs of "previous" manual systems; many banks said they did not have the required past data.

be highly tentative. Probably they will not rise as rapidly as in the 1950's, assuming a comparable increase in deposit activity. Certainly because fewer bookkeeping personnel are needed, overall employment in banking will rise less than would have been required with manual systems. Already, as a result of automation, some increase in average salaries can be detected. Some differences in opinions among banks concerning these cost effects may stem from the use of different methods of cost calculation; little is known about the methods presently used by individual banks. Moreover, there is the feeling among California banks that their methods of manual bookkeeping differed substantially. For some banks the availability of electronic equipment has prompted a rationalization of bookkeeping methods which could have been accomplished (albeit somewhat differently) with the use of manually operated equipment.

b. Effects of automation on the speed and accuracy of payments processing

Considerations besides costs and staffing influenced the decision to use high-speed electronic equipment in bank bookkeeping for demand deposits. With computers, banks are able to increase the speed of handling deposit accounting to what may be called a "current" basis. Deposits, checks, and other bookkeeping entries received during a given business day now can be reflected on the bank's books by the opening of the succeeding business day. Previously, many if not all items were posted on customers' accounts only by the following day. With the far-flung branch systems in California, a customer who made an interbranch transaction affecting his account might have noticed a lapse of one or more additional days before the final entries were made. As a sidelight, it may be noted that the practice of "check-kiting" has been restricted severely under computerized current-day bookkeeping.

The banks feel that computerized systems improve immensely the accuracy of deposit bookkeeping, although the degree cannot be specified precisely. The probable error of the computer's misreading the account number and/or the amount imprinted in magnetic ink on checks can be specified fairly accurately and controlled under present systems through the use of various transposition codes and customary balancing procedures. But computerized bookkeeping remains only as good as the documents presented. Computer-qualified items have been adopted by the general public more rapidly than was anticipated, although some bank customers have large supplies of checks without magnetic ink imprinting and are not expected to convert until these supplies are exhausted.[10] Customers do not always use imprinted checks and some imprinted items become mutilated and require special handling. Also, if a customer should use a check imprinted for the account of another customer, the chance of an inaccurate posting going undetected is not always eliminated in the final manual sorting and filing procedure. The principle remains that the more times an item requires human judgment in its handling, the greater is the likelihood of error.

c. Computers and transit processing

While the application of computer-based technology to banking is grounded in demand deposit bookkeeping, other aspects of the payments system are also susceptible to computer application. Some California banks use computers and related equipment for their transit or check collection operations, although others feel that this is not yet economically feasible or necessary. The advent of the computer, where necessary, is making possible a significant change in transit operations as well as reducing the personnel turnover problem.

The bulk of the checks received by the state's large branch systems is either "on us" items—checks drawn on accounts held by the branch initially receiving the check and on the other branches of the same bank—or items drawn on the other large California banks. In recent years these have been augmented further by direct sendings from out-of-state correspondent banks. Thus most banks find that 80 to 85 percent of total items received are "on us" or on the other large banks. Federal Reserve regulations require that interbranch "on us" items be collected through a bank's own facilities. In the recent past, where branches of banks A and B were in proximity, the most rapid settlement often was achieved if systemwide receipts by bank A of checks drawn on that particular branch of bank B were sent to the nearby bank A branch. Then bank A sent a clerk down the street to present them for payment.

---

[10] At present some difficulties are being encountered with warrants of states and political subdivisions. Prior to the introduction of magnetic ink encoding many of these warrants lacked even a bank designation and the customary routing symbol. Nevertheless, 89 percent of all checks flowing through the head office and Los Angeles facilities of the Federal Reserve Bank of San Francisco in August 1963 were preprinted with magnetic ink characters. This compares with 86 percent in February 1963 and 81 percent in August 1962. For Federal Reserve facilities in the United States as a whole, the respective percentages on these dates were 84 percent, 79 percent and 68 percent.

Where the volume or amounts involved did not warrant this type of exchange for more distant branches of another bank, the facilities of a correspondent bank or of the Federal Reserve were used.

d. "Parent bank" exchanges of checks

With the advent of automation, bookkeeping at the large banks has been centralized in a smaller number of end points. Even where regional service centers have been established by banks with far-flung systems, communications among the service centers, as among the branches, has been speeded up to achieve the current-day posting of items received systemwide. With these communications networks and the smaller number of end points for processing of accounts, it has become feasible for many large banks to undertake "parent bank" exchanges of cash items. An item received in a branch of one of these large banks, which is drawn on any branch of another large bank in the state, can be presented for collection on the same business day. This procedure is implemented through funneling the applicable transit items to the Los Angeles or San Francisco head offices of the banks involved. One or more days will be subtracted from the time of collection for applicable cash items as the result of these exchanges.

The advent of parent bank exchanges at the large California banks brought about sizable reductions in the volume of checks passing through the facilities of the formally organized clearing houses and Federal Reserve Bank offices. At the Los Angeles branch of the Federal Reserve the increase in check volume averaged 14 percent annually for many years, despite greater use of correspondent facilities. The check volume in Los Angeles and San Francisco zones has dropped more than 25 percent since 1962. Under this new system, survival of the twenty-one formally organized clearing houses in California will depend upon their usefulness for purposes other than the exchange of checks among the larger banks. Although a third of these have closed, and others may, some will remain as essentially public relations organizations representing banking to the rest of the community.

e. Computers and ancillary payment services

Because of their use of electronic data processing equipment in demand deposit accounting, the banks have been able to broaden the range of customer services related to the making of payments. Such ancillary customer services as payroll preparation, including employee account deposits and account reconciliation, have been offered even by banks with less sophisticated equipment. With computer equipment presently marketed, these services now can be offered economically to customers of virtually any size. Major California banks also offer "lock box" services by which depositors may arrange for direct bank processing of payments mailed by their customers to a post office lock box. A variety of reports and even of additional payments (as in the case of oil royalties and insurance premiums) flows from this processing. Savings and loan associations and credit unions are seeking arrangements for their routine savings share and loan accounting to be handled on bank computers.

For a number of years California banks have processed "automatic" deductions from customers' accounts for transfers to savings and Christmas Club accounts and for the payment of real estate and consumer loans. Insurance premiums also may be deducted "automatically" from customers' accounts through the use of drafts signed in advance by the customer and presented for payment each month by the insurance company. Arrangements are under way for magnetic ink preprinting of these drafts with the customer's account number and bank routing symbols. These types of services could be extended to other regularly recurring transactions, with resultant broad changes in future payments practices.

Computer applications in banking, of course not confined exclusively to payments mechanism activities and closely related services, are being extended to such routines as real estate, consumer loan, and savings deposit accounting, trust services, maintenance of the general ledger, and so on. In all of these functions programming requirements have challenged the banks to rethink the logic of traditional systems. Again, many monotonous clerical routines and the attendant staffing problems can be alleviated.

f. Automation and smaller banks

Tables 7 and 8 indicated that the main initial direct impact of computer-based technology was on the larger branch banks in California. What will be the impact of these developments on smaller banks within the state? Can the small bank survive in this new atmosphere?

The large California banks assert that bookkeeping and transit costs, variable according to scale of operation, will not prevent survival of efficient smaller banks. A variety of efficient bookkeeping and transit methods is open to these banks, including the more up-to-date manual equipment, semi-automated "tronics" and access to fully computerized systems, so that no great change in competitive relations can be foreseen as a direct result of this innovation in demand deposit accounting. Only relatively large computer systems were available initially to the banking community, but now there are systems adaptable to the needs of medium-sized banks. Also, access to full computer systems can be secured in several ways besides purchase or rental of equipment by the individual institution.

In other parts of the United States, small- and medium-sized banks have formed joint ventures to automate their processing. This institutional arrangement apparently will be unimportant in California, however, where joint ventures have not progressed past the thinking stage. The smaller banks are somewhat scattered, and even where the distance factor is surmountable, management problems are unresolved. The state's unlimited branching leaves even small banks as potential competitors, and there is no guarantee against encroachment on each other's market areas. Some smaller banks already use the facilities of independent service bureaus, although there are limitations on this means of benefiting from the new technology. Some bankers feel that independent bureaus at times lack the flexibility necessary to serve their needs, including the maintenance of banking standards of timing and accuracy. It may be also that independent bureaus lack an appreciation of the importance of these considerations to the banking business. For small California banks wishing to automate there may be greater appeal in the possibility of sharing the facilities of their larger correspondents. Several of the larger banks in the Los Angeles area extend deposit accounting services to small banks, and other large banks in the state expect to enter this field following the shake-down period for their own systems. Quite naturally, many small banks are hesitant to participate in this type of arrangement because they fear that too much reliance on outsiders may threaten their independence. Also there remains the possibility that the tradition of nonencroachment by correspondents might not be respected by a bank which seeks to expand its branch operations. Thus automation represents an important new challenge to the continuing workability of the correspondent banking system.

g. Present equipment will not impair competitive positions substantially

In the field of payments, related services, and other facets of bank operations, the introduction of high-speed electronic data processing equipment has begun to effect marked changes in bank methods. This discussion, based in part on views presented by personnel of large California banks, suggests that despite economies of large-scale automated operations, the competitive position of smaller banks will not be impaired. The present types of automated equipment may contribute moderate economies of scale to the payments system itself and somewhat greater scale economies to the provision of ancillary payments services which are not feasible under an atomistic or unit banking structure. Some technological gains in the payments field would have been impossible, or delayed longer, with an atomistic banking structure. In the future, smaller California banks which lack the flexibility of the more advanced automated systems may find it increasingly difficult (unless technology changes in their favor) to meet the growing needs of some of their customers, but they should continue to enjoy a strong demand for their services.

4. PAYMENTS MECHANISM DEVELOPMENTS IN THE MORE DISTANT FUTURE

The above statements apply to the California banking system as it is now and as it is likely to be for five to ten years. But already some members of the banking industry are beginning to consider the possibilities of more radical departures from traditional banking practices. Present types of computer equipment can be programmed for automatic entry against customer accounts of regularly recurring transactions such as utility bill, tax, charge account, and credit card payments, and the deposit of corporate dividends, rent receipts, and so on. Credit cards could be substituted for present-day checks in many other types of transactions. The difference between present credit card plans and bank checks is more one of degree than of substance. In the former case, the date of final payment customarily is deferred for a maximum of about a month (before interest becomes chargeable in many cases), and the customer must issue a check to settle his account. The customer's check will be reflected on his account with a delay of only a few days. But in most cases, credit is extended by someone for these few days or more even under present check usage. There is no reason why credit card billings themselves could not include an order for payment on a specified date. If bank credit card plans after the "end of the month" and revolving check credit plans are incorporated into regular checking accounts, banking practices will become analogous to the British practice of "overdraft" banking. Matters to be settled include the date from which interest will be chargeable and the recourse which banks will have against customers when satisfactory borrowing arrangements have not been made.[11]

---

[11] For some changes to occur, modifications of existing laws may be required. For example, Chapter 7, Paragraph 858 of the California Financial Code prohibits overdrafts of longer than 90 days' duration from being considered as assets of any bank.

Future potentialities extend much further than this and need not involve the extension of credit. Improvements in equipment have been rapid, and future and present equipment may differ markedly. Banks expect that data transmission between computer centers (probably over leased telephone lines) soon will become feasible economically. On the basis of present line charges, the volume of data and the speed of sending justify only limited use. When the economically feasible applications of data transmission by wire increase, California banks expect that the physical transmission of checks between banking offices, or even between different banks, will become superfluous. Physical presentation of cancelled checks to the depositor may be eliminated. Any questions arising about a transaction may be resolved by wire referral to the original document at its point of entry into the banking system.

Giant random-access computers are expected to become available at a later time for instantaneous recording of transactions when they enter the banking system. Computers with memory cores of the requisite size for economic feasibility are presently unavailable, but they are expected in perhaps ten years or before. Actually, something like this method of effecting payments is already encountered *in reverse* in current banking. Where large sums are involved, customers often use the bank wire network to transfer balances between their accounts and to the accounts of others. A future payment recipient will present cash items to a bank, and the money transfer will be effected by wire instantaneously.

What effect will these future innovations have on the payments system? Clearly, more thorough studies are required. It may be that these too will point toward no great change in the competitive relations among banks of different size classes. Or the position of the smaller banks may be strengthened by improvements in technology which increase their ability to offer a greater variety of payments services, either without cost disadvantages or with positive cost advantages relative to larger banks. Toward the other extreme, with larger computers and data transmission by wire, economies of scale may become so large— perhaps because overlapping wire networks, duplicated computer facilities, and intertie complexes prove very costly—that payments functions could be performed most efficiently by a few giant banks in each area. This would require virtually nationwide acceptance of compatible payments procedures. One cannot be sure of the path of future developments in a field where technology is advancing so rapidly, or for that matter, where so little is known about what payments methods the general public will consider acceptable. But within the time horizon of this study there is the potential for full scale transformations to occur within the payments field. Because this field includes important public utility aspects, regulatory agencies must be alert for situations where institutional changes are desirable in the interests of the general public. Moreover, it is incumbent upon regulatory agencies to acquaint themselves fully with the innovations before their actual introduction to the banks. Changes may be so extensive and rapid that society cannot afford "wait and see" policies.

Changes within the payments sphere cannot be considered by themselves. In the present banking system, payments functions and credit provision are intertwined. There may very well be tradeoffs between these two functions (or with others) in the sense that the minimum standards of performance considered acceptable in one phase of bank activity may be affected in another by the degree to which performance criteria are met. In the early 1930's, for example, the safety of bank-issued payments media might have been improved by the proposal for 100 percent reserve backing, but what would have been the effect on credit accommodation for business firms? This brings us back to the problem noted at the beginning of this paper; there is no general theoretical formulation of what should be expected of a national payments system and thus no adequate basis for judging how well the system is performing in various parts of the country.

a. Need for more information on bank costs

More precise information on bank costs is highly desirable as little is known about the extent to which the costs of demand deposit accounting, transit processing, and other payments-related operations vary according to the size of operation. Some of the data required are presently compiled for banks within the service areas of the Boston and New York Federal Reserve Banks. Only relatively small banks are included in "functional income and cost" studies in these two areas—the largest banks included have little more than $50 million in total deposits. In contrast, banking services in California are dominated by the eight largest banks which account for almost nine-tenths of total deposits. Each of these banks has total deposits well in excess of $500 million, and the largest had more than $13 billion in 1963. Even if the results of cost studies in other areas are applicable to comparable-sized banks in California, there remains a vast area of ignorance about the costs of the larger banks in conducting similar operations.

Cost studies at large banks necessarily would be elaborate because of their more complex overall operations and the extensive variety of their services. The regulatory authorities should be conversant with the cost effects of different scales of bank operation for such matters as new charters, new branch authorizations, mergers, and so on. They also should become informed about the effects on these costs of changes in methods of bank operation.

b. Banking jobs may grow more slowly in California

If, as now indicated, the future trend is for a marked increase in the use of capital relative to labor in many banking tasks, the number of new job openings at the banks themselves will grow somewhat less rapidly than it has since World War II. The Williams-National Planning Association estimate (see Williams, this volume, Table 5) projects a slower expansion to 1976 in the finance-real estate segment of California employment than in such fields as trade, services and construction. In the base year for these estimates, 1957, banking accounted for about 20 percent of total finance and real estate jobs. A modest future decline in this proportion would not be surprising; routine tasks capable of computer resolution are relatively greater in banking than in the other sub-industries included. Average salaries in banking will tend to increase because of the upgrading in job classifications which accompanies automation.

c. Cost reduction incentives will remain strong

With these future changes the speed of making transactions probably will be increased further. A given amount of cash balances held for transactions purposes will thus be able to mediate a progressively greater volume of exchanges. Even the accelerated growth in Gross National Product projected by Williams might not require comparable increases in the money supply in some years, particularly if "mail float" is reduced by such things as improvements in the speed of mail transportation and a greater use of lock box facilities at banks. Therefore, assuming that monetary instruments continue to be important in the nation's arsenal of economic controls, future growth in the money supply will depend largely on the extent to which the public holds money for other than transactions purposes. If faced with inflation, cautious monetary authorities may enhance the opportunities of nonbank intermediaries to substitute other stores of value for money. Briefly, no great acceleration in the growth rate of the money supply can be projected under foreseeable peacetime circumstances. The banks will remain under the pressure of minimizing unit costs of demand deposit administration as a major means of improving their net earnings. Innovations must breed further innovations or earnings will suffer.

The slowdown in California's growth relative to the rest of the country may have an adverse effect on the rate of expansion in demand deposit holdings at the state's banks. The effect of this on their gross earning capacity may be offset, at least in part, for net profits purposes by increased substitution of nationally-priced equipment for higher-salaried California labor.